EYEWITNESS *TRAVEL GUIDES*

IRELAND

EYEWITNESS *TRAVEL GUIDES*

IRELAND

Main Contributors:
LISA GERARD-SHARP AND TIM PERRY

DK

DORLING KINDERSLEY
LONDON • NEW YORK • SYDNEY • MOSCOW
www.dk.com

A DORLING KINDERSLEY BOOK

www.dk.com

PROJECT EDITOR Ferdie McDonald
ART EDITOR Lisa Kosky
EDITORS Maggie Crowley, Simon Farbrother, Emily Hatchwell,
Seán O'Connell, Jane Simmonds
DESIGNERS Joy FitzSimmons, Jaki Grosvenor,
Katie Peacock, Jan Richter
MAP CO-ORDINATORS Michael Ellis, David Pugh
RESEARCHERS John Breslin, Andrea Holmes

MANAGING EDITORS Vivien Crump, Helen Partington
MANAGING ART EDITOR Steve Knowlden
DEPUTY EDITORIAL DIRECTOR Douglas Amrine
DEPUTY ART DIRECTOR Gaye Allen

PRODUCTION David Proffit, Hilary Stephens
PICTURE RESEARCH Sue Mennell, Christine Rista
DTP DESIGNER Adam Moore

CONTRIBUTORS
Una Carlin, Polly Phillimore, Susan Poole, Martin Walters

MAPS
Gary Bowes, Margaret Slowey, Richard Toomey
(ERA-Maptec, Dublin, Ireland)

PHOTOGRAPHERS
Joe Cornish, Tim Daly, Alan Williams

ILLUSTRATORS
Draughtsman Maps, Maltings Partnership, Robbie Polley
•
Film outputting bureau PLS (London)
Reproduced by Colourscan (Singapore)
Printed and bound by G. Canale & C. (Italy)

First published in Great Britain in 1995
by Dorling Kindersley Limited
9 Henrietta Street, London WC2E 8PS
Reprinted with revisions 1996 (twice), 1997, 1999

Copyright 1995, 1999 © Dorling Kindersley Limited, London

•
Every effort has been made to ensure that the information in this
book is as up-to-date as possible at the time of going to press.
However, details such as telephone numbers, opening hours,
prices, gallery hanging arrangements and travel information are
liable to change. The publishers cannot accept responsibility for
any consequences arising from the use of this book.

We would be delighted to receive any corrections and suggestions
for incorporation in the next edition. Please write to:
Deputy Editorial Director, Eyewitness Travel Guides,
Dorling Kindersley, 9 Henrietta Street, London WC2E 8PS.

CONTENTS

An evangelical symbol from the
Book of Kells (see p62)

INTRODUCING IRELAND

DUBLIN AREA BY AREA

Georgian doorway in Fitzwilliam
Square, Dublin *(see p67)*

Lighthouse at Spanish Point near Mizen Head *(see p159)*

IRELAND REGION BY REGION

Detail of the Chorus Gate at Powerscourt *(see pp126–7)*

TRAVELLERS' NEEDS

SURVIVAL GUIDE

Façade of a pub in Dingle *(see p149)*

Bunratty Castle in County Clare

HOW TO USE THIS GUIDE

THIS GUIDE helps you to get the most from your visit to Ireland. It provides both expert recommendations and detailed practical information. *Introducing Ireland* maps the country and sets it in its historical and cultural context. The seven regional chapters, plus *Dublin Area* *by Area*, contain descriptions of all the important sights, with maps, pictures and illustrations. Restaurant and hotel recommendations can be found in *Travellers' Needs*. The *Survival Guide* has tips on everything from the telephone system to transport both in the Republic and in Northern Ireland.

DUBLIN AREA BY AREA

Central Dublin is divided into three sightseeing areas. Each has its own chapter, which opens with a list of the sights described. A fourth chapter, *Further Afield*, covers the suburbs and County Dublin. Sights are numbered and plotted on an *Area Map*. The descriptions of each sight follow the map's numerical order, making sights easy to locate within the chapter.

Sights at a Glance lists the chapter's sights by category: Churches, Museums and Galleries, Historic Buildings, Parks and Gardens.

All pages relating to Dublin have red thumb tabs.

A locator map shows where you are in relation to other areas of the city centre.

1 Area Map
For easy reference, the sights are numbered and located on a map. Sights in the city centre are also shown on the Dublin Street Finder *on pages 110–11.*

2 Street-by-Street Map
This gives a bird's-eye view of the key area in each chapter.

A suggested route for a walk is shown in red.

Stars indicate the sights that no visitor should miss.

3 Detailed information
The sights in Dublin are described individually with addresses, telephone numbers and information on opening hours and admission charges.

Story boxes highlight noteworthy features of the sights.

1 Introduction
The landscape, history and character of each region is described here, showing how the area has developed over the centuries and what it offers to the visitor today.

IRELAND REGION BY REGION
Apart from Dublin, Ireland has been divided into seven regions, each of which has a separate chapter. The most interesting towns and places to visit in each area have been numbered on a *Pictorial Map*.

Each region of Ireland can be quickly identified by its colour coding, shown on the inside front cover.

2 Pictorial Map
This shows the road network and gives an illustrated overview of the whole region. All interesting places to visit are numbered and there are also useful tips on getting around the region by car and train.

Getting Around gives tips on travel within the region.

3 Detailed information
All the important towns and other places to visit are described individually. They are listed in order, following the numbering on the Pictorial Map. Within each town or city, there is detailed information on important buildings and other sights.

The Visitors' Checklist provides all the practical information you will need to plan your visit for all the top sights.

4 Ireland's top sights
These are given two or more full pages. Historic buildings are dissected to reveal their interiors. The most interesting towns or city centres are shown in a bird's-eye view, with sights picked out and described.

INTRODUCING
IRELAND

Putting Ireland on the Map

T HE ISLAND OF IRELAND covers an area of 84,430 sq km (32,598 sq miles). Lying in the Atlantic Ocean to the northwest of mainland Europe, it is separated from Great Britain by the Irish Sea. The Republic of Ireland takes up 85 per cent of the island with a population of 3.5 milllion. Northern Ireland, part of the United Kingdom, has 1.5 million people. Dublin is the capital of the Republic and has good international communications.

Europe

Most visitors to Ireland come through Dublin, either on the ferry to Dun Laoghaire or by air. The main ferry routes are from Wales, Scotland and France. There are international flights to Shannon, Belfast and Cork airports as well as Dublin. Many European flights are routed via Great Britain, though flight times are generally only around an hour on from British airports.

0 kilometres   100

0 miles   50

KEY

✈	Airport
⛴	Ferry port
▬	Motorway
▬	Major road
—	Railway line

GREATER DUBLIN

Swords
Malahide
N1
N3
N2
Finglas
Dublin
Airport
M50
Glasnevin
Marino
Howth
Royal Canal
Liffey
N4
Lucan
Kilmainham
Dublin
Clondalkin
Grand Canal
Ballsbridge
Dublin Bay
N7
Rathmines
N81
Dundrum
Dun
Laoghaire
M50
N11
0 km   5
0 miles   5

Greater Dublin

Nearly one third of the Republic's population lives in Dublin. Nevertheless the city is relatively uncongested and access to the centre from the ports and airport is easy.

SCOTLAND
Islay
Glasgow
Arran
A83
A83

North   Channel

Coleraine
Cairnryan
A37
A6
A26
A36
A75
Larne
Stranraer
A77

THERN
LAND
Lough Neagh
Belfast
ENGLAND
A595
A4
M1
rmagh
A3
A1
A2
A65
Newry
N2
Isle of Man
M6
Dundalk
Douglas
OF
Irish   Sea
Manchester
M62
D
Boyne
Liverpool
M62
N1
N4   DUBLIN
M56
M7
M50
Dun Laoghaire
Holyhead
A55
A5
M6
N7
Liffey
N11
A5
Carlow
A487
A470
M54
N9
Slaney
N11
Severn
N25
M50
Wexford
Vaterford
Rosslare
WALES
St   George's   Channel
Fishguard
A487
M4
Le Havre/Cherbourg
A40   A477
Pembroke
Swansea
M4
CARDIFF
Bristol
M5

Bristol   Channel

A PORTRAIT OF IRELAND

MANY VISITORS *see Ireland as a lush green island, full of thatched cottages, pubs, music, wit and poetry. Like all stereotypes, this image of the country has a basis in truth and the tourist industry helps sustain it. The political and economic reality is, of course, rather less ideal, but the relaxed good humour of the people still makes Ireland a most welcoming place to visit.*

Ireland, at least for the time being, is a divided island. History and religion have created two hostile communities, with the Protestant majority in the North implacably opposed to the idea of a united Ireland. In recent years the focus of the world's attention has been the Troubles, the campaigns of bombings and shootings in Northern Ireland, but the cease-fire of 1994 has brought a new climate of hope.

Ireland has had more than its fair share of wars and disasters, culminating in the Great Famine of 1845–8, since when poverty and emigration have been part of the Irish way of life. More people of Irish descent live in

Cathleen ni Houlihan, personification of Ireland

the USA than in Ireland itself. Suffering and martyrdom in the cause of independence also play an important part in the Irish consciousness. The heroine of WB Yeats's play *Cathleen ni Houlihan* inspires young men to lay down their lives for Ireland. Her image appeared on the first bank note issued by the newly created Irish Free State in 1922.

Yet, in spite of the past, the Irish retain their traditional easy-going attitude to life. Both parts of the island have a young, highly educated population and are working hard to make their way in today's European Union. In the Republic, 50 per cent of the population is aged under 25.

Façade of Trinity College, Dublin, the Republic's most prestigious university

◁ Thatching a traditional cottage in Adare, County Limerick

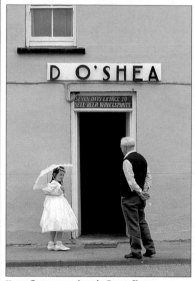

Young first communicant in County Kerry

Despite its high birth rate, rural Ireland is sparsely populated. The Industrial Revolution of the 19th century barely touched the South and the Republic seems an old-fashioned place, poorer than almost all its fellow members of the European Union. With large families and high unemployment, the ratio of dependants to wage-earners is the highest in Europe.

ECONOMIC DEVELOPMENT

Traditionally, Northern Ireland had far more industry than the South, but during the 25 years of the Troubles, old heavy industries, such as shipbuilding, have declined and new investors have been scared away. For both parts of Ireland, geography is a serious barrier to prosperity. Located on the periphery of Europe, the island is isolated from its main markets and thus saddled with high transport costs. Fortunately, subsidies from the European Union have helped improve the transport infrastructure in the Republic, especially the roads and ports.

Traditional Irish dancing

Tax breaks and low inflation have attracted foreign investment to the Republic and many multinationals, especially computing and chemical companies, have subsidiaries in Ireland. Even so, the economy still depends heavily on agriculture and there are more cattle than people on the island. Another important industry is tourism. The Republic receives over 3 million visitors a year and the North is well prepared for an influx of tourists, now the Troubles appear to be at an end.

RELIGION AND POLITICS

The influence of Catholicism is strong. In the Republic, the Church runs most schools, along with some hospitals and social services. Irish Catholicism runs the gamut from missionary zeal to simple piety. According to some estimates, over 90 per cent of the

Pavement artist on O'Connell Street, Dublin

population goes to Mass. Religion plays an important role in the politics of the Republic and moral conservatism is evident in attitudes to issues such as divorce, contraception, abortion and homosexuality.

The election of liberal lawyer Mary Robinson as President in 1990, the first woman to hold the post, was seen as a sign of more enlightened times by many people, not only women. A new political climate has favoured the quiet spread of feminism and challenged the old paternalism of Irish politics, not only in social issues

Traditional farming: a field of haystacks overlooking Clew Bay, County Mayo

but also in helping break down the clannish cronyism of the traditional parties Fianna Fáil and Fine Gael.

LANGUAGE AND CULTURE

Ireland was a Gaelic-speaking nation until the 16th century, since when the language has declined. Today, however, the Republic is officially bilingual and knowledge of Irish is a requirement for university entrance and a career in the public sector. While 11 per cent of the population speak Gaelic fluently, only three per cent use it regularly in daily life.

Connemara pony show

Irish culture, on the other hand, is in no danger of being eroded. The people have a genuine love of old folk legends, epic poetry and songs, and festivals play an important part in community life. Festivals may be dedicated to St Patrick or James Joyce, pubs or oysters, salmon or sailing, music or matchmaking. Music is a national passion – from the rock of U2 and the Cranberries to the folk music of Clannad, the Chieftains and Mary Black.

Another national passion is horse racing. Ireland's breeders and trainers are masters of their trade and enjoy astonishing international success for such a small country. Other sports are followed with equal intensity, as witnessed during the 1994 football World Cup. Drinking also plays an important part in Irish culture: social life centres on the pub and the "crack" (convivial chat) to be enjoyed there. When the Republic introduced stricter drink-driving laws in 1994, many rural publicans said traditional Irish society would collapse. Given the attachment to Guinness, gossip and music, this is extremely unlikely.

Matt Molloy's pub in Westport, County Mayo

The Landscape and Wildlife of Ireland

Corncrake

THE LANDSCAPE is one of the Ireland's greatest attractions. It varies from bogs and lakes in the central lowlands to mountains and rocky islands in the west. Between these two extremes, the island has abundant lush, green pastureland, the result of plentiful rainfall, but little natural woodland. Parts of the far west, where the land is farmed by traditional methods, are havens for threatened wildlife, including the corncrake, which needs undisturbed hay fields in which to nest.

THE FAUNA OF IRELAND

Natterjack toad

Many animals (including snakes) did not make it to Ireland before the Irish Sea rose after the Ice Age. Other surprising absentees are the mole, weasel and common toad (the natterjack, however, can be seen). The wood mouse is the only small native rodent, but the once common red squirrel has now been virtually taken over by the grey.

ROCKY COASTS

Chough

The Dingle Peninsula *(see pp150–51)* is part of a series of rocky promontories and inlets created when sea levels rose at the end of the Ice Age. Cliffs and islands offer many sites for sea birds, with some enormous colonies, such as the gannets of Little Skellig *(pp156–7)*. The chough still breeds on cliffs in the extreme west. Elsewhere in Europe, this rare species of crow is declining in numbers.

Thrift grows in cushion-like clumps, producing its papery pink flowerheads from spring right through to autumn.

Sea campion is a low-growing plant. Its large white flowers brighten up many a cliff top and seaside shingle bank.

LAKES, RIVERS AND WETLANDS

Great crested grebe

This watery landscape around Lough Oughter is typical of the lakelands of the River Erne *(pp262–3)*. Rainfall is high throughout the year, which results in many wetlands, especially along the Shannon *(pp176–7)* and the Erne. The elegant great crested grebe breeds mainly on the larger lakes in the north.

Water lobelia grows in the shallows of stony lakes. Its leaves remain below the water, while the pale lilac flowers are borne on leafless stems above the surface.

Fleabane, once used to repel fleas, thrives in wet meadows and marshes. It has yellow flowers like dandelions.

Grey seals *are a common sight in the waters off the Atlantic coast, feeding on fish and occasionally on sea birds.*

Otters *are more likely to be seen in the shallow seas off rocky coasts than in rivers and lakes, though they live in both habitats.*

Red deer *have been introduced into many areas, notably the hills of Connemara.*

Pine martens, *though mainly nocturnal, may be spotted in daytime during the summer.*

MOUNTAIN AND BLANKET BOG

Wheatear

As well as the raised bogs of the central lowlands (*p244*), much of Ireland's mountainous ground, particularly in the west, is covered by blanket bog such as that seen here in Connemara (*pp198–201*). On drier upland sites this grades into heather moor and poor grassland. The wheatear, which inhabits rocky scree and heathland, is a restless bird with an unmistakeable white rump. It flits about, dipping and bobbing in pursuit of flies.

Bog myrtle *is an aromatic shrub, locally common in Ireland's bogs. Its leaves can be used to flavour drinks.*

Bogbean, *a plant found in fens and wet bogland, has attractive white flowers splashed with pink. Its leaves were once used as a cure for boils.*

PASTURELAND

Rook

Rolling pastureland with grazing livestock, as seen here in the foot-hills of the Wicklow Mountains (*pp130–31*), is a very common sight throughout Ireland. The traditional farming methods employed in many parts of the island (particularly in the west) are of great benefit to wildlife. Rooks, for example, which feed on worms and insect larvae found in pasture, are very common.

Meadow vetchling *uses its tendrils to clamber up grasses and other plants. It has clusters of pretty pale yellow flowers.*

Marsh thistle *is a common flower of wet meadows and damp woodland. It is a tall species with small, purple flowerheads.*

Architecture in Ireland

Window of an Irish cottage

IRELAND'S TURBULENT HISTORY has done incalculable damage to its architectural heritage. Cromwell's forces, in particular, destroyed scores of castles, monasteries and towns in their three-year campaign against the Irish in the mid-17th century. However, many fascinating buildings and sites remain, with Iron Age forts being the earliest surviving settlements. Christianity in Ireland gave rise to monasteries, churches and round towers; conflict between Anglo-Norman barons and Irish chieftains created castles and tower houses. The later landlord class built luxurious country mansions, while their labourers had to make do with basic, one-roomed cottages.

LOCATOR MAP

	Iron Age forts
	Round towers
	Tower houses
	Georgian country houses

IRON AGE FORT

Ring forts *(raths) were Iron Age farmsteads enclosed by an earth bank, a timber fence and a ditch to protect against cattle-raiders. Inside, people lived in huts with a souterrain (underground passage) for storage and refuge. Some were in use as late as the 17th century, but all you can usually see today are low circular mounds. In the west, stone was used for cahers (stone ring forts) and promontory forts (semi-circular forts built on cliff tops using the sea as a natural defence).*

Thatched hut

Entrance   **Souterrain**

ROUND TOWER

Lookout window   **Conical roof**

Round towers, often over 30m (100 ft) tall, were built between the 10th and 12th centuries on monastic sites. They were bell towers, used as places of refuge and to store valuable manuscripts. The entrance, which could be as high as 4 m (13 ft) above ground, was reached by a ladder that was hauled up from the inside. Other moveable ladders connected the tower's wooden floors.

Wooden floor

Moveable ladder

TOWER HOUSE

Machicolation

Spiral staircase

Outer wall around bawn

Tower houses were small castles or fortified residences built between the 15th and 17th centuries. The tall square house was often surrounded by a stone wall forming a bawn (enclosure), used for defence and as a cattle pen. Machicolations (projecting parapets from which to drop missiles) were sited at the top of the house.

COTTAGE

One-roomed cottages, thatched or slate-roofed, are still a common feature of the Irish landscape. Built of local stone with small windows to retain heat, the cottages were inhabited by farm workers or smallholders.

Bog-oak timbers   **Thatched, clay-lined chimney**

Clay floor

IRON AGE FORTS

① Staigue Fort *p156*
② Dún Aonghasa *p206*
③ Craggaunowen *p182*
④ Grianán of Aileach *pp218–19*
⑤ Hill of Tara *p240*

ROUND TOWERS

⑥ Kilmacduagh *p204*
⑦ Ardmore *p137*
⑧ Clonmacnoise *pp242–3*
⑨ Devenish Island *p263*
⑩ Kilkenny *pp136*
⑪ Glendalough *pp132–3*

TOWER HOUSES

⑫ Aughnanure Castle *p201*
⑬ Thoor Ballylee *pp204–5*
⑭ Knappogue Castle *p181*
⑮ Blarney Castle *p163*
⑯ Donegal Castle *p222*

GEORGIAN COUNTRY HOUSES

⑰ Strokestown Park House *pp210–11*
⑱ Castle Coole *p264*
⑲ Emo Court *p245*
⑳ Russborough House *pp124–5*
㉑ Castletown House *pp122–3*

The well-preserved round tower at Ardmore

GEORGIAN COUNTRY HOUSE

Main house containing formal rooms

Pediment

Balustrade

Wing containing family rooms

Blind colonnade

Doric pillar

Portico

Ionic pillar

Between the 1720s and 1800, prosperous landlords commissioned palatial country mansions in the Palladian and Neo-Classical styles popular in England over that period. Castle Coole (above) has a Palladian layout, with the main house in the centre and a colonnade on either side leading to a small pavilion. The Neo-Classical influence can be seen in the unadorned façade and the Doric columns of the colonnades. Noted architects of Irish country houses include Richard Castle (1690–1751) and James Wyatt (1746–1813).

STUCCO

Stucco (decorative relief plasterwork), popular in the 18th century, is found in many Georgian country houses as well as town houses and public buildings. The Italian Francini brothers were particularly sought after for their intricate stuccowork (notably at Castletown and Russborough) as was Irish craftsman Michael Stapleton (Trinity College, Dublin and Dublin Writers Museum).

***Trompe l'oeil* detail at Emo Court**

Ceiling at Dublin Writers Museum

Stucco portrait at Castletown House

Stuccowork at Russborough House

OTHER TERMS USED IN THIS GUIDE

Beehive hut: Circular stone building with a domed roof created by corbelling (laying a series of stones so that each projects beyond the one below).

Cashel: Stone ring fort.

Crannog: Defensive, partly artificial island on a lake. Huts were often built on crannogs (*see p31*).

Curtain wall: Outer wall of a castle, usually incorporating towers at intervals.

Hiberno-Romanesque: Style of church architecture with rounded arches highly decorated with geometric designs and human and animal forms. Also called Irish-Romanesque.

Motte and bailey: Raised mound (motte) topped with a wooden tower, surrounded by a heavily fenced space (bailey). Built by the Normans in the 12th century, they were quickly erected in time of battle.

Tympanum: Decorated space over a door or window.

Literary Ireland

FOR A LAND the size of Ireland to have produced four Nobel prizewinners in Shaw, Yeats, Beckett and Séamus Heaney is a considerable feat. Yet it is not easy to speak of an "Irish literary tradition" as the concept embraces rural and urban experiences, Protestant and Catholic traditions and the Gaelic and English languages. Irish fiction today, as in the past, is characterized by a sense of community and history, a love of storytelling and a zest for language.

WB Yeats – Ireland's most famous poet

A first edition of *Ulysses*

The Blasket Islands, which provided inspiration for several writers

GAELIC LITERATURE

IRISH LITERATURE proclaims itself the oldest vernacular literature in Western Europe, dating back to early monastic times when Celtic folklore and sagas such as the epics of Cuchulainn *(see p24)* were written down for the first time. The disappearance of Gaelic literature followed the demise, in the 17th century, of the Irish aristocracy for whom it was written. Gaelic literature has had several revivals. Peig Sayers is famous for her accounts of the harsh life on the Blasket Islands *(see p150)* in the early 20th century.

Novelist Maria Edgeworth

ANGLO-IRISH LITERATURE

THE COLLAPSE of Gaelic culture and the Protestant Ascendancy led to English being the dominant language. Most literature was based around the privileged classes.

An early Anglo-Irish writer was satirist Jonathan Swift *(see p80)*, author of *Gulliver's Travels*, who was born in Dublin in 1667 of English parents. Anglo-Irish literature was strong in drama, the entertainment of the cultured classes, and owed little to Irish settings or sensibilities. By the 1700s, Ireland was producing an inordinate number of leading playwrights, many of whom were more at home in London. These included Oliver Goldsmith, remembered for his comedy *She Stoops to Conquer*, and Richard Brinsley Sheridan, whose plays include *The School for Scandal*. Near the end of the century, Maria Edgeworth set a precedent with novels such as *Castle Rackrent*, based on the class divide in Irish society.

The 19th century saw an exodus to England of Irish playwrights, including Oscar Wilde, who entered Oxford University in 1874 and later became the darling of London society with plays such as *The Importance of Being Earnest*. George Bernard Shaw *(see p98)*, writer of *St Joan* and *Pygmalion*, also made London his home. This dramatist, critic, socialist and pacifist continued to write until well into the 20th century.

Playwright George Bernard Shaw

20TH-CENTURY WRITERS

IN 1898, WB Yeats and Lady Gregory founded Dublin's Abbey Theatre *(see p86)*. Its opening, in 1904, heralded the Irish Revival, which focused on national and local themes. Playwright John Millington Synge drew inspiration from a love of the Aran Islands and Irish folklore, but the "immoral language" of his *Playboy of the Western World* caused a riot when first performed at the Abbey Theatre. Along with contemporaries, like Sean O'Casey and WB Yeats, Synge influenced subsequent generations of Irish writers, including novelist Seán O'Faolain, humorous writer and columnist Flann O'Brien, and hard-drinking, quarrelsome playwright Brendan Behan. The literary revival also produced many notable poets in the mid-20th century such as the gifted Patrick Kavanagh and Belfast-born Louis MacNeice, often considered to be one of the finest poets of his generation.

The writer Brendan Behan enjoying the company in a Dublin pub

Caricature of protesters at Dublin's Abbey Theatre in 1907

THREE LITERARY GIANTS

FROM the mass of talent to emerge in Irish literature, three figures stand out as visionaries in their fields. WB Yeats *(see p225)* spent half his life outside Ireland but is forever linked to its rural west. A writer of wistful, melancholic poetry, he was at the forefront of the Irish Revival, helping forge a new national cultural identity. James Joyce *(see p88)* was another trailblazer of Irish literature – his complex narrative and stream of consciousness techniques influenced the development of the modern novel. *Ulysses* describes a day in the life of Joyce's beloved Dublin and shaped the work of generations of writers. Bloomsday, which is named after one of the novel's characters, Leopold Bloom, is still celebrated annually in the city. The last of the three literary giants, novelist and playwright Samuel Beckett *(see p60)*, was another of Dublin's sons, though he later emigrated to France. His themes of alienation, despair, and the futility of human existence pervade his best-known plays, *Waiting for Godot* and *Endgame*.

The poet Patrick Kavanagh celebrating Bloomsday

CONTEMPORARY WRITERS

IRELAND'S proud literary tradition is today upheld by a stream of talented writers from both North and South. Among the finest are Cork-born William Trevor, regarded as a master of the short story, and Brian Moore, whose stories of personal and political disillusionment are often based in his native Belfast. Similarly, Dubliner Roddy Doyle mines his working-class origins in novels such as *The Snapper* and *Paddy Clarke Ha Ha Ha*. Other established Irish writers are Brian Friel and Edna O'Brien. Out of Ireland's contemporary poets, the Ulster-born writers Séamus Heaney and Derek Mahon are considered among the most outstanding.

IRELAND IN THE MOVIES

Ireland has long been fertile ground for the world's film makers. Hollywood invaded it as early as 1951 with *The Quiet Man*, starring John Wayne and set in the picturesque village of Cong. In recent years, Ireland and its people have been the subjects of several major films, notably *The Crying Game* (1992), *In the Name of the Father* (1994) and *Michael Collins* (1996). Another popular film was *The Commitments* (1991). Filmed on location in and around Dublin with an all-Irish cast, it was based on a novel by Roddy Doyle.

Cast of *The Commitments*, written by Roddy Doyle

The Music of Ireland

IRELAND IS THE ONLY COUNTRY in the world to have a musical instrument – the harp – as its national emblem. In this land, famous for its love of music, modern forms such as country-and-western and rock flourish, but it is traditional music that captures the essence of the country. Whether you are listening to Gaelic love songs that date back to medieval times or 17th- and 18th-century folk songs with their English and Scottish influences, the music is unmistakeably Irish. Dance is an equally important aspect of Irish traditional music, and some of the most popular airs are derived from centuries-old reels, jigs and hornpipes. Nowadays these are mainly performed at *fleadhs* (festivals) and *ceilidhs* (dances).

An Irish jig

Turlough O'Carolan (1670–1738) is the most famous Irish harper. The blind musician travelled the country playing his songs to both the rich and poor. Many of O'Carolan's melodies, such as The Lamentation of Owen O'Neill, *still survive.*

Piano accordion

The *bodhrán* is a hand-held goatskin drum that is usually played with a small stick. It is particularly effective when accompanying the flute.

Flute

Two-row button accordion

John F McCormack (1884–1945) was an Irish tenor who toured America to great acclaim during the early part of this century. His best-loved recordings were arias by Mozart. Another popular tenor was Derry-born Josef Locke. A singer of popular ballads in the 1940s and '50s, he was the subject of the 1992 film, Hear My Song.

THE CURRENT MUSIC SCENE

Mary Black

Ireland today is a melting pot of musical styles. The resurgence of Irish traditional music has produced many highly-respected musicians, such as the pipe-players Liam Ó Floin and Paddy Keenan from Dublin. Groups like the Chieftains and the Fureys have gained worldwide fame by melding old with new. Ireland is also firmly placed on the rock'n'roll map, thanks to bands such as Them in the 1960s and Thin Lizzy a decade later. The most famous rock band to come out of Ireland is Dublin's U2 who, in the 1980s, became one of the world's most popular groups. More recently, the series of albums entitled *A Woman's Heart* has been a showcase for talents such as Mary Black and Sinéad O'Connor, and bands like The Cranberries and Boyzone have conquered the world stage.

Bono of U2

Traditional Irish dancing is currently enjoying renewed popularity. From the 17th century the social focus in rural areas was the village dance held every Sunday. From these gatherings, Irish dancing became popular.

LIVE TRADITIONAL MUSIC

Wherever you go in Ireland, you won't be far from a pub with live music. For the Irish traditional musician, there are few set rules – the improvisational nature of the music means that no two performances of any piece are ever likely to be the same.

Violins, or fiddles, can either be tucked under the chin or held against the upper arm, shoulder or chest.

The New National Sons—

**ERIN
Remember
1916**

PRICE 2 NET

Published by
QUINN & COMPANY,
80 UPPER ABBEY ST.,
DUBLIN.

Irish folk songs, such as this one about the 1916 Easter Rising, tend to have a patriotic theme. But some of the most powerful songs have been written not just about the national struggle, but also on hardship, emigration and the longing for the homeland.

TRADITIONAL INSTRUMENTS

There is no set line-up in traditional Irish bands. The fiddle is probably the most common instrument used. Like the music, some instruments have Celtic origins – the uillean pipes are related to the bagpipes played in Scotland and Brittany today.

The melodeon is a basic version of the button accordion. Both these instruments are better suited to Irish music than the piano accordion.

The uillean pipes are similar to bagpipes and are generally considered to be one of the main instruments in Irish traditional music.

The harp has been played in Ireland since the 10th century. In recent years, there has been a keen revival of harp playing in Irish traditional music.

The banjo comes from the Deep South of the US and adds a new dimension to the sound of traditional bands.

Tin whistle

Flute

The flute and tin whistle are among the most common instruments used in traditional Irish music. The latter is often called the penny whistle.

The violin is called a fiddle by most musicians. The style of playing and sound produced varies from region to region.

Ireland's Celtic Heritage

I RELAND'S RICH TRADITION of storytelling embraces a folk heritage that abounds with myths and superstitions. Some stories have been in written form since the 8th century, but most originated over 2,000 years ago when druids passed on stories orally from one generation to the next. Like the Gaelic language itself, many of Ireland's legends have links with those of ancient Celtic races throughout Europe. As well as the heroic deeds and fearless warriors of mythology, Irish folklore is also rich in tales of fairies, leprechauns, banshees and other supernatural beings.

Stone carving on Boa Island

The formidable Queen Maeve of Connaught

single-handedly. However, Queen Maeve took revenge on Cuchulainn by using sorcerers to lure him to his death. Today, in Dublin's GPO *(see p87)*, a statue of Cuchulainn commemorates the heroes of the 1916 Easter Rising.

Part of the 2,300-year-old Gundestrup Cauldron unearthed in Denmark, which depicts Cuchulainn's triumph in the Cattle Raid of Cooley

CUCHULAINN

T HE MOST FAMOUS warrior in Irish mythology is Cuchulainn. At the age of seven, going by the name of Setanta, he killed the savage hound of Culainn the Smith by slaying it with a hurling stick (one of the first times the sport of hurling is mentioned in folklore). Culainn was upset at the loss so Setanta volunteered to guard the house,

earning himself the new name of Cuchulainn, meaning the hound of Culainn.

Before he went into battle, Cuchulainn swelled to magnificent proportions, turned different colours and one of his eyes grew huge. His greatest victory was in the "Cattle Raid of Cooley" when Queen Maeve of Connaught sent her troops to capture the coveted prize bull of Ulster. Cuchulainn learned of the plot and defeated them

FINN MACCOOL

T HE WARRIOR Finn MacCool is the most famous leader of the Fianna, an elite band of troops chosen for their strength and valour and who defended Ireland from foreign forces. Finn was not only strong and bold but also possessed the powers of a seer, and could obtain great wisdom by putting his thumb in his mouth and sucking on it. When they were not at war, the Fianna spent their time hunting. Finn had a hound called Bran which stood almost as high as himself and is said to be the original ancestor of the breed known today as the Irish wolfhound. Many of the

FAIRIES, LEPRECHAUNS AND BANSHEES

The existence of spirits, and in particular the "little people", plays a large part in Irish folklore. Centuries ago, it was believed that fairies lived under mounds of earth, or "fairy raths", and that touching one of these tiny figures brought bad luck. The most famous of the "little people" is the leprechaun. Legend has it that if you caught one of these, he would lead you to a crock of gold, but take your eyes off him and he would vanish into thin air. The banshee was a female spirit whose wailing presence outside a house was said to signal the imminent death of someone within.

The diminutive figure of the leprechaun

A banshee with long flowing hair

Fianna possessed supernatural powers and often ventured into the life beyond, known as the Otherworld. Among these was Finn's son Ossian who was not only a formidable warrior, like his father, but was also renowned as a wise and knowledgeable poet. Through time, Finn has come to be commonly portrayed as a giant. Legend has it that he constructed the Giant's Causeway in County Antrim *(see pp254–5)*.

The children of King Lir being turned into white swans

end of the children's 900-year ordeal coincided with the coming of Christianity. The four children regained human form but were wizened and weak. They died soon afterwards, but not before being baptized. King Lir then decreed that no swan in Ireland should be killed – an act which is still illegal today.

SAINT BRENDAN

BRENDAN THE NAVIGATOR, like many other 6th-century monks, travelled widely. It is known that although he lived in western Ireland he visited Wales, Scotland and France. It is likely, though, that his most famous journey is fictitious. This story tells of a shipload of monks who, after seven years of all kinds of strange encounters designed to test their faith, found the Land of Promise. It is essentially a Christian retelling of the common tales of the Celtic Otherworld. The Feast of St Brendan on 16 May is celebrated in Kerry by the climbing of Mount Brandon.

A 19th-century engraving of Finn MacCool dressed for battle

THE CHILDREN OF LIR

ONE OF the saddest tales in Irish folklore involves King Lir, who so adored his four children that their stepmother was driven wild with jealousy. One day she took the children to a lake and cast a spell on them, turning them into white swans confined to the waters of Ireland for 900 years. However, as soon as she had done the deed, she became racked with guilt and bestowed upon them the gift of exquisite song. The

ORIGINS OF IRISH PLACE NAMES

The names of many of Ireland's cities, towns and villages today are largely based on ancient Gaelic terms for prominent local landmarks, some of which no longer exist. Here are just a few elements of the place names the traveller may come across.

The fort on the Rock of Cashel that gives the town its name

Ar, ard – *high, height*
Ass, ess – *waterfall*
A, ah, ath – *ford*
Bal, bally – *town*
Beg – *small*
Ben – *peak, mountain*
Carrick, carrig – *rock*
Cashel – *stone fort*
Crock, knock – *hill*
Curra, curragh – *marsh*
Darry, derry – *oak tree*
Dun – *castle*
Eden – *hill brow*
Innis, inch – *island*
Inver – *river mouth*
Isk, iska – *water*
Glas, glass – *green*
Glen, glyn – *valley*
Kil, kill – *church*
Lough – *lake, sea inlet*
Mona, mone – *peat bog*
Mor – *great, large*
Mullen, mullin – *mill*
Rath, raha – *ring fort*
Slieve – *mountain*
Toom – *burial ground*
Tul, tulagh – *small hill*

St Canice's Cathedral in Kilkenny (the town's name means "church of Canice")

Engraving showing St Brendan and his monks encountering a siren

The Sporting Year

ALL MAJOR INTERNATIONAL team sports are played in Ireland, but the most popular games are the two uniquely native ones of Gaelic football and hurling. Most of the big games, plus soccer and rugby internationals, are sold out well in advance. However, if you can't get a ticket you'll find plenty of company with whom to watch the event in pubs. Horse racing, with over 240 days of racing a year, attracts fanatical support. For those keen on participatory sports, there are also Ireland's famous fishing waters and golf courses *(see pp332–3).*

The North West 200 *is the fastest motorcycle race in the world over public roads – held near Portstewart* (see p252).

Football Association of Ireland Cup – the Republic's football final

Round-Ireland Yacht Race – held every two years

Irish Gold Cup: steeplechase at Punchestown

The Irish Grand National *is a gruelling steeplechase run at Fairyhouse in County Meath.*

| January | February | March | April | May | June |

Irish Champion Hurdle, run at Leopardstown, County Dublin

The International Rally of the Lakes *is a prestigious car rally around the Lakes of Killarney (see pp154–5).*

Start of the salmon fishing season

The Five Nations Rugby Tournament, *between Ireland, Scotland, Wales, England and France, runs until April. Ireland play their home games at Lansdowne Road, Dublin.*

KEY TO SEASONS

- Hurling
- Gaelic football
- Flat racing
- National Hunt racing
- Rugby
- Association football
- Salmon fishing
- Equestrianism

Irish Football League Cup – Northern Ireland's final

The Irish Derby, *Ireland's premier flat race, attracts many of Europe's best three-year-olds to the Curragh (see p121).*

The All-Ireland Football Final *is held at Croke Park in Dublin. The top two counties play for this Gaelic football championship. More people watch the game than any other event in Ireland.*

Cork Week *is a biennial regatta, organized by Royal Cork Yacht Club, where crews and boats of all classes meet and compete.*

Greyhound Derby, run at Shelbourne Park, Dublin

The Dublin Marathon *is Ireland's foremost marathon event. It attracts a huge field including top-class athletes from around the world.*

Galway Race Week is one of Ireland's premier festival meetings and a popular social event.

Millstreet Indoor International showjumping event

July	August	September	October	November	December

The Dublin Horse Show *is Ireland's premier horse show and a major event in the social calendar.*

All-Ireland Hurling Final at Croke Park, Dublin

THE GAELIC ATHLETIC ASSOCIATION

The GAA was founded in 1884 to promote indigenous Irish sport and discourage British influences – members were once forbidden from playing foreign games such as cricket. Today, despite heavy competition from soccer, the most popular sport in Ireland remains Gaelic football. However, the more intriguing GAA game is hurling – a fast and physical field sport played with sticks – which is said to have originated in ancient Celtic times. Both Gaelic football and hurling are played at parish and county level on a wholly amateur basis. The season ends with the All-Ireland finals, which draw large and passionate crowds to Dublin.

Camogie, a version of hurling played by women

The Irish Open Golf Championship *is held at a different course each year and attracts a world-class field to courses such as Ballybunion in County Kerry.*

THE HISTORY OF IRELAND

IRELAND'S RELATIVE ISOLATION has cut it off from several of the major events of European history. Roman legions, for example, never invaded and the country's early history is shrouded in myths of warring Gods and heroic High Kings. Nevertheless, the bellicose Celtic tribes were quick to embrace Christianity after the arrival of St Patrick on the island in AD 432.

Until the Viking invasions of the 9th century, Ireland enjoyed an era of relative peace. Huge monasteries like Clonmacnoise and Glendalough were founded, where scholarship and art flourished. The Vikings never succeeded in gaining control of the island but in 1169 the Anglo-Normans arrived with greater ambitions. Many Irish chiefs submitted to Henry II of England, who declared himself Lord of Ireland. He left in 1172, and his knights shared out large baronies between themselves.

Matters changed when Henry VIII broke with the Catholic church in 1532. Ireland became a battleground between native Irish Catholics and the forces of the English Crown. Where the Irish were defeated, their lands were confiscated and granted to Protestants from England and Scotland. England's conquest was completed with the victory of William of Orange over James II at the Battle of the Boyne in 1690. The new order was backed up by repressive Penal Laws that denied the Irish the most basic freedoms, but opposition to English rule was never totally quashed.

The Famine of 1845 to 1848 was the bleakest period of Irish history. Over two million either died or were forced to emigrate. Many who stayed were evicted by absentee English landlords. A campaign for Home Rule gathered strength, but it took decades of parliamentary infighting and bloody battles before the Government of Ireland Act of 1920 divided the island. The South became the Irish Free State, gaining full independence in 1937. Northern Ireland, where Protestants have a majority, has remained, despite bombing campaigns, part of the United Kingdom.

South Cross, Clonmacnoise

Map of Ireland, printed in 1592, showing the four traditional provinces

◁ *The Feast of St Kevin amid the ruins of Glendalough* by Joseph Peacock (1813)

Prehistoric Ireland

UNTIL ABOUT 9,500 YEARS ago Ireland was uninhabited. The first people, who may have crossed by a land bridge from Scotland, were hunter-gatherers and left few traces of permanent settlement. The 4th millennium BC saw the arrival of Neolithic farmers and herdsmen who built stone field walls and monumental tombs such as Newgrange.

Early Bronze Age stone axe-head

Metalworking was brought from Europe around 2000 BC by the Bronze Age Beaker people, who also introduced new pottery skills. The Iron Age reached Ireland in the 3rd century BC along with the Celts, who migrated from Central Europe, via France and Britain, and soon established themselves as the dominant culture.

IRELAND c. 8000 BC

    Former coastline

    Present-day coastline

The terminal discs were worn on the shoulders.

GLENINSHEEN GORGET

Many remarkable pieces of gold jewellery were created in the late Bronze Age. This gold collar dates from about 700 BC. The Iron Age Celts produced similarly fine metalwork and ornaments.

Dolmens or Portal Tombs
These striking megalithic tombs date from around 2000 BC. Legananny Dolmen in the Mountains of Mourne (see p276) is a fine example.

Three strands of ropework

Wooden Idol
This Iron Age fetish would have played a role in pagan fertility rites.

Celtic Stone Idol
This mysterious three-faced head was found in County Cavan. In Celtic religion the number three has always had a special significance.

Bronze Bridle Bit
Celtic chiefs rode into battle on two-horse chariots with beautifully decorated harnesses.

TIMELINE

8000 BC	6000	4000	2000	1000
c. 7500 BC First inhabitants of Ireland *Extinct giant deer or "Irish Elk"*	**5000–3000** Ireland covered by dense woodland dominated by oak and elm		**2500** Building of Newgrange passage tomb *(see pp238–9)*	**1500** Major advances in metalworking, especially gold
6000 Date of huts excavated at Mount Sandel, Co Londonderry; oldest known dwellings in Europe	**3700** Neolithic farmers reach Ireland; they clear woods to plant cereals		**2050** Beaker people (so-called for their delicate pottery vessels) reach Ireland at the beginning of Bronze Age	

Pallisade (fence)

Thatched houses

Causeway to lake shore

Reconstruction of a Crannog
Originating in the Bronze Age, crannogs were artificial islands built in lakes. At first used for fishing, they soon developed into well-protected homesteads. Some remained in use up to the 17th century.

The raised bands on the collar were created by *repoussé* work, pushed through from the back. The delicate rope motifs were added from the front with a knife.

Bone Slip
(c. AD 50)
This may have been used for divination or for gambling.

Gold Boat
Part of a hoard of gold objects found at Broighter, County London-derry, the boat (1st century AD) was made as a votive offering.

WHERE TO SEE PREHISTORIC IRELAND

Prehistoric sites range from individual tombs such as Newgrange, Browne's Hill Dolmen *(see p133)* or Ossian's Grave to whole settlements, as at Céide Fields *(p196)* and Lough Gur *(p186)*. The largest Stone Age cemetery is at Carrowmore *(p226)*. Good reconstructions of prehistoric structures can be seen at Craggaunowen *(p182)* and the Ulster History Park *(p261)*. The National Museum in Dublin *(pp64–5)* houses the finest collection of artifacts, including wonderful gold objects from the Bronze Age.

Newgrange (pp238–9) *is Ireland's finest restored Neolithic tomb. At the entrance lie huge spiral-patterned boulders.*

Ossian's Grave *is a court grave, the earliest kind of Neolithic tomb (p259). An open court stood before the burial mound.*

600 First wave of Celtic invaders	**500** Intertribal warfare; chieftains vie for title of *Ard Ri* (High King)	**AD 80** Roman general Agricola considers invasion of Ireland from Britain		**367** Roman Britain attacked by Irish, Picts and Saxons
750	**500**	**250**	**AD 1**	**AD 250**
Bronze goad decorated with birds		**250** Second wave of Celts, who bring La Tène style of pottery		**c. 150** Greek geographer Ptolemy draws up map and account of Ireland
		Bronze sword hilt imported from southern France		

Celtic Christianity

CELTIC IRELAND was divided into as many as 100 chiefdoms, though these often owed allegiance to kings of larger provinces such as Munster or Connaught. At times, there was also a titular High King based at Tara (*see p240*). Ireland became Christian in the 5th century AD, heralding a golden age of scholarship centred on the new monasteries, while missionaries such as St Columba travelled abroad. At the end of the 8th century, Celtic Ireland was shattered by the arrival of the Vikings.

Monk illuminating a manuscript

IRELAND IN 1000

- Viking settlements
- Traditional Irish provinces

Ogham Stone
The earliest Irish script, Ogham, dates from about AD 300. The notches correspond to Roman letters, like a form of Morse code.

CELTIC MONASTERY

Monasteries were large centres of population. This reconstruction shows Glendalough (*see pp132–3*) in about 1100. The tall round tower served as a lookout for Viking raiders.

Craftmen's dwellings

Refectory and kitchen

Round tower

Abbot's house

St Mary's Church

The water-mill was used for grinding wheat and barley.

The Magnus Domus was a large communal building used by the abbot and the monks.

St Kevin's Church

Dry-stone bridge

A High Cross marks the monastery boundary.

Battle of Clontarf
After their defeat by the Irish High King, Brian Boru, in 1014, the Vikings began to integrate more fully with the native population. Brian Boru himself was killed in the battle.

TIMELINE

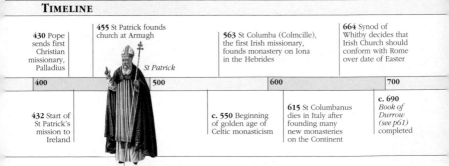

430 Pope sends first Christian missionary, Palladius

455 St Patrick founds church at Armagh

St Patrick

563 St Columba (Colmcille), the first Irish missionary, founds monastery on Iona in the Hebrides

664 Synod of Whitby decides that Irish Church should conform with Rome over date of Easter

400	500	600	700

432 Start of St Patrick's mission to Ireland

c. 550 Beginning of golden age of Celtic monasticism

615 St Columbanus dies in Italy after founding many new monasteries on the Continent

c. 690 *Book of Durrow* (*see p61*) completed

Viking Raids and Settlements
The first longships reached Ireland in 795. Though notorious for pillaging monasteries, the Vikings introduced new farming methods and coinage. They also founded walled cities such as Dublin, Waterford and Limerick.

Garryduff Gold Bird
Irish metalwork in the early Christian era was of very high quality. This gold ornament, possibly a wren, dates from around the 7th century AD.

WHERE TO SEE EARLY CHRISTIAN IRELAND

Important early monastic sites besides Glendalough include Clonmacnoise and Devenish Island. Churches from this period can also be seen at Gallarus (see p149), Clonfert (p205) and the Rock of Cashel (pp188–9), while High Crosses (p235) and round towers (p18) survive all over Ireland. Dublin's National Museum (pp64–5) has the best collection of ecclesiastical (and Viking) artifacts and Trinity College (pp60–62) houses the finest illuminated manuscripts.

***Devenish Island** has a fine 12th-century round tower and enjoys a peaceful setting on Lower Lough Erne (p263).*

Cathedral

Gatehouse

Guesthouse and stables

Monks' dwellings and barns

St Kieran's Church
and other important churches were built of stone, but most buildings were wood.

Clonmacnoise Crozier
This 11th-century bishop's staff is decorated with an ornate silver casing. The style of the incised patterns shows Viking influence.

***Clonmacnoise** (pp242–3) lies on the east bank of the Shannon. This Romanesque doorway is part of the ruined Nuns' Church.*

Viking silver brooch

795 First Viking invasion of coastal monasteries

807 Work starts on Kells monastery (see p233)

841 A large Viking fleet spends the winter at Dublin

967 Irish warriors sack Limerick and begin military campaign against Viking overlords

999 Sitric Silkenbeard, the Viking king of Dublin, surrenders to Brian Boru

1014 High King Brian Boru of Munster defeats joint army of Vikings and the King of Leinster at Clontarf

Viking coin

1134 Cormac's Chapel is built at Cashel (see pp188–9)

1142 Ireland's first Cistercian house founded at Mellifont (see p237)

1166 Dermot McMurrough, King of Leinster, flees overseas

| 800 | 900 | 1000 | 1100 |

Anglo-Norman Ireland

13th-century gold brooch

ANGLO-NORMAN NOBLES, led by Richard de Clare (nicknamed Strongbow), were invited to Ireland by the King of Leinster in 1169. They took control of the major towns and Henry II of England proclaimed himself overlord of Ireland. In succeeding centuries, however, English power declined and the Crown controlled just a small area around Dublin known as the Pale *(see p124)*. Many of the Anglo-Norman barons living outside the Pale opposed English rule just as strongly as did the native Irish clans.

IRELAND IN 1488

▨ *Extent of the Pale*

CARRICKFERGUS CASTLE

The first Anglo-Norman forts were wooden structures, but they soon started to build massive stone castles. Carrickfergus *(see p267)* was begun in the 1180s and by 1250 had acquired a keep and a gatehouse.

The keep contained a hall on the first floor and, above that, the lord's private apartments.

Guardroom

Storeroom

Stables

Bakery

Marriage of Strongbow
The King of Leinster gave his daughter to Strongbow for helping him regain his lands. Daniel Maclise's painting (1854) emphasizes Anglo-Norman power over the Irish.

Norman Weapons
These bows and arrows, unearthed at Waterford, may be relics of Strongbow's assault on the city in 1170.

TIMELINE

1172 Pope affirms King Henry II of England's lordship over Ireland

1177 John de Courcy's forces invade Ulster

Dermot McMurrough, King of Leinster, who invited Strongbow to come to his aid

1318 Bruce killed in battle

1315 Scots invade Ireland; Edward Bruce crowned king

1200	1250	1300

1169 Strongbow's Anglo-Normans arrive at invitation of exiled King of Leinster, Dermot McMurrough

1224 Dominican order enters Ireland and constructs friaries

1260 Powerful Irish chieftain Brian O'Neill killed at the Battle of Down

1297 First Irish Parliament meets in Dublin

Richard II's Fleet Returning to England in 1399
Richard made two trips to Ireland – in 1394 and 1399. On the first he defeated Art McMurrough, King of Leinster, and other Irish chiefs, but the second was inconclusive.

Kitchen

The gatehouse was the last addition made in the 13th century. The two towers have arrow loops for longbowmen.

Drawbridge

Chapel

The Hall was where the lord of the castle held public court and decided cases brought before him.

Éamonn Burke
The 14th-century Lord of Mayo was a typically independent chieftain of Anglo-Norman descent.

WHERE TO SEE ANGLO-NORMAN IRELAND

The strength of Norman fortifications is best seen in the castles at Carrickfergus, Limerick *(see p183)* and Trim *(p240)* and in Waterford's city walls. Gothic cathedrals that survive include Dublin's Christ Church *(pp78–9)* and St Patrick's *(pp80–81)* and St Canice's *(p136)* in Kilkenny. There are impressive ruins of medieval Cistercian abbeys at Jerpoint and Boyle *(p211)*.

Jerpoint Abbey (p137) *has a well-preserved 15th-century cloister decorated with carvings of curiously elongated figures.*

Waterford's *Anglo-Norman city walls include this sturdy watchtower* (pp138–9).

Great Charter Roll of Waterford (1372) showing portraits of the mayors of four medieval cities

1394 King Richard II lands with army to reassert control; returns five years later but with inconclusive results

1471 8th Earl of Kildare made Lord Deputy of Ireland

1496 Kildare regains Lord Deputy position

1491 Kildare supports Perkin Warbeck, pretender to the English throne

1350	1400	1450

1366 Statutes of Kilkenny forbid marriage between Anglo-Normans and Irish

1348 The Black Death: one third of population killed in three years

English forces (left) *confront Irish horsemen on Richard II's return expedition*

1487 Kildare crowns Lambert Simnel, Edward VI in Dublin

1494 Lord Deputy Edward Poynings forbids Irish Parliament to meet without royal consent

Protestant Conquest

Hugh O'Neill, Earl of Tyrone

ENGLAND'S BREAK with the Catholic Church, the dissolution of the monasteries and Henry VIII's assumption of the title King of Ireland incensed both the old Anglo-Norman dynasties and resurgent Irish clans such as the O'Neills. Resistance to foreign rule was fierce and it took over 150 years of war to establish the English Protestant ascendancy. Tudor and Stuart monarchs adopted a policy of military persuasion, then Plantation. Oliver Cromwell was even more forceful. Irish hopes were raised when the Catholic James II ascended to the English throne, but he was deposed and fled to Ireland, where he was defeated by William of Orange (William III) in 1690.

IRELAND IN 1625

◼ *Main areas of Plantation in the reign of James I*

The first relief ship to reach Londonderry was the *Phoenix*. For three months English ships had been prevented from sailing up the Foyle by a wooden barricade across the river.

Battle of the Boyne
This tapestry, from the Bank of Ireland (see p58), shows William of Orange leading his troops against the army of James II in 1690. His victory is still celebrated by Orangemen in Northern Ireland.

James II's army on the east bank of the Foyle attack the ship.

Silken Thomas Fitzgerald
Silken Thomas, head of the powerful Kildares, renounced his allegiance to Henry VIII in 1534. He was hanged along with his five uncles in 1537.

The artist's depiction of 17th-century weapons and uniforms is far from accurate.

TIMELINE

Henry VIII

Sir Thomas Lee, an officer in Elizabeth I's army, dressed in Irish fashion

1541 Henry VIII declared King of Ireland by Irish Parliament

1585 Ireland is mapped and divided into 32 counties

1592 Trinity College, Dublin founded

| 1500 | 1525 | 1550 | 1575 | 1(|

1534 Silken Thomas rebels against Henry VIII

1504 8th Earl of Kildare becomes master of Ireland after victory at Knocktoe

1539 Henry VIII dissolves monasteries

1557 Mary I orders first plantations in Offaly and Laois

1582 Desmond rebellion in Munster

1588 Spanish Armada wrecked off west coast

The Siege of Drogheda
Between 1649 and 1652 Cromwell's army avenged attacks on Protestant settlers with ruthless efficiency. Here Cromwell himself directs the gunners bombarding Drogheda.

PLANTATION IRELAND

James I realized that force alone could not stabilize Ireland. The Plantation programme uprooted the native Irish and gave their land to Protestant settlers from England and Scotland. London livery companies organized many of the new settlements. The policy created loyal garrisons who supported the Crown.

Bellaghy *in County Londonderry was settled by the Vintners Company. This map of the neatly planned town dates from 1622.*

The Walls of Derry have never been breached by any attacker and many of the original 17th-century gates and bastions that withstood the siege of 1689 are still in place *(see pp250–51).*

St George's flag

Ship Quay

Protestants emerge from the besieged city to greet the English relieving force and to engage the enemy.

Loftus Cup
Adam Loftus, Chancellor of Ireland, used his position to enrich his family. In 1593 he had the Great Seal of Ireland melted down and made into this silver-gilt cup.

THE RELIEF OF DERRY *(1689)*
Some 20,000 Protestants were besieged for 105 days in Londonderry by James II's forces. Thousands died from starvation, until relief finally came from English warships. This 18th-century painting by William Sadler II gives a rather fanciful picture of the ending of the siege.

1607 Flight of the Earls: old Irish leaders flee to the Continent; Plantation of Ulster

1632 Important Irish history, *The Annals of the Four Masters,* written by four Franciscan friars from Donegal

Protestant apprentice boys closing the gates of Derry before the siege of 1689

1690 William of Orange defeats James II at Battle of the Boyne; James's army surrenders the following year in Limerick

1625	1650	1675	1700

1603 Earl of Tyrone ends nine years of war by signing Treaty of Mellifont

1641 Armed rebellion in Ulster opposes Plantation

1649 Cromwell lands in Dublin; razes Drogheda and Wexford; Catholic landowners transplanted to far west

1688 James II, deposed Catholic king of England, flees to Ireland and raises army

1689 Siege of Derry

1695 Penal code severely reduces rights of Roman Catholics

Georgian Ireland

Lacquer cabinet in Castletown House

THE PROTESTANT ASCENDANCY was a period of great prosperity for the landed gentry, who built grand country houses and furnished them luxuriously. Catholics, meanwhile, were denied even the right to buy land. Towards the end of the century, radicals, influenced by events in America and France, started to demand independence from the English Crown. Prime Minister Henry Grattan tried a parliamentary route; Wolfe Tone and the United Irishmen opted for armed insurrection. Both approaches ultimately failed.

IRELAND IN 1703

Counties where Protestants owned over 75 per cent of land

The Irish House of Commons
This painting shows Irish leader Henry Grattan addressing the house (see p58). The "Grattan Parliament" lasted from 1782 to 1800, but was then abolished by the Act of Union.

State Bedroom

The saloon, the Casino's main room, was used for formal entertaining. It has a magnificent parquet floor.

Stone lions by Edward Smyth (1749–1812)

The basement contains the servants' hall, the kitchen, pantry and wine cellar.

Surveyors
The 18th century saw work begin on ambitious projects such as the Grand Canal, new roads and Dublin's network of wide streets and squares.

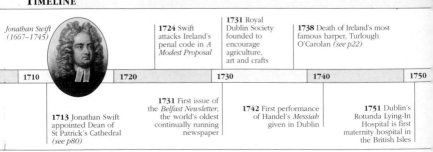

TIMELINE

Jonathan Swift (1667–1745)

1724 Swift attacks Ireland's penal code in *A Modest Proposal*

1731 Royal Dublin Society founded to encourage agriculture, art and crafts

1738 Death of Ireland's most famous harper, Turlough O'Carolan *(see p22)*

| 1710 | 1720 | 1730 | 1740 | 1750 |

1713 Jonathan Swift appointed Dean of St Patrick's Cathedral *(see p80)*

1731 First issue of the *Belfast Newsletter*, the world's oldest continually running newspaper

1742 First performance of Handel's *Messiah* given in Dublin

1751 Dublin's Rotunda Lying-In Hospital is first maternity hospital in the British Isles

Linen Bleaching
Ulster's linen industry flourished thanks to the expertise of Huguenot weavers from France. The woven cloth was spread out in fields or on river banks to bleach it (see p260).

The Classical urns on the roof conceal chimneys.

The china closet was originally designed as a bedroom.

Irish Painting
Aristocratic patronage encouraged the development of an Irish school of painting. This picture, by an unknown artist, shows Leixlip Castle in an idealized rural setting.

The hall ends in a semi-circular apse leading to the saloon.

Entrance

MARINO CASINO
This frivolous summer house was built in the 1760s for the first Earl of Charlemont on his estate just north of Dublin (*see p98*). Palladian architecture of this kind was popular among the Irish aristocracy, who followed 18th-century English fashions.

WHERE TO SEE GEORGIAN IRELAND

Dublin preserves many fine Georgian terraces and public buildings such as the Custom House *(see p86)* and the Four Courts *(p91)*. Around Dublin, the grand houses at Castletown *(pp122–3)*, Russborough and Powerscourt *(pp126–7)* are fascinating reminders of the lifestyle of the gentry. Other 18th-century country seats open to the public include Emo Court, Westport House *(pp196–7)* and Castle Coole *(p264)*.

Emo Court's *façade, with its plain Ionic portico, is by James Gandon, architect of many of Dublin's public buildings (p245).*

Russborough House *(p124) was built in 1741 by Richard Castle. Elegant niches with Classical busts flank the grand fireplace in the entrance hall.*

| 1760 | 1770 | 1780 | 1790 |

Guinness Brewery Gate

1782 Parliament gains greater degree of independence from Westminster

The Irish Volunteers, a local militia which pressed Parliament for reform

1798 Rebellion of Wolfe Tone's United Irishmen quashed

1759 Arthur Guinness buys the St James's Gate Brewery in Dublin

Custom House

1791 James Gandon's Custom House built in Dublin

1793 Limited emancipation for Irish Catholics

1795 Orange Order formed by Ulster Protestants

Famine and Emigration

Ration card from Famine period

THE HISTORY of 19th-century Ireland is dominated by the Great Famine of 1845–8, which was caused by the total failure of the potato crop. Although Irish grain was still being exported to England, around one million people died from hunger or disease, with even more fleeing to North America. By 1900, the pre-famine population of eight million had fallen by half. Rural hardship fuelled a campaign for tenants' rights which evolved into demands for independence from Britain. Great strides towards "Home Rule" were made in Parliament by the charismatic politician, Charles Stuart Parnell.

IRELAND IN 1851

☐ *Areas where population fell by over 25% during the Famine*

The ships that brought the Irish to America were overcrowded and fever-ridden, and known as "coffin ships".

Daniel O'Connell

Known as "The Liberator", O'Connell organized peaceful "monster rallies" of up to a million people in pursuit of Catholic emancipation. He was elected MP for Clare in 1828.

Castle Clinton was used for processing new arrivals to New York prior to the construction of the huge depot on Ellis Island.

The Boycotting of Landlords
In 1880, troops guarded the crops of Captain Boycott, the first notable victim of a campaign to ostracize landlords guilty of evicting tenants. His name later passed into the English language.

TIMELINE

Charles Bianconi's coach service, 1836

1815 First coach service begins in Ireland

1817 Royal Canal is completed

1838 Father Mathew founds temperance crusade – five million Irish take abstinence pledge and whiskey production is reduced by half

1845 Start Great Famine which lasts f four year

Father Mathew

1800	1810	1820	1830	1840

1803 Uprising, led by Robert Emmet, is crushed after feared Napoleonic invasion of England fails to materialize

1800 Act of Union: Ireland legally becomes part of Britain

1828 After a five-year campaign by Daniel O'Connell, Catholic Emancipation Act is passed, giving a limited number of Catholics the right to vote

Eviction of Irish Farmers
In the late 1870s, agricultural prices plummeted. Starving tenant farmers fell into arrears and were mercilessly evicted. Their plight spawned the Land League, which lobbied successfully for reform.

THE IRISH ABROAD

One result of the Famine was the growth of a strong Irish community in the USA. From the lowest rung of American society, the immigrants rose up the social scale and became rich by Irish Catholic standards. They sent money to causes back home, and as a well-organized lobby group put pressure on the American government to influence British policies in Ireland. A more militant group, Clan na Gael, sent veterans of the American Civil War to fight in the Fenian risings of 1865 and 1867.

New Yorkers *stage a huge St Patrick's Day parade, 17 March 1870.*

The Irish were widely perceived as illiterate peasants in the USA and often met with a hostile reception.

Charles Stuart Parnell
A campaigner for the Land League and Home Rule, Parnell saw his political career ruined in 1890, when he was cited as co-respondent in a divorce case.

IMMIGRANTS ARRIVE IN NEW YORK

The Irish who survived the journey to America landed at Castle Garden in New York, seen here in a painting by Samuel Waugh (1855). Although mainly country people, most new arrivals settled in Manhattan, often enduring horrific living conditions.

1853 Dublin Exhibition is opened by Queen Victoria

Dublin Exhibition

1877 Charles Stuart Parnell becomes leader of the new Home Rule Party

1884 Founding of Gaelic Athletic Association, first group to promote Irish traditions

1892 Second Home Rule Bill is defeated

1850	1860	1870	1880	1890

1867 Irish-Americans return home to fight in a rising led by the Irish Republican Brotherhood, also known as the Fenians

1881 Parnell is jailed in Kilmainham, Dublin

1886 British PM Gladstone sponsors first Home Rule Bill but is defeated by Parliament

1848 Failure of the Young Ireland Uprising – a spontaneous response to insurrections elsewhere in Europe

1879–82 Land War, led by Michael Davitt's Land League, campaigns for the reform of tenancy laws

War and Independence

Irish Free State stamp of 1922

Plans for Irish Home Rule were shelved because of World War I; however, the abortive Easter Rising of 1916 inspired new support for the Republican cause. In 1919 an unofficial Irish Parliament was established and a war began against the "occupying" British forces. The Anglo-Irish Treaty of 1921 divided the island in two, granting independence to the Irish Free State, while Northern Ireland remained in the United Kingdom. There followed a civil war between pro-Treaty and anti-Treaty factions in the South.

IRELAND IN 1922

⬛ *Northern Ireland*

☐ *Irish Free State*

The Unionist Party
Leader of the campaign against Home Rule was Dublin barrister Edward Carson. In 1913 the Ulster Volunteer Force was formed to demand that six counties in Ulster remain part of the UK.

Sean J Heuston

Major John McBride

Thomas McDonough

The 1916 Service Medal, issued to all who fought in the Easter Rising, depicts, on one side, the mythical Irish warrior Cuchulainn.

William Pearse

Patrick Pearse, a poet, read the Proclamation of the Republic from the steps of the GPO on Easter Monday.

The Black and Tans
Named for their makeshift uniforms, these British troops – mostly demobbed World War I soldiers – carried out savage reprisals against the Irish in 1920–21.

TIMELINE

The Titanic

1905 Sinn Féin (We Ourselves) party founded

1904 Dublin's Abbey Theatre opens

1912 Belfast-built *Titanic sinks on her maiden voyage*

1912 Edward Carson rallies Ulster Protestants; solemn covenant to defeat Home Rule signed by 471,414 people

Despatch bag carried by Constance Markievicz during Easter Rising

1913 General strike in Dublin

1916 Easter Rising quashed

1918 Sinn Féin wins 73 seats at Westminster; Constance Markievicz elected first woman MP

1919 Fi meeting indeper parliame (*Dáil Éi*

1920 Government of Ireland Act proposes partition of the island

1921 Anglo-Irish Treaty sigr de Valera resigns; south Ireland plunged into civil

1905	1910	1915	1

The General Post Office, Easter 1916
What was supposed to be a national uprising was confined to 2,500 armed insurgents in Dublin. They managed to hold the GPO and other public buildings for five days.

EAMON DE VALERA (1882–1975)
After escaping execution for his part in the Easter Rising, American-born de Valera went on to dominate Irish politics for almost 60 years. The opposition of his party, Sinn Fein, to the Anglo-Irish Treaty of 1921 plunged the new Irish Free State into civil war. After forming a new party, Fianna Fáil, he became Prime Minister (*Taioseach*) in 1932. De Valera remained in office until 1948, with further terms in the 1950s. Between 1959 and 1973 he was President of Ireland.

This Mauser rifle, smuggled in from Germany in 1914, was used by rebels in the Rising.

Tom Clarke

James Connolly

Joseph Plunkett

Mementoes of the Rising at Dublin's Kilmainham Gaol (*see p95*) include this crucifix made by a British soldier from rifle bullets.

Election Poster
Cumann na nGaedheal, the pro-Treaty party in the Civil War, won the Free State's first general election in 1923. It merged with other parties in 1933 to form Fine Gael.

LEADERS OF THE 1916 RISING
This collage portrait shows 14 leaders of the Easter Rising, who were all court-martialled and shot at Kilmainham Gaol. The brutality of their executions (the badly injured James Connolly was tied to a chair before being shot) changed public opinion of the Rising and guaranteed their status as martyrs.

22 Irish Free State inaugurated; Michael Collins shot dead in ambush in Co Cork

Michael Collins (1890–1922), hero of the War of Independence, became chairman of the Irish Free State and Commander-in-Chief of the Army

1932 Fianna Fáil sweep to victory in general election, and de Valera begins 16-year term as *Taioseach* (Prime Minister)

1936 IRA proscribed by Free State Government

1939 Éire declares neutrality during World War II

1925   1930   1935

1923 WB Yeats wins Nobel prize for Literature

1926 De Valera quits Sinn Féin; sets up Fianna Fáil (Soldiers of Destiny) party

1925 GB Shaw also receives Nobel prize

1929 Work started on River Shannon hydro-electric power scheme

1933 Fine Gael (United Ireland) party formed to oppose Fianna Fáil

1937 New constitution declares complete independence from Britain; country's name changes to Éire

Modern Ireland

Sᴉɴᴄᴇ ᴊᴏɪɴɪɴɢ the European Economic Community (now called the European Union) in 1973, the Irish Republic has done much to modernize its traditional rural-based economy. There have been social changes too, and laws prohibiting abortion and divorce have slowly been relaxed. Meanwhile, Northern Ireland has lived through more than 25 years of bombings and shootings, with British soldiers permanently on the streets.

Mary Robinson, Ireland's first woman President

Industry declined during the Troubles, but recent peace agreements have brought new hope to the province.

1972 Bloody Sunday – British soldiers shoot dead 13 demonstrators in Derry. Northern Ireland Parliament is suspended and direct rule from Westminster imposed

1970 Reverend Ian Paisley, a radical Protestant Unionist, wins the Bannside by-election

1969 Violent clashes between the police and demonstrators in Belfast and Derry. British troops sent to restore order

1956 IRA launches a terrorism campaign along the border with Northern Ireland which lasts until 1962

1967 Northern Ireland Civil Rights Association is set up to fight discrimination against Catholics

NORTHERN IRELAND		
1945	1955	1965
REPUBLIC OF IRELAND		

1959 Eamon de Valera resigns as *Taoiseach* (Prime Minister) and is later elected President

1949 New government under John A Costello. Country changes name from Éire to Republic of Ireland and leaves British Commonwealth

1955 Republic of Ireland joins United Nations. Irish troops have played an important role in UN peace-keeping missions around the world ever since

1963 John F Kennedy, the first American President of Irish Catholic descent, visits Ireland. He is pictured here with President Eamon de Valera

1969 Samuel Beckett, seen here rehearsing one of his own plays, is awarded the Nobel prize for literature, but does not go to Stockholm to receive it

1947 Statue of Queen Victoria is removed from the courtyard in front of the Irish Parliament in Dublin

1973 Republic of Ireland joins the European Economic Community at same time as the UK. Membership has given the country access to much-needed development grants

'74 Power-sharing experiment is ought down by a devastating ike, organized by Protestant orkers. Direct rule is reimposed

1985 Barry McGuigan beats the Panamanian, Eusebio Pedroza, for world featherweight boxing title

1976 Organizers of the Ulster Peace Movement, Mairead Corrigan and Betty Williams, are awarded the Nobel Peace Prize in Oslo

1982 De Lorean car factory in Belfast closes just four years after £17 million investment by British government

1981 Hunger-striker Bobbie Sands dies in Maze Prison

1986 Bitter Loyalist opposition follows the previous year's signing by the British and Irish governments of the Anglo-Irish Agreement

1987 IRA bomb explodes during Enniskillen's Remembrance Day parade, killing 11 people

1991 Peace talks instituted by Westminster between the main political parties of Northern Ireland (except Sinn Féin) and the British and Irish governments

1994 IRA and Protestant cease-fires. Gerry Adams, Sinn Féin leader, allowed to speak on British radio and television

1995 For the first time in 25 years, there are no troops on daylight patrols in Northern Ireland

1998 The Good Friday agreement sets out proposed framework for self-government in Northern Ireland

		NORTHERN IRELAND
1975	1985	1995
		REPUBLIC OF IRELAND

1988 Dublin's millennium is celebrated, boosting the city's image

1991 Mary Robinson becomes first female President of the Republic

1994 Republic of Ireland football team reaches quarterfinals of World Cup in the USA. Here, Ray Houghton is congratulated on scoring the winning goal against Italy

1992 In a referendum, 62 per cent of the Irish vote in favour of allowing pregnant women to seek an abortion abroad

1979 Pope John Paul II visits Ireland and celebrates Mass in Dublin's Phoenix Park, in front of more than a million people

1985 Irish pop singer Bob Geldof organizes Live Aid concerts in London and Philadelphia; £40 million is raised for African famine relief

1987 Dubliner Steven Roche wins the Tour de France, Giro d'Italia and World Championship in one incredible season

IRELAND THROUGH THE YEAR

POPULAR MONTHS for visiting Ireland are July and August, though whatever the season it's rarely crowded. June and September can be pleasant but never count on the weather, for Ireland's lush beauty is the product of a wet climate. Be aware that most tourist sights are open from Easter to September but have restricted opening hours or close in the low season. During spring and summer, festivals are held in

honour of everything from food to religion. A common thread is music, and few festivities are complete without musical accompaniment. Ireland is at its best when it has something to celebrate, so is an inspired choice for Christmas or New Year. Look out for the word *fleadh* (festival) on your travels but remember, too, that the Irish are a spontaneous people: festivities can spring from the air, or from a tune on a fiddle.

Ladies' Day at Dublin Horse Show

Dublin's annual parade to celebrate St Patrick's Day (17 March)

SPRING

ST PATRICK'S DAY is often said to mark the beginning of the tourist season. Later, the spring bank holiday weekend in May, when accommodation is in short supply, is celebrated with music in most places. After the quiet winter months, festivals and events start to become more common.

MARCH

Adare Jazz Festival *(mid-Mar, see p186)*. Staged in pubs and hotels throughout the town over five days.
St Patrick's Day *(17 Mar)*. Parades and pilgrimages held at Downpatrick, Armagh, Dublin, Cork, Limerick and many other places.
Horse Ploughing Match and Heavy Horse Show, Bally-castle *(17 Mar, see p258)*. The annual competition is more than 100 years old.

A St Patrick's Day float advertising Guinness

APRIL

Feis Ceoil, Dublin *(early Apr)*. A classical music festival held at many different venues throughout the city.
Pan Celtic Festival, Tralee *(mid-Apr, see p148)*. A lively celebration of Celtic culture, with music, dance and song.
Cork Choral Festival *(late Apr–May, see pp166–7)*.

MAY

Belfast Civic Festival and Lord Mayor's Show *(mid-May, see pp268–71)*. Street parade with bands and floats.
Royal Ulster Agriculture Society Show, Belfast *(mid-May)*. A three-day show with diverse events ranging from sheep-shearing competitions to fashion shows.
"A Taste of Baltimore" Shellfish Festival *(end May, see p162)*.
Fleadh Nua, Ennis, *end May, see p181)*. Four days of traditional Irish music, songs and dance.

SUMMER

FOR THE VISITOR, summer represents the height of the festive calendar. This is the busiest time of year for organized events, from music and arts festivals to lively local race meetings, summer schools and matchmaking festivals. Book accommodation if your plans include a popular festival.

Beach races at Laytown (June)

JUNE

Laytown Beach Races, Co Meath *(late May or early June)*. Horse races on the sand.
County Wicklow Garden Festival *(all month)*. Held at private and public gardens around the county, including Powerscourt *(see pp126–7)*.
An Tostal, Drumshanbo, Co Leitrim *(mid-Jun)*. A pageant of Irish music and dance.
Maracycle, Belfast and Dublin *(mid-Jun)*. Many thousands of people cycle each way between the two cities.
Bloomsday, Dublin *(16 Jun)*. Lectures, pub talks, readings, dramatizations and walks to celebrate James Joyce's greatest novel, *Ulysses*.

AVERAGE DAILY HOURS OF SUNSHINE

Hours

Sunshine Chart
The chart gives figures for Dublin, though conditions are similar around the country. The Southeast enjoys more sunshine hours than any other part of Ireland, while Northern Ireland receives marginally fewer hours of sun than the Republic.

Scurlogstown Olympiad Celtic Festival, Trim *(mid-Jun, see p240)*. Traditional Irish music, dance, fair and selection of a festival queen.
Music in Great Irish Houses *(second and third weeks)*. Classical music recitals in grand settings at various venues.
Castle Ward Opera, Strangford *(end Jun, see p276)*. Opera festival in the grounds of 18th-century stately home.
County Wexford Strawberry Fair; Enniscorthy *(end Jun–early Jul, see p141)*. Includes a craft fair, music, street theatre and, of course, strawberries.

JULY

Battle of the Boyne Day *(12 Jul, see p236)*. Members of the Orange Order march in towns across Northern Ireland to celebrate the Protestants' landmark victory over King James II's Catholic army in 1690.
Cork Regatta Week, Crosshaven, Co Cork *(mid-Jul)*.
Galway Arts Festival *(third & fourth weeks, see pp202–3)*. Processions, concerts, street theatre, children's shows and

Traditional sailing craft in the Cruinniú na mBad at Kinvarra (August)

many other events in the medieval city centre. Followed immediately by Galway's popular five-day race meeting.
Mary from Dungloe International Festival, Dungloe *(last week, see p220)*. Dancing, music and selection of "Mary", the beauty queen.
Lughnasa Fair, Carrickfergus Castle *(end Jul, see p267)*. A popular medieval-style fair.
Ballyshannon International Folk Festival *(end Jul, see p223)*. Three days of traditional Irish music.
O'Carolan Harp and Traditional Music Festival, Keadue, Co Roscommon *(end Jul–early Aug)*. Music and traditional dance.

AUGUST

Stradbally Steam-engine Rally, Co Laois *(early Aug)*. Many types of steam-engine join this rally.

Letterkenny Folk Festival, Co Donegal *(early Aug, see p219)*. A week of celebration.
Dublin Horse Show *(second week)*. A premier showjumping competition and important social event.
Puck Fair, Killorglin, Co Kerry *(mid-Aug, see p157)*. A wild goat is crowned "king" at this two-day-long traditional festival.
Blessing of the Sea *(second or third Sunday)*. Held in seaside towns all over Ireland.
Oul' Lammas Fair, Ballycastle *(mid-Aug, see p258)*. A popular fair that is particularly famous for its edible seaweed.
Kilkenny Arts Week *(fourth week, see pp134–6)*. A major arts festival including poetry, film, crafts and classical music.
Rose of Tralee Festival, *(end Aug, see p148)*. Bands, processions, dancing and selection of the "Rose".
Cruinniú na mBad, Kinvarra *(end Aug, see pp203–4)*. Various types of traditional sailing craft take part in this "gathering of the boats".

Orangemen parading on Battle of the Boyne Day

Steam-engine at Stradbally Rally (August)

AVERAGE MONTHLY RAINFALL

MM   Inches

Jan Feb Mar Apr May Jun Jul Aug Sep Oct Nov Dec

Rainfall Chart
Ireland is one of the wettest countries in Europe, with rainfall distributed evenly through the year – the figures displayed here are for Dublin. The West has the heaviest annual rainfall, while the Southeast receives marginally less rain than other regions.

Galway Oyster Festival (September)

AUTUMN

O YSTERS AND OPERA are the two big events in autumn. There are also festivals devoted to jazz, film and music. The October bank holiday weekend is celebrated with music in many towns; though it is low season, it can be difficult to find accommodation.

SEPTEMBER

All-Ireland Hurling Final, Croke Park, Dublin *(first Sunday, see p27)*.
Lisdoonvarna Matchmaking Festival *(all month and first week of Oct, see p180)*. Single people gather together for traditional music and dance.
Waterford International Festival of Light Opera *(mid-Sep –early Oct, see p329)*. Musicals and operettas at the Theatre Royal.
All-Ireland Football Final, Croke Park, Dublin *(3rd Sunday, see p27)*. Gaelic football final.
Sligo Arts Festival *(last week, see p226)*. Street entertainment, jazz, Irish music and dance.
Galway Oyster Festival *(end Sep, see pp202–3)*. Oyster tastings at different venues.

All-Ireland Hurling at Croke Park, Dublin

OCTOBER

Octoberfest, Londonderry *(all month, see pp250–51)*. Dance, poetry, film, comedy, theatre and music.
Cork Film Festival *(early Oct, see pp166–7)*. Irish and international films.
Kinsale Gourmet Festival *(early Oct, see pp164–5)*. Superb food is served in the

Horse and trap at Lisdoonvarna fair

hotels, restaurants and pubs of Ireland's "Gourmet Capital".
Ballinasloe Fair, Co Galway *(first week)*. One of Europe's oldest horse fairs, staged amid lively street entertainment.
Dublin Theatre Festival *(first and second week)*. Features works by both Irish and foreign playwrights.
Wexford Opera Festival *(last week Oct –first week Nov, see p329)*. A festival of lesser known operas.
Hallowe'en (Shamhana) *(31 Oct)*. An occasion celebrated all over the country.
Cork Jazz Festival *(end Oct, see pp166–7)*. An extremely popular festival, with music all over the city.

NOVEMBER

Sligo International Choral Festival *(early Nov, see p226)*. Choirs from around the world in concert and competition.
Carrick Theatre Festival, Carrick-on-Shannon, Co Leitrim *(mid-Nov, see p227)*. One-act plays in qualifying festival for the All-Ireland Drama Festival.
Belfast Festival at Queen's, Queen's University *(last three weeks, see pp268–71)*. Arts festival featuring drama, ballet, cinema and all types of music from classical to jazz.

Traditional horse fair at Ballinasloe in County Galway (October)

AVERAGE MONTHLY TEMPERATURE

Temperature Chart
This chart gives the average minimum and maximum temperatures for the city of Dublin. Winter is mild throughout Ireland, except in the high mountain ranges, while the warmest summer temperatures are in the Southeast.

WINTER

ALTHOUGH a quiet time for festivals, there's a range of entertainment including musical and theatrical events. Christmas is the busiest social period and there are plenty of informal celebrations. There is also a wide choice of National Hunt race meetings *(see p26)*.

DECEMBER

Pantomime Season *(Dec–Jan)*. Traditional pantomime performed at many theatres throughout Ireland.
Leopardstown Races *(26 Dec, see p121)*. The biggest meeting held on this traditional day for racing. There are other fixtures at Limerick and Down Royal.
St Stephen's Day *(26 Dec)*. Catholic boys traditionally dress up as Wren boys (chimney sweeps with blackened faces) and sing hymns to raise money for charitable causes.

Young boys dressed up as Wren boys on St Stephen's Day

JANUARY

Salmon and Sea Trout Season *(1 Jan–end Sep)*. Start of the season for one of the most popular pastimes in Ireland.

FEBRUARY

Dublin Film Festival *(end Feb–early Mar)*. International films at various venues.
Belfast Music Festival *(end Feb–mid-Mar)*. Young people take part in music (and speech and drama) competitions.
Five Nations Rugby Tournament, Lansdowne Road, Dublin *(varying Saturdays Feb–Apr, see p26)*.

PUBLIC HOLIDAYS

New Year's Day (1 Jan)
St Patrick's Day (17 Mar)
Good Friday
Easter Monday
May Day (1 May)
Spring Bank Holiday (Northern Ireland: last Mon in May)
June Bank Holiday (Republic: first Mon in Jun)
Battle of the Boyne Day (Northern Ireland: 12 Jul)
August Bank Holiday (first Mon in Aug)
Summer Bank Holiday (Northern Ireland: last Mon in Aug)
October Bank Holiday (last Mon in Oct)
Christmas Day (25 Dec)
St Stephen's Day (Republic: 26 Dec)
Boxing Day (Northern Ireland: 26 Dec)

Glendalough *(see pp132–3)* **in the snow**

DUBLIN AREA BY AREA

Dublin at a Glance

IRELAND'S CAPITAL has a wealth of attractions, most
within walking distance of each other. For the
purpose of this guide, central Dublin has been
divided into three sections: *Southeast Dublin*, heart
of the modern city and home to the prestigious
Trinity College; *Southwest Dublin*, site of the old
city around Dublin Castle; and *North of the Liffey*,
the area around the imposing O'Connell Street. The
map references given for sights in the city refer to
the *Dublin Street Finder* on pages 110–111.

Christ Church Cathedral
*was built by Dublin's Anglo-
Norman conquerors between
1172 and 1220. It stands on
high ground above the River
Liffey. Much of the
cathedral's present
appearance is due
to restoration carried
out in the 1870s.*
(See pp78–9.)

NORTH OF THE LIFFEY
Pages 82–91

**SOUTHWEST
DUBLIN**
Pages 70–81

Dublin Castle *stands in the heart of old
Dublin. St Patrick's Hall is part of the suite
of luxury State Apartments housed on the
upper floors on the south side of the castle.
Today, these rooms are used for functions of
national importance such as presidential
inaugurations.* (See pp74–5.)

St Patrick's Cathedral
*has a spectacular choir featuring
banners and stalls decorated with
the insignia of the Knights of St
Patrick. The cathedral also holds
Ireland's largest and most powerful
organ, as well as memorials to Dean
Jonathan Swift and prominent
Anglo-Irish families.* (See pp80–81.)

O'Connell Street, Dublin's main and busiest thoroughfare, has a fine mix of architectural styles and a grand central mall punctuated with statues of famous Irish citizens. Just off O'Connell Street, on Moore Street, is a colourful and lively market. (See pp86–7.)

The Custom House, a classic Georgian public building by James Gandon, was built between 1781 and 1791. The sculpted heads on the keystones are personifications of the rivers of Ireland; the one shown above represents the River Foyle. (See p86.)

Trinity College is home to the Old Library which contains priceless, illuminated manuscripts. These include the Book of Durrow which dates from the middle of the 7th century. (See pp60–62.)

SOUTHEAST DUBLIN
Pages 54–69

0 metres 400
0 yards 400

The National Gallery was opened in 1864. Housed on two floors, the well-organized gallery holds an eclectic collection, particularly strong on Irish and Italian paintings. The gallery's most prized painting is its recent acquisition The Taking of Christ by Caravaggio. (See pp68–9.)

The National Museum has an impressive collection of artifacts dating from the Stone Age to the 20th century. The Ardagh Chalice (c. 800 AD) is one of the many Celtic Christian treasures on display. (See pp64–5.)

SOUTHEAST DUBLIN

ESPITE ITS location close to the old walled city, this part of Dublin remained virtually undeveloped until the founding of Trinity College in 1592. Even then, it was almost a hundred years before the ancient common land further south was enclosed to create St Stephen's Green, a spacious city park.

The mid-18th century saw the beginning of a construction boom in the area. During this time, magnificent public buildings such as the Old Library at Trinity College, Leinster House and the Bank of Ireland were built. However, the most conspicuous reminders of Georgian Dublin are the beautiful squares and terraces around

Georgian doorknocker in Merrion Square

Merrion Square. Many of these buildings still have their original features, including doorknockers, fanlights and wrought-iron balconies.

Today, Southeast Dublin is very much the tourist heart of the city: few visitors can resist the lively atmosphere and attractive shops of Grafton Street. The area is also home to much of Ireland's cultural heritage. The National Gallery has a good collection of Irish and European paintings while the National Museum has superb displays of Irish Bronze Age gold and early Christian treasures. Nearby, the fascinating Natural History Museum has preserved its wonderful Victorian interior.

SIGHTS AT A GLANCE

Museums, Libraries and Galleries
National Gallery pp68–9 ⑪
National Library ⑧
National Museum pp64–5 ⑦
Natural History Museum ⑩
Royal Hibernian Academy ⑬

Historic Buildings
Bank of Ireland ①
Leinster House ⑨
Mansion House ⑤
Trinity College pp60–61 ②

Historic Streets
Fitzwilliam Square ⑭
Grafton Street ③
Merrion Square ⑫

Churches
St Ann's Church ⑥

Parks and Gardens
St Stephen's Green ④

KEY

▧	Street-by-Street map *See pp56–7*
🚆	Railway station
Ⓓ	DART station
Ⓟ	Parking
ℹ	Tourist information

0 metres 250
0 yards 250

◁ **Marble bust of Jonathan Swift in the Old Library, Trinity College**

Street-by-Street: Southeast Dublin

THE AREA AROUND COLLEGE GREEN, dominated by the façades of the Bank of Ireland and Trinity College, is very much the heart of Dublin. The alleys and malls cutting across busy pedestrianized Grafton Street boast many of Dublin's better shops, hotels and restaurants. Just off Kildare Street are the Irish Parliament, the National Library and the National Museum. To escape the city bustle many head for sanctuary in St Stephen's Green, which is overlooked by fine Georgian buildings.

To Dublin Castle

COLLEGE GREEN

Bank of Ireland
This grand Georgian building was originally built as the Irish Parliament ❶

Statue of Molly Malone (1988)

Grafton Street
Bewley's Oriental Café is the social hub of this busy pedestrian street, alive with talented buskers and pavement artists ❸

St Ann's Church
The striking façade of the 18th-century church was added in 1868. The interior features lovely stained-glass windows ❻

Mansion House
This has been the official residence of Dublin's Lord Mayor since 1715 ❺

Fusiliers' Arch (1907)

★ St Stephen's Green
The relaxing city park is surrounded by many grand buildings. In summer, lunch-time concerts attract tourists and workers alike ❹

To O'Connell Bridge

LOCATOR MAP
See Dublin map pp110–11

★ **Trinity College**
Pomodoro's sculpture,
Sphere within Sphere
*(1982), adds a modern
dimension to the
grand buildings
of the campus* ❷

National Library
*Saintly cherubs appear on the frieze
around the library's magnificent old
reading room, once a haunt of
novelist James Joyce* ❽

Leinster House
*This grand
house has been
the home of the
Irish Parliament
since 1922* ❾

★ **National Museum**
*The museum's
collection of Irish
antiquities includes a
mysterious bronze
object known as the
Petrie Crown (2nd
century AD)* ❼

NASSAU STREET

FREDERICK STREET

OLESWORTH STREET

KILDARE STREET

The Shelbourne Hotel,
built in 1867, dominates the
north side of St Stephen's Green.
It is a popular spot with tourists
and locals for afternoon tea.

STAR SIGHTS
★ **Trinity College**
★ **National Museum**
★ **St Stephen's Green**

0 metres 50
0 yards 50

KEY

– – – Suggested route

Original chamber of the Irish House of Lords at the Bank of Ireland

Bank of Ireland ❶

2 College Green. **Map** D3. 661
5933 ext 2265. 10am–4pm Mon–
Wed & Fri, 10am–5pm Thu. public
hols. **House of Lords** 10:30am,
11:30am & 1:45pm Tue or by appt.

THE PRESTIGIOUS offices of
Ireland's national bank
began life as the first purpose-
built parliament house in
Europe. The original central
section was started by Irish
architect Edward Lovett
Pearce and completed in 1739
after his death. Sadly, Pearce's
masterpiece, the great octagonal chamber of the House of
Commons (see p38), was
destroyed by fire in 1792. The
House of Lords, however,
remains gloriously intact.
Attendants lead tours that
point out the coffered ceiling
and oak panelling. There are
also huge tapestries of the
Battle of the Boyne and the
Siege of Londonderry, and a
splendid 1,233-piece crystal
chandelier dating from 1788.
   The east portico was added
by architect James Gandon in
1785. Further
additions to
the building
were made
around
1797.

Bronze statue of *Molly Malone* on Grafton Street

After the dissolution of the
Irish Parliament in 1800, the
Bank of Ireland bought the
building. The present structure
was then completed in 1808
with the transformation of the
former lobby of the House of
Commons into a magnificent
cash office and the addition
of a curving screen wall and
the Foster Place annexe.
   At the front of the bank on
College Green – common
grazing land in the 17th
century – is a statue (1879) by
John Foley of Henry Grattan
(see p38), the most formidable
leader of the old parliament.

Trinity College ❷

See pp60–61.

Grafton Street ❸

Map D4.

THE SPINE OF DUBLIN'S most
popular and stylish shop-
ping district runs south from
Trinity College to the glass St
Stephen's Green Shopping
Centre. At the junction with
Nassau Street is a statue by
Jean Rynhart of *Molly Malone*
(1988), the celebrated street
trader from the traditional
song "Molly Malone". This
busy pedestrianized strip,
characterized by energetic
buskers and talented street

theatre artists, boasts Brown
Thomas, one of Dublin's
finest department stores (see
p325). However, the street's
most famous landmark is
Bewley's Oriental Café at No.
78 (see p306). Although not
the oldest branch of this 150-
year-old Dublin institution,
this is Bewley's most popular
location. It stands on the site
of Samuel Whyte's school,
whose illustrious roll included
Robert Emmet (see p75),
leader of the 1803 Rebellion,
and the Duke of Wellington.
   Despite the removal of the
old wooden pews, the café
retains its Victorian ambience,
especially in the James Joyce
Room on the first floor.

St Stephen's Green ❹

Map D5. daylight hours.
Newman House 85–86 St Stephen's
Green. 706 7422. Jun–Aug:
noon–5pm Tue–Fri, 2–5pm Sat, 11am–
2pm Sun (Sep–May: by appointment).
public hols. obligatory.

Royal College of Surgeons, which
overlooks St Stephen's Green

ORIGINALLY one of three
ancient commons in the
old city, St Stephen's Green
was enclosed in 1664. The
9-ha (22-acre) green was laid
out in its present form in
1880, using a grant given by
Lord Ardilaun, a member of
the Guinness family. Landscaped with flowerbeds, trees,
a fountain and a lake, the
green is dotted with memorials
to eminent Dubliners, including
Ardilaun himself. There is a
bust of James Joyce (see p88),
and a memorial by Henry
Moore (1967) dedicated to
WB Yeats (see pp224–5). At

Dubliners relaxing by the lake in St Stephen's Green

the Merrion Row corner stands a massive monument (1967) by Edward Delaney to 18th-century nationalist leader Wolfe Tone – it is known locally as "Tonehenge". The 1887 bandstand is still the focal point for free daytime concerts in summer.

The imposing Royal College of Surgeons stands on the west side. Built in 1806, it was commandeered by rebel troops under Countess Constance Markievicz in the 1916 Rising (see pp42–3) and its columns still bear the marks of bullets from the fighting.

The busiest side of the Green is the north, known during the 19th century as the Beaux' Walk and still home to several gentlemen's clubs. The most prominent building is the venerable Shelbourne Hotel (see p287). Dating back to 1867, its entrance is adorned by statues of Nubian princesses and attendant slaves. It is well worth popping in for a look at the chandeliered foyer and for afternoon tea in the Lord Mayor's Lounge.

Situated on the south side is Newman House, home of the Catholic University of Ireland (now part of University College). Opened in 1854, its first rector was English theologian John Henry Newman. Famous past pupils include Patrick Pearse, a leader of the 1916 Rising, former Taoiseach Eamon de Valera (see p43) and author James Joyce.

Tours reveal some of the best Georgian interior decor to survive in the city. The walls and ceilings of the Apollo Room and Saloon at No. 85 are festooned with intricate Baroque stuccowork (1739) by the Swiss brothers Paolo and Filippo Francini. The Bishops' Room at No. 86 is decorated with heavy 19th-century furniture.

The small University Church (1856) next door has a colourful, richly marbled Byzantine interior. Also on the south side of St Stephen's Green is Iveagh House, a town house once owned by the Guinness family and now the Department of Foreign Affairs.

Mansion House ❺

Dawson St. **Map** E4. ◉ to the public.

SET BACK from Dawson Street by a neat cobbled forecourt, the Mansion House is an attractive Queen Anne-style building. It was built in 1710 for the aristocrat Joshua Dawson, after whom the street is named. The Dublin Corporation bought it from him five years later as the official residence of the city's Lord Mayor. A grey stucco façade was added in Victorian times.

The Dáil Éireann (see p63), which adopted the Declaration of Independence, first met here on 21 January 1919. The building is now used mostly for civic functions and receptions.

St Ann's Church ❻

Dawson St. **Map** E4. 📞 676 7727. ⭘ 10am–4pm Mon–Fri (also for Sun service, phone to check).

FOUNDED IN 1707, St Ann's striking Romanesque façade was added in 1868. Inside are colourful stained-glass windows, dating from the mid-19th century. The church has a long tradition of charity work: in 1723 Lord Newton left a bequest to buy bread for the poor. The original shelf for the bread still stands next to the altar.

Famous past parishioners include Wolfe Tone (see p39), who was married here in 1785, Douglas Hyde (see p43) and Bram Stoker (1847–1912), author of Dracula.

Detail of window depicting Faith, Hope and Charity, St Ann's Church

Trinity College ❷

Trinity College coat of arms

TRINITY COLLEGE was founded in 1592 by Queen Elizabeth I on the site of an Augustinian monastery. Originally a Protestant college, it only began to take Catholics in numbers after 1970, when the Catholic Church relaxed its opposition to their attending. Among Trinity's many famous students were playwrights Oliver Goldsmith and Samuel Beckett, and political writer Edmund Burke. The college's lawns and cobbled quads provide a pleasant haven in the heart of the city. The major attractions are the Old Library and the *Book of Kells*, housed in the Treasury.

★ Campanile
The 30-m (98-ft) bell tower was built in 1853 by Sir Charles Lanyon, architect of Queen's University, Belfast (see p270).

Reclining Connected Forms (1969) by Henry Moore

Dining Hall (1761)

Chapel *(1798)*
This was the first university chapel in the Republic to accept all denominations. The painted window above the altar is from 1867.

Parliament Square

Statue of Edmund Burke (1868) by John Foley

Main entrance

Statue of Oliver Goldsmith (1864) by John Foley

SAMUEL BECKETT (1906–89)

Nobel prizewinner Samuel Beckett was born at Foxrock, south of Dublin. In 1923 he entered Trinity, and later graduated with a first in modern languages and a gold medal. He was also a keen member of the college cricket team. Forsaking Ireland, Beckett moved to France in the early 1930s. Many of his major works such as *Waiting for Godot* (1951) were written first in French, and later translated, by Beckett, into English.

Provost's House (c. 1760)

Examination Hall
Completed in 1791 to a design by Sir William Chambers, the hall features a gilded oak chandelier and ornate ceilings by Michael Stapleton.

Library Square
The red-brick building (known as the Rubrics) on the east side of Library Square was built around 1700 and is the oldest surviving part of the college.

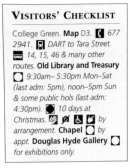

The Museum Building, completed in 1857, is noted for its Venetian exterior, and its magnificent multicoloured hall and double-domed roof.

Shop and entrance to Old Library

Sphere within Sphere
(1982) was given to the college by its sculptor Arnaldo Pomodoro.

New Square

Berkeley Library Building by Paul Koralek (1967)

Fellows' Square

Entrance from Nassau Street

The Douglas Hyde Gallery was built in the 1970s to house temporary art exhibitions.

★ **Old Library** *(1732)*
The spectacular Long Room measures 64 m (210 ft) from end to end. It houses 200,000 antiquarian texts, marble busts of scholars and the oldest surviving harp in Ireland.

★ **Treasury**
This detail is from the Book of Durrow, *one of the other magnificent illuminated manuscripts housed in the Treasury along with the celebrated* Book of Kells (see p62).

STAR FEATURES

★ **Old Library**

★ **Treasury**

★ **Campanile**

The Book of Kells

THE MOST RICHLY decorated of Ireland's medieval illuminated manuscripts, the *Book of Kells* may have been the work of monks from Iona, who fled to Kells *(see p233)* in AD 806 after a Viking raid. The book, which was moved to Trinity College *(see p60–61)* in the 17th century, contains the four gospels in Latin. The scribes who copied the texts also embellished their calligraphy with intricate interlacing spirals as well as human figures and animals. Some of the dyes used were imported from as far as the Middle East.

Pair of moths

Stylized angel

The Greek letter "X"

The symbols of the four evangelists are used as decoration throughout the book. The figure of the man symbolizes St Matthew.

The letter that looks like a "P" is a Greek "R".

The letter "I"

Interlacing motifs

Cat watching rats

A full-page portrait of St Matthew, shown standing barefoot in front of a throne, precedes the opening words of his gospel.

Rats eating bread could be a reference to sinners taking Holy Communion. The symbolism of the animals and people decorating the manuscript is often hard to interpret.

MONOGRAM PAGE

This, the most elaborate page of the book, contains the first three words of St Matthew's account of the birth of Christ. The first word "XRI" is an abbreviation of "Christi".

The text is in a beautifully rounded Celtic script with brightly ornamented initial letters. Animal and human forms are often used to decorate the end of a line.

The magnificent domed Reading Room on the first floor of the National Library

National Museum ❼

See pp64–5.

National Library ❽

Kildare St. **Map** E4. 661 8811.
10am–9pm Mon, 2–9pm Tue &
Wed, 10am–5pm Thu & Fri, 10am–
1pm Sat. public hols.

DESIGNED BY Sir Thomas
Deane, the National
Library was opened in 1890.
It was built to house the
collection of the Royal Dublin
Society, which was formed in
1731 to promote the arts and
sciences and improve conditions for the poor. On display
in the entrance hall are temporary exhibitions of treasures
from the library's archive. This
includes manuscripts by playwright George Bernard Shaw,
and politician and liberator,
Daniel O'Connell *(see p40).*
The 13th-century manuscript
of Giraldus Cambrensis's
Topographia Hiberniae is a
prized acquisition, as is the
huge collection of photo-
graphs of Victorian Ireland.
 The first-floor Reading Room
(where Joyce sited the literary
debate in *Ulysses*) has well-
worn desks and green-shaded
lamps. Simply ask an attendant
for a visitor's pass. There is
also a small genealogy exhibit;
a more extensive display,

along with details on how
to trace family trees, can be
found at the Heraldic Museum
in the Genealogical Office a
few doors down at Nos. 2
and 3 Kildare Street.

Leinster House ❾

Kildare St. **Map** E4. 618 3000.
to the public. by arrangement,
ask at Kildare St entrance or phone
for details.

THIS STATELY MANSION houses
the *Dáil* and the *Seanad* –
the two chambers of the Irish
Parliament. It was originally

built for the Duke of Leinster
in 1745. Designed by German-
born architect Richard Castle,
the Kildare Street façade
resembles that of a large town
house. However, the rear,
looking on to Merrion Square,
has the air of a country estate
complete with sweeping lawns.
The Royal Dublin Society
bought the building in 1815.
The government obtained a
part of it in 1922 for parliamentary use and bought the
entire building two years later.
 Visitors can arrange to tour
the main rooms, including the
Seanad chamber with its
heavily ornamented ceiling.

THE IRISH PARLIAMENT

The Irish Free State, forerunner of the Republic of Ireland,
was inaugurated in 1922 *(see p42)*, although an unofficial
Irish parliament, the *Dáil*, had already been in existence since
1919. Today, parliament is
made up of two houses:
the *Dáil* (House of Repre-
sentatives) and the *Seanad
Éireann* (Senate). The Prime
Minister is the *Taoiseach* and
the deputy, the *Tánaiste*.
The *Dáil's* 166 representa-
tives – *Teachta Dala,* known
as TDs – are elected by
proportional representation.
The 60-strong *Seanad* is
appointed by various
individuals and authorities,
including the *Taoiseach* and
the University of Dublin.

**Opening of the first parliament
of the Irish Free State in 1922**

National Museum ●

THE NATIONAL MUSEUM OF IRELAND was built in the 1880s to the design of Sir Thomas Deane. Its splendid domed rotunda features marble pillars and a zodiac mosaic floor. The Treasury houses priceless items such as the Broighter gold boat *(see p31)*, while *Ór – Ireland's Gold*, an exhibition focusing on Ireland's Bronze Age gold, contains beautiful jewellery such as the Gleninsheen Gorget *(see pp30–31)*. The museum's other permanent displays feature prehistoric Ireland, the Vikings in Ireland and ancient Egypt.

A curving portico, with a grandiose sweep of Classical-style columns, fronts the museum.

Flag from 1916 Rising
The Road to Independence *exhibition covers historical events between 1900 and 1921. This flag flew over Dublin's GPO during the Easter Rising* (see p87).

★ Ór – Ireland's Gold
This is one of the most extensive collections of Bronze Age gold in Western Europe. This gold lunula (c. 1800 BC) is one of many pieces of fine jewellery in the exhibition.

GALLERY GUIDE
The ground floor holds The Treasury, Ór – Ireland's Gold *exhibition,* The Road to Independence *and the* Prehistoric Ireland *display. The first floor houses Viking artifacts and the Ancient Egypt gallery. There may be other new displays, while some rooms may be closed to the public – this is due to the continuing reorganization of the museum.*

KEY TO FLOORPLAN

- ☐ The Road to Independence
- ☐ Ór – Ireland's Gold
- ☐ The Treasury
- ☐ Prehistoric Ireland
- ☐ Ancient Egypt
- ☐ Viking exhibition
- ☐ Temporary exhibitions
- ☐ Non-exhibition space

The domed rotunda, based on the design of the Altes Museum in Berlin, makes an impressive entrance hall.

Main entrance

The Treasury houses masterpieces of Irish crafts such as the Ardagh Chalice *(see p53)*.

First floor

The temporary exhibition space has changing displays of objects, usually from the museum's own collection.

★ **Cross of Cong** *Some 75 cm (30 inches) in height, this processional cross shows a high level of craftsmanship. Dating from 1123, its gilt-bronze plating is adorned with silver wire, crystals and enamelled studs.*

The Viking exhibition houses many items, including coins, pottery and swords uncovered in the 1970s from the Viking settlement, discovered beside the Liffey at Wood Quay *(see p76).*

Ground floor

Crucifixion Plaque
This plaque is one of the earliest depictions of the crucifixion found in Ireland. Dating from the late 7th century, it may have been decoration for a manuscript cover.

St Patrick's Bell, made of bronze-coated iron, is housed in a beautiful 12th-century shrine *(see inset p3).*

★ **Tara Brooch**
Found at Bettystown, County Meath, this ornate brooch dates from the 8th century AD. It is decorated on the front and rear with a filigree of gold wire entwined around settings of amber and enamel.

STAR EXHIBITS

★ **Ór – Ireland's Gold**

★ **Cross of Cong**

★ **Tara Brooch**

Natural History Museum ➓

Merrion St. **Map** E4. **[** 677 7444.
○ 10am–5pm Tue–Sat, 2–5pm Sun.
● public hols. ♿ ground floor only.
☑ May–Sep.

KNOWN AFFECTIONATELY as the "Dead Zoo", this museum is crammed with antique glass cabinets containing stuffed animals from around the world. The museum was opened to the public in 1857 with an inaugural lecture by Dr David Livingstone on African fauna. It remains virtually unchanged from Victorian times and is now a museum piece itself.

The Irish room on the ground floor holds exhibits on Irish wildlife. Inside the front door are three huge skeletons of the extinct giant deer, better known as the "Irish elk". Also on this floor are shelves stacked with jars of bizarre creatures such as octopuses, leeches and worms preserved in embalming fluid.

The upper gallery houses the noted Blaschka Collection of glass models of marine life, and a display of buffalo and deer trophies. Suspended from the ceiling are the skeletons of a fin whale, found at Bantry Bay *(see p159)* in 1862, and a humpback whale, which was found stranded at Inishcrone in County Sligo in 1893.

Lawn and front entrance of the Natural History Museum

National Gallery ⓫

See pp68–9.

Georgian town houses overlooking Merrion Square gardens

Merrion Square ⓬

Map F4.

MERRION SQUARE is one of Dublin's largest and grandest Georgian squares. Covering about 5 ha (12 acres), the square was laid out by John Ensor around 1762.

On the west side are the impressive façades of the Natural History Museum, the National Gallery and the front garden of Leinster House *(see p63)*. However, this august triumvirate does not compare with the lovely Georgian town houses on the other three sides of the square. Many have brightly painted doors with original features such as wrought-iron balconies, ornate doorknockers and fanlights. The oldest and finest houses are on the north side.

Many of the houses – now predominantly used as office space – have plaques detailing the rich and famous who once lived in them. These include Catholic emancipation leader Daniel O'Connell *(see p40)*, who lived at No. 58 and poet WB Yeats *(see pp224–5)*, who lived at No. 82. The playwright Oscar Wilde *(see p20)* spent his childhood at No. 1.

The attractive central park features colourful flower and shrub beds. In the 1840s it served a grim function as an emergency soup kitchen, feeding the hungry during the Great Famine *(see p211)*. On the northwest side of the park stands the restored Rutland Fountain. It was originally erected in 1791 for the sole use of Dublin's poor.

Just off the square, at No. 24 Merrion Street Upper, is the birthplace of the Duke of

Wellington, who, when teased about his Irish background, said, "Being born in a stable does not make one a horse."

Royal Hibernian Academy ⓭

15 Ely Place. **Map** E5. **[** 661 2558.
○ 11am–5pm Mon–Wed, Fri & Sat, 11am–9pm Thu, 2–5pm Sun.
● public & Christmas hols.

THE ACADEMY is one of the largest exhibition spaces in the city. It puts on touring exhibitions and mounts shows of painting, sculpture and other work by Ireland's best young art and design students. This modern brick-and-plate-glass building does, however, look out of place at the end of Ely Place, an attractive Georgian cul-de-sac.

Fitzwilliam Square ⓮

Map E5. **No. 29 Fitzwilliam St Lower**
[702 6165. ○ 10am–5pm Mon–Sat, 2–5pm Sun. ● 3 weeks at Christmas. ☑ ☑

DATING FROM 1825, this was one of the last Georgian squares to be laid out in central Dublin. Much smaller than Merrion Square, it is a popular location for medical practices.

In the 1960s, more than 20 town houses on Fitzwilliam Street Lower, a continuation of the east side of the square, were destroyed to make way for the headquarters of the Electricity Supply Board. The company has since tried to appease public indignation by renovating No. 29 as a Georgian showpiece home.

Dublin's Georgian Terraces

THE 18TH CENTURY was Dublin's Age of Elegance, a time of relative prosperity when the Irish gentry, keen not to appear as the poor relations of Britain, set about remodelling Dublin into one of the most elegant cities in Europe. Terraced town houses were built, forming handsome new streets and squares. During the 19th century the city's wealth declined,

Doorknocker, Merrion Square

forcing some middle-class families to divide their homes into tenements. Many of Dublin's once grand streets slowly deteriorated. A century later the property boom of the 1960s threatened to rip out what was left of Georgian Dublin. Fortunately, much has survived and some of the city's finest architecture can be seen in Merrion Square and Fitzwilliam Square.

Playroom

Attic

Wrought-iron balconies gave added prestige to the Georgian house. Those still in place today are mostly later Victorian additions.

The bedrooms were usually on the second floor, while the upper floors contained the servants' quarters and children's rooms.

Lavish stuccowork was an important way of showing an owner's wealth during the 18th century.

The drawing room was always on the first floor. The high ceiling was decorated with the finest plasterwork.

Architrave

The dining room was normally on the ground floor.

The kitchen contained a huge cooking range which was fired by either coal or wood. The adjoining pantry was used to store the household's groceries.

The doorway was usually crowned with a segmented fanlight. The principal decoration on the door itself was a heavy brass knocker.

GEORGIAN TERRACED HOUSE

While Georgian streetscapes may appear uniform, closer inspection reveals a diversity of styles in terms of details such as fanlights, architraves and balconies. The hallways usually had stone floors and, facing the hall door, a staircase rising to the upper floors. Many of the town houses did not have gardens – the railed-off parks in the centre of the squares were reserved for residents only and served as such.

National Gallery ⑪

THIS PURPOSE-BUILT gallery was opened to the public in 1864. It houses many excellent exhibits, largely due to generous bequests, such as the Milltown collection of works of art from Russborough House *(see p124)*. Playwright George Bernard Shaw was also a benefactor, leaving a third of his estate to the gallery. More than 600 works are on display in the gallery and, although there is much emphasis on Irish landscape art and portraits, every major school of European painting is well represented.

The Houseless Wanderer by John Foley

Pierrot
This Cubist-style work, by Spanish-born artist Juan Gris, is one of many variations he painted on the theme of Pierrot and Harlequin. This particular one dates from 1921.

First floor

★ For the Road
A whole room is dedicated to the works of Jack Yeats (1871–1957). This mysterious late painting reflects the artist's obsession with the Sligo countryside.

The Shaw Fund Gallery is an elegant hall, lined with full-length portraits, dating from the 17th century onwards, and lit by magnificent Waterford Crystal chandeliers.

GALLERY GUIDE

The collection is housed on two floors. On the ground floor are the Irish and British rooms: Room 32 has portraits of Irish sitters by artists from all schools. The maze-like first floor features works hung in broadly chronological order according to nation. The Italian, French, Dutch and Flemish collections account for most of the space.

19th-century façade

Main entrance

Lecture theatre

STAR PAINTINGS

★ **The Taking of Christ by Caravaggio**

★ **Castle of Bentheim by Ruisdael**

★ **For the Road by Jack Yeats**

The French Rooms hold works by artists such as Poussin, Monet and Degas, as well as a few Impressionist paintings.

The Spanish Room houses a broad collection, including works by Goya and Zurbarán.

Stairway

The Dutch, Flemish and German rooms feature works by Rubens, Rembrandt and Hobbema.

★ The Taking of Christ
Rediscovered in the Dublin Jesuit House of Study in 1990, this 1602 composition by Caravaggio has enhanced the gallery's reputation.

★ Castle of Bentheim
This 17th-century Dutch landscape was painted by Jacob van Ruisdael when he was only 24 years old.

Ground floor

Judith with the Head of Holofernes
Renaissance artist Andrea Mantegna (c. 1431–1506) used a monochrome scheme to depict this image of the decapitation of an Assyrian chief, in the style of a Classical Roman stone carving.

KEY TO FLOORPLAN

- Irish
- British
- Baroque
- French
- Italian
- Spanish
- Dutch, Flemish and German
- Non-exhibition space

The Sick Call
Painted in a Pre-Raphaelite style by Matthew James Lawless, this 1863 canvas evokes the suffering and poverty of the Irish population in the years following the Famine.

SOUTHWEST DUBLIN

THE AREA around Dublin Castle was first settled in prehistoric times, and it was from here that the city grew. Dublin gets its name from the dark pool *(Dubh Linn)* which formed at the confluence of the Liffey and the Poddle, a river which once ran through the site of Dublin Castle. It is now channelled underground and trickles out into the Liffey by Grattan Bridge. Archaeological excavations behind Wood Quay, on the banks of the Liffey, reveal that the Vikings established a trading settlement here around 841.

Memorial to Turlough O'Carolan in St Patrick's Cathedral

Following Strongbow's invasion of 1170, a medieval city began to emerge; the Anglo-Normans built strong defensive walls around the castle.

A small reconstructed section of these old city walls can be seen at St Audoen's Church. More conspicuous reminders of the Anglo-Normans are provided by the grand medieval Christ Church Cathedral and Ireland's largest church, St Patrick's Cathedral. When the city expanded to the north and east during the Georgian era, the narrow cobbled streets of Temple Bar became a quarter of skilled craftsmen and merchants. Today this area is considered to be the trendiest part of town, and is home to a variety of alternative shops and cafés. The Powerscourt Townhouse, an elegant 18th-century mansion, has been converted into one of the city's best shopping centres.

SIGHTS AT A GLANCE

Museums and Libraries
Chester Beatty Library and
 Gallery of Oriental Art ②
Dublinia ⑧
Marsh's Library ⑫

Historic Buildings
City Hall ③
Dublin Castle pp74–5 ①
Powerscourt Townhouse ④
Tailors' Hall ⑩

Historic Streets
Temple Bar ⑤
Wood
Quay ⑥

Churches
*Christ Church Cathedral
 pp78–9* ⑦
St Audoen's Church ⑨
St Patrick's Cathedral ⑪
Whitefriar Street Carmelite
 Church ⑬

KEY

▢ Street-by-Street map
  See pp72–3

P Parking

0 metres 250
0 yards 250

◁ **Temple Bar, a centre for the arts and a popular meeting spot for young Dubliners**

Street-by-Street: Southwest Dublin

D ESPITE ITS WEALTH of ancient buildings, such
as Dublin Castle and Christ Church
Cathedral, this part of Dublin lacks the sleek
appeal of the neighbouring streets around
Grafton Street. In recent years, however,
redevelopment has helped to rejuvenate the
area, especially around Temple Bar, where
the attractive cobbled streets are lined with
interesting shops, galleries and cafés.

Sunlight Chambers
were built in 1900 for
the Lever Brothers
company. The
delightful
terracotta deco-
ration on the
façade advertises
their main business
of soap manufacturing.

Wood Quay
*This is where the Vikings
established their first
permanent settlement in
Ireland around 841* **6**

★ **Christ Church Cathedral**
*Huge family monuments
including that of the 19th
Earl of Kildare can be
found in Ireland's oldest
cathedral, which also has
a fascinating crypt* **7**

**Chester Beatty Library and
Gallery of Oriental Art**
*Art and manuscripts from the Far
and Middle East are on display* **2**

City Hall
*Originally built as the
Royal Exchange in
1779, the city's muni-
cipal headquarters is
fronted by a huge
Corinthian portico* **3**

Dublinia
*Medieval Dublin is
the subject of this
interactive museum,
located in the
former Synod Hall
of the Church of
Ireland. It is linked
to Christ Church by
a bridge* **8**

★ **Dublin Castle**
*The Drawing Room, with its
Waterford crystal chandelier, is
part of a suite of luxurious rooms
built in the 18th century for the
Viceroys of Ireland* **1**

To O'Connell Bridge

Ha'penny Bridge

NORTH OF THE LIFFEY

SOUTHWEST DUBLIN

SOUTHEAST DUBLIN

LOCATOR MAP
See Dublin map pp110–11

★ **Temple Bar**
This arts and entertainments district occupies a maze of narrow, cobbled streets ❺

New Bank of Ireland building

The Covered Market between Drury Street and South Great George's Street is a popular spot for buying second-hand clothes and antique jewellery.

Powerscourt Townhouse
This shopping centre is one of the best places in Dublin to find fashion accessories and arts and crafts ❹

To Grafton Street

KEY

– – – Suggested route

Dublin Civic Museum, set in the former City Assembly House, has a wide range of displays covering the history of Dublin from pre-Viking times until the 1960s.

The Long Hall is a magnificent, old-fashioned, smoky pub. Behind the narrow room's long bar stands a bewildering array of antique clocks.

0 metres 50

0 yards 50

STAR SIGHTS

★ **Dublin Castle**

★ **Temple Bar**

★ **Christ Church Cathedral**

Dublin Castle ❶

FOR SEVEN CENTURIES Dublin Castle was a symbol of English rule, ever since the Anglo-Normans built a fortress here in the 13th century. Nothing remains of the original structure except the much modified Record Tower. Following a fire in 1684, the Surveyor-General, Sir William Robinson, laid down the plans for the Upper and Lower Castle Yards in their present form. On the first floor of the south side of the Upper Yard are the luxury State Apartments, including St Patrick's Hall. These rooms, with Killybegs carpets and chandeliers of Waterford glass, served as home to the British-appointed Viceroys of Ireland.

St Patrick by Edward Smyth

Figure of Justice
Facing the Upper Yard above the main entrance from Cork Hill, this statue roused much cynicism among Dubliners, who felt she was turning her back on the city.

★ **Throne Room**
Built in 1740, this room contains a throne said to have been presented by William of Orange after his victory at the Battle of the Boyne (see p236).

Wedgwood Room

Picture Gallery

Bedford Tower (1760)

Entrance from Cork Hill

Entrance to State Apartments

Upper Yard

Bermingham Tower dates from the 14th century. It was turned into an elegant supper room around 1740.

Entrance to Upper Yard

Octagonal Tower (c. 1812)

Record Tower (1258)

★ **St Patrick's Hall**
This hall, with its banners of the now defunct Knights of St Patrick, has ceiling paintings by Vincenzo Valdré (1778), symbolizing the relationship between Britain and Ireland.

The Church of the Most Holy Trinity was completed in 1814 by Francis Johnston. The 100 heads on the exterior of this Neo-Gothic church were carved by Edward Smyth.

ROBERT EMMET

Robert Emmet (1778–1803),
leader of the abortive 1803
rebellion, is remembered
as a heroic champion of
Irish liberty. His plan was
to capture Dublin Castle
as a signal for the country
to rise up against the Act
of Union (see p40). Emmet
was caught and publicly
hanged, but the defiant,
patriotic speech he made
from the dock helped to
inspire future generations
of Irish freedom fighters.

**Government
offices**

ver Yard

Dame Street →

STAR FEATURES

★ St Patrick's Hall

★ Throne Room

**Manuscript (1874) from the Holy Koran written by calligrapher
Ahmad Shaikh in Kashmir, Chester Beatty Library**

Chester Beatty Library and Gallery of Oriental Art ❷

Bermingham Tower, Dublin Castle.
677 7129. ring for details.

THIS COLLECTION of Oriental
manuscripts and art was
bequeathed to Ireland by the
American mining magnate and
art collector Sir Alfred Chester
Beatty, who died in 1968. This
generous act no doubt led to
his selection as Ireland's first
honorary citizen in 1957.
During his lifetime, Beatty
accumulated almost 300 copies
of the Koran, representing the
works of many master calli-
graphers. Among the other
exhibits are 6,000-year-old
Babylonian stone tablets,
Greek papyri and biblical
material written in Coptic, the
original language of Egypt.

Treasures from the Far East
include a collection of Chinese
jade books – each leaf of these
unique books is made from
thinly cut jade, engraved with
Chinese characters which are
then filled with gold. Burmese
and Siamese art is represented
by the collection of 18th-
century Parabaiks, books of
folk tales with colourful illustrations on mulberry leaf
paper. The Japanese collection
includes paintings, woodblock
prints and books and scrolls
from the 16th to 18th centuries, containing popular
stories. The illustrations were
painted by Buddhist monks
from the city of Nara.

Not to be overlooked is the
collection of western European
manuscripts. One of the most
beautiful is the Coëtivy Book
of Hours, an illuminated French
prayer book, which dates
from the 15th century.

City Hall ❸

Lord Edward St. **Map** C3. to the
public.

DESIGNED BY Thomas Cooley,
this imposing Corinthian-
style building was erected
between 1769 and 1779 as the
Royal Exchange. It was taken
over by Dublin Corporation
in 1852 as a meeting place for
the city council – a role it
keeps to this day.

Beyond the ornate balustrade
and columned façade is the
striking entrance rotunda. The
city's coat of arms with the
motto Obedientia Civium
Urbis Felicitas (Happy the city
where citizens obey) is depicted in mosaic form on the
floor of the rotunda.

City Hall from Parliament Street

Interior of Powerscourt Townhouse Shopping Centre

Powerscourt Townhouse ❹

South William St. **Map** D4. █ *679 4144.* ☐ *8am–6pm Mon–Sat (8am–7pm Thu). See also **Shopping in Ireland** pp322–5.*

COMPLETED IN 1774 by Robert Mack, this grand mansion was built as the city home of Viscount Powerscourt, who also had a country estate at Enniskerry *(see pp126–7).* Granite from the Powerscourt estate was used in its construction. Today the building houses one of Dublin's best shopping centres. Inside it still features the original grand mahogany staircase, and detailed plaster-work by Michael Stapleton.

The building became a drapery warehouse in the 1830s, and major restoration during the 1960s turned it into

a centre of specialist galleries, antique shops, jewellery stalls, cafés and other shop units. The enclosed central court-yard, topped by a glass dome, is where many Dubliners stop to have a snack. The centre can also be reached from Grafton Street down the narrow Johnson Court alley.

Temple Bar ❺

Map C3. **Temple Bar Information Centre** 18 Eustace St. █ *677 2255 or 671 5717 (recorded information).* ☐ *9am–5:30pm Mon–Fri.* ● *public hols.* ♿ *See also **Entertainment in Dublin** p106.*

SOME OF DUBLIN'S best night spots, restaurants and unusual shops line these narrow, cobbled streets run-ning between the Bank of Ireland *(see p58)* and Christ Church Cathedral. In the 18th century the area was home to many insalubrious characters – Fownes Street was noted for its brothels. It was also the birthplace of parliamentarian Henry Grattan *(see p38).* Skilled craftsmen and artisans, such as clockmakers and printers, lived and worked around Temple Bar until post-war industrialization led to a decline in the area's fortunes.

In the 1970s, the CIE (the national transport authority) bought up parcels of land in this area to build a major bus depot. While waiting to acquire the land and build-ings needed, the CIE rented out, on cheap leases, some of the old retail and warehouse

premises to young artists and to record, clothing and book shops. The area developed an "alternative" identity and a successful lobby by local residents persuaded the CIE to drop their plans.

As more cynical Dubliners put it, the area became the city's "officially designated arts zone". But while the new investment and planning may have added a slight air of contrivance, it's still an exciting, atmospheric and essentially very young place.

Organizations based here include the Irish Film Centre, the experimental Project Arts Centre and around a dozen galleries such as the popular DESIGNyard, an applied arts centre displaying contemporary Irish jewellery and furniture. There are also centres for music, multi-media and photography as well as a Children's Cultural Centre – an arts centre offering theatre, workshops and other entertainment for children.

A pub in Temple Bar

Wood Quay ❻

Map B3.

NAMED AFTER the strong timber supports used to reclaim the land during the 13th century, this is where the Vikings first settled in 841. Excavations in the 1970s revealed remains of Norse and Norman villages, and arti-facts including pottery, coins, swords and leatherwork. Many of these findings are at the National Museum *(see pp64–5)* and at the Dublinia exhibition.

However, the city chose not to develop this archaeological find, but instead built two large civic offices (known locally as "The Bunkers") on the site. Today all you will see is a plaque and a rather surrealistic picnic site in the shape of a Viking longboat.

Strolling through the streets of Temple Bar

Former Synod Hall, now home to the Dublinia exhibition

Christ Church Cathedral ❼

See pp78–9.

Dublinia ❽

St Michael's Hill. **Map** B3. █ 679 4611. ☐ Apr–Sep: 10am–5pm daily; Oct–Mar: 11am–4pm Mon–Sat, 10am–4:30pm Sun & public hols. ● 24–26 Dec. ▧ includes entry to Christ Church Cathedral via bridge. ♿

M ANAGED BY the non-profit-making Medieval Trust, the Dublinia exhibition covers the formative period of Dublin's history from the arrival of the Anglo-Normans in 1170 to the closure of the monasteries in the 1540s *(see p36).*

The exhibition is housed in the Neo-Gothic Synod Hall, which, up until 1983, was home to the ruling body of the Church of Ireland. The building and the hump-backed bridge linking it to Christ Church Cathedral date from the 1870s. Before Dublinia was established in 1993, the Synod Hall was briefly converted into a nightclub.

The exhibition is entered via the basement where an audiotape-guided tour takes visitors through exhibits of life-size reconstructions. These depict major events in Dublin's history, such as the Black Death and the rebellion of Silken Thomas *(see p36).* The ground floor houses a large scale model of Dublin around 1500, a display of artifacts from the Wood Quay excavation, and reconstructions including the inside of a late medieval merchant's kitchen. There are also information panels on the themes of trade, merchants and religion. On the first floor is the dark-wood panelled Great Hall, where there is a multi-screen presentation on Dublin's medieval history.

The 60-m (200-ft) high St Michael's Tower is one of the best vantage points in Dublin, offering a splendid bird's-eye view of the low-rise city.

St Audoen's Church ❾

High St. **Map** B3. ● for restoration.

Tower of St Audoen's Church

D ESIGNATED a national monument and currently under restoration, St Audoen's is Dublin's earliest surviving medieval church. The 12th-century tower is believed to be the oldest in Ireland, and its three bells date from 1423. The 15th-century nave also remains intact. The church stands in an attractive church-yard with well-maintained lawns and shrubs. To the rear, steps lead down to St Audoen's Arch, the only remaining gate-way of the old city. Flanking the gate are restored sections of the 13th-century city walls.

Next door stands St Audoen's Roman Catholic Church, completed in 1847. The two Pacific clam shells by the front door hold holy water. In the basement is an audiovisual presentation on pre-Viking Ireland.

THE VIKINGS IN DUBLIN

Viking raiders arrived in Ireland in the late 8th century and founded Dublin in 841. They built a fort where the River Poddle met the Liffey at a black pool *(Dubh Linn)*, on the site of Dublin Castle. They also established a settlement along the banks of the Liffey at Wood Quay. Much of their trade was based on silver, slaves and piracy.

Following their defeat by Brian Boru at the Battle of Clontarf in 1014 *(see p32),* the Vikings integrated fully with the local Irish, adopting Christian beliefs. After Strongbow's Anglo-Norman invasion in 1170 *(see p34),* the flourishing Hiberno-Viking trading community declined, and many were banished to a separate colony called Oxmanstown, just north of the river.

Artist's impression of a Viking ship in Dublin Bay

Christ Church Cathedral ❼

CHRIST CHURCH CATHEDRAL was commissioned in 1172 by Strongbow, Anglo-Norman conqueror of Dublin *(see p34)*, and Archbishop Laurence O'Toole. It replaced an earlier wooden church built by the Vikings in 1038. At the time of the Reformation *(see p36)*, the cathedral passed to the Protestant Church of Ireland. By the 19th century it was in a bad state of repair, but was completely remodelled by architect George Street in the 1870s. In the crypt are monuments removed from the cathedral during its restoration.

Arms on Lord Mayor's pew

★ **Medieval Lectern**
This beautiful brass lectern was hand-wrought during the Middle Ages. It stands on the left-hand side of the nave, in front of the pulpit. The matching lectern on the right-hand side is a copy, dating from the 19th century.

The Lord Mayor's pew is usually kept in the north aisle, but is moved to the front of the nave when used by Dublin's civic dignitaries. It features a carving of the city arms and a stand for the civic mace.

Great Nave
The 25-m (68-ft) high nave has some fine early Gothic arches. On the north side, the original 13th-century wall leans out by as much as 50 cm (18 in) due to subsidence.

Entrance

The bridge to the Synod Hall was added when the cathedral was being rebuilt in the 1870s.

★ **Strongbow Monument**
The large effigy in chain armour is probably not Strongbow. However, his remains are buried in the cathedral and the curious half-figure may be part of his original tomb.

STAR FEATURES

★ **Strongbow Monument**

★ **Crypt**

★ **Medieval Lectern**

Chapel of St Laud
The casket on the wall contains the heart of St Laurence O'Toole. The chapel features original medieval floor tiles.

VISITORS' CHECKLIST

Christ Church Place. **Map** B3.
677 8099. 50, 66, 77 & many other routes. 10am–5pm daily (summer: 6pm). 26 Dec.
Donation. 11am, 3:30pm Mon–Fri (also 6pm Wed & Thu), choral Evensong 5pm Sat.

The Lady Chapel is used for Eucharist celebrations and is the chapel of the St John Ambulance Brigade.

★ Crypt
The cavernous crypt contains several oddities, including this mummified cat and rat, found in an organ pipe in the 1860s.

Stairs to crypt

Crypt

The foundations of the original Chapter House date back to the early 13th century.

Romanesque Doorway
Leading to the south transept, this ornately carved doorway is one of the finest examples of 12th-century Irish stonework.

TIMELINE

1000	1200	1400	1600	1800
1038 Construction of original wooden Viking cathedral	**1240** Completion of stone cathedral	**1600** Shopkeepers rent crypt space	**1689** King James II of England worships in cathedral	**1983** Cathedral ceases using Synod Hall
		1541 King Henry VIII alters constitution of cathedral		
1172 St Laurence O'Toole and Strongbow commission the new stone cathedral	*Meeting between Lambert Simnel and the Earl of Kildare (see p35)*	**1487** Coronation of 10-year-old Lambert Simnel as King of England	**1742** Choir participates in first performance of Handel's *Messiah*	**1871** Major rebuilding of the cathedral begins, including Synod Hall and bridge

Tailors' Hall ⑩

Back Lane. **Map** B4. ● *to the public.*

DUBLIN'S only surviving guildhall preserves a delightful corner of old Dublin in an otherwise busy redevelopment zone. Built in 1706, it stands behind a limestone arch in a quiet cobbled yard. The building is the oldest guildhall in Ireland and was used by various trade groups including hosiers, saddlers and barber-surgeons as well as tailors. It also hosted many political meetings – Wolfe Tone addressed a public United Irishmen rally here before the 1798 rebellion (*see p39*). The building closed in the early 1960s due to neglect, but a successful appeal by Desmond Guinness saw the hall completely refurbished. It is now the home of *An Taisce* (the Irish National Trust).

Façade of Tailors' Hall, home of the Irish National Trust

St Patrick's Cathedral with Minot's Tower and spire

St Patrick's Cathedral ⑪

St Patrick's Close. **Map** B4.
🎫 *475 4817.* ◯ *Apr–Oct: 9am–6pm Mon–Fri, 9am–5pm Sat, 10–11am & 12:15–3pm Sun; Nov–Mar: 9am–6pm Mon–Fri, 9am–4pm Sat, 10am–11am & 12:15–3pm Sun.* 📷

IRELAND'S LARGEST CHURCH was founded beside a sacred well where St Patrick is said to have baptized converts around AD 450. A stone slab bearing a Celtic cross and covering the well was unearthed at the turn of the 20th century. It is now preserved in the west end of the cathedral's nave. The original building was just a wooden chapel and remained so until 1192 when Archbishop John Comyn rebuilt the cathedral in stone.

Over the centuries, St Patrick's came to be seen as the people's church, while the older Christ Church Cathedral (*see pp78–9*) nearby was more associated with the British establishment. In the mid-17th century, Huguenot refugees from France arrived in Dublin, and were given the Lady Chapel by the Dean and Chapter as their place of worship. The chapel was separated from the rest of the cathedral and used by the Huguenots until the late 18th century. Today St Patrick's Cathedral is the Protestant Church of Ireland's national cathedral.

Much of the present building dates back to work completed between 1254 and 1270. The cathedral suffered over the centuries from desecration, fire and neglect but, thanks to the generosity of Sir Benjamin Guinness, it underwent extensive restoration during the 1860s. The building is 91 m (300 ft) long; at the western end is a 43-m (141-ft) tower, restored by Archbishop Minot in 1370 and now known as Minot's Tower. The spire was added in the 18th century.

The interior is dotted with memorial busts, brasses and monuments. A leaflet available at the front desk helps identify and locate them. The largest, most colourful and elaborate tomb was dedicated to the Boyle family in the 17th century. Erected by Richard Boyle, Earl of Cork, in memory of his second wife Katherine, it is decorated with painted figures of his family,

JONATHAN SWIFT (1667–1745)

Jonathan Swift was born in Dublin and educated at Trinity College (*see pp60–61*). He left for England in 1689, but returned in 1694 when his political career failed. Back in Ireland he began a life in the church, becoming Dean of St Patrick's in 1713. In addition to his clerical duties, Swift was a prolific political commentator – his best-known work, *Gulliver's Travels*, contains a bitter satire on Anglo-Irish relations. Swift's personal life, particularly his friendship with two younger women, Ester Johnson, better known as Stella, and Hester Vanhomrigh, attracted criticism. In his final years, Swift suffered from Menière's disease – an illness of the ear which led many to believe him insane.

including his wife's parents. Other famous citizens remembered in the church include the harpist Turlough O'Carolan (1670–1738) and Douglas Hyde (1860–1949), the first President of Ireland.

Many visitors come to see the memorials associated with Jonathan Swift, the satirical writer and Dean of St Patrick's. In the north transept is "Swift's Corner", containing various memorabilia such as an altar table and a bookcase holding his death mask and various pamphlets. A self-penned epitaph can be found on the wall on the southwest side of the nave. A few steps away, two brass plates mark his grave and that of his beloved Stella, who died in 1728.

At the west end of the nave is an old door with a hole in it – a relic from a feud which took place between the Lords Kildare and Ormonde in 1492. The latter took refuge in the Chapter House, but a truce was soon made and a hole was cut in the door by Lord Kildare so that the two could shake hands in friendship.

Marsh's Library ⓬

St Patrick's Close. **Map** B4.
📞 454 3511. 🕐 10am–12.45pm & 2–5pm Mon & Wed–Fri, 10:30am–12:45pm Sat. ● 10 days at Christmas & public hols. 🈁

THE OLDEST public library in Ireland was built in 1701 for Archbishop Narcissus Marsh, a Dean of St Patrick's Cathedral. It was designed by Sir William Robinson, architect of much of Dublin Castle *(see pp74–5)* and the Royal Hospital Kilmainham *(see p95)*.

Inside, the bookcases are topped by a mitre and feature carved gables with lettering in gold leaf. To the rear of the library are wired alcoves (or "cages") where readers were locked in with rare books. The collection of books from the 16th, 17th and early 18th centuries includes irreplaceable volumes, such as Bishop Bedell's 1685 translation of the Old Testament into Irish. There is also a volume of Clarendon's *History of the Rebellion*, with anti-Scottish margin notes by Jonathan Swift.

Statue of Virgin and Child in Whitefriar Street Carmelite Church

Whitefriar Street Carmelite Church ⓭

56 Aungier St. **Map** C4. 📞 475 8821. 🕐 8am–6:30pm Mon & Wed–Fri, 8am–9pm Tue, 8am–7pm Sat, 8am–7:30pm Sun.

DESIGNED by George Papworth, this Catholic church was built in 1827. It stands on the site of a 16th-century Carmelite priory of which nothing remains.

In contrast to the two Church of Ireland cathedrals, St Patrick's and Christ Church, which are usually full of tourists, this church is frequented by local worshippers. Every day they come to light candles to various saints, including St Valentine – the patron saint of lovers. His remains, previously buried in the cemetery of St Hippolytus in Rome, were offered to the church as a gift from Pope Gregory XVI in 1836. Today they rest beneath the commemorative statue of St Valentine, which stands in the northeast corner of the church beside the high altar.

Nearby is a Flemish oak statue of the Virgin and Child, dating from the late 15th or early 16th century. It may have belonged to St Mary's Abbey *(see p91)* and is believed to be the only wooden statue of its kind to escape destruction when Ireland's monasteries were sacked at the time of the Reformation *(see p36)*.

Carved monument (1632) to the Boyle family in St Patrick's Cathedral

NORTH OF THE LIFFEY

Statue of James Joyce on Earl Street North

DUBLIN'S NORTHSIDE was the last part of the city to be developed during the 18th century. The city authorities envisioned an area of wide, leafy avenues, but the reality of today's heavy traffic has rather spoiled their original plans. Nonetheless, O'Connell Street, lined with fine statues and monuments, is an impressive thoroughfare. This is where Dubliners come to shop and some of the adjacent streets, particularly Moore Street, have a colourful parade of stalls and street vendors offering cut-price tobacco.

Some public buildings, such as James Gandon's glorious Custom House and majestic Four Courts, together with the historic General Post Office (see p87), add grace to the area. The Rotunda Hospital, Europe's first purpose-built maternity hospital, is another fine building. Dublin's two most celebrated theatres, the Abbey and the Gate, act as a cultural magnet, as do the Dublin Writers Museum and the James Joyce Cultural Centre, two museums dedicated to writers who lived in the city.

Some of the city's finest Georgian streetscapes are found in the north of the city. Many have been neglected for decades, but thankfully some areas, most notably North Great George's Street, are undergoing restoration.

SIGHTS AT A GLANCE

Museums and Galleries
Dublin Writers Museum ❾
Hugh Lane Municipal Gallery of Modern Art ❿
Old Jameson's Distillery ⓭
James Joyce Cultural Centre ❺

Historic Buildings
Custom House ❶
Four Courts ⓯
King's Inns ⓫
Rotunda Hospital ❼

Historic Streets and Bridges
Ha'penny Bridge ⓱
O'Connell Street ❸
Smithfield ⓬

Theatres
Abbey Theatre ❷
Gate Theatre ❻

Churches
St Mary's Abbey ⓰
St Mary's Pro-Cathedral ❹
St Michan's Church ⓮

Parks and Gardens
Garden of Remembrance ❽

KEY

	Street-by-Street map See pp84–5
🚍	Coach station
Ⓟ	Parking
ℹ	Tourist information

```
0 metres        250
0 yards         250
```

◁ **Portico of the Custom House, illuminated at night**

Street-by-Street: Around O'Connell Street

Throughout the Georgian era, O'Connell Street was very much the fashionable part of Dublin to live. However, the 1916 Easter Rising destroyed many of the fine buildings along the street, including much of the

Detail of pavement mosaic, Moore Street

General Post Office – only its original façade still stands. Today, this main thoroughfare is lined with shops and businesses. Other attractions nearby include St Mary's Pro-Cathedral and James Gandon's Custom House, overlooking the Liffey.

James Joyce Cultural Centre
This well-restored Georgian town house contains a small Joyce museum 5

Parnell Monument (1911)

Gate Theatre
Founded in 1928, the Gate is renowned for its productions of contemporary drama 6

Rotunda Hospital
Housed in the Rotunda Hospital is a chapel built in the 1750s to the design of Richard Castle. It features lovely stained-glass windows, fluted columns, panelling and intricate iron balustrades 7

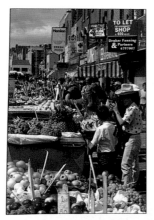

Moore Street Market
is the busiest of the streets off O'Connell. Be prepared for the shrill cries of the stall holders offering an enormous variety of fresh fruit, vegetables and cut flowers.

Anna Livia Fountain (1988)

The General Post Office, the grandest building on O'Connell Street, was the centre of the 1916 Rising.

James Larkin Statue (1981)

KEY

– – – Suggested route

0 metres   50

0 yards   50

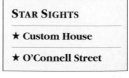

STAR SIGHTS

★ **Custom House**

★ **O'Connell Street**

St Mary's Pro-Cathedral
*Built around 1825, this is
Dublin's main place of
worship for Catholics. The
plaster relief above the
altar in the sanctuary
depicts The Ascension* ❹

LOCATOR MAP
See Dublin map pp110–11

The statue of James Joyce (1990), by
Marjorie Fitzgibbon, commemorates one
of Ireland's most famous novelists. Born in
Dublin in 1882, he catalogued the people
and streets of Dublin in *Dubliners* and in
his most celebrated work, *Ulysses*.

Abbey Theatre
*Ireland's national
theatre is known
throughout the world
for its productions by
Irish playwrights,
such as Sean O'Casey
and JM Synge* ❷

★ O'Connell Street
*This monument to Daniel
O'Connell by John Foley took
19 years to complete from the
laying of its foundation
stone in 1864* ❸

L ST

STREET NORTH

MARLBOROUGH ST.

SACKVILLE PL.

ABBEY STREET LR

EDEN QUAY

LIFFEY

CUSTOM HOUSE QUAY

Butt Bridge

**O'Connell
Bridge**

To Trinity College

★ Custom House
*This grotesque head, by
Edward Smyth, symbolizes
the River Liffey. It is one of
14 carved keystones that
adorn the building* ❶

Illuminated façade of the Custom House reflected in the Liffey

Custom House ❶

Custom House Quay. **Map** E2. ◐ *to the public.*

THIS MAJESTIC BUILDING was designed as the Custom House by the English architect James Gandon. However, just nine years after its completion, the 1800 Act of Union *(see p40)* transferred the custom and excise business to London, rendering the building practically obsolete. In 1921, supporters of Sinn Fein celebrated their election victory by setting light to what they saw as a symbol of British imperialism. The fire blazed for five days causing extensive damage. Reconstruction took place in 1926, although further deterioration meant that the building was not completely restored until 1991, when it re-opened as government offices.

The main façade is made up of pavilions at each end with a Doric portico in its centre. The arms of Ireland crown the two pavilions and a series of 14 allegorical heads, by Dublin sculptor Edward Smyth, form the keystones of arches and entrances. These heads depict Ireland's main rivers and the Atlantic Ocean. Topping the central copper dome is a statue of Commerce, while the north façade is decorated with figures representing Europe, Africa, America and Asia.

The best view of the building is from the south of the Liffey beyond Matt Talbot Bridge, especially at night when it is illuminated. Sadly, the Loop Line railway bridge spoils the view from O'Connell Bridge.

Abbey Theatre ❷

Lower Abbey St. **Map** E2. 🎟 *878 7222.* ◯ *for performances only.* **Box office** ◯ *10:30am–7pm Mon–Sat. See also* **Entertainment in Dublin** *p107.*

Logo of the Abbey Theatre

FOUNDED in 1898 with WB Yeats and Lady Gregory as co-directors, the Abbey staged its first play in 1904. The early years of this much lauded national theatre witnessed works by WB Yeats, JM Synge and Sean O'Casey. Many were controversial: nationalist sensitivities were severely tested in 1926 during the premiere of O'Casey's *The Plough and the Stars* when the flag of the Irish Free State appeared on stage in a scene which featured a pub frequented by prostitutes.

The Abbey remains best known for its productions of early 20th-century Irish work, though in recent years it has done much to encourage new writing talent, particularly in the small Peacock Theatre downstairs. One of the most acclaimed performances staged in the main theatre was Brian Friel's *Dancing At Lughnasa* (1990). The walls of the foyer and bar are lined with portraits of famous names linked with the theatre.

O'Connell Street ❸

Map D1–D2.

O'CONNELL STREET is very different from the original plans of Irish aristocrat Luke Gardiner. When he bought the land in the mid-18th century, Gardiner envisioned a grand residential parade with an elegant mall running along its centre. Such plans were short-lived. The construction of Carlisle (now O'Connell) Bridge in 1790 transformed the street into the city's main north-south route. Also, several buildings were destroyed during the 1916 Easter Rising and the Irish Civil War. Since the 1960s many of the old buildings have been replaced by the plate glass and neon of fast food joints, amusement arcades and chain stores.

A few venerable buildings remain, such as the General Post Office (1818), Gresham Hotel (1817), Clery's department store (1822) and the Royal Dublin Hotel, part of which occupies the street's only original town house.

A walk down the central mall is the most enjoyable way to see the street's mix of architectural styles and take a close look at the series of monuments lining the route. At the south end stands a massive monument to Daniel O'Connell *(see p40)*, unveiled in 1882. The street, which throughout the 19th century had been called Sackville Street, was renamed after O'Connell in 1922. Higher up, almost facing the General Post Office, is an animated statue of James Larkin (1867–1943), leader of the Dublin general strike in 1913. The next statue is of Father Theobald Mathew (1790–1856), founder of the Pioneer Total Abstinence

Statue of James Larkin (1981) in O'Connell Street

Movement. At the north end of the street is the obelisk-shaped monument to Charles Stewart Parnell (1846–91), who was leader of the Home Rule Party and known as the "uncrowned King of Ireland" *(see p41)*. Also on O'Connell Street, at the junction of Cathedral Street, is the ridiculous Anna Livia Millennium Fountain, which was unveiled during the city's millennium celebrations in 1988. It is supposed to represent the River Liffey but most Dubliners dismiss it as the "Floozie in the Jacuzzi".

St Mary's Pro-Cathedral ❹

Marlborough St. **Map** D2. 874 5441. 9:30am–5pm daily.

D EDICATED in 1825 before Catholic emancipation was fully effected *(see p40)*, St Mary's is Dublin's Catholic cathedral. Its backstreet site was the best the city's Anglo-Irish leaders would allow.

The façade is based on the Temple of Theseus in Athens. Its six Doric columns support a pediment with statues of St Laurence O'Toole, 12th-century Archbishop of Dublin and patron saint of the city, St Mary and St Patrick. The most striking feature of the interior is the intricately carved high altar.

St Mary's is home to the famous Palestrina Choir, started in 1902. In 1904 the great tenor, John McCormack *(see p22)*, began his career with the choir, which can be heard every Sunday at 11am.

Austere Neo-Classical interior of St Mary's Pro-Cathedral

THE GENERAL POST OFFICE (GPO)

Irish Life magazine cover showing the 1916 Easter Rising

Built in 1818 halfway along O'Connell Street, the GPO became a symbol of the 1916 Irish Rising. Members of the Irish Volunteers and Irish Citizen Army seized the building on Easter Monday, and Patrick Pearse *(see p42)* read out the Proclamation of the Irish Republic from its steps. The rebels remained inside for a week, but shelling from the British eventually forced them out. At first, many Irish people viewed the Rising unfavourably. However, as WB Yeats wrote, matters "changed utterly" and a "terrible beauty was born" when, during the following weeks, 14 of the leaders were caught and shot at Kilmainham Gaol *(see p95)*. Inside the building is a sculpture of the mythical Irish warrior Cuchulainn *(see p24)*, dedicated to those who died for their part in the Easter Rising.

South end of O'Connell Street with monument to Daniel O'Connell

James Joyce Cultural Centre ❺

35 North Great George's St. **Map** D1.
🔲 878 8547. ⭕ 9:30am–5pm
Mon–Fri, noon–5pm Sat & Sun.
⬤ Good Fri & 23–27 Dec. ◻ ◻

THIS AGREEABLE STOP on the literary tourist trail is primarily a meeting place for Joyce enthusiasts, but is also worth visiting for its remarkable Georgian interior. The centre is located in a 1784 town house which was built for the Earl of Kenmare. Michael Stapleton, one of the greatest stuccodores of his time, contributed to the plasterwork, of which the friezes are particularly noteworthy.

The main literary display is an absorbing set of biographies of around 50 characters from Joyce's novel *Ulysses*, who were based on real Dublin people. Professor Dennis J Maginni, a peripheral character in *Ulysses*, ran a dancing school from this town house. Leopold and Molly Bloom, the central characters of *Ulysses*, lived a short walk away at No. 7 Eccles Street. The centre also organizes walking tours of Joyce's Dublin, so a visit is a must for all Joycean zealots.

At the top of the road, on Great Denmark Street, is the Jesuit-run Belvedere College attended by Joyce between 1893 and 1898. He recalls his unhappy schooldays there in *A Portrait of the Artist as a Young Man*. The college's interior contains some of Stapleton's best and most colourful plasterwork (1785).

JAMES JOYCE (1882–1941)

Born in Dublin, Joyce spent most of his adult life in Europe. He used the city of Dublin as the setting for all his major works including *Dubliners*, *A Portrait of the Artist as a Young Man* and *Ulysses*. Joyce claimed that if the city was ever destroyed it could be re-created through the pages of *Ulysses*. However, the Irish branded the book pornographic and banned it until the 1960s.

Gate Theatre ❻

1 Cavendish Row. **Map** D1.
🔲 874 4368. ⭕ for performances only. **Box office** 🔲 874 4045.
⭕ 10am–7pm Mon–Sat. See also *Entertainment in Dublin pp102–7*.

Entrance to the Gate Theatre

RENOWNED FOR its staging of contemporary international drama in Dublin, the Gate Theatre was founded in 1928 by Hilton Edwards and Mícheál Mac Liammóir. The latter is now best remembered for *The Importance of Being Oscar*, his long-running one-man show about the writer Oscar Wilde *(see p20)*. An early success was Denis Johnston's *The Old Lady Says No*, so-called because of the margin notes made on one of his scripts by Lady Gregory, founding director of the Abbey Theatre *(see p86)*. Although still noted for staging new plays, the Gate's current output often includes classic Irish plays. Among the young talent to get their first break here were James Mason and a teenaged Orson Welles.

Rotunda Hospital ❼

Parnell Square West. **Map** D1.
🔲 873 0700.

STANDING in the middle of Parnell Square is Europe's first purpose-built maternity hospital. Founded in 1745 by Dr Bartholomew Mosse, the design of the hospital is similar to that of Leinster House *(see p63)*. German-born architect, Richard Castle, designed both.

At the east end of the hospital is the Rotunda, after which the hospital is named. It was built in 1764 by John Ensor as Assembly Rooms to host fundraising functions and concerts. Franz Liszt gave a concert here in 1843.

On the first floor is a chapel featuring striking stained-glass windows and exuberant Rococo plasterwork and ceiling (1755) by the stuccodore Bartholomew Cramillion.

Across the road from the hospital is Conway's Pub. Opened in 1745, it is a popular retreat for expectant fathers.

Stained-glass Venetian window (c. 1863) in Rotunda Hospital's chapel

Garden of Remembrance ❽

Parnell Square. **Map** C1.
◯ *dawn–dusk daily.*

AT THE NORTHERN END of Parnell Square is a small, peaceful park, dedicated to the men and women who have died in the pursuit of Irish freedom. The Garden of Remembrance marks the spot where several leaders of the 1916 Easter Rising were held overnight before being taken to Kilmainham Gaol *(see p95)*, and was also where the Irish Volunteers movement was formed in 1913.

Designed by Daithí Hanly, the garden was opened by President Eamon de Valera *(see p43)* in 1966, to mark the 50th anniversary of the Easter Rising. In the centre of the garden's well-kept lawns is a cruciform pool. A mosaic on the floor of the pool depicts abandoned, broken swords, spears and shields, symbolizing peace. The focal point at one end of the garden is a large bronze sculpture by Oisín Kelly (1971) of the legendary *Children of Lir*, who were changed into swans by their stepmother *(see p25)*.

Children of Lir in the Garden of Remembrance

Gallery of Writers at Dublin Writers Museum

Dublin Writers Museum ❾

18 Parnell Sq North. **Map** C1. 🅲 872 2077. ◯ *10am–5pm (Jun–Aug: 10am–6pm) Mon–Sat, 11am–5pm Sun & public hols.* ● *25 & 26 Dec.* 🖼

OPENED IN 1991, the museum occupies a tasteful 18th-century town house. There are displays relating to Irish literature in all its forms from around the 10th century to the present day. The exhibits include paintings, manuscripts, letters, rare editions and mementoes of many of Ireland's finest authors. There are a number of temporary exhibits and a sumptuously decorated Gallery of Writers upstairs. The museum also hosts frequent poetry readings and lectures. An excellent restaurant, the Chapter One *(see p307)*, and a specialist bookstore, providing an out-of-print search service, add to the relaxed, friendly ambience.

Hugh Lane Municipal Gallery of Modern Art ❿

Charlemont House, Parnell Square North. **Map** C1. 🅲 874 1903. ◯ *9:30am–6pm Tue–Thu, 9:30am–5pm Fri & Sat, 11am–5pm Sun.* ● *23–25 Dec & public hols.*

NOTED ART COLLECTOR Sir Hugh Lane donated his valuable collection of Impressionist paintings to Dublin Corporation in 1905. However, the failure to find a suitable location for them prompted Lane to consider transferring his gift to the National Gallery in London. The Corporation then proposed Charlemont House and Lane relented. However, in 1915, before Lane's revised will could be witnessed, he died on board the torpedoed liner *Lusitania (see p170)*. This led to a 50-year dispute which has been resolved by Dublin Corporation and the National Gallery swapping the collection every five years.

Besides the Lane bequest, which includes paintings by Degas, Courbet and Monet, the gallery also has a sculpture hall with work by Rodin and others. There is also an extensive collection of modern Irish canvasses, including Michael Farrell's *Madonna Irlanda* (1977) and Patrick Graham's disturbing *Ire/land III* (1982).

Beach Scene (c. 1876) by Edgar Degas, Hugh Lane Municipal Gallery

Detail of wood carving (c. 1724) at St Michan's Church

King's Inns ⓫

Henrietta St/Constitution Hill. **Map** B1. to the public.

THIS CLASSICALLY PROPORTIONED public building was founded in 1795 as a place of residence and study for barristers. To build it, James Gandon chose to seal off the end of Henrietta Street, which at the time was one of Dublin's most fashionable addresses. Francis Johnston added the graceful cupola in 1816, and the building was finally completed in 1817. Inside is a fine Dining Hall, and the Registry of Deeds (formerly the Prerogative Court). The west façade has two doorways flanked by Classical caryatids carved by Edward Smyth. The male figure, with book and quill, represents the law.

Sadly, much of the area around Constitution Hill is less attractive than it was in Georgian times. However, the gardens, which are open to the public, are still pleasing.

Caryatid, King's Inns

Smithfield ⓬

Map A2.

LAID OUT in the mid-17th century as a marketplace, this vast cobbled expanse is a welcome respite from Dublin's traffic-laden streets. Most of the time Smithfield is relatively tranquil, though it springs to life on the first Sunday of each month when it hosts a horse and pony sale. However, don't expect to see any thoroughbreds here; none of the animals on sale are likely to run in the Irish Derby. The occasion is a delightful cameo of Dublin life.

Old Jameson's Distillery ⓭

Bow St. **Map** A2. 807 2355.
9:30am–6pm daily (last tour: 5pm).
Good Friday & 25 Dec.

PROOF OF recent investment in the emerging Smithfield area is this large exhibition in a restored part of John Jameson's distillery, which produced whiskey from 1780 until 1971. A visit here is both entertaining and educational. It starts with a video, *Uisce Beatha* (the Water of Life), and further whiskey-related facts are then explained on a 20-minute tour. This takes you around displays set out as a working distillery, with different rooms devoted to the various stages of production.

The tour guides show how the Irish process differs from that of Scotch whisky: here the barley is dried with clean air, while in Scotland it is smoked over peat. The claim is that the Irish product is a smoother, less smoky tipple. After the tour, visitors can test this in the bar.

Sampling different brands at Old Jameson's Distillery

St Michan's Church ⓮

Church St. **Map** B3. 872 4154.
mid-Mar–Oct: 10am–12:45pm & 2–4:45pm Mon–Fri, 10am–12:45pm Sat; Nov–mid-Mar: 12:30–3:30pm Mon–Fri, 10am–12:45pm Sat.

LARGELY REBUILT in 1686 on the site of an 11th-century Hiberno-Viking church, the dull façade of St Michan's hides a more exciting interior. Deep in its vaults lie a number of bodies that have barely decomposed because of the dry atmosphere created by the church's magnesian limestone walls. Their wooden caskets, however, have cracked open, revealing the preserved bodies, complete with skin and strands of hair. Among those thought to have been mummified in this way are the brothers Henry and John Sheares, leaders of the 1798 rebellion *(see p39)*, who were executed that year.

Other less gory attractions include the magnificent wood carving of fruits and violins and other instruments above the choir. There is also an organ (1724) on which Handel is said to have played. It is thought that the churchyard contains the unmarked grave of United Irishman Robert Emmet *(see p75)*, leader of the abortive 1803 Rising.

Four Courts ⓯

Inns Quay. **Map** B3. 872 5555.
10am–1pm, 2–4:30pm Mon–Fri (when courts in session).

COMPLETED IN 1802 by James Gandon, this majestic public building overlooks the River Liffey. It was virtually gutted 120 years later during the Irish Civil War *(see pp42–3)* when government forces bombarded anti-Treaty rebels into submission. The adjacent Public Records Office, with its irreplaceable collection of historical and legal documents dating back to the 12th century, was destroyed by fire.

By 1932, the main buildings were sympathetically restored using Gandon's original design. An imposing copper-covered lantern dome rises above the six-columned Corinthian portico, which is crowned with the figures of Moses, Justice and Mercy. This central section is flanked by two wings containing the four original courts: Common Pleas, Chancery, Exchequer and King's Bench. It is possible to walk into the central waiting hall under the grand dome; an information panel to the right of the entrance gives details of the building's history and functions.

St Mary's Abbey 🟦

Meetinghouse Lane. **Map** C2.
📞 872 1490. ⬜ *mid-Jun–mid-Sep: 10am–5pm Wed.* 🈁

FOUNDED BY Benedictines in 1139, but transferred to the Cistercian order just eight years later, this was one of the largest and most important monasteries in medieval Ireland. As well as controlling extensive estates, including

The Ha'penny Bridge looking from Temple Bar to Liffey Street

whole villages, mills and fisheries, the abbey acted as state treasury and meeting place for the Council of Ireland. It was during a council meeting in St Mary's that "Silken Thomas" Fitzgerald *(see p36)* renounced his allegiance to Henry VIII and marched out to raise the short-lived rebellion of 1534. The monastery was dissolved in 1539 and during the 17th century the site served as a quarry. Stone from St Mary's was used in the construction of Essex Bridge (replaced by Grattan Bridge in 1874), just to the south of the abbey.

All that remains of the abbey today is the vaulted chamber of the Chapter House. This contains a historical display and a model of how the entire complex would have looked 800 years ago.

Ha'penny Bridge 🟦

Map D3.

LINKING the Temple Bar area *(see p76)* and Liffey Street, this high-arched cast-iron foot bridge is used by thousands of people every day. It was built by John Windsor, an ironworker from Shropshire, England. One of Dublin's most photographed sights, it was originally named the Wellington Bridge. It is now officially called the Liffey Bridge, but is also known as the Metal Bridge. Opened in 1816, the bridge got its better known nickname from the halfpenny toll that was levied on it up until 1919. A recent restoration, which included the installation of period lanterns, has made the bridge even more attractive.

James Gandon's Four Courts overlooking the River Liffey

FURTHER AFIELD

THERE ARE many interesting sights just outside the city centre. The best part of a day can be spent exploring the western suburbs taking in the modern art museum housed in the splendid setting of the Royal Kilmainham Hospital and the eerie Kilmainham Gaol. Phoenix Park, Europe's largest city park, offers the opportunity for an afternoon stroll. Further north are the National Botanic Gardens, home to over 20,000 plant species from around the world. Nearby is Marino Casino, one of the finest examples of Palladian architecture in Ireland.

Candelabra at Malahide Castle

The magnificent coastline with its stunning views of Dublin Bay is easily reached by the DART rail network. It encompasses the towering promontory of Howth, while the highlight of the riviera-like southern stretch is around Dalkey village, especially the lovely Killiney Bay. One of many Martello towers built along the coast to defend Ireland against Napoleonic attacks, now houses a collection of Joyce memorabilia and is known as the James Joyce Tower. To the northeast, slightly further from the city centre, is Malahide Castle, former home of the Talbot family.

SIGHTS AT A GLANCE

Museums and Galleries
Collins Barracks **9**
Guinness Hop Store **4**
Irish Museum of Modern Art **3**
James Joyce Tower **13**

Kilmainham Gaol **2**
Shaw's Birthplace **6**
Waterways Visitors' Centre **8**

Parks and Gardens
National Botanic Gardens **5**
Phoenix Park **1**

Historic Buildings
Malahide Castle **10**
Marino Casino **7**

Towns and Villages
Dalkey **14**
Dun Laoghaire **12**
Howth **11**
Killiney **15**

CENTRAL DUBLIN

GREATER DUBLIN AND ENVIRONS

KEY

▨	Main sightseeing areas
▢	Greater Dublin
═	Motorway
═	Major road
═	Minor road
—	Railway
✈	Airport
⛴	Ferry port

0 kilometres 4
0 miles 2

15 km = 10 miles

◁ **Martello tower at Howth Head**

Phoenix Park ●

Park Gate, Conyngham Rd, Dublin 8.
🚌 10, 25, 26, 37, 38, 39. ◯ 6:30am–
11pm daily. **Phoenix Park Visitor
Centre** 🎧 677 0095. ◯ Mar–May &
Oct: 9:30am–5:30pm daily; Jun–Sep:
9:30am–6:30pm daily; Nov to mid-
Mar: 9:30am–4:30pm Sat & Sun. 🎫
Zoo 🎧 677 1425. ◯ 9:30am–6pm
(4pm in winter) Mon–Sat, 10:30am–
6pm (5pm in winter) Sun. 🎫

A LITTLE to the west of the
city centre, ringed by a
wall 11 km (7 miles) long, is
Europe's largest enclosed city
park. The name "Phoenix" is
said to be a corruption of the
Gaelic *Fionn Uisce*, meaning
"clear water". This refers to
a spring that rises near the
Phoenix Column which, to
add confusion, is crowned by
a statue of the mythical bird.

Phoenix Park originated in
1662, when the Duke of
Ormonde turned the land into
a deer park. In 1745 it was
landscaped and opened to the
public by Lord Chesterfield.
Near Park Gate is the lakeside **People's Garden** – the
only part of the park which
has been cultivated. A little
further on are the **Zoological
Gardens**, established in 1830,
making them the third oldest
zoo in the world. The zoo is
renowned for the successful
breeding of lions, including
the one that appears at the
beginning of MGM movies.
In addition to the Phoenix
Column, the park has two
other conspicuous monuments.
The **Wellington Testimonial**,
a 63-m (204-ft) obelisk, was
begun in 1817 and completed
in 1861. Its bronze bas-reliefs
were made from cap-
tured French cannons.
The 27-m (90-ft) steel
Papal Cross marks
the spot where the
pope celebrated Mass
in front of one million
people in 1979.

**Pope John Paul II celebrating
Mass in Phoenix Park in 1979**

Buildings within the park
include two 18th-century
houses: **Áras an Uachtaráin**,
the Irish President's official
residence, and **Deerfield**,
home of the US Ambassador.
The only building open to the
public is **Ashtown Castle**, a
restored 17th-century tower
house which contains the
Phoenix Park Visitor Centre.
Five times the size of Hyde
Park in London, Phoenix Park
has playing fields for Gaelic
football, hurling and polo,
and running and cycling trails.

Jogger in Phoenix Park

PHOENIX PARK

Áras An Uachtaráin ⑤
Ashtown Castle ①
Deerfield ②
Papal Cross ③
People's Garden ⑧
Phoenix Column ④
Wellington Testimonial ⑦
Zoological Gardens ⑥

KEY

🚌 Bus stop

🅿 Parking

ℹ Tourist information

▭▭▭ Park wall

0 metres   500

0 yards   500

Restored central hall at Kilmainham Gaol

Kilmainham Gaol ❷

Inchicore Rd, Kilmainham, Dublin 8.
📞 453 5984. 🚌 23, 51, 51A, 78, 79.
🕐 Apr–Sep: 9:30am–6pm daily; Oct–
Mar: 9:30am–5pm Mon–Fri, 10am–
6pm Sun; all year: last adm 1 hr before
closing. ⬤ 25 & 26 Dec. 🎫 🍴

ALONG TREE-LINED avenue runs
from the Royal Hospital
Kilmainham to the grim, grey
bulk of Kilmainham Gaol. The
building dates from 1789, but
was restored in the 1960s.
During its 130 years as a
prison, it housed many of
those involved in the fight for
Irish independence, including
Robert Emmet (see p75) and
Charles Stewart Parnell (p41).
The last prisoner held was
Eamon de Valera (p43), who
was released on 16 July, 1924.
    Tours start in the chapel,
where Joseph Plunkett married
Grace Gifford just a few hours
before he faced the firing
squad for his part in the 1916
Rising (see pp42–3). The tours
end in the prison yard where
Plunkett's badly wounded
colleague James Connolly, unable to stand up, was strapped
into a chair before being shot.

You also pass the dank cells
of those involved in the 1798,
1803, 1848 and 1867 uprisings,
as well as the punishment cells
and hanging room. There is a
video presentation, and in the
central hall are exhibits depicting various events which took
place in the Gaol until it
closed in 1924. There are also
personal mementoes of some
of the former inmates.
    Standing in the courtyard
is the *Asgard*, a ship used to
deliver arms from Germany to
the Nationalists in 1914.

Irish Museum of Modern Art – Royal Hospital Kilmainham ❸

Military Road, Kilmainham, Dublin 8.
📞 612 9900. 🚌 68, 68A, 69, 78A,
79, 90, 123. **Irish Museum of
Modern Art** 🕐 10am–5:30pm
Tue–Sat, noon–5:30pm Sun & public
hols. ⬤ Good Fri & 24–26 Dec. 🍴

IRELAND'S FINEST surviving 17th-
century building was laid out
in 1680, styled on Les Invalides
in Paris. It was built by Sir
William Robinson as a home
for 300 wounded soldiers – a
role it kept until 1927. When
it was completed, people were
so impressed by its Classical
symmetry that it was suggested it would be better used as
a campus for Trinity College.
In contrast to the functional
design of the building, the
Baroque chapel has fine carvings and intricate stained glass.
The plaster ceiling is a replica
of the original, which fell in
1902. The hospital's Formal
Gardens, restored using many
of the 17th-century designs,
are now open to the public.
    In 1991, the hospital's former
residential quarters became the
Irish Museum of Modern Art.
Corridors were painted white
and floors covered in grey to
create a stunning home for the
museum. Since its opening it
has established a collection
through purchases, donations
and loans. The exhibits include
a cross section of Irish and
international art and are shown
on a rotating basis.

The Royal Hospital Kilmainham

Sampling Guinness at the Hop Store

Guinness Hop Store **4**

Crane St, Dublin 8. **[** 453 6700 ext 5155. **==** 51B, 78A, 123. **○** Apr–Sep: 9:30am–5pm Mon–Sat, 10:30am–4:30pm Sun; Oct–Mar: 9:30am–4:30pm Mon–Sat, noon–4pm Sun. **●** public hols. **🎦 📷 ♿**

THE WORLD OF GUINNESS exhibition is housed in a 19th-century warehouse, which was used for storing bales of hops until the 1950s.

A self-guided tour takes the visitor through displays which chronicle 200 years of brewing at St James's Gate. The tour starts in a Victorian kieve (or mash tun), and goes on to examine all other stages of the brewing process. Displays show how production has changed over the years from when Arthur Guinness took over the backstreet brewery in 1759, to today's state-of-the-art techniques. There is also a cooperage display with life-size models showing the craftmen's skills involved in making the wooden barrels used for storage. Since the 1950s metal containers have been used.

On the ground floor, in the Transport Gallery, is a narrow-gauge steam locomotive which once ferried materials around the factory site. Other displays include models of the company's fleet of barges that plied the Grand Canal, ocean tankers, and the once familiar dray horses which transported the stout to the ports.

The tour ends with an audio-visual show on the company's development, followed by a visit to the sampling bar where you can enjoy a couple of glasses of draught Guinness.

The Brewing of Guinness

Label from a Guinness bottle

GUINNESS IS A BLACK BEER, known as "stout", renowned for its distinctive malty flavour and smooth creamy head. From its humble beginnings over 200 years ago, the Guinness brewery site at St James's Gate now sprawls across 26 ha (65 acres). It is the largest brewery in Europe and exports beers to more than 120 countries throughout the world. Other famous brands owned by Guinness include Harp Lager and Smithwick's Ale.

HOW GUINNESS IS MADE
The four main ingredients used to brew Guinness are barley, hops, yeast and water which, contrary to popular belief, comes from the Wicklow Mountains rather than the River Liffey.

Barley

Flaked barley

Malted barley

Roasted barley

Water

Masher

Grist

Grist mill

Kieve

Sweet wort

1 Irish barley is prepared in three ways – malted, flaked and roasted (to give the distinctive tint). These are all ground together in a grist mill to form a grist.

2 The grist is mixed together with hot water and mashed into a porridge-like consistency. The mixture is strained into a kieve, or mash tun, and left to stand for an hour. Here starches are turned into sugars, producing a dark, sweet wort.

Residual husks are removed

Guinness advertising has become almost as famous as the product itself. Since 1929, when the first advertisement announced that "Guinness is Good for You", poster and television advertising campaigns have employed many amusing images of both animals and people.

ARTHUR GUINNESS

Arthur Guinness

In December 1759, 34-year-old Arthur Guinness signed a 9,000-year lease at an annual rent of £45 to take over St James's Gate Brewery, which had lain vacant for almost ten years. At the time the brewing industry in Dublin was at a low ebb – the standard of ale was much criticized and in rural Ireland beer was virtually unknown, as whiskey, gin and poteen were the more favoured drinks. Furthermore, Irish beer was under threat from imports. Guinness started brewing ale, but was also aware of a black

ale called porter, produced in London. This new beer was so called because of its popularity with porters at Billingsgate and Covent Garden markets. Guinness decided to stop making ales and develop his own recipe for porter (the word "stout" was not used until the 1920s). So successful was the switch that he made his first export shipment in 1769.

Engraving (c. 1794) of a satisfied customer

Hops

Yeast

5 The liquid has now become a stout. The Guinness is matured and conditioned for up to ten days in tall storage tanks. It is then pumped into tankers or kegs to be sold throughout the world.

Stainless steel kegs

Kettle

Hopped wort

Stout

Centrifuge

3 Hops, which provide the tangy taste in Guinness, are added to the wort in huge 20-tonne kettles. The ingredients are boiled to very high temperatures for about 90 minutes and then strained.

4 The hopped wort is cooled and the yeast is added. The mixture is passed to a fermenting vessel where some sugars are turned to alcohol. It is left to ferment for 48 hours and the yeast is removed by centrifuge.

Draught and bottled Guinness

The Guinness brewery has relied heavily on water transport since its first export was shipped to England in 1769. The barges, which up until 1961 made the short trip with their cargo up the Liffey to Dublin Port, were a familiar sight on the river. Once at port, the stout would be loaded on to huge tanker ships for worldwide distribution.

Steel kettles used in modern-day brewing

Giant water lilies in the Lily House, National Botanic Gardens

National Botanic Gardens **5**

Botanic Ave, Glasnevin, Dublin 9.
[837 4388. ▥ 13, 19, 19A, 134.
◯ Mar–Oct: 9am–6pm Mon–Sat,
11am–6pm Sun; Nov–Feb: 10am–
4:30pm Mon–Sat, 11am–4:30pm Sun.
◑ 25 Dec. **Glasnevin Cemetery**
Finglas Rd. ◯ Apr–Oct: 8am–5pm
Mon–Fri, 8am–4pm Sat, 9:30am–5pm
(Nov–Mar: 9:30am–4:30pm) Sun.

Opened in 1795, the gardens are home to Ireland's foremost centre of botany and horticulture. They still possess an old-world feel, thanks to the beautiful cast-iron Palm House and other curvilinear glasshouses. These were built between 1843 and 1869 by Richard Turner, who was also responsible for the Palm House at Kew Gardens, London, and the glasshouses at Belfast's Botanic Gardens (see p270).

The 20-ha (49-acre) park contains over 20,000 different plant species. A particularly attractive feature is the display of colourful, old-fashioned Victorian carpet bedding. Other highlights include a renowned rose garden and rich collections of cacti and orchids. There is also a 30-m (100-ft) high redwood tree.

The gardens back on to the huge Glasnevin or Prospect Cemetery where many of Ireland's political figures are buried, including Charles Stewart Parnell (see p41) and Daniel O'Connell (see p40).

Shaw's Birthplace **6**

33 Synge St, Dublin 8. [475 0854.
▥ 16, 19, 22. ◯ May–Oct: 10am–
1pm, 2–5pm Mon–Sat & 11:30am–
1pm, 2–6pm Sun & public hols. ▨

Kitchen at Shaw's Birthplace

Playwright and Nobel prize-winner George Bernard Shaw was born in this house on 26 July 1856. In 1876 he followed his mother to London. She had left four years earlier with her daughters, fed up with her husband's drinking habits. It was in London that Shaw met his wife Charlotte Payne-Townsend. He stayed in England until his death in 1950.

Inside the house visitors can see the young Shaw's bedroom and the kitchen where the author remembered he drank "much tea out of brown delft left to 'draw' on the hob until it was pure tannin". Although there is little on Shaw's productive years, the home gives a fair idea of the lifestyle of a Victorian middle-class family.

Marino Casino **7**

Fairview Park, off Malahide Rd,
Dublin 3. [833 1618. ▥ 20A, 20B,
27, 42, 42B, 43. ◯ May–Oct: 10am–
6:30pm daily; Nov, Feb–Apr: noon–
4pm Wed & Sun. ▨ ▣ obligatory.

This delightful little villa (see pp38–9), built by Sir William Chambers in the 1760s for Lord Charlemont, now sits rather incongruously next to a busy road and a housing estate. Originally built as a summer house for the Marino Estate, the villa survives today although the main house was pulled down in 1921. The Casino is acknowledged to be one of the finest examples of Palladian architecture in Ireland. Some fascinating innovative features were used in its construction, including chimneys disguised as urns and hollow columns that accommodate drains. Outside, four fine carved stone lions, thought to be by English sculptor Joseph Wilton, stand guard at each of the corners.

Carved stone lion at Marino Casino

The building's squat, compact exterior conceals eight rooms built on three floors around a central staircase. The ground floor comprises a spacious hall and a saloon, with beautiful silk hangings, elaborate parquet flooring and a coffered ceiling. On the first floor is the ostentatious State Room, decorated in green and white.

Waterways Visitors' Centre ❽

Grand Canal Quay, Dublin 2.
📞 677 7510. 🚌 3. ⬤ Jun–Sep:
9:30am–6:30pm daily; Oct–May:
12:30–5pm Wed–Sun. ⬤ 25 Dec.
📷 📹 on request

Fifteen minutes' walk from Trinity College along Pearse Street, this building overlooks the Grand Canal Basin. Audiovisual displays and models illustrate Ireland's inland waterways. One of the most interesting displays focuses on their construction: in the 18th century, canals were often called "navigations" and the men who built them were "navigators", a term shortened to "navvies". There are also exhibits on the wildlife found on and around the canals.

DUBLIN'S CANALS

The affluent Georgian era witnessed the building of the Grand and Royal canals linking Dublin with the River Shannon and the west coast. These two canals became the main arteries of trade and public transport in Ireland from the 1760s until the coming of the railways, which took much of the passenger business, almost a century later. However, the canals continued to carry freight until after World War II, finally closing to commercial traffic in 1960. Today the canals are well maintained and used mainly for pleasure-boating, cruising and fishing.

Late 18th-century engraving of passenger ferry passing Harcourt Lock on the Grand Canal, taken from a painting by James Barralet

Stretch of the Grand Canal near Waterways Visitors' Centre

Collins Barracks ❾

Benburb St, Dublin 7. 📞 677
7444. 🚌 25, 25A, 66, 67, 90.
⬤ 10am–5pm Tue–Sat, 2–5pm Sun.
⬤ 25 Dec, Good Fri. 📷 ♿ 🚫

Close to Phoenix Park and just across the Liffey from the Guinness Brewery, stands the wonderful annexe of the National Museum *(see pp64–5)*. Its setting in this historic building is an inspired move. The massive complex was commissioned by King William III in 1700, just ten years after victory at the Battle of the Boyne, and was the largest barracks in his domain, with living accommodation for over 5,000 people. It was in continuous use right up to the 1990s. Originally known as Dublin Barracks, the prefix was changed to "Royal" in 1803. After Irish independence the barracks was finally named for Michael Collins, the first commander-in-chief of the Irish Army.

The large central courtyard, measured at one hundred marching paces, is an object lesson in simplicity. In marked contrast to the grey institutional exterior, the museum's interior presents the exhibits in an innovative way that makes use of the latest technology.

Furniture, silver and scientific instrument collections form the bulk of items on show in the South Block. In the West Block, however, visitors get an insight into the history, work and development of the National Museum. The Out of Storage exhibit brings together a wide array of artefacts from around the world, with background information obtainable from banks of interactive multimedia computers. One of the highlights of the museum is the Curator's Choice section where 25 unusual exhibits – such as, for instance, an early hurling stick and ball – are displayed with a story line that explains their cultural significance.

There is also a large hall set aside for temporary displays. It is planned that the museum will in future expand to occupy all four barracks blocks.

An 18th-century, gilded wooden chair on display at Collins Barracks

The oak-beamed Great Hall at Malahide Castle

Malahide Castle ⑩

Malahide, Co Dublin. 🚉 🚌 *42 from Dublin.* 🕿 *846 2184.* 🕐 *Apr–Oct: 10am–5pm Mon–Sat, 11am–6pm Sun & public hols; Nov–Mar: 10am–5pm Mon–Fri, 2–5pm Sat, Sun & public hols.* **Fry Model Railway** 🕐 *Jun–Sep: 10am–6pm Mon–Fri, 10am–5pm Sat, 2–6pm Sun & public hols (Apr & May: Mon–Thu, Sat, Sun & public hols); Oct–Mar: 2–5pm Sat, Sun & public hols.* 🎟 *Combined ticket available.*

NEAR THE SEASIDE dormitory town of Malahide stands a huge castle set in 100 ha (250 acres) of grounds. The castle's core dates from the 14th century but later additions, such as its rounded towers, have given it a classic fairytale appearance. Originally a fortress, the building served as a stately home for the Talbot family until 1973. They were staunch supporters of James II: the story goes that on the day of the Battle of the Boyne in 1690 *(see p236)*, 14 members of the family breakfasted here; none came back for supper.

Guided tours take you round the castle's collection of 18th-century Irish furniture. You will also see the oak-beamed Great Hall and the carved panelling of the Oak Room.

Part of the Portrait Collection, on loan from the National Gallery *(see pp68–9)*, can be seen at the castle. It includes portraits of the Talbot family, as well as other figures such as Wolfe Tone *(see p39)*.

In the old corn store is the Fry Model Railway, started in the 1920s by Cyril Fry, a local railway engineer. The 240 sq m (2,500 sq ft) exhibit contains models of Irish trains, miniatures of stations, streets and local landmarks such as the River Liffey and Howth Head.

Howth ⑪

Co Dublin. 🚉 *DART.* **Howth Castle grounds** 🕐 *8am–sunset daily.*

THE COMMERCIAL fishing town of Howth marks the northern limit of Dublin Bay. Howth Head, a huge rocky mass, has lovely views of the bay. A footpath runs around the tip of Howth Head, which is known as the "Nose". Nearby is Baily Lighthouse (1814). Sadly, much of this area – some of Ireland's prime real estate – has suffered from building development.

To the west of the town is Howth Castle, which dates back to Norman times. Its grounds are particularly beautiful in May and June when the rhododendrons and azaleas are in full bloom.

A short boat ride out from the harbour is the rocky islet, Ireland's Eye, which is a bird sanctuary where puffins nest. Boat trips from Howth run there throughout the summer.

Dun Laoghaire ⑫

Co Dublin. 🚉 *DART.* **National Maritime Museum of Ireland** 🕿 *280 0969.* 🕐 *May–Sep: 1–5pm Tue–Sun (Oct: 1–5pm Sun).* 🎟

IRELAND'S MAJOR passenger ferry port and yachting centre, with its brightly painted villas, parks and palm trees, makes a surprising introduction to Ireland. On a

Baily Lighthouse on the southeastern tip of Howth Head

Yachts anchored in Dun Laoghaire harbour

good day it exudes a decidedly continental feel. Many visitors head straight out of Dun Laoghaire (pronounced Dunleary) from the ferry. However, the town offers some magnificent walks around the harbour and to the lighthouse along the east pier. The villages of Sandycove and Dalkey can be reached via "The Metals" footpath which runs along a disused railway.

Located in the 1837 Mariners' Church is the National Maritime Museum. Exhibits tell the story of Robert Halpin, who captained the ship that laid the first transatlantic telegraph cable in 1866. Also on display are a huge clockwork-driven lighthouse lens formerly used at Howth, and a longboat used by French officers during Wolfe Tone's unsuccessful invasion at Bantry in 1796 *(see pp160–61).*

years later James Joyce *(see p88)* stayed here for a week as the guest of Oliver St John Gogarty, poet and model for the *Ulysses* character Buck Mulligan. Gogarty rented the tower for a mere £8 per year. Inside the squat 12-m (40-ft) tower's granite walls is a small museum with some of Joyce's correspondence, personal belongings, such as his guitar, cigar case and walking stick, and his death mask. There are also photographs and first editions of his works, including a de luxe edition (1935) of *Ulysses* illustrated by Henri Matisse. The roof, originally a gun platform but later used as a sunbathing deck by Gogarty, affords marvellous views of Dublin Bay. Directly below the tower is Forty Foot Pool, traditionally an all-male nude bathing spot, but now open to all.

Guitar at James Joyce Tower

James Joyce Tower ⓭

Sandycove, Co Dublin. █ 280 9265. ▣ *DART to Sandycove.* ◯ *Apr–Oct: 10am–1pm & 2–5pm Mon–Sat, 2–6pm Sun & public hols.* ▨

STANDING on a rocky promontory above the village of Sandycove is this Martello tower. It is one of 15 defensive towers which were erected between Dublin and Bray in 1804 to withstand a threatened invasion by Napoleon. One hundred

Dalkey ⓮

Co Dublin. ▣ *DART.*

DALKEY was once known as the "Town of Seven Castles", but only two of these now remain. They are both on the main street of this attractive village whose tight, winding roads and charming villas give it a Mediterranean feel.

A little way offshore is tiny Dalkey Island, a rocky bird sanctuary with a Martello tower and a medieval Benedictine church, both now in a poor state of repair. In summer the island can be reached by a boat ride from the town's Coliemore Harbour.

Killiney ⓯

Co Dublin. ▣ *DART to Dalkey or Killiney.*

SOUTH OF DALKEY, the coastal road climbs uphill before tumbling down into the village of Killiney. The route offers one of the most scenic vistas on this stretch of the east coast, with views often compared to those across the Bay of Naples. Howth Head is clearly visible to the north, with Bray Head *(see p125)* and the foothills of the Wicklow Mountains *(see pp130–31)* to the south. There is another exhilarating view from the top of Killiney Hill Park, off Victoria Road – well worth tackling the short steep trail for. Down below is the popular pebbly beach, Killiney Strand.

Shopfronts on the main street of Dalkey

ENTERTAINMENT IN DUBLIN

ALTHOUGH DUBLIN is well served by theatres, cinemas, nightclubs and rock venues, what sets the city apart from other European capitals is its pubs. Lively banter, impromptu music sessions and great Guinness are the essential ingredients for an enjoyable night in any one of dozens of atmospheric hostelries.

Olympia Theatre façade

One of the most popular entertainment districts is the rejuvenated Temple Bar area. Along this narrow network of cobbled streets you can find everything from traditional music in grand old pubs to the latest dance tracks in a postindustrial setting. The many pubs and venues around this area make the city centre south of the Liffey the place to be at night. The north side does, however, boast the two most illustrious theatres, the largest cinemas and the 7,000-seater Point Theatre, a converted 19th-century rail terminal beside the docks. It is now the venue for all major rock concerts and stage musicals as well as a number of classical music performances.

Buskers playing near Grafton Street in southeast Dublin

ENTERTAINMENT LISTINGS

THE MAIN LISTINGS magazine, *In Dublin*, comes out every two weeks and is readily available from all newsagents. *Hot Press*, a national bimonthly newspaper that covers both rock and traditional music, has comprehensive listings for Dublin. The *Dublin Event Guide* is a free sheet available from pubs, cafés, restaurants and record shops. Also published every two weeks, it is particularly strong on music and nightclubs.

BOOKING TICKETS

TICKETS FOR MANY EVENTS are available on the night, but it is usually safer to book in advance. All the major venues take credit card payment over the telephone. The **Ticket Shop** accepts phone bookings by credit card for many of the major shows and events in and around Dublin, while the main branches of **HMV** sell tickets over the counter for some of the top theatre shows and most major rock gigs.

THEATRE

ALTHOUGH DUBLIN has only a limited number of theatres, there is almost always something worth seeing and the productions are of a very high standard. Most of Dublin's theatres are closed on Sunday.

The most famous venue is Ireland's national theatre, the **Abbey** *(see p86)*, which concentrates on major new Irish productions as well as revivals of work by Irish playwrights such as Brendan Behan, Sean O'Casey, JM Synge and WB Yeats. The smaller Peacock Theatre downstairs covers more experimental works. Also on the north side is the **Gate Theatre** *(see p88)* founded in 1929 and noted for its interpretations of well-known international plays.

The main venue south of the Liffey, the **Gaiety Theatre**, stages a mainstream mix of plays, emphasizing the work of Irish playwrights. Some of the best fringe theatre and modern dance in Dublin can be seen at the **Project Arts Centre** in Temple Bar and the **City Arts Centre**, which sometimes has midnight performances. **Andrews Lane Theatre** provides a forum for new writers and directors. The **Olympia Theatre** has the feel of a Victorian music hall. It specializes in comedy and popular drama and occasionally stages rock and Irish music concerts.

Every October the **Dublin Theatre Festival** takes over all the venues in the city with mainstream, fringe, Irish and international plays.

Record shop and ticket office in Crown Alley, Temple Bar

Crowds enjoying the Temple Bar Blues Festival

CLASSICAL MUSIC, OPERA AND DANCE

DUBLIN may not have the range of classical concerts of other European capitals, but it has a great venue in the **National Concert Hall**. In the 1980s, this 19th-century exhibition hall was completely redesigned and acoustically adapted, and is where the National Symphony Orchestra plays most Friday evenings. The National Concert Hall's programme also includes opera, chamber music, jazz, dance and some traditional music.

The **Hugh Lane Municipal Gallery of Modern Art** (see p89) has regular Sunday lunchtime concerts. Other classical venues include the **Royal Hospital Kilmainham** (see p95) and the **Royal Dublin Society (RDS)** main hall and showground. International opera is staged in the **Point Theatre**. The DGOS (Dublin Grand Opera Society) performs every April and November at the Gaiety Theatre.

TRADITIONAL MUSIC AND DANCE

TO MANY IRISH PEOPLE the standard of music in a pub is just as important as the quality of the Guinness. Central Dublin has a host of pubs reverberating to the sound of bodhráns, fiddles and uilleann pipes. One of the most famous is **O'Donoghue's**, where the

The listings magazine
In Dublin

legendary Dubliners started out in the early 1960s. **Slattery's** and the **Auld Dubliner** are also renowned venues. Established acts play venues such as **Mother Redcap's Tavern**, which is a fun place occupying an old factory. **Jury's Hotel** and the **Castle Inn** stage nightly Irish cabaret featuring dancing, singing and music.

ROCK, JAZZ, BLUES AND COUNTRY

DUBLIN has had a thriving rock scene ever since local band Thin Lizzy made it big in the early 1970s. U2's international success has acted as a further catalyst for local bands, and each night there's usually an interesting gig somewhere in the city. **Whelan's** and the **Baggot Inn** feature the best up-and-coming Irish bands

nightly. The upstairs room at the likeable **International Bar** caters mostly for acoustic acts and singer-songwriters, while **Break for the Border** is a popular nightclub that also features a wide variety of live bands. All the big names play at either the Point Theatre or, in summer, local sports stadia. The Olympia Theatre attracts some top performers with its more intimate setting.

Jazz and blues musicians play occasionally in large and small venues; an annual highlight is the **Temple Bar Blues Festival** in July. Country music enjoys a massive following in Ireland, and country acts play regularly at several Dublin pubs. **Bad Bob's Backstage Bar** is a lively country music nightclub where there's usually lots of dancing.

NIGHTCLUBS

UNTIL A CLUSTER of new dance venues opened in the early 1990s, Dublin's club-life was fairly unremarkable. Nowadays the **POD** (Place of Dance) attracts visiting stars taking time out from their film shoots in the city. Another extremely trendy place is the **Kitchen**, downstairs in the (U2-owned) Clarence Hotel. **Ri-Rá** and **The Da Club** are at the cutting edge of dance music, while **River Club** and **Lillie's Bordello** provide a more mainstream dance sound.

Most clubs close at 2am. For further action, head for clubs like **Buck Whaleys** on Leeson Street which stay open until 5am. Admission is free, but drinks prices are high.

A traditional Irish music session in O'Donoghue's

Traditional façade of Doheny and Nesbitt

PUBS AND BARS

Dublin's pubs are a slice of living history. These are the places where some of the best-known scenes in Irish literature have been set, where rebellious politicians have met and where world-famous music acts have made their debuts. Today, as well as the memorabilia on the walls, it's the singing, dancing, talk and laughter that make a pub tour of Dublin an absolute must.

There are nearly 1,000 pubs inside the city limits. Among the best of the traditional bars are **Neary's**, popular with actors and featuring a gorgeous marble bar, the atmospheric **Long Hall** and the friendly **Stag's Head**, dating from 1770. **The Bailey**, recently renovated, is another old favourite and is mentioned in *Ulysses*.

Cosy snugs – where drinkers could lock themselves away for private conversation – were an important feature of 19th-century bars. A few remain, notably at the tiny, journalists' haunt of **Doheny and Nesbitt** and the intimate **Kehoe's**.

The **Brazen Head** claims to be the city's oldest pub, dating back to 1198. The present pub, built in the 1750s, is lined with old photographs and dark wood panelling. Every pub prides itself on the quality of its Guinness, though most locals acknowledge that **Mulligan's**, founded in 1782, serves one of the best pints in the city.

The range extends beyond smoky pubs with nicotine-stained ceilings: the splendid decor of the **Shelbourne Bar**, in the Shelbourne Hotel, pulls in a sophisticated crowd. Good bars abound in the Trinity College and Temple Bar areas, including **The Norseman** and **Oliver St John Gogarty**.

A LITERARY PUB CRAWL

Pubs with strong literary associations abound in Dublin, particularly around Grafton Street. **McDaid's**, an old pub with an Art Deco interior, still retains some of the Bohemian air from the time when famous writer-drinkers such as Patrick Kavanagh and Brendan Behan were regulars. **Davy Byrne's** has much plusher decor than when Leopold Bloom dropped in for a gorgonzola and mustard sandwich in *Ulysses*, but it is still well worth paying a visit.

These and about six other pubs, once frequented by Ireland's most famous authors

GUINNESS TIME

A Guinness sign on the outside of a Dublin pub

and playwrights, are featured on the excellent **Dublin Literary Pub Crawl**. This is by far the most entertaining way to get a real feel for the city's booze-fuelled literary heritage. The two-and-a-half-hour tours, led by actors, start with a beer in the Duke, Duke Street. Tours take place daily in summer, but are usually only at weekends in winter.

CINEMA

Dublin's cinemas have had a boost thanks to the success of Dublin-based films such as *My Left Foot* (1989) and *The Commitments* (1991) and a huge growth in the country's movie production industry.

The **Irish Film Centre** opened its doors in 1992 and is a most welcome addition to the city's entertainment scene. Showing mostly independent and foreign films, along with a programme of lectures and seminars, it boasts two screens, as well as a bar and restaurant. Another cinema whose repertoire is mostly art house is the **Screen**, situated close to Trinity College. The large first-run cinemas are all located on the north side. These usually offer tickets at reduced prices for their afternoon screenings and show late-night films at the weekend. The **Dublin Film Festival**, which is held over ten days between late February and early March, shows a varied selection of the latest international and Irish releases.

Bustling interior of the Oliver St John Gogarty pub in Temple Bar

DIRECTORY

BOOKING TICKETS

HMV
18 Henry St. **Map** D2.
【 873 2899.
65 Grafton St. **Map** D4.
【 677 5930.

Ticket Shop
2nd Floor, Grafton House,
70 Grafton St. **Map** D4.
【 456 9569.

THEATRE

Abbey Theatre
Abbey St Lower. **Map** E2.
【 878 7222.

Andrews Lane Theatre
9–11 St Andrew's Lane.
Map D3.
【 679 5720.

City Arts Centre
23–25 Moss St. **Map** E2.
【 677 0643.

Dublin Theatre Festival
47 Nassau St. **Map** D3.
【 677 8439.

Gaiety Theatre
King St South. **Map** D4.
【 677 1717.

Gate Theatre
Cavendish Row. **Map** D1.
【 874 4368.

Olympia Theatre
Dame St. **Map** C3.
【 677 7744.

Project Arts Centre
The Mint, Henry Place.
Map D2.
【 671 2321.

Riverbank Theatre
Merchant's Quay. **Map** B3.
【 677 3370.

CLASSICAL MUSIC, OPERA AND DANCE

Hugh Lane Municipal Gallery of Modern Art
Charlemont House, Parnell
Sq North. **Map** C1.
【 874 1903.

Irish Museum of Modern Art
Kilmainham.
【 612 9900.

National Concert Hall
Earlsfort Terrace. **Map** D5.
【 475 1666.

Point Theatre
East Link Bridge, North
Wall Quay. **Map** D1.
【 836 3633.

Royal Dublin Society (RDS)
Ballsbridge.
【 668 0866.

TRADITIONAL MUSIC AND DANCE

Auld Dubliner
24–25 Temple Bar.
Map D3.
【 677 0527.

Castle Inn
5–7 Lord Edward St.
Map C3.
【 475 1122.

Jury's Hotel
Pembroke Rd, Ballsbridge.
【 660 5000.

Mother Redcap's Tavern
Back Lane, Christchurch.
Map B4.
【 453 8306.

O'Donoghue's
15 Merrion Row. **Map** E5.
【 660 7194.

Slattery's
129 Capel St. **Map** C2.
【 872 7971.

ROCK, JAZZ, BLUES AND COUNTRY

Bad Bob's Backstage Bar
35 East Essex St. **Map** C3.
【 677 5482.

Baggot Inn
143 Baggot St Lower.
Map E5.
【 676 1430.

Break for the Border
Grafton Plaza Hotel,
Johnson's Place. **Map** D4.
【 478 0300.

International Bar
23 Wicklow St. **Map** D3.
【 677 9250.

Temple Bar Blues Festival
Temple Bar Information
Centre, 18 Eustace St.
Map C3.
【 671 5717.

Whelan's
25 Wexford St. **Map** C5.
【 478 0766.

NIGHTCLUBS

Buck Whaleys
67 Lower Leeson St.
【 676 1755.

The Da Club
2 Johnson's Place. **Map** D4.
【 670 3137.

Kitchen
6–8 Wellington Quay.
Map C3.
【 677 6635.

Lillie's Bordello
Adam Court, off Grafton
St. **Map** D4.
【 679 9204.

POD
Harcourt St. **Map** D5.
【 478 0166.

Ri-Rá
11 South Great George's
St. **Map** C3.
【 677 4835.

River Club
Merchants' Arch. **Map** D3.
【 677 2382.

PUBS AND BARS

The Bailey
2 Duke St. **Map** D4.
【 679 3734.

Brazen Head
20 Bridge St Lower.
Map A3.
【 677 9549.

Davy Byrne's
21 Duke St. **Map** D4.
【 677 5217.

Doheny and Nesbitt
5 Lower Baggot St.
Map E5.
【 676 2945.

Dublin Literary Pub Crawl
35 Heytesbury St. **Map** C5.
【 454 0228.

Kehoe's
9 South Anne St. **Map** D4.
【 677 8312.

Long Hall
51 South Great George's
St. **Map** C4.
【 475 1590.

McDaid's
3 Harry St, off Grafton St.
Map D4.
【 679 4395.

Mulligan's
8 Poolbeg St. **Map** E3.
【 677 5582.

Neary's
1 Chatham St. **Map** D4.
【 677 8596.

The Norseman
29 East Essex St, Temple
Bar. **Map** C3.
【 671 5135.

Oliver St John Gogarty
58–59 Fleet St, Temple Bar.
Map D3.
【 671 1822.

Queen's
12 Castle St, Dalkey.
【 285 4569.

Shelbourne Bar
27 St Stephen's Green
North. **Map** E4.
【 676 6471.

Stag's Head
1 Dame Court, off Dame
Lane. **Map** D3.
【 679 3701.

Toner's
139 Lower Baggot St.
Map E5.
【 676 3090.

CINEMA

Dublin Film Festival
1 Suffolk St. **Map** D3.
【 679 2937.

Irish Film Centre
6 Eustace St, Temple Bar.
Map C3.
【 679 5744.

MGM 9 Screen Multiplex
Parnell St. **Map** C2.
【 872 8444.

Screen
D'Olier St. **Map** D3.
【 671 4988.

Dublin's Best: Entertainment

IT'S EASY TO PACK a lot into a night out in Dublin.
Most of the best nightspots are situated close
to each other and, in the Temple Bar area alone,
there are plenty of exciting haunts to try out.
The city offers something to suit every taste and
pocket: choose from world-class theatre, excellent
concert venues, designer café-bars and lively or
laid-back clubs hosting nights of traditional, country,
jazz or rock music. Even when there is no specific
event that appeals, you can simply enjoy Dublin's
inexhaustible supply of great traditional pubs.

Gate Theatre
*The Gate puts on both foreign
plays and Irish classics such as
Sean O'Casey's* Juno and the
Paycock. (See p88.)

NORTH OF
THE LIFFEY

SOUTHWEST
DUBLIN

Stag's Head
*This gorgeous Victorian pub has a long,
mahogany bar and has retained its original
mirrors and stained glass. Located down
an out-of-the-way alley, this atmospheric
pub is well worth seeking out.* (See p105.)

| 0 metres | 500 |
| 0 yards | 500 |

THE TEMPLE BAR AREA

It will take more than a couple of
evenings to explore fully all that
these narrow streets have to offer.
Many of Dublin's
best mid-priced
restaurants are here,
while modern bars
sit next to traditional
pubs hosting fiddle
sessions. There are
also theatres and the
Irish Film Centre.
Later, clubs play
music ranging from
country to the latest
dance sounds.

HA'PENNY BRIDGE

L I F F E Y

WELLINGTON QUAY

THE GARAGE BAR

PROJECT

BAD BOBS

MEETING HOUSE SQUARE

Irish Film Centre

OLYMPIA

ESSEX STREET EAST

SYCAMORE ST

TEMPLE LANE

FOWNNES STREET

CROW ST

THE AULD DUBLINER

TEMPLE BAR

CROWN ALLEY

THE BAD ASS CAFE

COPE STREET

D A M E   S T R E E T

| 0 metres | 100 |
| 0 yards | 100 |

Queuing for a concert in Temple Bar

Street theatre events take
place throughout the summer
in Temple Bar. This actor is
portraying George Bernard Shaw
in a typical street performance.

Abbey Theatre
Despite recurring financial problems, Ireland's prestigious national theatre still manages to stage compelling new drama, such as Dancing at Lughnasa *by Brian Friel. (See p86.)*

Point Theatre
Once a Victorian railway terminus, this is now the country's top live music arena. Major acts, including Van Morrison (above) and Luciano Pavarotti, have appeared here and it's also a popular venue for hit musicals. (See p105.)

LIFFEY

SOUTHEAST DUBLIN

McDaid's
Playwright Brendan Behan (see p21) downed many a pint in this pub, which dates from 1779. Though firmly on the tourist trail, McDaid's retains its bohemian charm, and bars upstairs and downstairs provide space for a leisurely drink. (See p105.)

National Concert Hall
The National Symphony Orchestra performs most Friday evenings. A combination of dance, chamber music and other performance arts makes up a full programme of events. From May to July, inexpensive Tuesday lunch-time concerts are held. (See p103.)

Street Finder Index

KEY TO THE STREET FINDER

▪ Major sight	🚕 Taxi rank	⊠ Post office
▪ Place of interest	🅿 Main car park	═ Railway line
▪ Railway station	ℹ Tourist information office	— One-way street
🚊 DART station	✚ Hospital with casualty unit	▬ Pedestrian street
🚌 Main bus stop	🚓 Police station	0 metres 200
🚍 Coach station	✝ Church	0 yards 200 1:11,500

KEY TO ABBREVIATIONS USED IN THE STREET FINDER

Ave	Avenue	**E**	East	**Pde**	Parade	**Sth**	South
Br	Bridge	**La**	Lane	**Pl**	Place	**Tce**	Terrace
Cl	Close	**Lr**	Lower	**Rd**	Road	**Up**	Upper
Ct	Court	**Nth**	North	**St**	Street/Saint	**W**	West

A

Abbey Street Lower	D2
Abbey Street Middle	D2
Abbey Street Old	E2
Abbey Street Upper	C2
Abbey Theatre	D2
Adair Lane	D3
Adelaide Hospital	C4
Amiens Street	F1
Anglesea Row	C2
Anglesea Street	D3
Anne Street North	B2
Anne Street South	D4
Anne's Lane	D4
Ardee Row	A5
Ardee Street	A5
Arran Quay	A3
Arran Street East	B2
Asdill's Row	D3
Ash Street	A4
Aston Place	D3
Aston Quay	D3
Aungier Place	C5
Aungier Street	C5

B

Bachelors Walk	D3
Back Lane	B4
Baggot Court	F5
Baggot Rath Place	E5
Baggot Street Lower	F5
Ball's Lane	B2
Bank of Ireland	D3
Bass Place	F4
Beaver Street	F1
Bedford Row	D3
Bella Place	F1
Bella Street	E1
Bell's Lane	E5
Benburb Street	A2
Beresford Lane	E2
Beresford Place	E2
Beresford Street	B2
Bewley's Oriental Café	D4
Bishop Street	C5
Blackhall Parade	A2
Blackhall Place	A2
Blackhall Street	A2
Blackpitts	B5
Bolton Street	C1
Bonham Street	A3
Borris Court	B3
Bow Lane East	C4
Bow Street	A2
Boyne Street	F4
Brabazon Row	A5
Brabazon Street	A4
Bracken's Lane	E3
Braithwaite Street	A4
Bride Road	B4
Bride Street	C4

Bride Street New	C5
Bridge Street Lower	A3
Bridge Street Upper	A3
Bridgefoot Street	A3
Britain Place	D1
Brown Street North	A2
Brown Street South	A5
Brunswick Street North	A2
Buckingham Street Lower	F1
Bull Alley Street	B4
Burgh Quay	D3
Busáras	E2
Butt Bridge	E2
Byrne's Lane	C2

C

Camden Place	C5
Camden Row	C5
Camden Street Lower	C5
Capel Street	C2
Carman's Hall	A4
Castle Market	D4
Castle Steps	C3
Castle Street	C3
Cathal Brugha Street	D1
Cathedral Lane	B5
Cathedral Street	D2
Cathedral View Court	B5
Chamber Street	A5
Chancery Lane	C4
Chancery Place	B3
Chancery Street	B3
Chapel Lane	C2
Charles Street West	B3
Chatham Row	D4
Chatham Street	D4
Christ Church Cathedral	B3
Christchurch Place	B4
Church Avenue West	B2
Church Lane South	C5
Church Street	B3
Church Street New	A2
Church Street Upper	B2
Church Terrace	B2
City Hall	C3
City Quay	F2
Clanbrassil Street Lower	B5
Clare Lane	E4
Clare Street	E4
Clarence Mangan Road	A5
Clarendon Row	D4
Clarendon Street	D4
Clonmel Street	D5
Coke Lane	A3
Coleraine Street	B1
College Green	D3
College Lane	E3
College Street	D3
Commons Street	F2
Connolly Station	F1

Constitution Hill	B1
Convent Close	F5
Cook Street	B3
Coombe Court	A4
Cope Street	D3
Copper Alley	C3
Cork Hill	C3
Cork Street	A5
Corporation Street	E1
Crane Lane	C3
Creighton Street	F3
Crown Alley	D3
Cuckoo Lane	B2
Cuffe Street	C5
Cumberland Street North	D1
Cumberland Street South	F4
Custom House	E2
Custom House Quay	E2

D

D'Olier Street	D3
Dame Lane	C3
Dame Street	C3
Dawson Lane	D4
Dawson Street	D4
Dean Street	B4
Dean Swift Square	B4
Denzille Lane	F4
Diamond Park	E1
Digges Street Upper	C5
Dominick Lane	C1
Dominick Place	C1
Dominick Street Lower	C1
Dominick Street Upper	B1
Donore Road	A5
Dorset Street Upper	C1
Dowlings Court	F3
Drury Street	D4
Dublin Castle	C3
Dublin Civic Museum	D4
Dublin Writers Museum	C1
Dublinia	B4
Duke Lane	D4
Duke Street	D4

E

Earl Place	D2
Earl Street North	D2
Earl Street South	A4
Earlsfort Terrace	D5
Ebenezer Terrace	A5
Eden Quay	D2
Ellis Quay	A3
Ely Place	E5
Erne Place Lower	F3
Erne Street Upper	F4
Erne Terrace Front	F3
Essex Quay	C3
Essex Street East	C3
Essex Street West	C3

Eustace Street	C3
Exchange Street Lower	C3
Exchange Street Upper	C3
Exchequer Street	D3

F

Fade Street	C4
Father Mathew Bridge	A3
Father Mathew Square	B2
Fenian Street	F4
Fishamble Street	B3
Fitzwilliam Lane	E5
Fitzwilliam Square	E5
Fitzwilliam Square North	E5
Fitzwilliam Square West	E5
Fitzwilliam Street Lower	F5
Fitzwilliam Street Upper	F5
Fleet Street	D3
Foley Street	E1
Foster Place	D3
Fountain Place	A2
Four Courts	B3
Fownes Street	D3
Francis Street	B4
Frederick Street South	E4
Frenchman's Lane	E2
Friary Avenue	A2
Fumbally Lane	B5

G

Garden Lane	A4
Garden of Remembrance	C1
Gardiner Street Lower	E1
Gardiner Street Middle	D1
Gate Theatre	D1
General Post Office	D2
Geoffrey Keating Road	A5
George's Dock	F2
George's Hill	B2
George's Lane	A2
George's Quay	E2
Gloucester Diamond	E1
Gloucester Place	E1
Gloucester Street South	E3
Glover's Alley	D4
Golden Lane	C4
Grafton Street	D4
Granby Lane	C1
Granby Place	C1
Granby Row	C1
Grangegorman Upper	A1
Grant's Row	F4
Grattan Bridge	C3
Gray Street	A4
Greek Street	B2
Green Street	B2

A   **B**   **C**

1

KIRWAN STREET

STANHOPE STREET

GRANGEGORMAN UPPER

PHIBSBOROUGH RD

CONSTITUTION HILL

CHURCH ST UPPER

KING'S INNS PARK

King's Inns

PRESEND STREET

TEMPLE COTTAGES

DOMINICK STREET UPPER

MOUNTJOY ST MIDDLE

HAMILTON

WESTERN WAY

MOUNTJOY ST

HENRIETTA LANE

HENRIETTA STREET

HENRIETTA PLACE

KING'S INNS ST

LINENHALL TCE

COLERAINE STREET

LISBURN STREET

LINENHALL PDE

MENHALL STREET

NEWPORT

DORSET ST UPPER

Dublin W
Muse
Hugh Kane
Municipal Gallery
of Modern Art
GRANBY ROW   GAR
REMEMBE

GRANBY ROW

PARNELL S

DOMINICK PLACE

DOMINICK STREET LOWER

DOMINICK LANE

BOLTON STREET

PARNELL STREET

LOFTUS LANE

CAPEL STREET

RYDER'S ROW

CHAPEL LANE

P

JERVIS LANE UP

WOLFE TONE ST

JERVIS STREET

STREET

2

BLACKHALL PLACE

ST PAUL STREET

BLACKHALL PDE

BLACKHALL ST

OXMANTOWN LA

HENDRICK STREET

BENBURB STREET

JOHN STREET

KING

BRUNSWICK STREET NORTH

FOUNTAIN PLACE

STREET

SMITHFIELD

FRIARY AVENUE

QUEEN STREET

HAYMARKET

CHURCH ST NEW

MAY LANE

P

Old
Jameson's
Distillery

St Michan's
Church

CHURCH STREET

CHURCH ST NTH

STIRRUP LANE

NEW ST NTH

CHURCH TCE

FATHER
MATHEW
SQUARE

CHURCH AVE W

NORTH

BERESFORD STREET

HALL'S LA

ANNE STREET NORTH

CUCKOO LANE

GREEK STREET

LITTLE

GREEN STREET

GEORGE'S HILL

LITTLE BRITAIN STREET

LITTLE GREEN ST

HALSTON STREET

MARY'S LANE

MARY ST LITTLE

LYNCH'S LANE

ARRAN

ANGLESEA ROW

St
Mary's
Abbey

STREET

MEETINGHOUSE LANE

MARY'S ABBEY

JERVIS LANE LR

WOLFE
TONE
PARK

JERVIS ST

ABBEY STREET UP

BYRNE'S LA

3

ELLIS QUAY

Mellowes
Bridge

USHER'S ISLAND

COKE LA

ARRAN

STABLE LA

Liffey

PHOENIX STH

QUAY

HAMMOND LANE

CHANCERY

CHANCERY PL

Four
Courts

CHANCERY ST

INNS QUAY

Father Mathew
Bridge

STREET

STRAND STREET

STRAND STREET

LITTLE

ORMOND SQUARE

ORMOND QUAY UPPER

O'Donovan
Rossa Bridge

Bridge

Grattan

ORMOND QUAY L

WELLINGTON Q

ISLAND STREET

BONHAM STREET

USHER STREET

USHER'S QUAY

BRIDGEFOOT STREET

AUGUSTINE ST

BRIDGE ST LOWER

MERCHANT'S QUAY

WOOD QUAY

ESSEX QUAY

ESSEX STREET EAST

EXCHANGE ST LOWER

PARLIAMENT ST

CRANE LA

SYCAMORE ST

ESSEX STREET WEST

4

MARSHALL LANE

OLIVER BOND STREET

THOMAS STREET WEST

THOMAS COURT LANE

CATHEDRAL LANE

HANBURY LANE

MEATH STREET

EARL STREET SOUTH

BRAITHWAITE ST

PIMLICO

REGINALD STREET

GRAY STREET

MEATH PLACE

BRIDGE ST UPPER

COOK STREET

St Audoen's
Church

HIGH STREET

JOHN'S LANE WEST

VICAR STREET

SWIFT'S ALLEY

DEAN SWIFT SQ

THOMAS DAVIS ST STH

GARDEN LANE

FRANCIS STREET

LAMB ALLEY

Dublinia

Tailors'
Hall

ST MICHAEL'S CL

BORRIS CT

SCHOOLHOUSE LANE

BACK LANE

ST AUGUSTINE ST

JOHN DILLON STREET

CARMAN'S HALL

ASH STREET

HANOVER LANE

MARK'S ALLEY W

Christ
Church
Cathedral

CHRISTCHURCH PL

St Werburgh's
Church

WERBURGH STREET

NICHOLAS STREET

ROSS ROAD

BRIDE ROAD

BULL ALLEY STREET

LORD EDWARD ST

DAME

City Hall

DAME

Dublin
Castle

CASTLE STREET

WERBURGH STREET

SHIP ST LITTLE

SHIP STREET GREAT

CHANCERY LANE

STEPHEN ST UP

STEPHEN

GOLDEN LANE

WHITEFRIAR ST

LONGFORD ST GREAT

Whitefriar
Street
Carmelite
Church

AUNGIER STREET SOUTH

YO

5

JOHN ST SOUTH

CORK STREET

BROWN ST SOUTH

ARDEE STREET

ARDEE ROW

WATKINS
BUILDINGS

O'DONOVAN'S

CHAMBER STREET

OSCAR SQUARE

O'CURRY AVE

O'CAROLAN RD

EBENEZER TERRACE

SUSAN TERRACE

GEOFFREY KEATING ROAD

MADDEN RD

DONORE RD

ST THOMAS ROAD

CLARENCE MANGAN RD

MILL STREET

THE COOMBE

COOMBE COURT

WEAVER'S SQUARE

NEWMARKET

WARDS HILL

FUMBALLY LANE

BLACKPITTS

MALPAS STREET

ST KEVIN'S AVE

MICHAEL'S TCE

HAMMOND ST

CLANBRASSIL ST LR

WILLIAM'S PL STH

DEAN ST

NEW ROW SOUTH

NEW STREET SOUTH

KEVIN STREET UPPER

CATHEDRAL VIEW CT

St Patrick's
Cathedral

ST PATRICK'S

PATRICK STREET

ST PATRICK'S
PARK

Marsh's
Library

ST PATRICK'S CLOSE

Adelaide Hospital

WOOD ST

PETER STREET

PETER ROW

WHITEFRIAR PLACE

PETER ST

BISHOP STREET

KEVIN STREET LOWER

BRIDE STREET NEW

LONG LANE

HEYTESBURY ST

CAMDEN ROW

Meath
Hospital

PLEASANTS STREET

LIBERTY LANE

CHURCH LANE

REDMOND'S

DIGGES LA

AUNGIER ST L

WEXFORD ST

CUFFE

CAMDEN ST

A   **B**   **C**

IRELAND REGION BY REGION

Ireland at a Glance

THE LURE of Ireland's much-vaunted Atlantic shores, from the wild coastline of Cork and Kerry to the remote peninsulas of the Northwest, is strong. However, to neglect the interior would be to miss out on Ireland's equally characteristic landscapes of lush valleys, dark peatlands and unruffled loughs. Most regions are rich in historic sights: from world-famous Neolithic sites in the Midlands to imposing Norman castles in the North and Palladian mansions in the Southeast.

Yeats Country *is a charming part of County Sligo closely associated with WB Yeats. The poet was born here and is buried within sight of Ben Bulben's ridge.* (See pp224–5.)

NORTHWEST IRELAND
(See pp212–27)

Connemara National Park *in County Galway boasts stunning landscapes in which mountains and lakes are combined with a dramatic Atlantic coastline. The extensive blanket bogs and moorland are rich in wildlife and unusual plants.* (See p200.)

THE WEST OF IRELAND
(See pp192–211)

Bunratty Castle
(See pp184–5)

The Rock of Cashel, *a fortified medieval abbey, perches on a limestone outcrop in the heart of County Tipperary. It boasts some of Ireland's finest Romanesque sculpture.* (See pp188–9.)

THE LOWER SHANNON
(See pp172–91)

CORK AND KERRY
(See pp144–71)

Bantry House
(See pp160–61)

The Lakes of Killarney, *flanked by the lush, wooded slopes of some of the country's highest mountains, are the principal attraction in the southwest of Ireland.* (See pp154–5.)

The Giant's Causeway, where ancient lava flows have been eroded to reveal columns of unnatural regularity, is Northern Ireland's most curious sight. According to local mythology, the rocks were placed here by a giant called Finn MacCool to enable him to walk across the sea to Scotland. (See pp254–5.)

NORTHERN IRELAND
(See pp246–77)

THE MIDLANDS
(See pp228–45)

Newgrange
(See pp238–9)

Mount Stewart House, a 19th-century mansion, is most renowned for its magnificent gardens. These were created as recently as the 1920s, but a colourful array of exotic plants has thrived in the warm microclimate enjoyed in this part of County Down. (See pp274–5.)

SOUTHEAST IRELAND
(See pp116–43)

0 kilometres   50

0 miles   25

Powerscourt is a large estate in superb countryside on the edge of the Wicklow Mountains. Its grounds rank among the last great formal gardens of Europe. Originally planted in the 1730s, they were restored and embellished in the 19th century. (See pp126–7.)

Kilkenny Castle was for centuries the stronghold of the Butler dynasty, which controlled much of southeast Ireland in the Middle Ages. The vast Norman fortress was remodelled during the Victorian period and still dominates Kilkenny – one of the country's most historic and pleasant towns. (See pp134–6.)

SOUTHEAST IRELAND

KILDARE · WICKLOW · CARLOW · KILKENNY
WATERFORD · WEXFORD

B LESSED WITH *the warmest climate in Ireland, the Southeast has always presented an attractive prospect for settlers. Landscapes of gently rolling hills have been tamed by centuries of cultivation, with lush farmland, imposing medieval castles and great houses enhancing the region's atmosphere of prosperity.*

The Southeast's proximity to Britain meant that it was often the first port of call for foreign invaders. Viking raiders arrived here in the 9th century and founded some of Ireland's earliest towns, including Waterford and Wexford. They were followed in 1169 by the Anglo-Normans *(see pp34–5)*, who shaped the region's subsequent development.

Given its strategic importance, the Southeast was heavily protected, mostly by Anglo-Norman lords loyal to the English Crown. Remains of impressive castles attest to the power of the Fitzgeralds of Kildare and the Butlers of Kilkenny, who between them virtually controlled the Southeast throughout the Middle Ages. English influence was stronger here than in any other part of the island.

From the 18th century, wealthy Anglo-Irish families were drawn to what they saw as a stable zone, and felt confident enough to build fine mansions like the Palladian masterpieces of Russborough and Castletown. English rule was not universally accepted, however. The Wicklow Mountains became a popular refuge for opponents to the Crown, including the rebels who fled the town of Enniscorthy after a bloody battle during the uprising against the English in 1798 *(see p39)*.

This mountainous region is still the only real wilderness in the Southeast, in contrast to the flat grasslands that spread across Kildare to the west. To the east, sandy beaches stretch almost unbroken along the shore between Dublin and Rosslare in Wexford.

Traditional thatched cottages in Dunmore East, County Waterford

◁ **Staircase hall with ornate 18th-century stuccowork in Castletown House, County Kildare**

Exploring Southeast Ireland

T HE SOUTHEAST has something for everyone, from busy seaside resorts to quaint canalside villages, Norman abbeys and bird sanctuaries. The Wicklow Mountains, the location of several major sights such as the monastic complex of Glendalough and the magnificent gardens of Powerscourt, provide perfect touring and walking territory. Further south, the most scenic routes cut through the valleys of the Slaney, Barrow and Nore rivers, flanked by historic ports such as New Ross, from where you can explore local waterways by boat. Along the south coast, which is more varied than the region's eastern shore, beaches are interspersed with rocky headlands, and quiet coastal villages provide good alternative bases to the busy towns of Waterford and Wexford. Further inland, the best places to stay include Lismore and Kilkenny, which is one of the finest historic towns in Ireland.

Atb

PEATLAND WORLD

RATHANGA

MONASTEREVIN ❹

Portl

Graiguenamanagh, on the Barrow north of New Ross

SIGHTS AT A GLANCE

Ardmore ⓳
Avondale House ⓮
Bray ❽
Browne's Hill Dolmen ⓯
Castletown House pp122–3 ❶
Dunmore East ㉑
Enniscorthy ㉔
Glendalough ⓭
Hook Peninsula ㉒
Irish National Heritage Park ㉕
Jerpoint Abbey ⓱
Johnstown Castle ㉗
Kildare ❺
Kilkenny pp134–6 ⓰
Killruddery House ❾
Lismore ⓲
Monasterevin ❹
Mount Usher Gardens ⓬
New Ross ㉓
Peatland World ❸
Powerscourt pp126–7 ❼
Robertstown ❷
Rosslare ㉙

Russborough House ❻
Saltee Islands ㉘
Waterford pp138–9 ⓴
Wexford ㉖
Wicklow Mountains ⓫

Tours
Military Road ❿

Portlaoise

Casbel

KILKENNY ⓰

N10

CALLAN

JERPOINT ABBEY ⓱

INISTIC

Fermoy

Suir

WATERFORD ⓴

N25

R666

R675

LISMORE ⓲

Mallow

DUNGARVAN

Blackwater

⓳ ARDMORE

Cork

CASTLETOWN HOUSE ①

② **ROBERTSTOWN**

R403   Grand Canal   Dublin

KILDARE   Liffey   M7

⑧ **BRAY**

⑦ **POWERSCOURT**

⑥   R759   ⑨ **KILLRUDDERY HOUSE**

RUSSBOROUGH HOUSE

⑩ **MILITARY ROAD**

N81   R756   W I C K L O W   M O U N T A I N S   ⑪

⑫ **MOUNT USHER GARDENS**

⑬ **GLENDALOUGH**

● **WICKLOW**

● **BALTINGLASS**   N9   R755

Avonmore

⑭ **AVONDALE HOUSE**   Avoca

CARLOW

⑮ **BROWNE'S HILL DOLMEN**   W I C K L O W   W A Y   Bann   R747

● **ARKLOW**

Slaney   N80

● **GOREY**

N11   R741

GRAIGUENAMANAGH   R703   R702

ENNISCORTHY

⑳ ④

N9

NEW ROSS   N25

IRISH NATIONAL HERITAGE PARK

㉕

㉖ **WEXFORD**

㉗ **JOHNSTOWN CASTLE**   **ROSSLARE**

㉙

N25   **ROSSLARE HARBOUR**

R733   R736   R739

KILMORE QUAY

HOOK PENINSULA ㉒

㉘ **SALTEE ISLANDS**

A 19th-century winged horse at Powerscourt

GETTING AROUND

Routes N11, N9 and N7 fan out from Dublin, serving Wexford, Waterford and Kildare respectively. Rail lines follow a similar course: the eastern coastal towns are served by the Dublin–Rosslare railway, and there are good train services to Kildare and Kilkenny. You will need a car to explore the south coast; the Passage East–Ballyhack ferry is a useful shortcut between Waterford and Wexford.

SEE ALSO

• *Where to Stay* pp289–91

• *Restaurants, Cafés and Pubs* pp308–9 & 318–19

KEY

▰	Motorway
▰	Major road
▬	Minor road
▰	Scenic route
～	River
– –	Walk
⚡	Viewpoint

0 kilometres   15

0 miles   15

The seaside resort of Bray on the east coast

Castletown House ❶

See pp122–3.

Robertstown ❷

Road map D4. Co Kildare. 🏛 *240*. 🚌

TEN LOCKS WEST along the Grand Canal from Dublin, Robertstown is a characteristic 19th-century canalside village, with warehouses and cottages flanking the waterfront. Freight barges plied the route until about 1960, but pleasure boats have since replaced them. Visitors can take barge cruises from the quay and the Grand Canal Company's Hotel, built in 1801 for canal passengers, is now used for banquets.

Near Sallins, about 8 km (5 miles) east of Robertstown, the canal is carried over the River Liffey along the **Leinster Aqueduct**, an impressive structure built in 1783.

Peatland World ❸

Road map D4. Lullymore, Co Kildare. 📞 *045 860133*. 🚌 🚌 *to Newbridge.* ⏰ *9am–4:30pm Mon–Fri (Apr–Oct: 2–6pm Sat, Sun also).* 🔴 *10 days at Christmas.* 💶 ♿ *limited.*

ANYONE INTERESTED in the natural history of Irish bogs should visit Peatland World, an exhibition in an old farm at Lullymore, 9 km (6 miles) northeast of Rathangan. It lies at the heart of the Bog of Allen, a expanse of raised bog *(see p244)* that extends across the counties of Offaly, Laois and Kildare.

The Grand Canal Company's Hotel in Robertstown

There is an exhibition of the history and ecology of the bog, with displays of flora and fauna and archaeological finds from the surrounding area. Guided walks across the peatlands are also organized to introduce visitors to the bog's delicate ecosystem.

Stacking peat for use as fuel

Monasterevin ❹

Road map D4. Co Kildare. 🏛 *2,200.* 🚌

THIS GEORGIAN market town lies west of Kildare, where the Grand Canal crosses the River Barrow. Waterborne trade brought prosperity to Monasterevin in the 18th century, but the locks now see little traffic. However, you can still admire the aqueduct, which is a superb example of canal engineering.

Moore Abbey, next to the church, was built in the 18th century on the site of a monastic foundation, but the grand Gothic mansion owes much to Victorian remodelling. Once the ancestral seat of the Earls of Drogheda, in the 1920s Moore Abbey became the home of the celebrated tenor, John McCormack *(see p24)*. It is now a hospital.

Kildare ❺

Road map D4. Co Kildare. 🏛 *4,200.* 🚌 🚌 ℹ *Market House (May–Sep: 045 522696).* 🚌 *Thu.*

THE CHARMING and tidy town of Kildare is dominated by **St Brigid's Cathedral**, which commemorates the saint who founded a religious community on this site in 490. Unusually, monks and nuns lived there under the same roof, but this was not the only unorthodox practice associated with the community. Curious pagan rituals, including the burning of a perpetual fire, continued until the 16th century. The fire pit is visible in the grounds today. So too is a round tower, which was probably built in the 12th century and has

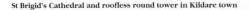

St Brigid's Cathedral and roofless round tower in Kildare town

Japanese Gardens at Tully near Kildare

a Romanesque doorway. The cathedral was rebuilt in the Victorian era, but the restorers largely adhered to the original 13th-century design.

🏠 St Brigid's Cathedral
Market Square. 📞 045 521229.
🕐 May–Oct: daily. **Donation**. ♿

ENVIRONS: Kildare lies at the heart of racing country: the Curragh racecourse is nearby, stables are scattered all around and bloodstock sales take place at Kill, northeast of town.

The **National Stud** is a state-run bloodstock farm at Tully, just south of Kildare. It was founded in 1900 by an eccentric Anglo-Irish colonel called William Walker. He sold his foals on the basis of their astrological charts, and put skylights in the stables to allow the horses to be "touched" by sunlight or moonbeams. Walker received the title Lord Wavertree in reward for bequeathing the farm to the British Crown in 1915.

Visitors can explore the 400-ha (1,000-acre) grounds and watch the horses being exercised. Mares are normally kept in a separate paddock from the stallions, though a "teaser" stallion is introduced to discover when the mares come into season. Breeding stallions wait in the covering shed: each one is expected to cover 50 mares per season. There is a special foaling unit where the mare and foal can remain undisturbed for a few days after the birth.

The farm has its own forge and saddlery, and also a Horse Museum. Housed in an old stable block, this illustrates the importance of horses in Irish life. Exhibits include the frail skeleton of Arkle, the champion steeplechaser who shot to fame in the 1960s.

Sharing the same estate as the National Stud are the **Japanese Gardens**, created by Lord Wavertree at the height of the Edwardian penchant for Orientalism. The gardens were laid out in 1906–10 by a Japanese landscape gardener called Tassa Eida, with the help of his son Minoru and 40 assistants. The impressive array of trees and shrubs includes maples, mulberries, bonsai, magnolias, sacred bamboos and cherry trees.

The gardens take the form of an allegorical journey from the cradle to the grave, beginning with life emerging from the Gate of Oblivion (a cave) and leading to the Gateway of Eternity, a contemplative Zen rock garden. The route incorporates a variety of elaborate rockeries, symbolic stone lanterns and miniature bridges.

🌿 National Stud and Japanese Gardens
Tully. 📞 045 521617. 🕐 Feb–Nov:
9:30am–6pm daily. 🎫 ♿
🎦 National Stud only. 🖥 🚻

HORSE RACING IN IRELAND

Ireland has a strong racing culture and, thanks to its non-elitist image, the sport is enjoyed by all. Much of the thoroughbred industry centres around the Curragh, a grassy plain in County Kildare stretching unfenced for more than 2,000 ha (5,000 acres). This area is home to many of the country's studs and training yards, and every morning horses are put through their paces on the gallops. Most of the major flat races, including the Irish Derby, take place at the Curragh racecourse just east of Kildare. Other popular fixtures are held at nearby Punchestown – most famously the steeplechase festival in April – and at Leopardstown, which also hosts major National Hunt races *(see pp26–7)*.

Finishing straight at the Curragh racecourse

Castletown House ➊

B UILT IN 1722–32 for William Conolly, Speaker
of the Irish Parliament, Castletown was the
grandest house in the country at the time. The
work of Florentine architect, Alessandro Galilei,
the building gave Ireland its first taste of
Palladianism. The magnificent interiors date
from the second half of the 18th century. They
were commissioned by Lady Louisa Lennox,
wife of William Conolly's great-nephew, Tom,
who took up residence here in 1758.
Castletown remained in the family until 1965,
when it was taken over by the Irish Georgian Society. The
house now belongs to the state and is open to the public.

**Conolly crest
on an armchair**

★ Long Gallery
*Pompeiian-style friezes adorn
the cobalt-blue walls of this
magnificent room. The niches
frame statues of figures from
Classical mythology.*

**Green Drawing
Room**

Red Drawing Room
*The room takes its name from the red damask
on the walls, which is probably French and
dates from the 1820s. This exquisite mahogany
bureau was made for Lady Louisa in the 1760s.*

**West wing
with kitchen**

Boudoir Wall Paintings
*The boudoir's decorative panels,
moved here from the Long Gallery,
were inspired by the Raphael
Loggia in the Vatican.*

The Dining Room was
designed by William Chambers,
architect of the Marino Casino
(see pp38–9). The mantelpiece
and door cases show his strong
Neo-Classical inspiration.

★ **Print Room**
In this, the last surviving print room in Ireland, Lady Louisa indulged her taste for Italian engravings. In the 18th century, it was fashionable for ladies to paste prints directly on to the wall and frame them with elaborate festoons.

VISITORS' CHECKLIST

Road map D4. Celbridge, Co Kildare. 01 6288252. 67, 67A from Dublin. *Reopening mid-1999 after restoration work.* Apr–Sep: daily; Oct: Mon–Fri & Sun; Nov–Mar: Sun. *Call for exact opening times.* obligatory. **Concerts.**

The Boar Hunt, painted by Paul de Vos (1596–1678)

★ **Staircase Hall**
This portrait of Lady Louisa is part of the superb Rococo stuccowork by the Francini brothers which decorates the staircase.

The east wing originally housed the stables.

Entrance

The Entrance Hall is an austere Neo-Classical room. Its most decorative feature is the delicate carving on the pilasters of the upper gallery.

STAR FEATURES

★ **Long Gallery**

★ **Print Room**

★ **Staircase Hall**

CONOLLY'S FOLLY

This folly, which lies just beyond the grounds of Castletown House, provides the focus of the view from the Long Gallery. Speaker Conolly's widow, Katherine, commissioned it in 1740 as a memorial to her late husband, and to provide employment after a harsh winter. The unusual structure of superimposed arches crowned by an obelisk was designed by Richard Castle, architect of Russborough House *(see p124).*

Saloon in Russborough House with original fireplace and stuccowork

Russborough House ⑥

Road map D4. Blessington, Co Wicklow.
📞 045 865239. 🚌 65 from Dublin.
🕐 May–Sep: daily; Easter–Apr & Oct: Sun & public hols. 🏷️ 📷 ♿

THIS PALLADIAN MANSION, built in the 1740s for Joseph Leeson, Earl of Milltown, is one of Ireland's finest houses. Its architect, an anglicized German called Richard Castle, also designed Powerscourt House *(see pp126–7)* and is credited with introducing the Palladian style to Ireland.

Unlike many grand estates in the Pale, Russborough has survived magnificently, both inside and out. The house claims the longest frontage in Ireland, with a façade adorned by heraldic lions and curved colonnades. The interior is even more impressive. Many rooms feature superb stucco decoration, which was done largely by the Italian Francini brothers, who also worked on Castletown House *(see pp122–3)*. The best examples are found in the music room, saloon and library, which are embellished with exuberant foliage and cherubs. Around the main staircase, a riot of Rococo plasterwork

Vernet seascape in the drawing room

depicts a hunt, with hounds clasping garlands of flowers. The stucco mouldings in the drawing room were designed especially to enclose marine scenes by the French artist, Joseph Vernet (1714–89). The paintings were sold in 1926, but were tracked down more than 40 years afterwards and returned to the house.

Russborough has many other treasures, including finely worked fireplaces of Italian marble, imposing mahogany doorways and priceless collections of silver, porcelain and Gobelins tapestries.

Such riches aside, one of the principal reasons to visit Russborough is to see the **Beit Art Collection**, famous for its Flemish, Dutch and Spanish Old Master paintings. These include fine works by Goya, Velázquez, Hals, Rubens and Vermeer. Sir Alfred Beit, who bought the house in 1952, inherited the pictures from his uncle – also named Alfred Beit and co-founder of the de Beer diamond mining empire in South Africa. In 1974, several masterpieces were taken by the IRA, but they were later retrieved. Several pictures are still missing, following a second robbery in 1986. Only a selection of paintings is on view in the house at any one time, while

---

THE HISTORY OF THE PALE

The term "Pale" refers to an area around Dublin which marked the limits of English influence from Norman to Tudor times. The frontier fluctuated, but at its largest the Pale stretched from Dundalk in County Louth to Waterford town. Gaelic chieftains outside the area could keep their lands provided they agreed to bring up their heirs within the Pale.

The Palesmen supported their rulers' interests and considered themselves the upholders of English values. This widened the gap between the Gaelic majority and the Anglo-Irish, a foretaste of England's doomed involvement in the country. Long after its fortifications were dismantled, the idea of the Pale lived on as a state of mind. The expression "beyond the pale" survives as a definition of those outside the bounds of civilized society.

An 18th-century family enjoying the privileged lifestyle typical within the Pale

Tourist road train on the beachfront esplanade at Bray

others are on permanent loan to the National Gallery in Dublin (see pp68–9).

Russborough enjoys a fine position near the village of **Blessington**, with a good view across to the Wicklow Mountains. The house lies amid wooded parkland rather than elaborate flower gardens. As Alfred Beit said of Irish Palladianism, "Fine architecture standing in a green sward was considered enough."

ENVIRONS: The **Poulaphouca Reservoir**, which was formed by the damming of the River Liffey, extends south from Blessington. The placid lake is popular with watersports enthusiasts, while other visitors come simply to enjoy the lovely mountain views.

Powerscourt ➐

See pp126–7.

Bray ➑

Road map D4. Co Wicklow.
🏠 33,000. 🚆 DART. 🚌 ℹ️ Old Court House, Main St (01 2867128).

O NCE A REFINED Victorian resort, Bray is nowadays a brash holiday town, with amusement arcades and fish and chip shops lining the seafront. Its beach attracts large crowds in summer, including many young families. Anyone in search of peace and quiet can escape to nearby Bray Head, where there is scope for bracing cliffside walks. Bray also makes a good base from which to explore Powerscourt Gardens, the Wicklow Mountains and the delightful coastal villages of Killiney and Dalkey (see p101).

Killruddery House ➒

Road map D4. Bray, Co Wicklow.
📞 01 2867128. 🕐 May–Jun & Sep: daily (pm only). 🅿️ ♿ limited.

K ILLRUDDERY HOUSE lies just to the south of Bray, in the shadow of Little Sugar Loaf Mountain. Built in 1651, it has been the family seat of the Earls of Meath ever since, although the original mansion was remodelled in an Elizabethan Revival style in the early 19th century.

The house contains some good carving and stuccowork, but it is a rather faded stately home. The real charm of Killruddery stems from the 17th-century formal gardens, which are regarded as the finest French Classical gardens in the country. They were laid out in the 1680s by a French gardener named Bonet, who also worked at Versailles.

The gardens, planted with great precision, feature romantic parterres, a whole array of different hedges and many fine trees and shrubs, both native and foreign. The sylvan theatre, a small enclosure surrounded by a bay hedge, is the only known example of its kind in Ireland.

The garden centres on the Long Ponds, a pair of canals which extend 165 m (550 ft) and were once used to stock fish. Beyond, a pool enclosed by two circular hedges leads to a Victorian arrangement of paths flanked by statues and neat hedges of yew, beech, lime and hornbeam.

View across the Long Ponds to Killruddery House

Powerscourt **7**

THE GARDENS AT POWERSCOURT are probably the finest in Ireland, both for their design and their dramatic setting at the foot of Great Sugar Loaf Mountain. The house and grounds were commissioned in the 1730s by Richard Wingfield, the 1st Viscount Powerscourt. The gardens fell into decline, but in 1840 the original scheme was revived. New ornamental gardens were completed in 1858–75 by the 7th Viscount, who added gates, urns and statues collected during his travels on the Continent. Gutted by an accidental fire in 1974, the ground floor and the ballroom on the first floor have now been beautifully renovated.

Laocoon statue on upper terrace

Bamberg Gate
Made in Vienna in the 1770s, this gilded wrought-iron gate was brought to Powerscourt by the 7th Viscount from Bamberg Church in Bavaria.

The Walled Gardens include a formal arrangement of clipped laurel trees but are also used for growing plants for Powerscourt's nursery.

The Pets' Cemetery contains the graves of Wingfield family dogs, cats and even horses and cattle.

Statue of Laocoon

Dolphin Pond
This pool, designed as a fish pond in the 18th century, is enclosed by exotic conifers in a lovely secluded garden.

POWERSCOURT HOUSE

In 1974 a fire at the Palladian mansion at Powerscourt left the fine building a burnt-out shell. In recent years the Slazenger family, who now own the estate, have restored the ground floor and the ballroom upstairs, although much work remains to be done to the rest of the house. Originally built in 1731 on the site of a Norman castle, the house was designed by Richard Castle, who was also the architect of Russborough House (see p124).

Powerscourt ablaze in 1974

★ The Perron
Leading down to Triton Lake is the Perron, a beautiful Italianate stairway added in 1874. Beside the lake, it is guarded by two statues of Pegasus – the mythical winged horse and emblem of the Wingfield family.

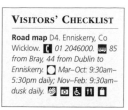

The Italian Garden
is laid out on terraces which were first cut into the steep hillside in the 1730s.

Pebble Mosaic
Many tonnes of pebbles were gathered from nearby Bray beach to build the Perron and to make this mosaic on the terrace.

The Pepper Pot Tower was built in 1911.

★ Triton Lake
Made for the first garden, the lake takes its name from its central fountain, which is modelled on a 17th-century work by Bernini in Rome.

★ Japanese Gardens
These enchanting Edwardian gardens, created out of bogland, contain Chinese conifers and bamboo trees.

STAR FEATURES

★ The Perron

★ Japanese Gardens

★ Triton Lake

Powerscourt Gardens with Great Sugar Loaf Mountain beyond ▷

A Tour of the Military Road ❿

Rare red squirrel

THE BRITISH BUILT the Military Road through the heart of the Wicklow Mountains during a campaign to flush out Irish rebels after an uprising in 1798 *(see p141)*. Now known as the R115, this road takes you through the emptiest and most rugged landscapes of County Wicklow. Fine countryside, in which deer and other wildlife flourish, is characteristic of the whole of this tour.

Glencree ①
The former British barracks in Glencree are among several found along the Military Road.

Powerscourt Waterfall ⑨
The River Dargle cascades 130 m (425 ft) over a granite escarpment to form Ireland's highest waterfall.

Great Sugar Loaf ⑧
The granite cone of Great Sugar Loaf Mountain can be climbed in under an hour from the car park on its southern side.

Sally Gap ②
This remote pass is surrounded by a vast expanse of blanket bog dotted with pools and streams.

Glenmacnass ③
After Sally Gap, the road drops into a deep glen where a waterfall spills dramatically over rocks.

Lough Tay ⑦
Stark, rocky slopes plunge down to the dark waters of Lough Tay. Though it lies within a Guinness-owned estate, the lake is accessible to walkers.

Roundwood ⑥
The highest village in Ireland at 238 m (780 ft) above sea level, Roundwood enjoys a fine setting. Its main street is lined with pubs, cafés and craft shops.

Glendalough ④
This ancient lakeside monastery *(see pp132–3)*, enclosed by wooded slopes, is the prime historical sight in the Wicklow Mountains.

TIPS FOR DRIVERS

Length: 96 km (60 miles).
Stopping-off points: There are several pubs and cafés in Enniskerry (including Poppies, an old-fashioned tearoom), and also in Roundwood, but this area is better for picnics. There are several marked picnic spots south of Enniskerry. (See also pp355–7.)

0 kilometres   5
0 miles   3

KEY

▬▬ Tour route
══ Other roads
🔆 Viewpoint

Vale of Clara ⑤
This picturesque wooded valley follows the River Avonmore. It contains the tiny village of Clara, which consists of two houses, a church and a school.

Wicklow Mountains ⓫

Road map D4. � *to Rathdrum & Wicklow.* 🚏 *to Enniskerry, Wicklow, Glendalough, Rathdrum & Avoca.* 🛈 *Rialto House, Fitzwilliam Square, Wicklow (0404 69117).*

STANDING AMID the rugged wilderness of the Wicklow Mountains, it can be hard to believe that Dublin is under an hour's drive away. The inaccessibility of the mountains meant that they once provided a safe hideout for opponents of English rule. When much of the Southeast was obedient to the English Crown, within an area known as the Pale *(see p124)*, warlords such as the O'Tooles held sway in the Wicklow Mountains. Rebels who took part in the 1798 uprising *(see p39)* sought refuge here too. One of their leaders, Michael Dwyer, remained at liberty in the hills around Sally Gap until 1803.

The building of the **Military Road**, started in 1800, made the area more accessible, but the mountains are still thinly populated. There is little traffic to disturb enjoyment of the exhilarating scenery of rock-strewn glens, lush forest and bogland where heather gives a purple sheen to the land. Turf-cutting is still a thriving cottage industry, and

Road sign in the Wicklow Mountains

you often see peat stacked up by the road. Numerous walking trails weave through these landscapes. Among them is the **Wicklow Way**, which extends 132 km (82 miles) from Marlay Park in Dublin to Clonegal in County Carlow. It is marked but not always easy to follow, so do not set out without a decent map. Although no peak exceeds 915 m (3,000 ft), the Wicklow Mountains can be dangerous in bad weather.

Hiking apart, there is plenty to see and do in this region. A good starting point for exploring the northern area is the picture-postcard estate village of **Enniskerry**. In summer, it is busy with tourists who come to visit the gardens at Powerscourt *(see pp126–7)*. From Laragh, to the south, you can reach Glendalough *(see pp132–3)* and the **Vale of Avoca**, where cherry trees are laden with blossom in the spring. The beauty of this gentle valley was captured in the poetry of Thomas Moore (1779–1852): "There is not in the wide world a valley so sweet as that vale in whose bosom the bright waters meet" – a reference to the confluence of the Avonbeg and Avonmore rivers, the so-called **Meeting of the Waters** beyond Avondale House *(see p132)*. Nestled among wooded

Mount Usher Gardens, on the banks of the River Vartry

hills at the heart of the valley is the hamlet of Avoca, where the **Avoca Handweavers** produce colourful tweeds in the oldest hand-weaving mill in Ireland, in operation since 1723.

Further north, towards the coast near Ashford, the River Vartry rushes through the deep chasm of the **Devil's Glen**. On entering the valley, the river falls 30 m (100 ft) into a pool known as the Devil's Punchbowl. There are good walks around here, with fine views of the coast.

🏠 **Avoca Handweavers**
Avoca. 🕻 *0402 35105.* ⭘ *daily.* ⬤ *25 & 26 Dec.* 🍴 🏠

Mount Usher Gardens ⓬

Road map D4. Ashford, Co Wicklow. 🕻 *0404 40205.* 🚏 *to Ashford.* ⭘ *Mar–Nov: daily.* 🍃 ♿ *limited.*

SET BESIDE the River Vartry just east of Ashford are the Mount Usher Gardens. They were designed in 1868 by a Dubliner, Edward Walpole, who imbued them with his strong sense of romanticism.

The gardens contain many rare shrubs and trees, from Chinese conifers and bamboos to Mexican pines and pampas grass. There is also a Maple Walk, which is glorious in autumn. The river provides the main focus of the Mount Usher Gardens, and amid the exotic vegetation you can glimpse herons on the weirs.

Colourful moorland around Sally Gap in the Wicklow Mountains

Glendalough ⓭

Road map D4. Co Wicklow.
St Kevin's Bus from Dublin.
Ruins ☐ *daily.* ◪ *in summer.*
Visitors' Centre ◖ 0404 45325.
☐ *daily.* ● *23–31 Dec.* ◪ ♿

THE STEEP, WOODED slopes of Glendalough, the "valley of the two lakes", harbour one of Ireland's most atmospheric monastic sites. Established by St Kevin in the 6th century, the settlement was sacked time and again by the Vikings but nevertheless flourished for over 600 years. Decline set in only after English forces partially razed the site in 1398, though it functioned as a monastic centre until the Dissolution of the Monasteries in 1539 *(see p36)*. Pilgrims kept on coming to Glendalough even after that, particularly on St Kevin's feast day, 3 June, which was often a riotous event *(see p28)*.

The age of the buildings is uncertain, but most date from the 8th to 12th centuries. Many were restored during the 1870s.

View along the Upper Lake at Glendalough

The main group of ruins lies east of the Lower Lake, but the earliest buildings associated with St Kevin are by the Upper Lake. Here, where the scenery is much wilder, you are better able to enjoy the tranquillity of Glendalough and to escape the crowds which inevitably descend on the site. Try to arrive as early as possible in the day, particularly during the peak tourist season. You enter the monastery through the double stone arch of the **Gatehouse**, the only surviving example in Ireland of a gateway into a monastic enclosure.

A short walk leads to a graveyard with a **Round tower** in one corner. Reaching 33 m (110 ft) in height, this is one of the finest of its kind in the country. Its cap was rebuilt in the 1870s using stones found inside the tower. The roofless **Cathedral** nearby dates mainly from the 12th century and is

Remains of the Gatehouse, the original entrance to Glendalough

St Kevin's Kitchen

the valley's largest ruin. At the centre of the churchyard stands the tiny **Priest's House**, whose name derives from the fact that it was a burial place for local clergy. The worn carving of a robed figure above the door is possibly of St Kevin, flanked by two disciples. East of here, **St Kevin's Cross** dates from the 12th century and is one of the best preserved of Glendalough's various High Crosses. Made of granite, the cross may once have marked the boundary of the monastic cemetery. Below, nestled in the lush valley, a minuscule oratory with a steeply pitched stone roof is a charming sight. Erected in the 11th century or even earlier, it is popularly known as **St Kevin's Kitchen**; this is perhaps because its belfry, thought to be a later addition, resembles a chimney. One of the earliest churches at Glendalough, **St Mary's**, lies across a field to the west.

PLAN OF GLENDALOUGH

The Visitors' Centre explains the history of the monastery and is the best place to start a tour. You can see both groups of ruins, which lie less than 1.5 km (1 mile) apart, in about two hours, but to make the most of the site allow a full day.

R756

LARAGH

Round tower ●   ● Gatehouse
St Mary's Church ●   ● Cathedral   🅿 ℹ
St Kevin's Kitchen ●

Glendassan

R757   Lower Lake

Glenealo

🅿

Upper Lake

Teampall-na-Skellig   ● Reefert Church
● St Kevin's   ● St Kevin's
Bed   Cell

0 metres   500
0 yards   500

KEY

═══ Road

--- Path

🅿 Parking

ℹ Visitors' Centre

Round tower at Glendalough

ST KEVIN AT GLENDALOUGH

St Kevin was born in 498, a descendant of the royal house of Leinster. He rejected his life of privilege, however, choosing to live instead as a hermit in a cave at Glendalough. He later founded a monastery here, and went on to create a notable centre of learning devoted to the care of the sick and the copying and illumination of manuscripts. St Kevin attracted many disciples to Glendalough during his lifetime, but the monastery became more celebrated as a place of pilgrimage after his death in around 618.

Colourful legends about the saint make up for the dearth of facts about him. That he lived to the age of 120 is just one of the stories told about him. Another tale claims that one day, when St Kevin was at prayer, a blackbird laid an egg in one of his outstretched hands. The saint remained in the same position until it was hatched.

Some traces of Romanesque moulding are visible outside the east window. Following the path along the south bank of the river, you reach the Upper Lake. This is the site of more monastic ruins and is also the chief starting point for walks through the valley and to a number of abandoned lead and zinc mines.

Situated in a grove not far from the Poulanass waterfall are the ruins of the **Reefert Church**, a simple Romanesque building. Its unusual name is a corruption of *Righ Fearta*, meaning "burial place of the kings"; the church may mark the site of an ancient cemetery. Near here, on a rocky spur overlooking the Upper Lake, stands **St Kevin's Cell**, the ruins of a beehive-shaped structure which is thought to have been the hermit's home.

There are two sites on the south side of the lake which cannot be reached on foot but are visible from the opposite shore. **Teampall-na-Skellig**, or the "church on the rock", was supposedly built on the site of the first church that St Kevin founded at Glendalough. To the east of it, carved into the cliff, is **St Kevin's Bed**. This small cave, in reality little more than a rocky ledge, may have been used as a tomb in the Bronze Age, but it is more famous as St Kevin's favourite retreat. It was from here that the saint allegedly rejected the advances of a naked woman by tossing her into the lake.

Avondale House ⓮

Road map D4. Co Wicklow. 🚌 0404 46111. 🚉 🚌 to Rathdrum. **House** 🔲 daily. ● Good Fri & 23–28 Dec. 🎦 **Grounds** 🔲 daily.

LYING JUST south of Rathdrum, Avondale House was the birthplace of the 19th-century politician and patriot, Charles Stewart Parnell *(see p41)*. The Georgian mansion is now a museum dedicated to Parnell and the fight for Home Rule.

The state owns Avondale and runs a forestry school here, but the public is free to explore the grounds. Known as **Avondale Forest Park**, the former estate includes an impressive arboretum first planted in the 18th century and much added to since 1900. There are some lovely walks through the woods, with pleasant views along the River Avonmore.

Browne's Hill Dolmen ⓯

Road map D4. Co Carlow. 🚉 🚌 to Carlow. 🔲 daily.

IN A FIELD 3 km (2 miles) east of Carlow, along the R726, stands a dolmen boasting the biggest capstone in Ireland. Weighing a reputed 100 tonnes, this massive stone is embedded in the earth at one end and supported at the other by three much smaller stones. Dating back to 2000 BC, Browne's Hill Dolmen is thought to mark the tomb of a local chieftain. A path leads to it from the road.

Browne's Hill Dolmen, famous for its enormous capstone

Street-by-Street: Kilkenny ⑯

Kilkenny coat of arms

KILKENNY is undoubtedly Ireland's loveliest inland city. It rose to prominence in the 13th century, when the Irish Parliament often met at Kilkenny Castle. The Anglo-Norman Butler family came to power in the 1390s and held sway over the city for 500 years. Their power has gone but their legacy is visible in the city's historic buildings, many of which have been restored. Kilkenny is proud of its heritage and every August hosts the Republic's top arts festival.

To Irishtown, St Canice's Cathedral

Grace's Castle was built in 1210 and later converted into a jail. Remodelled in the 18th century, it has functioned as a courthouse ever since.

PARLIAMENT STREET

ST KIERAN'S STREET

HIGH STREET

Marble City Bar

Narrow alleyways, known locally as "slips", are part of Kilkenny's medieval heritage. Several slips survive, and these are currently undergoing restoration.

Tholsel (City Hall)

★ Rothe House
This fine Tudor merchant's house, built around two court-yards, is fronted by arcades once typical of Kilkenny's main streets. A small museum inside the house contains a display of local archaeological artifacts and a costume collection.

Butter Slip
The alley is named after the butter stalls that once lined this small market place.

View of the High Street
The 18th-century Tholsel, with its distinctive clock tower and arcade, is the main landmark on the High Street. Its elegant Georgian chamber is used by city councillors to this day.

STAR SIGHTS

★ **Kilkenny Castle**

★ **Rothe House**

Kyteler's Inn
This medieval coaching inn (see p318) is named after Dame Alice Kyteler, a 14th-century witch who once lived in the building. Like most of the pubs in the city, Kyteler's Inn sells Smithwick's beer, which has been brewed in Kilkenny since 1710.

VISITORS' CHECKLIST

Road map C4. Co Kilkenny.
18,000. Dublin Road (056 22024). Dublin Road (056 64933). Shee Almshouse, Rose Inn St (056 51500). Kilkenny Arts Week (Aug). Rothe House 056 22893. Mar–Dec: daily; Jan–Feb: Sat–Sun (pm only).

The Shee Almshouse
is one of Ireland's few surviving Tudor alms-houses. Inside, the Cityscope Exhibition illustrates life in 17th-century Kilkenny using a model of the city.

St Mary's Hall

St John's Bridge

To train and bus stations, Dublin

★ **Kilkenny Castle**
Set in a commanding position overlooking the River Nore, this Norman fortress is one of Ireland's most famous castles. The Long Gallery, the finest room in the house, has a striking 19th-century hammer beam and glass roof.

CANAL SQ

NORE

ROSE INN STREET

THE PARADE

PATRICK STREET

To Cork, Waterford

0 metres   50
0 yards   50

KEY
P Parking
i Tourist information
– – – Suggested route

Kilkenny Design Centre
Housed in Kilkenny Castle's stable block, the centre has a nationwide reputation. You can see craftspeople in action and also buy their work.

Exploring Kilkenny

In a lovely spot beside a kink in the River Nore, Kilkenny is of great architectural interest, with much use made of the distinctive local black limestone, known as Kilkenny marble. A tour of the town also reveals many unexpected treasures: a Georgian façade often seems to conceal a Tudor chimney, a Classical interior or some other surprise.

The survival of the Irishtown district, now dominated by St Canice's Cathedral, recalls past segregation in Kilkenny. The area once known as Englishtown still boasts the city's grandest public buildings.

As a brewery city, Kilkenny is a paradise for keen drinkers. Not counting the popular private drinking clubs, there are about 80 official pubs.

Sign of the Marble City Bar on Kilkenny's High Street

♠ Kilkenny Castle

The Parade. 【 056 21450.
◯ Apr–Sep: daily; Oct–Mar: Tue–Sun. ● 10 days at Christmas.
obligatory. limited.

Built in the 1190s, Kilkenny Castle was occupied right up until 1935. The powerful Butler family (see p134) lived in it from the late 14th century, but because of the exorbitant running costs, their descendants eventually donated Kilkenny Castle to the nation in 1967. With its drum towers and solid walls, the castle retains its

North side of Kilkenny Castle showing Victorian crenellations

medieval form, but has undergone many alterations. The Victorian changes made in Gothic Revival style have had the most enduring impact, and are even more impressive since recent restoration work. The castle is a tremendously popular sight, so be prepared to queue during the summer.

High spots of a tour include the library, the wood-panelled dining room and the Chinese bedroom. Best of all, however, is the Long Gallery, rebuilt in the 1820s to house the Butler art collection. Its elaborate painted ceiling has a strong Pre-Raphaelite feel, with many of the motifs inspired by the *Book of Kells (see p62)*.

The castle grounds have shrunk over the centuries, but the French Classical gardens remain, with terraces opening onto a woodland walk and pleasant rolling parkland.

🔒 St Canice's Cathedral

Irishtown. ◯ daily. **Donation.**
The hilltop cathedral, flanked by a round tower that you can climb for a good view over Kilkenny, was built in the 13th century in an Early English

Gothic style. It was sacked by Cromwell's forces in 1650, but has survived as one of Ireland's medieval treasures. Walls of the local Kilkenny marble and pillars of pale sandstone combine to create an interior of simple grandeur. There is a finely sculpted west door, but the cream of the carving lies inside. An array of splendid 16th-century tombs includes the beautiful effigies of the Butler family in the south transept.

🔒 Black Abbey

Abbey St. 【 056 21279. ◯ daily.
Lying just west of Parliament Street, this Dominican abbey was founded in 1225. It was turned into a courthouse in the 16th century, but is once again a working monastery. The church boasts a fine vaulted undercroft and distinctive, though perhaps over-restored, stonework. There are also some beautiful stained-glass windows, several of which date back to the 14th century.

ENVIRONS: Just north of the town lies **Dunmore Cave**, a limestone cavern with an impressive series of chambers, noted for its steep descent and curious rock formations.

Bennettsbridge, on the Nore 8 km (5 miles) south of Kilkenny, is famous for its ceramics. The Nicholas Mosse Pottery (see p327) specializes in colourful earthenware made from the local clay.

🐚 Dunmore Cave

Ballyfoyle. 【 056 67726. ◯ Mar–mid-Jun: Tue–Sun; mid-Jun–Oct: daily; Nov–Feb: Sat, Sun & public hols.

Tomb of 2nd Marquess of Ormonde in St Canice's Cathedral

Jerpoint Abbey ⑰

Road map D5. Thomastown, Co
Kilkenny. ☏ 056 24623. 🚌 🚌 to
Thomastown. ☐ mid–Jun–Oct: daily;
Apr–mid-Jun: Tue–Sun. 🏛 🅿 ♿

LYING ON THE BANKS of the
Little Arrigle just south of
Thomastown, Jerpoint Abbey
ranks among the finest
Cistercian ruins in Ireland,
despite the loss of many of its
domestic buildings. Founded
in about 1160, the fortified
medieval complex rivalled
nearby Duiske Abbey (see
p141) in prestige. Jerpoint
flourished until the Dissolution of the Monasteries (see
pp34–5), when it passed to
the Earl of Ormonde.

The 15th-century cloisters
have not survived as well as
some earlier parts of
the abbey. Even so,
they are the highlight
of Jerpoint, with their
amusing sculptures of
knights, courtly ladies,
bishops and dragons.
The church itself is
well preserved. The
Irish-Romanesque
transepts date back to
the earliest period and
contain several 16th-
century tombs with
exquisite stylized
carvings. The north
side of the nave is
also intact, with a rich
array of decorated
Romanesque capitals.
There are tombs and
effigies of early
bishops and patrons
throughout the abbey. The
battlemented crossing tower
was added during the 1400s.

Stylized carving of saints on 16th-century tomb in Jerpoint Abbey

**Burne-Jones window
in St Carthage's
Cathedral, Lismore**

Lismore ⑱

Road map C5. Co Waterford.
🏛 1,100. 🚌 ℹ Apr–Oct: Lismore
Heritage Centre (058 54975).

THIS GENTEEL riverside town
is dwarfed by **Lismore
Castle**, perched romantically
above the River Blackwater.
Built in 1185 but re-
modelled in the 19th
century, the castle is the
Irish seat of the Duke
of Devonshire and is
closed to the public.
However, you can visit
the sumptuous gardens,
which include a lovely
riverside walk. **Lismore
Heritage Centre** tells
the story of St Carthage,
who founded a monas-
tic centre here in the
7th century. The town
has two cathedrals
dedicated to him. The
Protestant **Cathedral
of St Carthage** is
the more interesting.
It dates from 1633
but incorporates
older elements and
was later altered to suit the
Neo-Gothic tastes of the
Victorians. There is some fine
Gothic vaulting, and two
stained-glass windows in the
south transept are by the Pre-
Raphaelite artist, Sir Edward
Burne-Jones.

⚜ **Lismore Castle
Gardens** ☏ 058 54424. ☐ May–
Sep: daily (pm only). 🏛

ENVIRONS: From Lismore you
can follow a picturesque
route through the **Blackwater
Valley** (see p169). This runs
from Cappoquin, in an idyllic
woodland setting just east of
Lismore, down to the estuary
at Youghal (see p171).

Ardmore ⑲

Road map C5. Co Waterford. 🏛 380.
🚌 ℹ May–Sep: Main St (024 94444).

ARDMORE is a popular seaside
resort with a splendid
beach, lively pubs, good cliff
walks and some interesting
architecture. The hill beside
the village, which provides
fine views of the beach, is the
site of a monastery established
in the 5th century by St Declan,
the first missionary to bring
Christianity to this area.

Most of the buildings, including the ruined **St Declan's
Cathedral**, date from the
12th century. The cathedral's
west wall has fine Romanesque
sculptures, arranged in a
series of arcades. The scenes
include The *Archangel
Michael Weighing Souls* in the
upper row, and below this
The Adoration of the Magi and
The Judgment of Solomon.
The adjacent round tower is
one of the best preserved
examples in Ireland, and rises
to a height of 30 m (95 ft). An
oratory nearby is said to mark
the site of St Declan's grave.

St Declan's Cathedral at Ardmore, with its near-perfect round tower

Waterford ⑳

Waterford city coat of arms

WATERFORD WAS FOUNDED in 853 by the Vikings and later extended by the Anglo-Normans. Set in a commanding position by the estuary of the River Suir, it became southeast Ireland's main seaport. From the 18th century, the city's prosperity was consolidated by local industries, including the glassworks for which Waterford is famous. The strong commercial tradition persists today and Waterford's port is still one of Ireland's busiest. While the city has been somewhat tarnished by industrialization, great efforts are now being made to salvage what remains of its heritage, with further excavations of the old Viking city and the creation of pedestrian precincts in the historic quarter.

Reginald's Tower on the quayside

Jenkin's Lane, a quiet corner of Waterford off George's Street

Exploring Waterford

The extensive remains of the city walls clearly define the area originally fortified by the Vikings. The best-preserved section runs northwest from the **Watch Tower** on Castle Street, although Reginald's Tower, overlooking the river, is the largest structure in the old defences. In the Reginald Bar *(see p318)* you can see the arches through which boats sallied forth down the river; these sallyports are one of several Viking sections of the largely Norman fortifications.

Although Waterford retains its medieval layout, most of the city's finest buildings are Georgian. Some of the best examples can be seen on the Mall, which runs southwest from Reginald's Tower, and in the lovely Cathedral Square. The latter takes its name from **Christchurch Cathedral**, which was built in the 1770s to a design by John Roberts, a local architect who contributed much to the city's Georgian heritage. It is fronted by a fine Corinthian colonnade. A grim 15th-century effigy of a rotting corpse is an unexpected sight inside. Heading down towards the river, you pass the 13th-century ruins of **Grey Friars**, often known as the French Church after it became a Huguenot chapel in 1693.

West along the waterfront, a Victorian clock tower stands at the top of Barronstrand Street. Rising above the busy shops is the **Holy Trinity Cathedral**, which has a rich Neo-Classical interior. George's Street, which runs west from here, is dotted with period houses and cosy pubs. It leads to O'Connell Street, whose partially restored warehouses contrast with the shabbier buildings on the quay. In the summer, you can enjoy another view of the waterfront by taking a cruise on the river.

♣ Reginald's Tower

The Quay. **[** 051 873501.
○ Apr–Oct: daily.
The Vikings erected a tower on this spot in 1003, but it was the Normans who built the solid structure you see now. With impregnable walls 3 m (10 ft) thick, it is said to be the first Irish building to use mortar, a primitive concoction of blood, lime, fur and mud. The tower has in its time been a fortress, a mint, an arsenal and a prison. It also contains Waterford's civic museum.

⋔ Waterford Heritage Museum

Grey Friars St. **[** 051 871227.
○ Apr–Oct: daily; Nov–Mar: Mon–Fri.
This excellent museum tells the story of Waterford using models and a reconstruction of the early city. It has a fine display of Viking and medieval artifacts which were discovered during recent excavations.

View of the city of Waterford across the River Suir

Waterford Crystal Factory

Kilbarry. 051 373311. Apr–Oct: daily; Nov–Mar: Mon–Fri.

A visit to the Waterford Crystal Factory, just 2.5 km (1.5 miles) south of the centre, is strongly recommended for the insight it gives into the city's special process of crystal-making.

The original glass factory was founded in 1783 by two brothers, George and William Penrose, who chose Waterford because of its port. For many

Craftsman engraving a vase at the Waterford Crystal Factory

decades their crystal enjoyed an unrivalled reputation, but draconian taxes caused the firm to close in 1851. A new factory was opened in 1947, however, and master blowers and engravers were brought from the Continent to train local apprentices. Competition from Tipperary and Galway Crystal hit sales in the early 1990s, but these have revived recently, largely due to an upturn in the North American market.

Visitors can follow all stages of production, observing the process by which sand, lead and potash are transformed by fire into sparkling crystal. The main difference between ordinary glass and crystal is the latter's high lead content, 30 per cent in Waterford's case. The glass-blowers require great skill to create walls of the right thickness to take the heavy incisions typical of Waterford Crystal. The factory's other main hallmark is the Waterford signature, which is engraved on the base of each piece.

In the gallery showroom, a crystal chandelier lights up a dining table laden with Wedgwood pottery and Waterford glass, tempting visitors to buy.

VISITORS' CHECKLIST

Road map D5. Co Waterford.
42,000. 6 km (4 miles) S.
Plunkett Station, The Bridge
(051 873401). 41 The Quay
(051 879000). Plunkett Station
(051 875788). (051 21723):
Jun–Aug. Fri. International
Festival of Light Opera (Sep).

Ballyhack port, across Waterford Harbour from Passage East

ENVIRONS: The small port of **Passage East**, 12 km (7 miles) east of Waterford, witnessed the landing of the Normans in 1170 (see p34), but little has happened since. A car ferry links the village to Ballyhack in County Wexford, providing a scenic shortcut across Waterford Harbour as well as an excellent entry point to the Hook Peninsula (see p140).

WATERFORD CITY CENTRE

Christchurch Cathedral ④
Clock Tower ①
Holy Trinity Cathedral ②
Reginald's Tower ⑥
Watch Tower ③
Waterford Heritage Centre ⑤

KEY

River boat service
Parking
Tourist information
Church
City walls

0 metres 200
0 yards 200

Waterford Crystal Factory
CORK

Dunmore East ㉑

Road map D5. Co Waterford.
🚶 *1,100.* 🚌

THE APPEAL of Dunmore East, Waterford's most charming fishing village, lies chiefly in its red sandstone cliffs and bustling harbour. Paths run along the foot of the cliffs, but for the best views take the road that winds uphill from the beach, past tidy cottages and the ivy-clad Ship Inn to the Haven Hotel. A gate nearby leads to delightful gardens overlooking the fishing boats below. Climbing further, up steps cut into the rock, you are rewarded by views of the cliffs and noisy kittiwake colonies.

Hook Peninsula ㉒

Road map D5. Co. Wexford. 🚌 *to Duncannon.* 🚢 *from Passage East to Ballyhack (051 382480).* 🛈 *Jun–Sep: Fethard-on-Sea (051 397502).*

THIS TAPERING HEADLAND of gentle landscapes scattered with ancient ruins and quiet villages is perfect for a circular tour. The "Ring of Hook" route begins south of New Ross at **Dunbrody Abbey**, the ruins of a 12th-century Cistercian church, but **Ballyhack** is another good place to start. Once a fortified crossing point into County Waterford, the town still has a ferry service to neighbouring Passage East *(see p139).* **Ballyhack Castle**, built by the Knights Templar in about 1450, contains a small museum. About 4 km (2.5 miles) beyond is the small

Busy fishing harbour at Dunmore East

resort of **Duncannon**, with a broad sandy beach and a star-shaped fort, which was built in 1588 in expectation of an attack by the Spanish Armada.

The coast road continues south to **Hook Head**. Here, perched on red sandstone, sits what is almost certainly the oldest lighthouse in Europe, dating from 1172. Paths skirt the coast, which attracts many seabirds and seals and is also famous for its fossils.

Just 2 km (1.5 miles) east is the picturesque village of **Slade**. A ruined 15th-century tower house, **Slade Castle**, presides over the tiny harbour where fishing boats cluster around the slipways. The road proceeds along the rugged coastline, past the resort of Fethard-on-Sea and Saltmills to the dramatic ruin of **Tintern Abbey**. This 13th-century Cistercian foundation was built by William Marshall, Earl of Pembroke, in fulfilment of a vow made when his boat was caught in a storm off the coast nearby. The west end has been restored, but excavation work

continues. Fields lead to an old stone bridge and views over **Bannow Bay**, where it is thought the Normans made their first landing in 1169.

🏚 Dunbrody Abbey
Campile. 🖀 *051 388603.* ☐ *Apr–Sep: daily.* 🅿

⚓ Ballyhack Castle
Ballyhack. 🖀 *051 389468.* ☐ *Jul–Aug: daily; Apr–Jun & Sep: Wed–Sun.*

Norman lighthouse at Hook Head, on the tip of the Hook Peninsula

New Ross ㉓

Road map D5. Co Wexford.
🚶 *6,000.* 🚌 🛈 *The Quay (051 421857).* 🛒 *Tue.* **Galley Cruising Restaurants** *The Quay (051 421723).*

LYING ON the banks of the River Barrow, New Ross is one of the oldest towns in the county. Its importance, now as in the past, stems from its status as a port. In summer there is much activity on the river. Cruises run by Galley Cruising Restaurants ply both the Barrow and Nore rivers. Traditional shopfronts line the streets, which rise steeply

Castle ruins and harbour at Slade on the Hook Peninsula

from the quayside. The **Tholsel**, now the town hall but originally a tollhouse, was occupied by the British during the 1798 rebellion *(see pp38–9)*. Opposite, a monument to a Wexford pikeman commemorates the bravery of the Irish rebels who faced the British cannons.

Nearby is **St Mary's** which, when founded in the 13th century, was the largest parish church in Ireland. A modern church occupies the site, but the original (now roofless) south transept remains, as do many medieval tombstones.

ENVIRONS: A popular trip up the meandering Barrow goes 16 km (10 miles) north to **Graiguenamanagh**. The main attraction of this market town is **Duiske Abbey**, the largest Cistercian church in Ireland. Founded in 1207, it has been extensively restored and now acts as the parish church. The most striking features include a Romanesque door in the south transept, the great oak roof and traces of a medieval pavement below floor level. There is also a cross-legged statue of the Knight of Duiske, which is one of the finest medieval effigies in Ireland. Outside are two 9th-century granite High Crosses.

Trips along the Nore take you to **Inistioge**. Lying in a deep, wooded valley, this is an idyllic village, with neat 18th-century houses, a square planted with lime trees and a ten-arched bridge spanning the Nore. On a rock above the river stands a ruined Norman fort, a popular place for picnics.

From Inistioge you can walk along the river or up to **Woodstock House Demesne**, a national park. Among the

View over Enniscorthy and St Aidan's cathedral from Vinegar Hill

beech woods stands an 18th-century mansion, reduced to a ruin by a fire in 1922.

On a hill 12 km (7.5 miles) south of New Ross, a large area of woodland is enclosed within the **John F Kennedy Park and Arboretum**. Founded in 1968, near the late president's ancestral home in Dunganstown, the park boasts more than 4,500 types of tree and provides splendid panoramic views. There are marked paths and nature trails, and it is also possible to go horse riding.

🏠 **Duiske Abbey**
Graiguenamanagh, Co Kilkenny.
📞 0503 24238. ☐ daily. ♿
🌷 **John F Kennedy Park and Arboretum**
New Ross, Co Wexford. 📞 051 388171. ☐ daily. 🎫 ♿

Enniscorthy ㉔

Road map D5. Co Wexford. 👥
4,500. 🚌 🚆 🅷 County Museum, The Castle (054 35926).

THE STREETS of Enniscorthy, on the banks of the River Slaney, are full of character and redolent of the town's turbulent past. In 1798, Enniscorthy

witnessed the last stand of the Wexford pikemen, when a fierce battle was fought against a British force of 20,000 on nearby **Vinegar Hill**. The events of that year are told in full at the excellent County Museum inside **Enniscorthy Castle** – an imposing presence in the town, founded by the Normans but then altered in the 16th century.

Enniscorthy's other main sight is **St Aidan's Cathedral**, a Neo-Gothic creation designed in the 1840s by AWN Pugin (1812–52), most famous for his work on the Houses of Parliament in London.

Granaries and mills overlook the Slaney, along with several potteries for which the town is famous. Carley's Bridge was founded in 1654 and is still producing terracotta pots.

Enniscorthy's historic pubs are another big attraction. They include the Antique Tavern *(see p318)*, a half-timbered building which is hung with pikes used during the Battle of Vinegar Hill in 1798.

♣ **Enniscorthy Castle**
Castle Hill. 📞 054 35926.
☐ Mar–Sep: daily; Oct–Feb: Sun.
🎫 ♿ limited.

The inland port of New Ross seen from the west bank of the River Barrow

View across the harbour to Wexford town

Irish National Heritage Park 25

Road map D5. Ferrycarrig, Co Wexford. from Wexford in summer. 053 20733. Mar–Oct: daily. 25–26 & 31 Dec.

Built on former marshland near Ferrycarrig, just north of Wexford, the Irish National Heritage Park is a bold open-air museum. Trails lead visitors through woods to replicas of homesteads, places of worship and burial sites. These provide a good introduction to the country's ancient history (*see pp30–31*), and the section which deals with the Celtic period is particularly interesting. Other highlights include the Viking boatyard, complete with raiding ship, and a 7th-century horizontal watermill.

Wexford 26

Road map D5. Co Wexford. 15,000. Crescent Quay (053 23111).

Wexford's name derives from *Waesfjord*, a Norse word meaning "estuary of the mud flats". It thrived as a port for centuries but the silting of the harbour in the Victorian era put an end to most sea traffic. Wexford's quays, from where ships once sailed to Bristol, Tenby and Liverpool, are now used mainly by a fleet of humble mussel dredgers.

Wexford is a vibrant place, packed with fine pubs and boasting a varied arts scene. The town's singular style is often linked to its linguistic heritage. The *yola* dialect, which was spoken by early settlers, survives in the local pronunciation of certain words.

Wexford retains few traces of its past, but the Viking fishbone street pattern still exists, with narrow alleys fanning off the meandering Main Street. Keyser's Lane, linking South Main Street with the lively Commodore pub on Paul Quay, is a tiny tunnel-like Viking alley which once led to the Norse waterfront. The Normans were responsible for Wexford's town walls, remnants of which include one of the original gateways. This houses the **Westgate Heritage Centre**, which traces the history of Wexford. Behind it lies **Selskar Abbey**, the ruin of a 12th-century Augustinian monastery. King Henry II is said to have done penance here for the murder of Thomas à Becket in 1170.

Wexford also has several handsome buildings dating from a later period, including the 18th-century market house, known as the **Cornmarket**, on Main Street. The nearby square, the **Bull Ring**, is notable only for its history: it was used for bull-baiting in Norman times and was the scene of a cruel massacre by Cromwell's men in 1649.

Wexford Opera Festival, held in October, is the leading operatic event in the country. Aficionados praise it for its intimate atmosphere – both

Sign of a popular Wexford pub

during performances and afterwards, when artists and audience mingle together in the pubs: the Centenary Stores off Main Street is a favourite, though the Wren's Nest, on Custom House Quay, is better for traditional music.

🏛 Westgate Heritage Centre
Westgate. 053 46506. Jun–Aug: daily; Sep–May: Mon–Sat. 25 & 26 Dec.

ENVIRONS: Skirting the shore just east of the town is the **Wexford Wildfowl Reserve**. It covers 100 ha (250 acres) of reclaimed land and is noted in particular for its geese: over a third of the world's entire population of Greenland white-fronted geese winter here between October and April.

The mudflats also attract large numbers of swans and waders, and provide a rich hunting ground for birds of prey. The birds can be viewed from a number of hides and an observation tower.

🦢 Wexford Wildfowl Reserve
Wexford. 053 23129. daily. at weekends.

Johnstown Castle 27

Road map D5. Co Wexford. 053 42888. to Wexford. **Gardens** daily. 24 & 25 Dec.

Façade of Johnstown Castle

Johnstown castle, a splendid Gothic Revival mansion, lies amid ornamental gardens and mature woodland 6 km (4 miles) southwest of Wexford. In state hands since 1945, the house now functions as an

Vast crescent of sand and shingle beach at Rosslare

agricultural research centre. It is not open to the public, but it is possible to visit the **Irish Agriculture Museum**, housed in the castle's farm buildings. Reconstructions illustrate the work of a wheelwright and other traditional trades.

The real glory of Johnstown Castle are the grounds, from the sunken Italian garden and ornamental lakes to the woodlands and shrubberies. Azaleas and camellias flourish alongside an impressive array of trees including Japanese cedars, redwoods and Scots pine.

Hidden among the dense woods west of the house lurk the ruins of **Rathlannon Castle**, a medieval tower house.

🏛 Irish Agriculture Museum
Johnstown Castle. ◯ Apr–mid-Nov: daily (Sat & Sun pm only); mid-Nov– Mar: Mon–Fri. 🅿 🅳 limited.

Saltee Islands ㉘

Road map D5. Co Wexford. 🚢 from Wexford to Kilmore Quay: Wed & Sat. 🚤 from Kilmore Quay: Jul & Aug (weather permitting). 📞 053 29684.

THESE ISLANDS off the south coast of Wexford are a haven for sea birds. Great and Little Saltee together form Ireland's largest bird sanctuary, nurturing an impressive array of birds, from gannets and gulls to puffins and Manx shearwaters. Great Saltee particularly is famous for its colonies of cormorants. It also has more than 1,000 pairs of guillemots and is a popular stopping-off place for spring and autumn migrations. A bird-monitoring and research programme is in progress, and a close watch is also kept on the colony of grey seals.

The two uninhabited islands are privately owned, but visitors are welcome. Boat trips are run in fine weather from **Kilmore Quay**. These leave in late morning and return mid-afternoon.

Kilmore Quay is a small fishing village built on rare Precambrian gneiss rock – the oldest rock in Ireland. Pretty thatched cottages nestle above a fine sandy beach and the harbour, where a moored lightship houses a **Maritime Museum**. The boat's original fittings are just as interesting as the exhibits.

🏛 Maritime Museum
Kilmore Quay. 📞 053 29655. ◯ Jun– Oct: daily (pm only); Nov– May: by appt. 🅿

Rosslare ㉙

Road map D5. Co Wexford. 🏘 1,200. 🚍 🚌 ℹ Ferry terminal, Rosslare Harbour (053 33623).

ROSSLARE REPLACED Wexford as the area's main port after the decline of the original Viking city harbour. The port is so active today that people tend to associate the name Rosslare more with the ferry terminal for France and Wales than with the town lying 8 km (5 miles) further north.

Rosslare town is one of the sunniest spots in Ireland and draws many holidaymakers. It boasts a fine beach stretching for 9.5 km (6 miles), lively pubs and an excellent golf course fringed by sand dunes. There are good walks north to Rosslare Point.

ENVIRONS: At Tagoat, 6 km (4 miles) south of Rosslare, an old farmhouse called **Yola Farmstead** contains displays of traditional crafts such as thatching, glass-blowing and bread-and butter-making.

🏛 Yola Farmstead
Tagoat. 📞 053 31177. ◯ May–Sep: daily. 🅿 🅳

Colony of gannets nesting on the cliffs of Great Saltee Island

CORK AND KERRY

CORK · KERRY

MAGNIFICENT SCENERY *has attracted visitors to this region since Victorian times. Rocky headlands jut out into the Atlantic and colourful fishing villages nestle in the shelter of the bays. County Kerry offers dramatic landscapes and a wealth of prehistoric and early Christian sites, whereas County Cork's gentle charm has enticed many a casual visitor into becoming a permanent resident.*

Killarney and its romantic lakes are a powerful magnet for tourists, and so are Cork's attractive coastal towns and villages. Yet the region remains remarkably unspoilt, with a friendly atmosphere and authentic culture still alive in Irish-speaking pockets. There is also a long tradition of arts and crafts in the area.

This corner of Ireland used to be the main point of contact with the Continent. In the 17th century, in response to the threat of invasions from France and Spain, the English built a line of forts along the Cork coast, including the massive Charles Fort at Kinsale.

In the 19th century, the city of Cork was an important departure point for people fleeing from the Famine *(see p211)*, with Cobh the main port for emigrants to the New World. Cork's importance as a port has diminished, but it is still the Republic's second city with a lively cultural scene.

Poverty and temperament helped foster a powerful Republican spirit in the southwest. The region saw much guerrilla action in the War of Independence and the subsequent Civil War. In 1920, the centre of Cork city was burned in an uncontrolled act of reprisal by the notorious Black and Tans *(see pp42–3)*.

Kerry is known as "the Kingdom" on account of its tradition of independence and disregard for Dublin rule. The Irish recognize a distinctive Kerry character, with a boisterous sense of living life to the full. They also make Kerrymen the butt of countless jokes.

As well as the friendliest people in Ireland, the region has some of the finest scenery. Cork has lush valleys and a beautiful coast while Kerry is wilder and more mountainous. The islands off the Kerry coast appear bleak and inhospitable, but many were once inhabited. Remote, rocky Skellig Michael, for example, was the site of a 6th-century Christian monastery.

Puffins on the island of Skellig Michael off the coast of Kerry

◁ **Beach at Barley Cove near Mizen Head, County Cork**

Exploring Cork and Kerry

KILLARNEY IS A POPULAR BASE with tourists for exploring Cork and Kerry, especially for touring the Ring of Kerry and the archaeological remains of the Dingle Peninsula. Despite the changeable weather, the region attracts many visitors who come to see its dramatic scenery and lush vegetation. As you pass through quiet fishing villages and genteel towns, such as Kenmare, you will always encounter a friendly welcome from the locals. For the adventurous there are plenty of opportunities to go riding, hiking or cycling. Cork city offers a more cosmopolitan atmosphere, with its art galleries and craft shops.

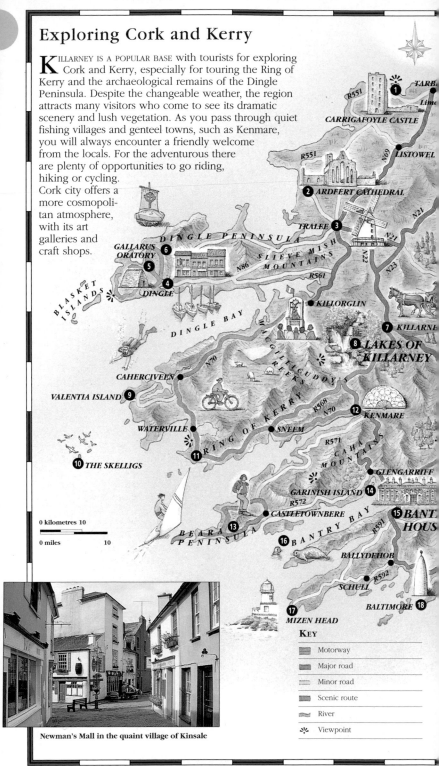

CARRIGAFOYLE CASTLE

TARB

Lime

R551

R551

N69

LISTOWEL

② ARDFERT CATHEDRAL

N21

N21

TRALEE ③

DINGLE PENINSULA

GALLARUS ORATORY ⑥

⑤

④ DINGLE

SLIEVE MISH MOUNTAINS

N86

R561

N22

N23

BLASKET ISLANDS

KILLORGLIN

DINGLE BAY

⑦ KILLARNE

⑧ LAKES OF KILLARNEY

CAHERCIVEEN

MACGILLICUDDY'S REEKS

VALENTIA ISLAND ⑨

R568

N70

⑫ KENMARE

WATERVILLE

SNEEM

R571

CAHA MOUNTAINS

⑪ RING OF KERRY

⑩ THE SKELLIGS

GLENGARRIFF

GARINISH ISLAND ⑭

R572

0 kilometres 10

0 miles 10

CASTLETOWNBERE

⑮ BANT HOUS

BEARA PENINSULA ⑬

⑯ BANTRY BAY

R591

BALLYDEHOB

SCHULL

R592

BALTIMORE ⑱

⑰ MIZEN HEAD

KEY

▬	Motorway
▬	Major road
▭	Minor road
▬	Scenic route
⌇	River
☀	Viewpoint

Newman's Mall in the quaint village of Kinsale

Cattle grazing near Ardfert Cathedral

SIGHTS AT A GLANCE

Ardfert Cathedral **2**
Baltimore **18**
Bantry Bay **16**
Bantry House pp160–61 **15**
Beara Peninsula **13**
Blarney Castle **23**
Carrigafoyle Castle **1**
Clonakilty **20**
Cobh **27**
Cork pp166–9 **25**
Dingle **4**
Drombeg Stone Circle **19**
Gallarus Oratory **5**

Garinish Island **14**
Jameson Heritage Centre **28**
Kenmare **12**
Killarney **7**
Kinsale pp164–5 **24**
Lakes of Killarney pp154–5 **8**
Mizen Head **17**
River Blackwater **26**
River Lee **22**
The Skelligs **10**
Timoleague Abbey **21**
Tralee **3**
Valentia Island **9**
Youghal **29**

Tours

Dingle Peninsula **6**
Ring of Kerry **11**

GETTING AROUND

To explore the region a car is essential. The N22 connects Cork, Killarney and Tralee while the N71 follows the coastline via Clonakilty, Bantry and on to Killarney. In the more remote parts the road signs may only be written in Irish. Killarney is the base for organized coach tours of the area. The train service from Cork to Dublin is efficient, and trains also connect Killarney with Dublin and Cork, but you may have to change trains en route. Buses run throughout the region, but services to the smaller sights may be infrequent.

SEE ALSO

• *Where to Stay* pp291–3

• *Restaurants, Cafés and Pubs* pp310–12 & p319

Kissing the Blarney Stone at Blarney Castle near Cork

Ardfert Cathedral and the ruins of Teampall na Hoe and Teampall na Griffin

Carrigafoyle Castle ❶

Road map B5. Co Kerry.
🚌 *to Listowel.*

Ruined keep of Carrigafoyle Castle

HIGH ABOVE the Shannon estuary, just west of Ballylongford, this 15th-century castle belonged to the O'Connor clan, who ruled much of northern Kerry. The English besieged or sacked it repeatedly but the body blow was delivered in 1649 by Cromwellian forces *(see p37)*. The ruins include a keep and walled courtyard, with romantic views of the estuary from the top of the tower, reached by a spiral staircase.

Ardfert Cathedral ❷

Road map A5. Co Kerry.
🚌 *to Ardfert.* ⭕ *daily.* 🏞 ♿

THIS COMPLEX of churches is linked to the cult of St Brendan the Navigator *(see p205)*, who was born nearby

in 484 and founded a monastery here. The ruined cathedral dates back to the 12th century and retains a delicate Romanesque doorway and blind arcading. Inside, an effigy of a 14th-century bishop occupies a niche in the northwestern corner. In the graveyard stand the remains of a Romanesque nave-and-chancel church, Teampall na Hoe, and a late Gothic chapel, Teampall na Griffin. The latter is named after the curious griffins carved beside an interior window.

A short walk away are the ruins of a Franciscan friary. It was founded by Thomas Fitzmaurice in 1253, but the cloisters and south chapel date from the 15th century.

ENVIRONS: Just northwest of Ardfert is **Banna Strand**. Irish patriot Roger Casement landed here in 1916 on a German U-boat, bringing in rifles for the Easter Rising *(see pp42–3)*. He was arrested as soon as he landed and a memorial stands

on the site of his capture. This beach was also used for the filming of David Lean's *Ryan's Daughter* (1970).

Tralee ❸

Road map B5. Co Kerry. 🚶 *20,000.*
🚌 🚉 ℹ️ *Ashe Memorial Hall, Denny St (066 21288).* 🅰 *Thu.*

HOST TO the renowned Rose of Tralee International Festival *(see p47)*, Tralee has made great strides in promoting its cultural and leisure facilities. The town's main attraction is **Kerry County Museum** with its theme park, "Kerry the Kingdom". It offers three exhibitions: an audio-visual show on Kerry scenery; a display of archaeological finds and interactive models; and a "time travel experience" through Anglo-Norman Tralee, complete with medieval smells.

Also based in Tralee is the **Siamsa Tíre** folklore theatre, an internationally celebrated

Steam train on the narrow gauge railway between Tralee and Blennerville, with Blennerville Windmill in the background

ambassador for Irish culture. Traditional song and dance performances take place here throughout the summer.

Just outside Tralee is the authentic **Blennerville Windmill**. Built in 1800, it is Ireland's largest working mill and one of Tralee's most popular attractions. The **Steam Railway** connects Blennerville with Tralee along a narrow gauge track. There are trips on the train with multilingual commentary, from Ballyard Station to the windmill.

🏛 **Kerry County Museum**
Ashe Memorial Hall, Denny St.
📞 066 27777. ⏰ mid-Mar–Dec: daily. 🔴 25 & 26 Dec. 📷 ♿

🎭 **Siamsa Tíre**
Town Park. 📞 066 23055. ⏰ for performances only May–Sep. 📷 ♿

🏛 **Blennerville Windmill**
📞 066 21064. ⏰ Apr–Oct: daily. 📷

🚂 **Steam Railway**
Ballyard Station. 📞 066 21064.
⏰ May–Oct: daily. 📷 ♿

Dingle ❹

Road map A5. Co Kerry. 👥 1,300.
🚌 May–Oct: Main St (066 51188).
🛍 Sat.

THIS ONCE REMOTE Irish-speaking town is today a thriving fishing port and an increasingly popular tourist

Gallarus Oratory, a dry-stone early Christian church

centre. Brightly painted craft shops and cafés abound, often with slightly hippy overtones.

Dingle Bay is attractive with a somewhat ramshackle harbour lined with fishing trawlers. Along the quayside are lively bars offering music and seafood. The harbour is home to Dingle's biggest star: Fungie, the dolphin, who has been a permanent resident since 1983 and can be visited by boat or on swimming trips.

Although Dingle has few architectural attractions, it makes an engaging base for exploring the archaeological remains on the Dingle Peninsula (see pp150–51).

Gallarus Oratory ❺

Road map A5. Co Kerry.
🚌 to Dingle.

SHAPED LIKE an upturned boat, this miniature church overlooks Smerwick harbour. Gallarus was built some time between the 6th and 9th centuries and is the best preserved early Christian church in Ireland. It represents the apogee of dry-stone corbelling, using techniques first developed by Neolithic tomb-makers. The stones were laid at a slight angle, lower on the outside than the inside, allowing water to run off.

Fishing trawlers moored alongside the quay at Dingle

A Tour of the Dingle Peninsula ❻

GUINNESS
Mar is gnách

Pub sign,
Ballyferriter

THE DINGLE PENINSULA offers some of Ireland's most beautiful scenery. To the north rises the towering Brandon Mountain, while the west coast has some spectacular seascapes. A drive around the area, which takes at least half a day, reveals fascinating antiquities ranging from Iron Age stone forts to inscribed stones, early Christian oratories and beehive huts. These are sometimes found on private land, so you may be asked for a small fee by the farmer to see them. Some parts of the peninsula – especially the more remote areas – are still Gaelic speaking, so many road signs are written only in Irish.

View from Clogher Head

Riasc (An Riasc) ⑦
This excavated monastic settlement dates from the 7th century. The enclosure contains the remains of an oratory, several crosses and an inscribed pillar stone *(see p235)*.

Ballyferriter
(Baile an Fheirtéaraigh) ⑥
The attractions of this friendly village include the pastel-coloured cottages, Louis Mulcahy's pottery and a museum featuring the cultural heritage of the area.

Blasket Centre
(Ionad an Bhlascaoid) ⑤
Overlooking Blasket Sound, the centre explains the literature, language and way of life of the inhabitants of the Blasket Islands. The islanders moved to the mainland in 1953.

R559

Clogher Head

Dunquin
(Dún Chaoin)

Mount Eagle

R559

Ve
(Ceann

Ven

DINGLE BA

BLASKET ISLANDS

Blasket Sound

Dunmore Head
(Ceann an Dúin Mhoir) ④
Mainland Ireland's most westerly point offers dramatic views of the Blaskets.

Slea Head
(Ceann Sléibe) ③
As you round the Slea Head promontory, the Blasket Islands come into full view. The sculpture of the Crucifixion beside the road is known locally as the Cross *(An Cros)*.

KEY

▬▬ Tour route

═══ Other roads

🌿 Viewpoint

0 kilometres   2

0 miles   1

Kilmalkedar *(Cill Maolchéadair)* ⑨
Once a pagan centre of worship,
Kilmalkedar is home to a ruined Irish
Romanesque church with stone carvings.
The graveyard still contains primitive
pagan stones, a cross and a sundial.

⑨

**Gallarus Oratory
(Séipéilín Ghallrois) ⑧**
This tiny, dry-stone church
(see p149) is a relic of early
Irish Christianity.

Dingle *(An Daingean)* ①
Dingle, famous for local resident
Fungie the dolphin, is a good
place to eat, drink or stay the
night *(see p149)*.

Dingle Harbour

R559

TRALEE
N86

-bour

DINGLE BAY

**Dunbeg Fort
(An Dún Beag) ②**
Dating from the Iron Age, this
is one of the best preserved
promontory forts in Ireland.
Just beyond are the Fahan beehive huts, early Christian huts
thought to have been built
for pilgrims visiting the area.

TIPS FOR DRIVERS

Length: 40 km (25 miles).
Stopping-off points: Most
villages on the route, such as
Dunquin and Ballyferriter, have
friendly bars offering pub meals.
There are also many opportunities
to stop for a picnic. On the
winding coast road around Slea
Head stop only at the safe and
clearly marked coastal viewing
points. (See also pp355–7.)

**Jaunting cars waiting to take
visitors to sights around Killarney**

Killarney ❼

Road map B5. Co Kerry. 🏃 *7,500.*
🚉 🚌 ℹ️ *Town Hall, Main St (064
31633).*

KILLARNEY is commonly
derided as "a tourist town"
but this has not dented the
town's open, cheerful atmosphere. The infectious Kerry
humour is personified by the
wise-cracking jarveys whose
families have run jaunting cars
(pony and trap rides) here for
generations. The town has
much to offer, with shops
open until 10pm in summer,
several excellent restaurants,
and a sprinkling of prestigious
hotels around the lake and
the heights. From the town
visitors can explore the sights
around the Lakes of Killarney
(see pp154–5) and the surrounding heather-covered hills.

ENVIRONS: Overlooking the
lakes and a short drive from
Killarney is **Muckross House**.
This imposing Victorian
mansion was built in 1843 in
Elizabethan style. Inside, the
elegant rooms are decorated
with period furnishings. There
is also a museum of Kerry Life,
with displays on the history of
southwest Ireland, and a craft
centre with numerous workshops. The landscaped gardens
are especially beautiful in
spring when the rhododen-
drons and azaleas are in
bloom. A short walk away is
Muckross Farm – a working
farm which still uses traditional
farming techniques.

🏛 **Muckross House**
4 km (2.5 miles) S of Killarney.
📞 064 31440. ⏰ daily. ● 10 days
at Christmas. 🎫 📷 🚻 🎥

Stunning mountain scenery near Moll's Gap on the Ring of Kerry ▷

Lakes of Killarney ❽

Fruit of the strawberry tree

RENOWNED FOR ITS splendid scenery, the area is one of Ireland's most popular tourist attractions. The three lakes are contained within Killarney National Park. Although the landscape is dotted with ruined castles and abbeys, the lakes are the focus of attention: the moody watery scenery is subject to subtle shifts of light and colour. The area has entranced many artists and writers including Thackeray, who praised "a precipice covered with a thousand trees ... and other mountains rising as far as we could see". In autumn, the bright red fruits of the strawberry tree colour the shores of the lakes.

Meeting of the Waters
This beauty spot, best seen from Dinis Island, is where the waters from the Upper Lake meet Muckross Lake and Lough Leane. At the Old Weir Bridge, boats shoot the rapids.

Long Range River

Torc Waterfall
The Owengarriff River cascades through the wooded Friars' Glen into Muckross Lake. A pretty path winds up to the top of this 18-m (60-ft) high waterfall, revealing views of Torc Mountain.

Muckross Lake

Dinis Island

Lough Leane

Innisfallen Island

Muckross Abbey was founded by the Franciscans in 1448, but was burnt down by Cromwellian forces in 1653.

Killarney *(see p151)* is the main town from which tourists visit the sights around the lakes.

N22 to Tralee *(see pp148–9)*

Ross Castle, built around 1420, was the last stronghold under Irish control to be taken by Cromwellian forces in 1653.

★ Muckross House
The 19th-century manor (see p151) enjoys a lovely location overlooking the lakes. Visit the wildlife centre for an introduction to the flora and fauna of the National Park.

Upper Lake

This narrow lake is the smallest of the three lakes. It flows into the Long Range River to the Meeting of the Waters.

Ladies' View gets its name from the
delight it gave Queen Victoria's ladies-in-
waiting when they visited the spot in 1861.

**N71 to
Moll's Gap
and Kenmare
(see pp156–8)**

Upper Lake

**Purple
Mountain,
832 m
(2,730 ft)**

★ **Gap of Dunloe**

*Glaciers carved this dramatic mountain
pass which is popular with walkers, cyclists
and horse riders. The route through the
gap offers fabulous views of the boulder-
strewn gorge and three small lakes.*

**Tomies
Mountain,
735 m
(2,411 ft)**

Kate Kearney's Cottage was home
to a local beauty who ran an illegal
drinking house for passing travellers
in the mid-19th century.

**R562 to Killorglin
(see pp156–7)**

0 kilometres   2

0 miles   1

STAR SIGHTS

★ **Muckross House**

★ **Gap of Dunloe**

Lough Leane
*The largest lake is
dotted with un-
inhabited islands
and fringed with
wooded slopes.
Boat trips run
between Ross Castle
and Innisfallen.*

Valentia Island ❾

Road map A5. Co Kerry. 🚌 *to Caherciveen.* ℹ️ *Caherciveen (066 72589).*

ALTHOUGH it feels like the mainland, Valentia is an island, albeit linked by a cause-way to Portmagee. It is 11 km (7 miles) long and noted for its water sports,

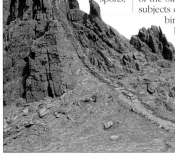

Stairway leading to Skellig Michael monastery

seascapes and views from Geokaun Mountain. Valentia is also popular for its proximity to the Skellig Islands which lie around 15 km (10 miles) south-west of the Iveragh Peninsula.

The **Skellig Experience Centre**, near the causeway linking Valentia to the main-land, houses an audiovisual display about the construction and history of the monastery on Skellig Michael, the largest of the Skellig Islands. Other subjects covered include sea birds and the marine life around the islands, a reminder that the Skellig cliffs lie underwater for a depth of 50 m (165 ft), providing a habitat for giant basking sharks, dolphins and turtles. The centre also operates cruises around the islands.

The main village on Valentia is **Knightstown**, which offers accommodation and lively pubs with music and dancing.

The first transatlantic cable was laid from the southwest point of the island to New-foundland, Canada, in 1866.

🏛 **Skellig Experience Centre**
Valentia Island. 📞 *066 76306.*
🕐 *Apr–Sep: daily.* 💰 ♿

The Skelligs ❿

Road map A6. Co Kerry. 🚤 *Apr–Oct: from Valentia Island.* 📞 *066 77156 (ring two or three days ahead).*

SKELLIG MICHAEL, also known as Great Skellig, is an inhospitable pinnacle of rock rising out of the Atlantic and covering an area of 17 ha (44 acres). Perched on a ledge almost 218 m (714 ft) above sea level and reached by an amazing 1,000-year-old

---

A Tour of the Ring of Kerry ⓫

THIS LONG-ESTABLISHED ROUTE around the Iveragh Peninsula, which can be taken in either direction, is always referred to as the Ring of Kerry. Allow a day to see its captivating mountain and coastal scenery, dotted with slate-roofed fishing villages. Set out early to avoid the mass of coach tours which converge on the towns for lunch and tea. There are interesting detours across the spine of the peninsula.

Glenbeigh ③
Stop here to visit the Kerry Bog Village, a cluster of reconstructed cottages dating from the 1800s.

Caherciveen ④
The main town on the peninsula is home to a local heritage centre.

Beach at Ballinskelligs

● *Little Skellig*
◗ *Skellig Michael*

KEY

▬▬▬	Tour route
═══	Other roads
🚤	Boats to the Skelligs
☀	Viewpoint

Derrynane House ⑤
Dating from the 17th century, the former home of Daniel O'Connell *(see p40)* now houses a museum featuring his memorabilia.

Staigue Fort ⑥
Set on a hill up a narrow track, this Iron Age, dry-stone fort *(caher)* is the best preserved in Ireland.

VALENTIA ISLAND

🚤 *Skellig Experience Centre*

Ballinskelligs

Waterville

Ballinskelligs Bay

Coomakista Pass

R565 N70 R567 R566 Inny

stairway is an isolated early Christian monastery. Monks settled for solitude on Skellig Michael during the 6th century, building a cluster of six corbelled beehive cells and two boat-shaped oratories. These dry-stone structures are still standing, despite being raked by storms over the centuries. The monks were totally self-sufficient, trading eggs, feathers and seal meat with passing boats in return for cereals, tools and animal skins. The skins were needed to produce the vellum on which the monks copied their religious manuscripts. They remained on this bleak island until the 12th century, when they retreated to the Augustinian priory at Ballinskelligs on the mainland.

Today the only residents on Skellig Michael are the thousands of sea birds which nest

Gannets flying around the precipitous cliffs of Little Skellig

and breed on the high cliffs, including storm petrels, puffins and Manx shearwaters. The huge breeding colonies are protected from predators by the sea and rocky shores.

Slightly closer to the mainland is Little Skellig. Covering an area of 7 ha (17 acres), the island has steep cliffs. Home to a variety of sea birds, it has one of the largest colonies of gannets (about 22,000 breeding pairs) in the British Isles.

A cruiser from Valentia Island circles the Skelligs but does not dock. Except for a pier on Skellig Michael, there are no proper landing stages on the islands. This is to discourage visitors from disturbing the birdlife, fragile plant cover and archaeological remains.

Atlantic gales permitting, local fishermen may run unofficial trips around the islands from Portmagee or Ballinskelligs, during the summer.

Killorglin ② This pretty village, sitting on the slopes above a river, is famous for its Puck Fair *(see p47)*.

Killarney ①
Visitors touring the Ring of Kerry usually start and finish here. The route passes lovely views of the Lakes of Killarney *(see pp154–5)*.

Moll's Gap ⑧
Cutting through bleak bogland and high mountainous terrain, Moll's Gap offers some stunning views.

Sneem ⑦
Brightly painted cottages line the streets of this charming town which also has a quaint village green.

0 kilometres   10

0 miles   5

TIPS FOR DRIVERS

Length: 180 km (112 miles).
Stopping off points: Many towns such as Killorglin or Caherciveen offer pub snacks. Finish the day in one of the excellent gourmet restaurants in Kenmare. (See also pp355–7.)

Lace making at Kenmare

Kenmare **12**

Road map B5. Co Kerry. ⚄ 1,400.
🚌 ℹ Apr–Oct: Main St (064
41233). 🚏 Wed.

THIS TOWN, on the mouth of
the River Sheen, was
founded in 1670 by William
Petty, Cromwell's surveyor
general. However, Kenmare's
appearance owes more to his
descendant, the first Marquess
of Lansdowne who, in 1775,
made it a model landlord's
town of neat stone façades
with decorative plasterwork.
  Today Kenmare is renowned
for its traditional lace. During
the famine years, nuns from
the local convent, St Clare's,
introduced lace making to
create work for the women
and girls. Other attractions
include the fine hotels (see
p292) and gourmet restaurants
(p311). The town is also an

excellent base for exploring
the Beara Peninsula and the
Ring of Kerry (see pp156–7).
  Set in a riverside glade off
Market Street is the **Druid's
Circle**, a prehistoric ring of
15 stones associated with
human sacrifice.

Beara Peninsula **13**

Road map A6. Co Cork & Co Kerry.
🚌 to Glengarriff & Castletownbere
(Fri only). ℹ Castletownbere (027
70344).

DOTTED WITH sparsely
populated fishing villages
surrounded by bleak moor-
land, this peninsula is remote.
It used to be a refuge for
smugglers, with the Irish
getting the better deal in their
exchange of pilchards for
contraband French brandy.
  The peninsula offers some
spectacular scenery and
wonderful walking country.
From the **Healy Pass**, which
cuts a jagged path across the
spine of the Caha Mountains,
there are some fine views of
Bantry Bay and the rugged
landscape of West Cork. To
the west of the pass is
Hungry Hill, the highest
mountain in the Caha range
and popular with hill walkers.
  Encircled by the Caha and
Slieve Miskish Mountains is
Castletownbere, the main
town on the peninsula. This
sheltered port was once a
haven for smugglers, but is
now awash with foreign
fishing trawlers. McCarthey's

Bar on Town Square features
an authentic matchmaking
booth, where Cork families
used to agree marriage terms
until a generation ago.
  West of Castletownbere
stands the shell of **Puxley
Mansion**, home of the Puxley
family who owned the mines
at nearby **Allihies**. Centre of
the copper-mining district until
the 1930s, it is now a desolate
place, with tall Cornish-style
chimneys and piles of ochre-
coloured spoil; beware of
unguarded mine shafts.
  From the tip of the peninsula
a cable car travels across to
Dursey Island, with its
ruined castle and colonies of
sea birds. Licensed to carry
three passengers and one cow,
the cable car swings across
the strait, offering views of
Bull, Cow and Calf islands.
  From the headland the R757
road back to Kenmare passes
through the pretty villages of
Eyeries, noted for its brightly
painted cottages and crafts,
and **Ardgroom**, a centre for
mussel farming and a base for
exploring the scenic glacial
valley around **Glenbeg Lough**.

Garinish Island **14**

Road map B6. Co Cork. 🚤 from
Glengarriff. **Gardens** 🔲 027 63040.
⭕ Mar–Oct: daily. 🔲 🔲 limited.

ALSO KNOWN as Ilnacullin, this
small island was turned
into an exotic garden in 1910
by Harold Peto for Annan
Bryce, a Belfast businessman.

View of Caha Mountains from the Healy Pass, Beara Peninsula

Italianate garden with lily pool and folly on Garinish Island

Framed by views of Bantry Bay, the gardens are landscaped with Neo-Classical follies and planted with rich subtropical flora. The microclimate and peaty soil provide the damp, warm conditions needed for these ornamental plants to flourish.

Exotic shrubberies abound especially during the summer months. Throughout May and June, visitors can admire the beautiful camellia beds, azaleas and rhododendrons. There is also a New Zealand fernery and a Japanese rockery, as well as a rare collection of Bonsai trees. A Martello tower crowns the island and among the follies are a clock tower and a Grecian temple.

The centrepiece is a colonnaded Italianate garden, with a Classical folly and ornamental lily pool. Much of its charm resides in the contrast between the cultivated lushness of the garden and the glimpses of wild seascape and barren mountains beyond. An added attraction of the boat trip across to this Gulf Stream paradise is the chance to see cavorting seals in Bantry Bay.

Bantry House ⑮

See pp160–61.

Bantry Bay ⑯

Road map A6. Co Cork. 🚌 *to Bantry and Glengarriff.* ℹ️ *Jun–Sep: The Square, Bantry (027 50229).*

BANTRY BAY ENCOMPASSES the resorts of **Bantry** and **Glengarriff**. It is also a springboard for trips to Mizen Head and the Beara Peninsula.

Bantry nestles beneath the hills which run down to the bay. Just offshore you can see **Whiddy Island**, the original home of the White family, who moved to Bantry House in the early 18th century. Further along is **Bere Island**, a British base until World War II which still boasts Martello towers on its southern side.

Glengarriff at the head the bay, exudes an air of Victorian gentility with its neatly painted shopfronts and craft shops. On the coast is the Eccles Hotel, a haunt of Queen Victoria and where George Bernard Shaw supposedly wrote *Saint Joan*.

The wooded hinterland to the north of Glengarriff is set in a bowl of the Caha Mountains. There are some pleasant walks leading to waterfalls.

Mizen Head ⑰

Road map A6. Co Cork.
🚌 *to Goleen.* ℹ️ *Town Hall, Main St, Skibbereen (028 21766).*

MIZEN HEAD, the most south-westerly tip of Ireland, has steep cliffs, which are often lashed by storms. Here, a lighthouse and new visitors' centre, **Mizen Vision**, are reached by a bridge across a rocky chasm. From the car park, a fine headland walk takes in views of vertiginous cliffs and Atlantic breakers. The sandy beaches of nearby **Barley Cove** attract bathers and walkers alike, and to the east is **Crookhaven**, a pretty yachting harbour. From here, a walk to Brow Head offers views of the lighthouse.

Mizen Head can be reached either from Bantry via Durrus or from the market town of **Skibbereen**, on the R592, via the charming crafts centre of **Ballydehob** and the village of **Schull**. Trips to Clear Island *(see p162)* leave from Schull.

🏛 Mizen Vision
Mizen Head. 📞 *028 35115.* ○ *Apr–Oct: daily; Nov–Mar: Sat & Sun.* 🈺

Rocky cliffs at Mizen Head

Bantry House ⑮

BANTRY HOUSE has been the home of the White family, formerly Earls of Bantry, since 1739. The original house was built in 1720, but the north façade overlooking the bay was a later addition. Inside there is an eclectic collection of art and furnishings brought from all over Europe by the 2nd Earl of Bantry. In the carriage house and stable block behind the house is the French Armada Centre, which explains the events surrounding Wolfe Tone's attempted invasion in 1796.

William and Mary clock in anteroom

North façade

The anteroom contains family mementoes, china and a collection of 18th-century prints.

Loggia

To car park

Tearoom and shop

Gobelins Room
The subject of this 18th-century Gobelins tapestry is The Bath of Cupid and Psyche. *The room also contains an early 19th-century piano.*

The Rose Garden, laid out in the early 18th century, is, in the words of the 1st Earl of Bantry, "a parterre after the English manner".

1st Earl of Bantry (1767–1851)

Richard White, 1st Earl of Bantry, played a leading role in defending Ireland against an attempted invasion by Wolfe Tone and the United Irishmen *(see pp38–9)*. On 16 December 1796, Tone sailed from Brest in Brittany with a fleet of 43 French ships bound for Ireland. White chose strategic spots around Bantry Bay and mustered volunteers to fight. His efforts proved unnecessary as the French fleet was forced back by bad weather. Nonetheless, White was rewarded with a peerage by George III for his "spirited conduct and important services". In 1801 he was made Viscount Bantry, becoming Earl of Bantry in 1816.

★ **Dining Room**
This room is dominated by portraits of King George III and Queen Charlotte by court painter, Allan Ramsay. The Spanish chandelier is decorated with Meissen china flowers.

Entrance hall

★ **Rose Room**
The rose-coloured tapestries (c. 1770) hanging in this room are thought to have been made for Marie Antoinette on her marriage to the Dauphin of France.

VISITORS' CHECKLIST

Road map B6. Bantry, Co Cork.
027 50047. from Cork to
Bantry (Mon–Sat).
late Mar–late Oct: 9am–6pm
daily. 25 Dec.
limited.
Concerts (summer only).
See also *Hotels* p291.
1796 French Armada Centre
027 51796. Apr–Sep:
10am–6pm daily (last adm:
5:40pm). limited.
Joint tickets for House and
Armada Centre available.

**Statue of
Diana
(1840)**

**South
façade**

**To 1796 French
Armada Centre**

Library

★ **View of House and Bantry Bay**
Bantry House enjoys a magnificent location overlooking Bantry Bay. This lovely view, from the terraces above the house, shows the harbour with Whiddy Island and the Caha Mountains beyond.

Italian Garden
Inspired by the Boboli Gardens in Florence, this garden encircles a pool decorated in Classical Grotesque style. It was designed in the early 1850s by the 2nd Earl.

STAR FEATURES

★ View of House and
Bantry Bay

★ Rose Room

★ Dining Room

The steps, known as the "Staircase to the Sky", lead to a series of terraces with fabulous views over the house and across the bay.

Baltimore ⑱

Road map B6. Co Cork. 🚶 220.
🚌 ⛴ to Sherkin Island (028 20125);
to Clear Island (028 39135).

BALTIMORE's most bizarre claim to fame dates back to 1631 when more than 100 citizens were carried off as slaves by Algerian pirates. Now that the threat of being kidnapped has gone, this village appeals to the yachting fraternity and island-hoppers. Like neighbouring Schull and Castletownshend, the town bustles with summer festivals.

Overlooking the harbour is a ruined 15th-century castle, once the stronghold of the O'Driscoll clan. Also worth a visit are the seafood pubs, including Bushe's Bar, an atmospheric inn hung with nautical memorabilia. Behind the village, cliff walks lead to splendid views of Carbery's Hundred Isles – mere specks on Roaringwater Bay. Baltimore Beacon is an important marker for boats in the bay.

A short ferry ride away is **Sherkin Island** with its sandy beaches in the west, a ruined 15th-century abbey, marine station and pubs. The ferry ride to **Clear Island** is more dramatic, as the boat weaves between sharp black rocks to this remote, Irish-speaking island, noted for its bird observatory in the North Harbour. There are some spectacular views of the mainland from Clear Island.

Distinctive white beacon for boats approaching Baltimore

Drombeg Stone Circle, erected around the 2nd century BC

Drombeg Stone Circle ⑲

Road map B6. Co Cork. 🚌 to Skibbereen or Clonakilty.

SITUATED ON the Glandore road 16 km (10 miles) west of Clonakilty, Drombeg is the finest of the many stone circles in County Cork. Dating back to about 150 BC, this circle of 17 standing stones is 9 m (30 ft) in diameter. At the winter solstice, the rays of the setting sun fall on the flat altar stone which faces the entrance to the circle, marked by two upright stones.

Nearby is a small stream with a Stone Age cooking pit *(fulacht fiadh)*, similar to one at Craggaunowen *(see p182)*. A fire was made in the hearth and hot stones from the fire were dropped into the cooking pit to heat the water. Once the water boiled, the meat, usually venison, was added.

Clonakilty ⑳

Road map B6. Co Cork. 🚶 3,000.
🚌 ℹ Jun–Sep: Astna Street (023 33226) .

FOUNDED as an English outpost around 1588, this market town has a typically hearty West Cork atmosphere. The **West Cork Regional Museum**, housed in an old schoolhouse, pays tribute to the town's industrial heritage. A number of the quayside

Sign for Clonakilty black pudding

buildings, linked to the town's industrial past, have been restored. Particularly pleasant is the neat Georgian nucleus of Emmet Square.

Until the 19th century Clonakilty was a noted linen producer. Today, however, it is renowned for its rich black puddings, hand-painted Irish signs and traditional music pubs. A short walk from the town centre is a model village exhibition, depicting Clonakilty as it was during the 1940s. Just east of town is the reconstructed **Lisnagun Ring Fort**, with earthworks, huts and souterrains *(see p18)*. A causeway links Clonakilty to **Inchydoney** beach.

🏛 **West Cork Regional Museum**
Western Road. ⬜ Mon–Sat. 📷 ♿

Timoleague Abbey ㉑

Road map B6. Co Cork.
🚌 to Clonakilty or Courtmacsherry.
⬜ daily.

TIMOLEAGUE ABBEY enjoys a waterside setting overlooking an inlet where the Argideen estuary opens into Courtmacsherry Bay. Founded around the late 13th century, the abbey is a ruined Franciscan friary. The buildings have been extended at various times. The earliest section is the chancel of the Gothic church. The most recent addition, the 16th-century tower, was added by the Franciscan Bishop of Ross. The friary was ransacked by the English in 1642 but much of significance remains, including the church, infirmary, fine lancet windows, refectory and a walled courtyard in the west. There are also sections of cloisters and wine cellars. In keeping with Franciscan tradition, the complex is plain to the point of austerity. Yet

Lancet window in ruined church at Timoleague Abbey

such restraint belied the friars' penchant for high living: the friary prospered on trade in Spanish wines, easily delivered thanks to its position on the then navigable creek.

River Lee ②

Road map B6. Co Cork. 🚃 🚌 to Cork. ℹ Cork (021 273251).

CARVING A COURSE through farm- and woodland to Cork city *(see pp166–9)*, the River Lee begins its journey in the lake of the enchanting **Gougane Barra Park**. The shores of the lake are linked by a causeway to **Holy Island**, where St Finbarr, the patron saint of Cork, founded a monastery. The Feast of St Finbarr, on 25 September,

signals celebrations that climax in a pilgrimage to the island on the following Sunday.

The Lee flows through several Irish-speaking market towns and villages. Some, such as **Ballingeary**, with its fine lakeside views, have good angling. The town is also noted for its Irish language college. Further east, near the town of Inchigeela, stand the ruins of **Carrignacurra Castle**. Further downstream lies the Gearagh, an alluvial stretch of marsh and woods which has been designated a wildlife sanctuary.

The river then passes through the Sullane valley, home of the thriving market town of **Macroom**. The hulk of a medieval castle, with its restored entrance, lies just off the main square. In 1654, Cromwell granted the castle to Sir William Penn. His son, who was to found the American state of Pennsylvania, also lived there for a time.

Between Macroom and Cork, the Lee Valley passes through a hydroelectric power scheme surrounded by artificial lakes, water meadows and wooded banks. Just outside Cork, on the south bank of the river is **Ballincollig**, home to the fascinating Royal Gunpowder Mills museum *(see p169)*.

Blarney Castle ㉓

Road map B5. Blarney, Co Cork. ☎ 021 385252. 🚌 to Cork. 🚌 to Blarney. ◯ daily. ● 24 & 25 Dec. 🖼 ♿

VISITORS from all over the world flock to this ruined castle to see the legendary Blarney Stone. Kissing the stone is a long-standing tradition, intended to confer a magical eloquence. It is set in the wall below the castle battlements and, in order to kiss it, the visitor is grasped by the feet and suspended backwards under the parapet.

Little remains of the castle today except the keep, built in 1446 by Dermot McCarthy. Its design is typical of a 15th-century tower house *(see p18)*. The vaulted first floor was once the Great Hall.

Next to the castle is **Blarney House**, a Scottish baronial mansion and the residence of the Colthurst family since the 18th century. The turreted façade is matched by a period interior, with its grand stairwell, family portraits and Victorian decor. The grounds include an arboretum and landscaped gardens.

Blarney also has a pretty village green with welcoming pubs and craft shops. The **Blarney Woollen Mills** sell quality garments and souvenirs.

🏛 Blarney House
Blarney Estate. ☎ 021 385252. ◯ Jul–Aug: noon–6:30pm Mon–Sat. 🖼 ♿

Battlemented keep and ruined towers of Blarney Castle

Street-by-Street: Kinsale ㉔

Old office sign
in Kinsale

FOR MANY VISITORS to Ireland, Kinsale heads the list of places to see. One of the prettiest small towns in Ireland, it has had a long and chequered history. The defeat of the Irish forces and their Spanish allies in the Battle of Kinsale in 1601 signified the end of the old Gaelic order. An important naval base in the 17th and 18th centuries, Kinsale today is a popular yachting centre. It is also famous for the quality of its cuisine – the town's annual Gourmet Festival attracts food lovers from far and wide. As well as its many wonderful restaurants, the town has pubs and wine bars to cater for all tastes.

Desmond Castle was built around 1500. It is known locally as the "French Prison".

★ **Old Courthouse**
The courthouse, now the regional museum, has a toll board listing the local taxes in 1788.

Market
Square

CHARLES FORT

The star-shaped fort is 3 km (2 miles) east of town in Summercove, but can be reached by taking the signposted coastal walk from the quayside, past the village of Scilly. The fort was built in the 1670s by the English to protect Kinsale harbour against foreign naval forces but, because of its vulnerability to land attack, was taken during the siege of 1690 by William of Orange's army. Nonetheless, it remained in service until 1922 when the British forces left the town and handed it over to the Irish Government. Charles Fort remains one of the finest remaining examples of a star-shaped bastion fort in Europe.

Kieran's
House Inn

★ **St Multose Church**
This much-altered Norman church is named after an obscure 6th-century saint and marks the centre of the medieval town.

Walls and bastions of Charles Fort

| 0 metres | | 50 |
| 0 yards | | 50 |

KEY

P Parking

i Tourist information

— — — Suggested route

Kinsale Harbour
Situated on the estuary of the Bandon River, this is one of Ireland's most scenic harbours. Kinsale is host to a number of international sailing events throughout the year.

VISITORS' CHECKLIST

Road map B6. Co Cork. 👤 1,800. 🚌 ℹ️ *Emmet Place (021 772234)*. 🎉 *Annual Regatta (Aug); Kinsale Fringe Jazz Festival (Oct); Gourmet Festival (Oct)*. **Old Courthouse** 📞 *021 772044*. ◯ *May–Sep: daily; Oct–May: by appt*. 🏛 **St Multose Church** 📞 *021 772220*. ◯ *Jun–Sep: daily; Oct–May: by appt*. ♿ **Desmond Castle and Wine Museum** 📞 *021 774855*. ◯ *Apr–Oct: daily*. 🏰 **Charles Fort** 📞 *021 772263*. ◯ *mid–Apr–mid-Oct: daily*. 🎉

Mother Hubbard's, one of Kinsale's most popular cafés, is situated in the heart of town on Market Street.

To Charles Fort

The Blue Haven, easily identified by the ornate clock above the entrance, is one of Kinsale's finest seafood restaurants.

To Kinsale Harbour, Denis Quay and Compass Hill

To Bandon

STAR SIGHTS

★ Old Courthouse

★ Main Street

★ St Multose Church

★ **Main Street**
Many of Kinsale's best eating and drinking places can be found on this picturesque street.

Cork ㉕

Sign outside a Cork pub

CORK CITY derives its name from the marshy land on the banks of the River Lee – its Irish name *Corcaigh* means marsh – on which St Finbarr founded a monastery around AD 650. The narrow alleys, waterways and Georgian architecture gives the city a Continental feel. Since the 19th century, when Cork was a base for the National Fenian movement *(see p41)*, the city has had a reputation for political rebelliousness. Today this mood is reflected in the city's attitude to the arts and its bohemian spirit, much in evidence at the lively October jazz festival.

St Ann's Shandon
Church St. 021 505906. ◯ daily. ● 25 Dec.

This famous Cork landmark stands on the hilly slopes of the city, north of the River Lee. Built in 1722, the church has a façade made of limestone on two sides, and of red sandstone on the other two. The steeple is topped by a weather vane in the shape of a salmon. The clock face is known by the locals as the "four-faced liar" because, up until 1986 when it was repaired, each face showed slightly different times. Visitors can climb the tower and, for a small fee, ring the famous Shandon bells.

Butter Exchange
John Redman St. ◯ daily.
Just a short walk away from St Ann's Shandon is the Butter Exchange. Opened in 1770, it was where butter was graded before it was exported to the rest of the world. It also supplied butter to the British navy. By 1892 the exchange was exporting around 500,000 casks of butter a year, bringing prosperity to the city. The exchange closed in 1924.

Part of the building was re-opened in the 1980s to house the Shandon Craft Centre. Here visitors can watch artists and craft workers, such as crystal cutters and weavers, at work.

Crawford Art Gallery
Emmet Place. 021 273377. ◯ Mon–Sat.
The red brick and limestone building that houses Cork's major art gallery dates back to 1724. Built as the city's original custom house, it became a school of design in 1850. In 1884, art patron William Horatio Crawford extended the building to accommodate studios, and sculpture and picture galleries. It served as a school and art gallery until the school moved in 1979.

The gallery houses some fine examples of late 19th- and early 20th-century Irish art including paintings by Jack Yeats.

Clock tower and weather vane of St Ann's Shandon

Detail of stained-glass window *The Meeting of St Brendan and the Unhappy Judas* (1911) by Harry Clarke, Crawford Art Gallery

SIGHTS AT A GLANCE

Butter Exchange ②
Crawford Art Gallery ④
Elizabeth Fort ⑩
English Market ⑥
Father Mathew Statue ⑤
National Monument ⑦
Parliament Bridge ⑧
Red Abbey ⑨
St Ann's Shandon ①
St Finbarr's Cathedral ⑪
St Mary's Dominican Church ③

There are also three excellent windows by Ireland's foremost stained-glass artist, Harry Clarke (1889–1931), including *The Meeting of St Brendan and the Unhappy Judas* (1911). Another attraction is the small collection by British artists and international works by artists such as Miró and Rouault.

The gallery is well known for its excellent restaurant which is run by the Ballymaloe cookery school *(see p331)*, the exponents of authentic Irish cooking with a modern twist.

Richly decorated apse ceiling of St Finbarr's Cathedral

🔒 St Finbarr's Cathedral
Bishop Street. **☎** 021 963387.
◯ *daily*. **Donation**. ♿
Situated in a quiet part of town south of the Lee, St Finbarr's Cathedral is dedicated to the founder and patron saint of the city. Completed in 1878 to the design of William Burges, it is an exuberant

triple-spired edifice built in Gothic Revival style, and decorated with stone tracery. Inside, the painted and gilded apse ceiling shows Christ in Glory surrounded by angels. The stained-glass windows below tell the story of Christ's life.

🏛 Cork City Gaol
Convent Avenue, Sunday's Well.
☎ 021 305022. ◯ *daily*.
A pretty, 20-minute walk west of the city centre leads to the restored City Gaol, complete with its furnished cells. The exhibition and audiovisual display trace the lives of individual inmates imprisoned here during the 19th and 20th centuries. Conditions were miserable and, for punishment, prisoners were made to run on a human treadmill that was used to grind grain.

There is also a café in the gaol which employs an amusing gimmick: visitors can choose between sampling the Victorian prisoners' fare or the prison governor's menu.

KEY

🚌	Coach station
🅿	Parking
🛈	Tourist information
🕀	Church

0 metres 250
0 yards 250

South Channel of the River Lee, looking towards Parliament Bridge

Exploring Cork

ONE OF CORK's great attractions is that it is a city built on water. Its heart lies on an island between two arms of the River Lee, and many of today's streets were in fact once waterways lined with warehouses and merchants' residences. Although the Dutch canalside appearance has faded, picturesque quays and bridges remain. Steep lanes rise to the north and south of the central island to the city's 19th-century suburbs, offering wonderful views of the city and its fine buildings.

The Quays

Although the river now plays only a minor part in the city's economy, much of Cork's commercial activity still takes place around the Quays (pronounced "kays" in the Cork accent). The South Mall, which covers an arm of the River Lee, was a waterway until the late 18th century. Boats were once moored at the foot of a series of stone steps, some of which are still intact today. These led to merchants' domestic quarters above. The arches below led to warehouses where goods were unloaded.

Near South Mall is **Parliament Bridge**, built in 1806 to commemorate the Act of Union *(see p40)*. Walk across the bridge to George's Quay to see Fitzpatrick's second-hand shop, with its bizarre display of bicycles, cartwheels, farm implements and other assorted bric-a-brac on its façade. A short walk away, on Sullivan's Quay, is the Quay Co-Op, a popular restaurant and meeting place. From Sullivan's Quay an elegant footbridge, built in 1985, crosses the river to the south end of Grand Parade.

Grand Parade and St Patrick's Street

On Grand Parade, also once a waterway, stands the grandiose **National Monument**, recalling the Irish patriots who died between 1798 and 1867. Bishop Lucey Park, off Grand Parade, has a section of city walls and a fine gateway from the old corn-market. Between St Patrick's Street and Grand Parade is the well-restored **English Market**, a covered fruit and vegetable market established in 1610. Bustling St Patrick's Street, the backbone of the city, was a waterway until 1800 when boats were moored under the steps of gracious houses such as the Chateau Bar *(see p319)*. A landmark at the top of the street, near Patrick Bridge, is the **Father Mathew Statue**, a monument to the founder the Temperance Movement.

National Monument, Grand Parade

Fitzpatrick's second-hand shop on George's Quay

Paul Street

Noted for its ethnic restaurants, chic bars, bookshops and trendy boutiques, Paul Street is the hub of the liveliest district in town. Just off Paul Street are the busy backstreets of Carey's Lane and French Church Street. In the early 18th century, Huguenots (French Protestants) settled in these streets and set themselves up as butter exporters, brewers and wholesale merchants. This area is Cork's equivalent to Dublin's Temple Bar *(see p76)*.

Shandon Quarter

Crossing the Christy Ring Bridge to Pope's Quay, you will see on your left **St Mary's Dominican Church**, with its portico of Ionic columns topped by a huge pediment. John Redmond Street leads to the northern slopes of Cork, dominated by the spire of St Ann's Shandon *(see p166)* with its fine views of the city. To the northeast lies the lofty Montenotte district, once the epitome of Victorian gentility.

St Finbarr's Quarter

South of the river, rising above the city, this area's distinctive landmark is St Finbarr's Cathedral *(see p167)*. Nearby is the ivy-clad **Elizabeth Fort**, a 16th-century structure which was converted into a prison in 1835 and later a *Garda* (police) station. A short walk to the east lies the **Red Abbey**, a 13th-century relic from an Augustinian abbey – the oldest building in Cork.

Selling fruit and vegetables at the English Market

ENVIRONS: Some beautiful countryside surrounds the city of Cork, especially along the lush valley of the River Lee *(see p163)*. The landscape of East Cork is much gentler than the wild, rocky coastline of West Cork and County Kerry, and the land is much more fertile. Many local attractions make good day trips and there are also plenty of opportunities for outdoor activities such as walking, riding and fishing.

♠ Blackrock Castle

Blackrock. **C** 021 357414.
O Tue–Sun. & ☐
On the banks of the River Lee 1.5 km (1 mile) downstream from the city centre stands Blackrock Castle. Originally built in 1582 by Lord Mountjoy as a harbour fortification, the castle was destroyed by fire in 1827. It was rebuilt in 1830 to the design of architects J and GR Pain. The riverside castle now houses a banqueting hall which can hold up to 150 guests, a bar and a restaurant. Visitors can admire the fine views from the mock battlements, or enjoy a pleasant walk along the river banks.

Blackrock Castle standing on the banks of the River Lee

⚜ Dunkathel House

Glanmire. **C** 021 821014.
O May–mid-Oct: Wed–Sun (pm only).
☐ & ground floor.
Standing just outside the village of Glanmire, 6 km (3.5 miles) northeast of Cork, is this gracious Neo-Classical country house. The building was totally remodelled around 1785 for Abraham Morris, a wealthy Cork merchant, but retains a few features from an earlier

Copy of *The Three Graces* by Antonio Canova, Dunkathel House

house, including some Italianate stuccowork. The interior is decorated with Adam fireplaces and a fine collection of Irish furniture. In the spacious entrance hall is an elegant Bath stone staircase with an iron balustrade. On the half landing stands a plaster copy of Canova's *The Three Graces*, thought to have been cast in the early 19th century. The drawing room, hung with Victorian watercolours, offers lovely views of the wooded banks of the River Glanmire. Charming parkland surrounds the house.

⛲ Royal Gunpowder Mills

Ballincollig. **C** 021 874430.
O mid-Mar–mid-Apr: Sat & Sun;
mid-Apr–Sep: daily. ☐ ☐ &
This unusual museum is 10 km (6 miles) west of Cork. Covering 320 ha (130 acres) of landscaped grounds, it is an impressive heritage project featuring canals, weirs, sluice gates, mills and workers' cottages. The mills were established in 1794 and flourished during the Napoleonic Wars, when they were also used as a British military base. By the 1850s, gunpowder production had become one of Cork's foremost industries. The mills finally closed in 1903, at the end of the Boer War. A guided tour covers the production of gunpowder in the main mills, and visitors are free to explore the rest of the complex.

River Blackwater ㉖

Road map B5. Co Cork. ☐ to Mallow. ☐ to Fermoy, Mallow or Kanturk. ☐ Jun–Sep: 10 Pearse Square, Fermoy (025 31811).

THE SECOND LONGEST RIVER in Ireland after the Shannon *(see p177)*, the Blackwater rises in high bogland in County Kerry. It then flows eastwards through County Cork until it reaches Cappoquin, County Waterford, where it changes course south through wooded sandstone gorges to the sea at Youghal *(see p171)*. Much of the valley is wooded, a reminder that the entire area was forested until the 17th century. The river passes some magnificent country houses and pastoral views. However, the region is best known for its fishing – the Blackwater's tributaries are filled with fine brown trout.

The best way to see the valley is to take the scenic Blackwater Valley Drive from Youghal to Mallow. The route passes through **Fermoy**, a town founded by Scottish merchant John Anderson in 1789. Angling is the town's main appeal, especially for roach, rudd, perch and pike. Further west is **Mallow**, a prosperous town noted for its fishing, golf and horse racing. Inviting detours along the tributaries include **Kanturk**, a pleasant market town with a castle, on the River Allow.

Weirs and bridge at Fermoy on the River Blackwater

Cobh ⑳

Road map C6. Co Cork. 👥 *10,000.*
📷 ℹ️ *Old Yacht Club (021 813301).*

COBH (pronounced "cove") lies on Great Island, one of the three islands in Cork harbour which are now linked by causeways. The Victorian seafront has rows of steeply terraced houses overlooked by **St Colman's**, an imposing Gothic Revival cathedral.

Following a visit by Queen Victoria in 1849, Cobh was renamed Queenstown but reverted to its original name in 1921. The town commands one of the world's largest natural harbours – the reason for its rise to prominence as a naval base in the 18th century. It was also a major port for merchant shipping and the main port from which Irish emigrants left for America.

Cobh was also a port of call for luxury passenger liners. In 1838, the *Sirius* made the first transatlantic crossing under steam power from here. Cobh was also the last stop for the *Titanic*, before its doomed Atlantic crossing in 1912. Three years later, the *Lusitania* was torpedoed and sunk by a German submarine just off Kinsale *(see pp164–5)*, southwest of Cobh. A memorial on the promenade is dedicated to all those who died in the attack.

IRISH EMIGRATION

Between 1848 and 1950 almost six million people emigrated from Ireland – two and a half million of them leaving from Cobh. The famine years of 1844–8 *(see p211)* triggered mass emigration as the impoverished made horrific transatlantic journeys in cramped, insanitary conditions. Many headed for the United States and Canada, and a few risked the long journey to Australia. Up until the early 20th century, emigrants waiting to board the ships were a familiar sight in Cobh. However, by the 1930s world recession and immigration restrictions in the United States and Canada led to a fall in the numbers leaving Ireland.

19th-century engraving of emigrants gathering in Cobh harbour

🏛 The Queenstown Story

Cobh Heritage Centre. 📞 *021 813591.* ⭕ *daily.* 📷 ♿
Housed in a Victorian railway station, *The Queenstown Story* is an exhibition detailing the town's marine history. Exhibits and audiovisual displays recall the part Cobh played in Irish emigration and the transportation of convicts. Between 1791 and 1853, 40,000 convicts were sent to Australian penal colonies in notorious "coffin ships"; many prisoners were also kept in floating jails in Cork Harbour.

On a happier note, the exhibition also documents Cobh's role as a port of call for glamorous transatlantic liners.

ENVIRONS: North of Cobh is the 280-ha (700-acre) Fota Estate. Surrounding the Regency mansion is the **Fota Wildlife Park and Arboretum**, which concentrates on breeding and reintroducing animals to their natural habitat. The white-tailed sea eagle is one native species that has been saved from extinction in Ireland. The landscaped park boasts

Cobh harbour with the steeple of St Colman's rising above the town

over 70 species of animal, including giraffes, flamingoes, and zebras. Only the cheetahs, subject to a long-term breeding programme, are restricted in enclosures. A train links the various sections of the park.

The arboretum has rare trees and shrubs from Japan, China, South America, the Himalayas and North America.

🦌 Fota Wildlife Park and Arboretum
Carrigtuohill. **[** 021 812678.
○ Apr–Oct: daily. 🅿️ **&**

Jameson Heritage Centre ㉘

Road map C5. Distillery Walk, Midleton, Co Cork. **[** 021 613594.
🚌 to Midleton. **○** daily. 🅿️ **& ✓**

A SENSITIVELY RESTORED 18th-century distillery, Jameson Heritage Centre is part of the vast Irish Distillers group at Midleton. Bushmills *(see p258)* is the oldest distillery in Ireland but Midleton is the largest. It comprises a series of separate distilleries each producing a different Irish whiskey, including Jameson and Tullamore Dew.

The story of Irish whiskey is presented through audiovisual displays, working models and authentic machinery. A tour of the old distillery takes in the mills, maltings, still-houses, kilns, granaries and warehouses. Visitors can take part in whiskey tasting and try to distinguish between various brands of Irish whiskey and Scotch. Highlights of the visit include the world's largest pot still, with a capacity of over 30,000 gallons, and the water wheel, which is still in good working order.

Clock tower on the main street of Youghal

Youghal ㉙

Road map C5. Co Cork.
🚶 9,300. 🚌 **i** Market House, Market Square (024 92390).

YOUGHAL (pronounced "yawl") is a historic walled town and thriving fishing port. The town was granted to Sir Walter Raleigh by Queen Elizabeth I but later sold to the Earl of Cork. In Cromwellian times, Youghal became a closed borough – an English Protestant garrison town.

The picturesque, four-storey **Clock tower** was originally the city gate, but was recast as a prison. Steep steps beside the tower lead up to a well-preserved section of the medieval town wall and fine views across the Blackwater estuary. Through the tower, in the sombre North Main Street, is the **Red House**. This authentic Dutch mansion was built in 1710. Virtually next door are some forbidding Elizabethan almshouses and, on the far side of the road, a 15th-century tower, known as **Tynte's Castle**.

Nestling in the town walls opposite is **Myrtle Grove**, one of the few unfortified Tudor manor houses to survive in Ireland. It has a triple-gabled façade and exquisite interior oak panelling. Just uphill is the Gothic **Church of St Mary**. Inside are tomb effigies and stained-glass windows depicting the coats of arms of local families.

Grain truck (c. 1940) at the Jameson Heritage Centre

THE LOWER SHANNON

CLARE · LIMERICK · TIPPERARY

*I*N THE THREE COUNTIES *which flank the lower reaches of the Shannon, Ireland's longest river, the scenery ranges from the rolling farmland of Tipperary to the eerie limestone plateau of the Burren. The Shannon's bustling riverside resorts draw many visitors, and there are medieval strongholds and atmospheric towns of great historic interest. The region also boasts a vibrant music scene.*

The River Shannon has long made this area an attractive prospect for settlers. There are several important Stone Age sites, including a major settlement by Lough Gur. From the 5th century, the region lay at the heart of Munster, one of Ireland's four Celtic provinces. The Rock of Cashel, a remarkable fortified abbey in county Tipperary, was the seat of the Kings of Munster for more than 700 years.

The Vikings penetrated the Shannon in the 10th century, but Gaelic clans put up stern resistance. During the Norman period, the chieftains of these clans built Bunratty Castle and other fortresses that were impressive enough to rival the strongholds erected by the Anglo-Irish dynasties. Foremost among the latter families were the Butlers, the Earls of Ormonde, who held much land in Tipperary, and the Fitzgeralds, the main landowners in the Limerick area. From the Middle Ages, Limerick was often at the centre of events in the Lower Shannon. In 1691, the army of William of Orange laid siege to the town, heralding the Treaty of Limerick that triggered the Catholic nobility's departure for Europe – the so-called "Flight of the Wild Geese".

Lush grassland, which has turned the Lower Shannon into prime dairy country, is typical of the region. In places this gives way to picturesque glens and mountains, such as the Galty range in southern Tipperary. The region's most dramatic scenery, however, is found along the coast of Clare, a county otherwise best known for its thriving traditional music scene.

Ruins of Dysert O'Dea monastery in County Clare with an outstanding 12th-century High Cross

◁ Traditional musicians playing at Feakle in County Clare

Exploring the Lower Shannon

THE CENTRAL LOCATION of Limerick city makes it a natural focus for visitors to the region. However, there are many charming towns that make pleasanter bases, such as Adare, Cashel and also Killaloe, which is well placed for exploring the River Shannon. Most places of interest in Tipperary lie in the southern part of the county, where historic towns such as Clonmel and Cahir overlook the River Suir. By contrast, County Clare has few towns of any size, though it boasts the major attraction of Bunratty Castle. Beyond Ennis, the landscape becomes steadily bleaker until you reach the Burren.

Looking up at the Cliffs of Moher

DOOLIN

R478

R477

N67

THE BURREN ❶

Galway

CLIFFS OF MOHER ❷

KILFENORA

R481

N67

ENNISTIMON

N85

DYSERT O'DEA ❼

FEAKI

ENNIS ❽

N18

N68

CRAGGAUNOWEN ❿

KNAPPOGUE CASTLE ❾

N7

SHANNON ❻

BUNRATT ❸ CASTLE

LIMERICK

KILRUSH ❸

R483

N68

R487

FOYNES ❺

N69

GLIN ❹

R521

N21

ADARE ⓯

GETTING AROUND

Roads extend from Limerick into every corner of the region, providing good access for motorists; the car ferry from Tarbert in Kerry to Killimer, near Kilrush in Clare, is a convenient route across the Shannon. Trains from Limerick serve Cahir, Clonmel and Carrick, but in other areas you must rely on the bus network. This is rather limited, especially in County Clare, although buses to the Burren from Limerick pass the Cliffs of Moher. Some of the most popular sights, such as Bunratty Castle and the Burren, can be reached on bus tours from Limerick.

NEWCASTLE WEST

R522

N20

N21

MULLAGHAREIRK MOUNTAINS

Tralee

Cork

Maigue

0 kilometres   25

0 miles   25

KEY

▬	Major road
=	Minor road
▬	Scenic route
～	River
☀	Viewpoint

Boats sailing on Lough Derg near Mountshannon

SEE ALSO

• *Where to Stay* pp294–5

• *Restaurants, Cafés and Pubs*
pp312–13 & 319–20

Painted pub sign in Cashel

Looking south along the Cliffs of Moher, one of the most dramatic stretches of Ireland's west coast

The Burren **●**

See pp178–9.

Cliffs of Moher **❷**

Road map B4. Co Clare. 🚌 *from Ennis & Limerick.* **Visitors' Centre** 📞 *065 81171.* ⭘ *Easter–Sep: daily.* **O'Brien's Tower** 📞 *065 81171.* ⭘ *Apr–Oct: daily.* 🅿️

EVEN WHEN SHROUDED in mist or buffeted by Atlantic gales, the Cliffs of Moher are breathtaking, rising to a height of 200 m (650 ft) out of the sea and extending for 8 km (5 miles). The sheer rock face, with its layers of black shale and sandstone, provides sheltered ledges where guillemots and other sea birds nest.

Well-worn paths lead along the cliffs. From the **Visitors' Centre**, 5 km (3 miles) northwest of Liscannor, you can walk south to **Hag's Head** in an hour. To the north, a good alternative is the three-hour walk along the coast between **O'Brien's Tower** – a viewing point built for the benefit of Victorian tourists – and Fisherstreet near **Doolin** *(see p180)*.

Kilrush **❸**

Road map B4. Co Clare. 🚶 *2,800.* 🚌 ℹ️ *Heritage Centre, Market House (065 51577).* ⭘ *Jun–Sep.*

WITH A NEW MARINA and the promotion of Kilrush as a heritage town, the fortunes of this 18th-century estate town have been greatly revived. It now has a **Heritage Centre**, where an exhibition covers the Great Famine *(see p211)* and the landlord evictions of 1888

(see pp40–41). A well-marked walking trail around the town's historic sights also starts here.

ENVIRONS: From Kilrush, boats take visitors dolphin-spotting or to nearby **Scattery Island**, site of a medieval monastery. The ruins include five churches and one of the tallest round towers in the country.

The **Loop Head Drive** is a 27-km (17-mile) route which begins at the resort of Kilkee, west of Kilrush. It winds south past dramatic coastal scenery to Loop Head, from where you can enjoy superb views.

Glin **❹**

Road map B5. Co Limerick. 🚶 *600.* 🚌 *from Limerick.*

THIS CHARMING village on the banks of the Shannon is the seat of the Knights of Glin, a branch of the Fitzgeralds who have lived in the district for seven centuries. Their first medieval castle is a ruin, but west of the village you can see

Rare 18th-century double "flying" staircase in Glin Castle

their newer ancestral home, **Glin Castle**. Originally built in 1780, the Georgian manor succumbed to the vogue for Gothic romance in the 1820s, when it acquired battlements and gingerbread lodges. There is some fine stuccowork and 18th-century furniture inside.

♠ **Glin Castle**
📞 *068 34173.* ⭘ *May–Jun: daily.* 🅿️ 🎫 *obligatory.*

Foynes **❺**

Road map B5. Co Limerick. 🚶 *650.* 🚌 *from Limerick.*

FOYNES ENJOYED short-lived fame in the 1930s and 1940s as the eastern terminus of the first airline passenger route across the Atlantic. **Foynes Flying Boat Museum** presents a detailed history of the seaplane service. The original Radio and Weather Room and a 1940s-style tea room are particularly evocative of the era.

🏛 **Foynes Flying Boat Museum**
Aras Ide, Foynes. 📞 *069 65416.* ⭘ *Apr–Oct: daily.* 🅿️ ♿

ENVIRONS: The historic town of **Askeaton**, 11 km (7 miles) east of Foynes, has a castle and Franciscan friary founded by the Fitzgeralds. The friary is particularly interesting, with a 15th-century cloister of black marble. In Rathkeale, 8 km (5 miles) south, **Castle Matrix** is a restored 15th-century tower house renowned for the fine library in the Great Hall.

♠ **Castle Matrix**
Rathkeale. 📞 *069 64284.* ⭘ *May–Sep: Sat–Thu.* 🅿️

Fishing on Lough Derg, the largest of the lakes on the Shannon

River Shannon ❻

Road map B4, C4, C3. 🚆 *to Limerick or Athlone.* 🚌 *to Carrick-on-Shannon, Athlone or Limerick.* 🛈 *Arthur's Quay, Limerick (061 317522).*

THE SHANNON IS the longest river in Ireland, rising in County Cavan and meandering down to the Atlantic. Flowing through the heart of the island, it has traditionally marked the border between the provinces of Leinster and Connaught. In medieval times, castles guarded the major fords from Limerick to Portumna, and numerous monasteries were built along the riverbanks, including the celebrated Clonmacnoise *(see pp242–3)*. Work began on the Shannon navigation system in the 1750s, but it fell into disuse with the advent of the railways. It has since been revived, with an additional boost given by the recent restoration of the Shannon-Erne Waterway *(see p227)*.

There are subtle changes of landscape along the length of the river. South of **Lough Allen**, the countryside is covered with the drumlins or low hills typical of the northern Midlands. Towards **Lough Ree**, islands stud the river in an area of ecological importance which is home to otters, geese, grey herons and whooper swans. Continuing south beyond **Athlone** *(see p241)*, the river flows through flood plains and bog before reaching **Lough**

Grey heron on the Shannon

EXPLORING THE SHANNON

Carrick-on-Shannon is the main centre for boating on the upper reaches of the river, while Portumna and the atmospheric ports of Mountshannon and Killaloe are the principal bases for exploring Lough Derg.

Cruiser on the Shannon

KEY

🛈	Tourist information
🚤	Cruiser hire
🚢	Water-bus tour

Derg, the biggest of the lakes on the Shannon. The scenery is more dramatic here, with the lough's southern end edged by wooded mountains. From **Killaloe** *(see p182)*, the river gains speed on its rush towards **Limerick** *(see p183)* and the sea. The mudflats of the Shannon estuary attract a great variety of birdlife. The port of **Carrick-on-Shannon** *(see p227)* is the cruising centre of Ireland, but there are bases all along the river – especially around Lough Derg, which is the lake most geared to boating. Water-buses connect most ports south of Athlone. If you hire a cruiser, enquire about the weather conditions before setting out, particularly on Loughs Ree and Derg, which are very exposed. The calm stretch from **Portumna** *(see p205)* to Athlone is easier for inexperienced sailors.

Walkers can enjoy the Lough Derg Way, a signposted route around the lake. The woods by **Lough Key** *(see p211)* also provide good walking territory.

Athlone and the southern reaches of Lough Ree

The Burren ❶

Dark red helleborine

THE WORD BURREN derives from *boireann*, which means "rocky land" in Gaelic – an apt name for this vast limestone plateau in northwest County Clare. In the 1640s, Cromwell's surveyor described it as "a savage land, yielding neither water enough to drown a man, nor tree to hang him, nor soil enough to bury". Few trees manage to grow in this desolate place, yet other plants thrive. The Burren is a unique botanical environment in which Mediterranean and alpine plants rare to Ireland grow side by side. From May to August, an astonishing array of flowers adds splashes of colour to the austere landscape. These plants grow most abundantly around the region's shallow lakes and pastures, but they also take root in the crevices of the limestone pavements which are the most striking geological feature of the rocky plateau. In the southern part of the Burren, limestone gives way to the black shale and sandstone that form the dramatic Cliffs of Moher *(see p176)*.

Grazing in the Burren
A quirk in the local climate means that, in winter, the hills are warmer than the valleys – hence the unusual practice in the Burren of letting cattle graze on high ground in winter.

FAUNA OF THE BURREN

The Burren is one of the best places in Ireland for butterflies, with 28 species found in the area. The birdlife is also varied. Skylarks and cuckoos are common on the hills and in the meadows, while the coast is a good place for razorbills, guillemots, puffins and other sea birds. Mammals are harder to spot. Badgers, foxes and stoats live here, but you are much more likely to see a herd of shaggy-coated wild goats or an Irish hare.

Turloughs are shallow lakes which are dry in summer but flood in winter, when they attract wildfowl and waders.

Spring gentian

The pearl-bordered fritillary, *one of a number of fritillaries found in the Burren, can be seen in no other part of Ireland.*

An Irish hare's *white and brown winter coat turns to reddish-brown in the summer.*

Whooper swans *from Iceland flock to the wetlands of the Burren in winter.*

The hooded crow *is easily identified by its grey and black plumage.*

Bloody Cranesbill
This striking plant, common in the Burren, is a member of the geranium family. It flowers in June.

Limestone Pavement
Glaciation and wind and rain erosion have formed limestone pavements with deep crevices known as "grykes". The porous rock is easily penetrated by rainwater, which has gouged out an extensive cave system beneath the rocky plateau.

Hawthorn is one of the few trees which manages to grow in the Burren, although the plants are usually twisted and stunted.

Exposed layers of limestone

Stone-built Burren cottage

Dry-stone wall

Limestone slabs, or "clints"

The hoary rock rose is one of several rare plants to grow abundantly in the Burren.

Holly trees can gain a foothold in the pavement, but grazing and wind restrict their growth.

Maidenhair fern thrives in the damp crevices of the Burren.

Mountain Avens
Normally a mountain plant, this flower grows here at sea level.

Exploring the Burren

If you are interested in the unique geology and natural history of the Burren, head for **Mullaghmore**, which is one of the wildest parts of the plateau and has some of the best limestone pavements in the area. A proposal to build a visitors' centre here is now causing a major controversy.

A good place to begin a tour of the more accessible parts of the Burren is at the **Cliffs of Moher** *(see p176)*. From here it is a short drive north to **Doolin**, near the port for the Aran Islands *(see pp206–7)*. This rather spread-out village is renowned for its traditional music; Gus O'Connor's pub *(see p320)* acts as a focus for music-lovers in the area. The coastal road runs north from Doolin to a desolate limestone outcrop at **Black Head**, while turning inland you will reach **Lisdoonvarna**. The Victorians developed the town as a spa, but it is now most renowned for its colourful pubs and its matchmaking festival *(see p48)*.

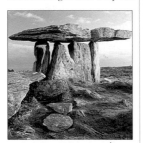

Poulnabrone Dolmen in the heart of the Burren's limestone plateau

Music shop in Doolin

To the north along the N67 lies **Ballyvaughan**, a fishing village dotted with slate-roofed cottages and busy with tourists in summer. It is well placed for reaching a number of sights. Nearby **Bishop's Quarter** has a sheltered beach with glorious views across a lagoon towards Galway Bay. **Aillwee Cave**, to the south, is just one of thousands of caves in the Burren, but is the only one open to the public. It consists of a tunnel which opens into a series of caverns. In the first, known as Bear Haven, the remains of hibernation pits used by bears are still visible.

Ruined forts and castles and numerous prehistoric sites dot the landscape. Just west of Aillwee Cave is **Cahermore Stone Fort**, with a lintelled doorway, and to the south

Gleninsheen Wedge Tomb, a style of grave which marks the transition between Stone and Bronze Age cultures. The more famous **Poulnabrone Dolmen** nearby is a striking portal tomb dating back to 2500–2000 BC. Continuing south you reach the ghostly shell of **Leamaneagh Castle**, a 17th-century mansion that incorporates an earlier tower house built by the O'Briens.

On the southern fringe of the Burren lies **Kilfenora**, a Catholic diocese which, by a curious historical quirk, has the Pope for its bishop. The village's modest cathedral, one of many 12th-century churches in the Burren, has a roofless chancel with finely sculpted capitals. Kilfenora, however, is more famous for its High Crosses, of which there are several in the graveyard. Best preserved is the Doorty Cross, with a carving of a bishop and two other clerics on the east face. Next door, the **Burren Centre** offers an excellent introduction to the geology and flora of the region, as well as to man's impact on the landcape. The displays include a model of the limestone plateau.

Carved capital in Kilfenora Cathedral

🏛 **Aillwee Cave**
Ballyvaughan. 📞 *065 77036.*
⭕ *daily.* 🈲 🗂

🏛 **Burren Centre**
Kilfenora. 📞 *065 88030.* ⭕ *Mar–Oct: daily.* 🈲

THE BURREN REGION

KEY

▨	Exposed limestone
=	Minor roads
▬	Major roads
ℹ	Tourist information
⚘	Viewpoint

0 kilometres　　　10

0 miles　　　5

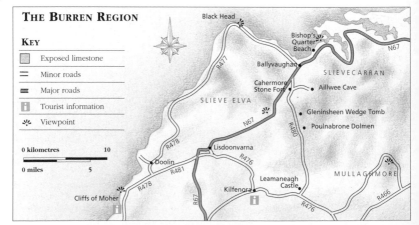

Black Head

Bishop's Quarter Beach

N67

Ballyvaughan

SLIEVECARRAN

R477

Cahermore Stone Fort

Aillwee Cave

SLIEVE ELVA

Gleninsheen Wedge Tomb

N67

R480

Poulnabrone Dolmen

R478

Lisdoonvarna

Doolin

R481

R476

Leamaneagh Castle

MULLAGHMORE

R67

R478

Kilfenora

R476

R466

Cliffs of Moher

Dysert O'Dea **7**

Road map 4B. Corrofin, Co Clare.
🚌 *from Ennis.* **Archaeology Centre**
☎ *065 37722.* ☐ *May–Sep: daily.*

Colourful exterior of Michael Kerins pub in Ennis

DYSERT O'DEA CASTLE stands on a rocky outcrop 9 km (6 miles) north of Ennis. This tower house, erected in the 15th century, is home to the **Archaeology Centre**, which includes a small museum and also marks the start of a trail around nearby historic sights. A map of the path, designed for both walkers and cyclists, is available from the tea room.

Across a field from the castle is a monastic site said to have been founded by the obscure St Tola in the 8th century. The ruins are overgrown and rather worn, but the Romanesque carving above one doorway is still clear, and there is also an impressive 12th-century High Cross, with a bishop sculpted on the east side *(see p235).*

Further south, the trail leads past the remains of two stone forts, a ruined castle and the site of a 14th-century battle.

Ennis **8**

Road map 4B. Co Clare. 🚶 *18,000.*
🚌 **i** *Clare Rd (065 28366).*

CLARE'S COUNTY TOWN, on the banks of the River Fergus, is a charming place. Narrow, winding lanes are particularly characteristic and recall Ennis's medieval beginnings. The town is also renowned for its painted shopfronts and folk music festivals (known as *fleadh* in Gaelic). It abounds in "singing" pubs and traditional music shops.

Ennis can trace its origins to the 13th century and to the O'Briens, Kings of Thomond, who were the area's feudal overlords in the Middle Ages. The Franciscan friary that they founded here in the 1240s is now the town's main attraction. Dating largely from the 14th and 15th centuries, the ruined **Ennis Friary** is famous for its rich carvings and decorated tombs in the chancel – above all the 15th century MacMahon tomb, whose carved alabaster panels have been incorporated into the later Creagh tomb.

Next door to the friary is a delightful 17th-century house, now Cruise's restaurant *(see p312),* and on the corner of nearby Francis Street stands the Queen's Hotel – featured in James Joyce's *Ulysses.* To the south, O'Connell Square has a monument to Daniel O'Connell *(see p40),* who was elected MP for Clare in 1828. He also gave his name to the town's main street, where, among the pubs and shops, you can spot a medieval tower, a Jacobean chimney stack and an 18th-century arch.

Finely carved Romanesque doorway at Dysert O'Dea

fi **Ennis Friary**
Abbey St. ☎ *065 29100.* ☐ *May–Sep: daily.* 🎧 ♿

ENVIRONS: The area around Ennis is rich in monastic ruins. Just 3 km (2 miles) south of the town is **Clare Abbey**, an Augustinian foundation set up by the O'Briens in 1189 but dating mainly from the 1400s.

Quin Franciscan Friary, set in meadows 13 km (8 miles) southeast of Ennis, was also built in the 15th century, and incorporates the romantic ruins of a Norman castle. The well-preserved cloister is one of the finest of its kind in Ireland.

Knappogue Castle **9**

Road map 4B. Quin, Co Clare.
☎ *061 360788.* 🚌 *to Ennis.*
☐ *Apr–Oct: daily.* 🎧 ♿

A POWERFUL LOCAL CLAN called the MacNamaras erected Knappogue Castle in 1467. Apart from a ten-year spell in Cromwellian times, it stayed in their hands until 1815. During the War of Independence *(see pp42–3),* the castle was used by the revolutionary forces.

Knappogue, now owned by Texans, has been restored with meticulous care and is one of the country's most charmingly furnished castles. The central tower house is original, but the rest is Neo-Gothic. Inside are fine Elizabethan fireplaces and linenfold wood panelling.

Medieval banquets are staged in the castle *(see p330),* with storytelling and singing forming part of the entertainment.

Craggaunowen ⑩

Road map B4. Kilmurry, Co Clare.
🚗 🚆 *to Ennis.* 📞 *061 360788.*
🕐 *Apr–Oct: daily.* 🎫 ♿

T HE CRAGGAUNOWEN PROJECT,
known as "Craggaunowen:
the Living Past" and designed
to bring Bronze Age and Celtic
culture to life, is a shining
example of a recreated prehistoric site. The centre was
created in the grounds of
Craggaunowen Castle in the
1960s by John Hunt, a noted
archaeologist who had been
inspired by his excavations at
Lough Gur *(see p186)*. The
castle's tower house contains
bronzes and other objects
from Hunt's archaeological
collection, the rest of which
can be seen in Limerick.

At Craggaunowen, people
in costume act out particular
trades, such as spinning or
potting, or serve as guides. A
French slave describes how
communities lived in the ring
fort, a typical early Christian
homestead. You can also see
meat being prepared in the
fulacht fiadh, a traditional
hunter's cooking hole.

The complex includes part
of a *togher*, an original Iron
Age timber road that was discovered in Longford. The most
eye-catching sight, however,
is the crannog *(see p31)*, a
man-made island enclosing
wattle and daub houses – a
style of defensive homestead
that survived until around 1600.

Another interesting exhibit
is a leather-hulled boat built in
the 1970s by the explorer, Tim
Severin. He used it to retrace

A woman in peasant costume spinning wool at Craggaunowen

the route which legend says
St Brendan took in a similar
vessel across the Atlantic in
the 6th century *(see p25)*.

Mountshannon ⑪

Road map C4. Co Clare. 🚶 240.

T HIS PRETTY VILLAGE on the
banks of Lough Derg *(see
p177)* seems to have its back
turned to the lake but is nevertheless a major angling centre.
Solid 18th-century stone houses
and churches cluster around
the harbour, together with
some good pubs: Madden's is
a prime venue for Irish music.

Mountshannon is well placed
for exploring the lake's western
shores, with plenty of scope
for walks and bicycle rides.
Fishing boats are available for
hire, and in summer you can
go by boat to **Holy Island**, the
site of a monastery founded
in the 7th century. The ruins
include four chapels and a
graveyard of medieval tombs.

Killaloe ⑫

Road map C4. Co Clare. 🚶 950.
🚆 ℹ️ *May–Sep: Heritage Centre,
The Bridge (061 376866).*

K ILLALOE, which enjoys a
beautiful setting close to
where the Shannon emerges
from Lough Derg, is the lake's
most prosperous pleasure port.
An attractive 17th-century stone
bridge divides Killaloe in two,
with its twin town of Ballina
lying on the opposite bank in
Tipperary. Ballina has better
pubs, including Goosers on
the waterfront *(see p320)*, but
Killaloe is the main boating
centre *(see p335)* and also has
more of historical interest.

Killaloe's grandest site is **St
Flannan's Cathedral**, founded
in around 1182. Though a
rather plain, solid church, it has
a richly carved Romanesque
doorway, which was rescued
from an earlier chapel. The
church also has an ancient
Ogham Stone *(see p32)*, unusual because the inscription
is in both Nordic runes and
Ogham. Outside stands St
Flannan's Oratory, built around
the same time as the cathedral.

The Heritage Centre, in a
converted boathouse on the
bridge, contains an exhibition
about the Shannon and Lough
Derg, and is the starting point
for a marked walk along
sections of the old Killaloe
Canal. It is also possible to
arrange for local fishermen to
take you out on the lake.

Bunratty Castle ⑬

See pp184–5.

Bicycle hire and boat trips at Mountshannon

Limerick ⓯

Road map B4. Co Limerick. 👥 90,000.
🚶 *Shannon.* 🚌 🚊 ℹ️ *Arthur's Quay (061 317522).* 🛍️ *Fri & Sat.*

THE THIRD LARGEST CITY in the Republic, Limerick was founded by the Vikings. Given its strategic point on the River Shannon, it thrived under the Normans, but later bore the brunt of English oppression. After the Battle of the Boyne *(see p236)*, the rump of the defeated Jacobite army withdrew here. The siege which followed has entered Irish folklore as a heroic defeat, sealed by the Treaty of Limerick in 1691. English treachery in reneging on most of the terms of the treaty still rankles. It is no coincidence that Catholicism and nationalism are strong in the city.

Limerick has a reputation for high unemployment, crime and general neglect. However, it is fast acquiring a new image as a commercial city, revitalized by new industries and laudable restoration projects. Even so, visitors may still have to dig a little to appreciate its charm.

The city centre consists of three historic districts. King's Island was the first area to be settled by the Vikings and was later the heart of the medieval city, when it was known as Englishtown. The island boasts Limerick's two main landmarks, King John's Castle and St Mary's Cathedral. The old Irishtown, south of the Abbey River, has its fair share of drab houses and shops, but also has its own historic buildings and a pocket of Georgian elegance in St John's Square. Near here is Limerick's most conspicuous sight, St John's Cathedral, built in 1861. Its 85-m (280-ft) spire is the tallest in the country.

The most pleasant part of Limerick in which to stroll is Newtown Pery – a grid of gracious Georgian terraces focused on O'Connell Street.

⚓ King John's Castle
Nicholas St. 📞 *061 411201.*
◯ *Apr–Oct: daily.* 🅿️ ♿
Supposedly founded by King John in 1200, not long after the Normans arrived, this castle is an imposing sight with five drum towers and solid curtain walls. Architecturally, the castle is less interesting inside, but it houses a good exhibition on the history of the city. Replicas of siege machinery are based on finds from the castle. Ongoing excavations have

Carved misericord in St Mary's Cathedral

unearthed jewellery and pots, and you can also see Viking houses and later fortifications. One of the most dramatic discoveries was a soldier's diary recording the horrors of the Siege of Limerick.

Across the nearby Thomond Bridge, the Treaty Stone marks the spot where the Treaty of Limerick was signed in 1691.

⛪ St Mary's Cathedral
Bridge Street. 📞 *061 416238.*
◯ *Jun–Aug: 9am–5pm daily; Sep–May: 9am–noon daily.*
Built in 1172, this is the oldest structure in the city. Except for a fine Romanesque doorway and the nave, however, little remains of the early church.

Characteristic Georgian doorway in St John's Square

The 15th-century misericords in the choir stalls are the pride of St Mary's, with superb carvings in black oak of angels, griffins and other creatures both real and imaginary.

Nearby, George's Quay is a pleasant street with restaurants and outdoor cafés and good views across the river.

🏛️ Hunt Museum
Rutland St. ◯ *Mon–Sat.* 🅿️ ♿
Recently moved from Limerick University to the Old Customs House, this museum has one of the greatest collections of antiquities in Ireland, gathered by the archaeologist, John Hunt. The best exhibits, dating from the Bronze Age, include gold jewellery, weapons and a magnificent shield. Among the other artifacts are Celtic brooches and the Antrim Cross, a masterpiece of 9th-century metalwork.

🏛️ Limerick Museum
St John's Sq. 📞 *061 417826.* ◯ *Tue–Sat.* ⬤ *10 days at Christmas.* ♿
A handsome Georgian house provides a fine setting for the city museum. Its displays cover Limerick's history, its traditions and passions, from silver- and lace-making to rugby.

View of Limerick showing Thomond Bridge across the Shannon and King John's Castle

Bunratty Castle ⓭

THIS FORMIDABLE CASTLE, built in the 15th century, is one of Ireland's major tourist attractions. Its most important residents were the O'Briens, Earls of Thomond, who lived here from around 1500 until the 1640s. The present interior looks much as it did under the so-called "Great Earl", who died in 1624. Abandoned last century, the castle was derelict when Lord Gort bought it in the 1950s, but it has been beautifully restored to its original state. The adjacent Folk Park and mock medieval banquets held in the castle attract many coach parties, giving Bunratty a rather commercialized atmosphere, but it is still well worth visiting.

The chimney is a replica in wood of the stone original. It provided a vent for the smoke given off by the fire in the centre of the Great Hall.

★ North Solar
This 17th-century German chandelier is the most curious feature in the Great Earl's private apartments. The term "solar" was used during the Middle Ages to describe an upper chamber.

The Murder Hole was designed for pouring boiling water or pitch on to the heads of attackers.

Entrance

The basement, with walls 3 m (10 ft) thick, was probably used for storage or as a stable.

North Front
Bunratty Castle is unusual for the high arches on both the north and south sides of the keep. However, the first-floor entrance, designed to deter invaders, was typical of castles of the period.

STAR FEATURES

★ **Great Hall**

★ **Main Guard**

★ **North Solar**

★ Main Guard

Now used for medieval-style banquets, this was the room where Bunratty's soldiers ate, slept and relaxed. Music was played to them from the Minstrels' Gallery, and a gate in one corner gave instant access to the dungeons.

Anteroom

The Robing Room
was where the earls put on their gowns before an audience in the Great Hall. They also used it for private interviews.

South Solar
These guest apartments have fine linenfold wood panelling, a form of decoration popular during the Tudor period. The elaborate fan-vaulted ceiling is partly a reconstruction.

A spiral staircase is found in each of the four towers.

★ Great Hall

This Tudor standard was among the many furnishings that Lord Gort brought to the castle. It stands in the Great Hall, once the banqueting hall and audience chamber, and still Bunratty's grandest room.

BUNRATTY FOLK PARK

A meticulous recreation of rural life in Ireland at the turn of the century, this Folk Park began with the reconstruction of a farmhouse which was saved during the building of nearby Shannon Airport. It now consists of a complete village, incorporating shops and a whole range of domestic architecture from a labourer's cottage to an elegant Georgian house. Other buildings include a farmhouse typical of the Moher region in the Burren *(see p176)* and a working corn mill. During the main summer season, people in authentic costume wander through the streets and demonstrate traditional crafts and trades from weaving to butter-making.

Main street of Bunratty Folk Park village

Typical thatched cottage in the village of Adare

Adare ⓯

Road map B5. Co Limerick. 🏚 *900.*
🚌 ℹ️ *Heritage Centre, Main St
(061 396255).*

ADARE IS BILLED as Ireland's prettiest village. Cynics call it the prettiest "English" village since its manicured perfection is at odds with normal notions of national beauty. Originally a fief of the Fitzgeralds, the Earls of Kildare, Adare owes its present appearance more to the Earls of Dunraven, who restored the estate village in the 1820s and 1830s. The long, thin village is a picture of neat stonework and thatched roofs punctuated by picturesque ruins, all in a woodland setting.

The tourist office is at the new Heritage Centre, which includes a good exhibition on Adare's monastic history. Next door is the **Trinitarian Priory**, founded by the Fitzgeralds in 1230 and over-restored by the first Earl of Dunraven; it is now a Catholic church and convent. Opposite, by a stone-arched bridge, is the Washing Pool, a restored wash-house site.

By the main bridge, on the Limerick road, is the **Augustinian Priory** which was founded by the Fitzgeralds in 1315. Also known as Black Abbey, this well-restored priory has a central tower, subtle carvings, delightful cloisters and a graceful sedilia – a carved triple seat. Just over the bridge, from where it is best viewed, is **Desmond Castle**, a 13th-century feudal castle set on the banks of the River Maigue.

Nearby stands the main gate to **Adare Manor**, a luxury hotel and golf course *(see p294)*. Within its 900 ha (365 acres) of parkland lie two evocative ruins. The **St Nicholas Church** and **Chantry Chapel** date back to the 12th century; both are accessible by path. The graceful 15th-century **Franciscan Abbey**, however, is surrounded by the golf course, though it can be seen clearly from the pathway.

In the heart of the village is the elegant Dunraven Arms Hotel *(see p294)* from where the local hunt rides to hounds. Some of the nearby cottages, originally built by the Earl of Dunraven in 1828 for his estate workers, have been converted into restaurants, including the cosy Inn-Between *(see p312)*.

Lough Gur ⓰

Road map B5. Co Limerick. 🚌
Visitors' Centre 📞 *061 385186.*
⭕ *May–Sep: daily.* 🎫 ♿

THIS STONE AGE settlement, 26 km (16 miles) south of Limerick, was extensively inhabited in 3000 BC. Today the horseshoe-shaped lough and surrounding hills enclose an intriguing if rather inscrutable archaeological park. All around Lough Gur are standing stones and burial mounds, including megalithic tombs. One of the most impressive sights is the 4,000-year-old **Great Stone Circle**, just outside the park, by the Limerick–Kilmallock road. Excavations in the 1970s unearthed rectangular, oval and rounded Stone Age huts with stone foundations. The

Colourfully painted shopfronts on Main Street in Adare

Façade of Cashel Palace Hotel

interpretive centre, which is housed in mock Stone Age huts on the site of the original settlement, offers a range of audiovisual displays, models of stone circles, burial chambers and tools and weapons.

As well as the various prehistoric sights scattered all over the Knockadoon Peninsula, there are also some sights from more modern times. Beside the lough are two castle ruins, the 15th-century **Bourchier's Castle** and **Black Castle**, a 13th-century seat of the Earls of Desmond.

Roscrea ⑰

Road map C4. Co Tipperary.
🚶 4,200. 🚌 🚆 🛈 Heritage Centre, Castle St (0505 21850).

THIS MONASTIC TOWN on the banks of the River Bunnow, though marred by heavy through traffic, has an interesting historic centre. The 13th-century Anglo-Norman **Roscrea Castle** consists of a gate tower, curtain walls and two corner towers. In the courtyard stands Damer House, a Queen Anne-style residence with a magnificent staircase and Georgian garden. Just over the river lies **St Cronan's Monastery** with a High Cross, Romanesque church gable and a truncated round tower. There are remains of a 15th-century **Franciscan Friary** on Abbey Street and nearby in St Cronan's churchyard is **Roscrea Pillar**, an enigmatic early Christian stone.

♣ **Roscrea Castle**
Castle Street. 📞 0505 21850. 🔲 Jun–Sep: daily; Oct–May: Sat & Sun. 🖼

Holy Cross Abbey ⑱

Road map C5. Thurles, Co Tipperary.
📞 0504 43241. 🚌 🚆 to Thurles.
🔲 May–Sep: daily; Oct–Apr: Sun. 🖼 🚻 🔖

FOUNDED IN 1169 by the Benedictines, Holy Cross was supposedly endowed with a splinter from the True Cross, hence its name. Now it has been completely restored, and the church is once again a popular place of worship and pilgrimage. Most of the present structure dates from the 15th century. It was built by the Cistercians, who took over the abbey in 1180. This gracious cruciform church, embellished with mullioned windows and sculpted pillars, is one of the finest examples of late Gothic architecture in Ireland.

Crucifixion carving at Holy Cross Abbey

The chancel has fine ribbed vaulting and, in the south wall, an exquisitely carved sedilia, which is rather oddly called "the tomb of the Good Woman's son". The abbey complex, set in charming gardens, also houses an old-fashioned pub.

Cashel ⑲

Road map C5. Co Tipperary.
🚶 2,500. 🚌 🛈 Town Hall (062 61333).

THE GREAT ATTRACTION of the town is the magnificent medieval **Rock of Cashel** (see pp188–9). Many people stay overnight to enjoy eerie floodlit views of the Rock. A private path leads to it from **Cashel Palace Hotel** (see p294), an opulent Queen Anne residence that was once the Bishop's Palace. Nearby, the remnant of a 12th-century castle has been turned into Kearney Castle Hotel. In the evening you can sample traditional Irish culture at the **Brú Ború Heritage Centre**. Named after Brian Boru, the 10th-century king of Munster (see pp32–3), the centre offers folk theatre, traditional music, banquets, and a craft shop.

At the foot of the Rock is the 13th-century **Dominican Friary**. This austere sandstone church has a fine west door, a 15th-century tower and lancet windows. On farmland outside Cashel lie the scant remains of **Hore Abbey**, a 13th-century Cistercian foundation. The abbey was largely remodelled and a tower added in the 15th century, but the barrel-vaulted sacristy, the nave, choir and chapter house are all original.

🏛 **Brú Ború Heritage Centre**
Cashel. 📞 062 61122. 🔲 daily (mid-Sep–mid-May: Mon–Fri). 🔖
🛈 **Dominican Friary**
Dominic Street. 🔖 limited.

Ruins of Hore Abbey (1272) with the Rock of Cashel in the background

Rock of Cashel

T HIS ROCKY STRONGHOLD, which rises dramatically out of the Tipperary plain, was a symbol of royal and priestly power for more than a millennium. From the 5th century it was the seat of the Kings of Munster, whose kingdom extended over much of southern Ireland. In 1101, they handed Cashel over to the Church, and it flourished as a religious centre until a siege by a Cromwellian army in 1647 culminated in the massacre of its 3,000 occupants. The abbey was finally abandoned in the late 18th century.

Two hundred years on, the Rock of Cashel is besieged by visitors. A good proportion of the medieval complex is still standing, and Cormac's Chapel is one of the most outstanding examples of Romanesque architecture in the country.

★ St Patrick's Cross
The carving on the east face of this cross is said to be of St Patrick, who visited Cashel in 450. The cross is a copy of the original which stood here until 1982 and is now in the museum.

Hall of the Vicars' Choral
This hall was built in the 15th century for Cashel's most privileged choristers. The ceiling, a modern reconstruction based on medieval designs, features several decorative corbels including this painted angel.

Dormitory block

Entrance

The Museum
in the undercroft contains a display of stone carvings, including the original St Patrick's Cross.

★ Cormac's Chapel
Superb Romanesque carving adorns this chapel – the jewel of Cashel. The tympanum over the north door shows a centaur in a helmet aiming his bow and arrow at a lion.

Limestone rock

Outer wall

STAR FEATURES

★ Cormac's Chapel

★ St Patrick's Cross

★ Cathedral

KEY

- ☐ **12th Century**
- **4** St Patrick's Cross (replica)
- **12** Cormac's Chapel
- **13** Round tower
- ☐ **13th Century**
- **6** Cathedral porch
- **7** Nave
- **8** Crossing
- **9** South transept
- **10** Choir
- **11** North transept
- ☐ **15th Century**
- **1** Ticket office
- **2** Hall of the Vicars' Choral (museum)
- **3** Dormitory
- **5** Castle

| 0 metres | 50 |
| 0 yards | 50 |

VISITORS' CHECKLIST

Road map C5. Cashel. ☎ 062 61437. 🚌 to Thurles. 🚌 to Cashel. ⏰ mid-Jun–mid-Sep: 9am–7:30pm: daily; mid-Sep–mid-Mar: 9:30am–4:30pm; mid-Mar–mid-Jun: 9:30am–5:30pm. ● 24–28 Dec. 🎫 📷 ♿ ✉

The Rock
The 28-m (92-ft) round tower, the oldest and tallest building on the rock, enabled Cashel's inhabitants to scour the surrounding plain for potential attackers.

Round tower

Crossing

The Choir contains the 17th-century tomb of Miler Magrath, who caused a scandal by being both a Protestant and Catholic archbishop at the same time.

Graveyard

The O'Scully Monument, an ornate memorial erected in 1870 by a local landowning family, was damaged during a storm in 1976.

North Transept
Panels from three 16th-century tombs in the north transept are decorated with remarkably fresh and intricate carvings. This one, against the north wall, features a vine-leaf design and strange stylized beasts.

★ Cathedral
The roofless Gothic cathedral has thick walls riddled with hidden passages; in the north transept these are seen emerging at the base of the windows.

Athassel Priory ⑳

Road map C5. 8 km (5 miles) W of Cashel, Co Tipperary. 🚌 *to Tipperary.* 🕐 *daily.*

THIS RUINED Augustinian priory is situated on the west bank of the River Suir. The tomb of William de Burgh, the Norman founder of the priory, lies in the church. Established in 1192, Athassel is believed to have been the largest medieval priory in Ireland until it burned down in 1447. The scattered monastic site conveys a tranquil atmosphere, from the gatehouse and church to the remains of the cloisters and chapter house. The church has a fine west doorway, nave and chancel walls, as well as a 15th-century central tower.

The ruins of Athassel Priory, on the banks of the River Suir

Glen of Aherlow ㉑

Road map C5. Co Tipperary. 🚌 *to Bansha or Tipperary.* ℹ️ *Coach Road Inn, on R663 8 km (5 miles) E of Galbally (062 56331).*

THE LUSH VALLEY of the River Aherlow runs between the Galty Mountains and the wooded ridge of Slievenamuck. Bounded by the villages of **Galbally** and **Bansha**, the glen was historically an important pass between Limerick and Tipperary and a notorious hideout for outlaws.

Today there are opportunities for riding, cycling, rambling and fishing. Lowland walks follow the trout-filled river along the valley floor. More adventurous walkers will be tempted by the Galty range, which offers more rugged hill-walking, past wooded foothills, mountain streams, tiny corrie lakes and splendid sandstone peaks.

Cahir ㉒

Road map C5. Co Tipperary. 👥 *2,100.* 🚌 🚌 ℹ️ *Apr–Sep: Castle Street (052 41453).* 🚍 *Fri.*

ONCE A GARRISON and mill town, Cahir is today a busy market town. The publined Castle Street is the most appealing area. It leads to the Suir River, Cahir Castle and the well-signposted rural walk to the Swiss Cottage.

On the edge of town lies the ruined **Cahir Abbey**, a 13th-century Augustinian priory. Its fine windows are decorated with carved heads.

♜ Cahir Castle

Castle Street. 📞 *052 41011.* 🕐 *daily.* 📷 🚻 ♿ *limited.*
Built on a rocky island in the River Suir, Cahir is one of the most formidable castles in Ireland and a popular film set. This well-preserved fortress dates from the 13th century but is inextricably linked to its later owners, the Butlers. A powerful family in Ireland since the Anglo-Norman invasion, they were considered trusty lieges of the English crown and were granted the Cahir barony in 1375. Under their command, the castle was renovated and extended throughout the 15th and 16th centuries. It remained in the Butler family until 1964.

The castle is divided into outer, middle and inner wards, with a barbican at the outer entrance. The inner ward is on the site of the original Norman castle; the foundations are 13th century, as are the curtain walls and keep. The restored interior includes the striking great hall, which dates largely from the 1840s, though one of the walls is original and the windows are 15th century. From the ramparts there are views over the river and millrace.

▦ Swiss Cottage

Ardfinnan Road, Cahir. 📞 *052 41144.* 🕐 *May–Sep: daily; Mar–Apr & Oct–Nov: Tue–Sun.* 📷 *obligatory.*
The Swiss Cottage is a superb example of a *cottage orné,* a rustic folly. It was designed for the Butlers by the Regency architect John Nash in 1810. Here, Lord and Lady Cahir played at bucolic bliss, enjoying picnics dressed as peasants. Fashion dictated a *cottage orné* should blend in with the

View across the unspoilt Glen of Aherlow

countryside and all designs should be drawn from nature with nothing matching, so the windows and sloping eaves are all of different sizes and design. The enchantingly furnished cottage contains a tea room, gracious music room and two bedrooms, all beautifully restored.

Clonmel ㉓

Road map C5. Co Tipperary.
🏘 17,500. 🚌 🚉 ℹ 6 Sarsfield St (052 22960).

SET ON THE RIVER SUIR and framed by the Comeragh Mountains, Clonmel is Tipperary's main town. This Anglo-Norman stronghold was a fief of the Desmonds and eventually of the Butlers. Its prosperity was founded on milling and brewing; attractive mills still line the quays. Today, Clonmel is a bustling, brash town with quirky architecture and lively nightlife.

The **Franciscan Friary** by the quays was remodelled in Early English style in Victorian times but retains a 15th-century tower and houses 16th-century Butler tomb effigies. Nearby is O'Connell Street, Clonmel's main shopping street, which is straddled by the West Gate, built in 1831. Visitors to **Hearn's**

Clonmel's mock Tudor West Gate, spanning O'Connell Street

The Swiss Cottage at Cahir, beautifully restored to its original state

Hotel on Parnell Street can see memorabilia of Charles Bianconi (1786 –1875), including pictures of the horse-drawn coach service he established between Clonmel and Cahir. Eventually this developed into a nationwide passenger service.

Carrick-on-Suir ㉔

Road map C5. Co Tipperary.
🏘 5,100. 🚌

THIS SLEEPY MARKET TOWN has a distinctly old-fashioned air. In the 15th century, it was a strategic site commanding access west to Clonmel and southeast to Waterford, but after Tudor times the town sank into oblivion. Apart from Ormond Castle, there are few specific sights. However, you can stroll by the old waterside warehouses or shop for Tipperary Crystal (see p323), which is made nearby.

♠ Ormond Castle
Castle Park. 🕻 051 640787.
◯ Jun–Sep: daily. 🈲 🅖 limited.
Although once a fortress, Ormond Castle is the finest surviving Tudor manor house in Ireland. It was built by the powerful Butler family, the Earls of Ormonde, who were given their title by the English crown in 1328. The castle has a gracious Elizabethan façade overlaying the medieval original; the battlemented towers on the south side sit oddly with the gabled façade and its mullioned and oriel windows.

The finest room is the Long Gallery, which has a stuccoed ceiling studded with heraldic crests, and two ornately carved fireplaces. The Elizabethan section was added by Black Tom Butler, the 10th Earl of Ormonde, a loyal subject to Elizabeth Tudor. On his death, the Ormondes abandoned Carrick for Kilkenny (see pp134 –6).

Intricate wood carving on a four-poster bed at Ormond Castle

ENVIRONS: In the churchyard at **Ahenny**, about 10 km (6 miles) north of Carrick, stand two magnificent High Crosses (see p235). Both are crowned by "caps" or "bishops' mitres" and have intricate cable, spiral and fret patterns.

At **Kilkieran**, 5 km (3 miles) north of Carrick, are three other interesting High Crosses, dating from the 9th century. The Plain Cross is unadorned but capped; the West Cross is profusely ornamented though weathered; the Long Shaft Cross has an odd design of stumpy arms on a long shaft.

THE WEST OF IRELAND

MAYO · GALWAY · ROSCOMMON

T HIS IS THE HEART OF CONNAUGHT, *Ireland's historic western province. The West lives up to its image as a traditional, rural, sparsely populated land, with windswept mountains and countryside speckled with low stone walls and peat bogs. Yet it also encompasses Galway, a fast-growing university town whose youthful population brings life to the medieval streets and snug pubs.*

The rugged Atlantic coastline of the West has been occupied for over 5,000 years. It is rich in prehistoric sites such as the land enclosures of Céide Fields and the ring forts on the Aran Islands. Evidence of the monastic period can be seen in the mysterious and beautiful remains at Kilmacduagh and Clonfert; and the region's religious associations still exert an influence, apparent in the pilgrimages to Knock and Croagh Patrick in County Mayo.

In medieval times, the city of Galway was an Anglo-Norman stronghold, surrounded by warring Gaelic clans. After the Cromwellian victories of the 1640s, many Irish were dispossessed of their fertile lands and dispatched "to hell or Connacht". Landlords made their mark in the 17th and 18th centuries, building impressive country houses at Clonalis, Strokestown Park and Westport. During the Great Famine, the West – especially County Mayo – suffered most from emigration, a trend that continues to this day. In spite of this, strong Gaelic traditions have survived in County Galway, the country's largest Gaeltacht *(see p221)*, where almost half the population speaks Irish as a first language.

The bracken browns and soft violets of Connemara in the west of Galway and the fertile farmland, extensive bogs and placid lakes of County Roscommon are in striking contrast to the magnificent cliff scenery of the remote islands off the coast. This region is often shrouded in a misty drizzle or else battered by Atlantic winds and accompanying heavy downpours.

Summer is a time for festivities: the Galway Races in July, traditional sailing ship races off Kinvarra in August and the Galway Oyster Festival in September are all lively events that attract a stream of visitors.

Swans by the quayside of the Claddagh area of Galway

◁ Typical Connemara landscape dominated by the peaks of the Twelve Bens

Exploring the West of Ireland

GALWAY CITY, CLIFDEN AND WESTPORT make the best bases for exploring the region, with cosy pubs, good walks and access to the scenic islands. Connemara and the wilds of County Mayo attract nature lovers, while the islands of Achill, Aran, Clare and Inishbofin appeal to water-sports enthusiasts and ramblers. The lakes of County Roscommon are popular with anglers, and Lough Corrib and Lough Key offer relaxing cruises.

Decorative stuccowork in Westport House

SEE ALSO

- *Where to Stay* pp295–7

- *Restaurants, Cafés and Pubs* pp313–14 & 320–21

GETTING AROUND

The tiny airport near Rossaveal runs flights to the Aran Islands, which can also be reached by ferry from Rossaveal, Galway or Doolin (County Clare). Ferries run from Cleggan to Inishbofin and Louisburgh to Clare. There is no rail service between Galway and Westport but the towns are linked by reliable (if slow) buses. Connemara is reached by Bus Éireann services from Galway and Clifden (via Oughterard or Cong) or can be explored on day-long minibus tours also from Galway or Clifden.

0 kilometres   20

0 miles   10

River valley at Delphi in northern Connemara

SIGHTS AT A GLANCE

Colourful shopfronts lining
Quay Street, Galway

KEY

▬	Major road
═	Minor road
▬	Scenic route
～	River
☀	Viewpoint

Bogwood centrepiece in Céide Fields interpretative centre

Céide Fields ❶

Road map B2. 8 km (5 miles) W of Ballycastle, Co Mayo. ☎ 096 43325. 🚌 from Ballycastle. ◯ mid-Mar–Nov: daily. 🚻 ♿ ground floor.

Surrounded by heather-clad moorlands and mountains along a bleak, dramatic stretch of north Mayo coastline is Europe's largest Stone Age land enclosure. Over 10 sq km (4 sq miles) were enclosed by walls to make fields suitable for growing wheat and barley, and grazing cattle. Remains of farm buildings indicate that it was an extensive community. The fields were slowly buried below the creeping bog formation, where they have been preserved for 5,000 years.

Part of the bog has been cut away to reveal the collapsed stone walls of the ancient fields. The remains are simple rather than spectacular, but excellent guides help visitors to find and recognize key features. Stone Age pottery and a primitive plough have been found in recent excavations. The striking, pyramid-shaped interpretative centre has a viewing platform overlooking the site, audiovisual presentations and displays on local geology and botany.

ENVIRONS: Scattered around the wilderness of the spectacular north Mayo coast from Ballina to the end of the Mullet peninsula is a series of sculptures forming the **North Mayo Sculpture Trail**. Created by 12 sculptors from three continents, the 15 works, often on a huge scale, are made from earth, stone and other natural materials; additional sculptures are planned. They aim to highlight the coast's grandeur and enduring nature.

Achill Island ❷

Road map A3. Co Mayo. 🚌 from Westport. ℹ Jun–Sep: The Sound (098 45384).

Ireland's largest island, 22 km (13.5 miles) long and 19 km (12 miles) wide, is reached by a road bridge that can be raised for boats to pass through. Achill offers moorland, mountains, rugged cliffs and long beaches, and is a popular spot for angling and water sports.

For motorists, the best introduction is the **Atlantic Coast Drive**, a circular, signposted route from Achill Sound, by the bridge. The road goes to the island's southern tip, then north around the rest of Achill. Between Doeega and Keel in the southwest, run the dramatic Minaun Cliffs and Cathedral Rocks. In the north is Slievemore, a mountain overlooking the village of Slievemore, which was abandoned during the Great Famine *(see p211)*. Sharks can be spotted off Keem Bay in the west.

Westport ❸

Road map B3. Co Mayo. 🏠 3,700. 🚊 🚌 ℹ The Mall (098 25711). 🛒 Thu.

The *Angel of Welcome* above the marble staircase at Westport House

Westport is a neat landlord town and has a prosperous air. In the 1770s, architect James Wyatt laid out the wide, tree-lined streets, including the North and South Mall on either side of Carrowbeg River. The town traded in yarn, cloth, beer and slate, but industrialization and the Great Famine *(see p211)* spelt long-term decline. The trend was reversed only in the 1950s when new industry and visitors were attracted to the area.

Beyond the South Mall is Bridge Street, lined with cafés and pubs; the most appealing is Matt Molloy's *(see p320)*, named after and owned by the flautist from The Chieftains.

🏛 Westport House

Off Louisburgh Rd. ☎ 098 25430. ◯ Easter, May–Sep: daily. 🚻 Just west of the town is the Carrowbeg estuary and Clew Bay. At the head of the bay stands Westport House, the

The deserted village of Slievemore on Achill Island

Statue of St Patrick at the foot of Croagh Patrick, looking out to Clew Bay

seat of the Earls of Altamont, descendants of the Browne family, who were Tudor settlers. The town of Westport itself was started in the 1750s by John Browne, first Lord Altamont, to complement the house. Designed in 1732 by Richard Castle, and completed by James Wyatt in 1778, the limestone mansion stands on the site of an O'Malley castle. Its imposing interior includes a sweeping marble staircase and an elegant James Wyatt dining room and is adorned with family portraits, antique Waterford chandeliers and 18th-century Chinese wallpaper. Recently the estate has become heavily commercialized, with a small boating lake, miniature railway, children's zoo, an amusement arcade and several shops.

Bog oak and silver bowl from Westport House

Foxford 4

Road map B3. Co Mayo. ▓ 1,000. ⊟ from Galway. ⓘ Westport (098 25711).

THIS TRANQUIL market town is known for good angling in nearby Lough Conn and for its woven rugs and tweeds. In the town centre is **Foxford Woollen Mills**, founded in 1892 by an Irish nun, Mother Arsenius (originally named Agnes). The thriving mill now supplies top fashion houses. An audiovisual tour traces the mill's history, and visitors can see craftspeople at work.

Foxford Woollen Mills and Visitor Centre

St Joseph's Place. ⓘ 094 56756. ◯ daily. ● Good Fri, 24–26 Dec. ▨ ▥

Knock 5

Road map B3. Co Mayo. ▓ 440. ✈ 15 km (9 miles) N of Knock. ⊟ ⓘ May–Sep: Knock (094 88193).

IN 1879, two local women saw an apparition of the Virgin, St Joseph and St John the Evangelist by the gable of the Church of St John the Baptist. It was witnessed by 13 more onlookers and validated by the Catholic Church amid claims of miracle cures. Every year, a million and a half believers make the pilgrimage to the shrine, including Pope John Paul II in 1979 and Mother Teresa in 1993. Its focal point is the gable where the apparition was seen, which is now covered over to form a chapel. Nearby is the Basilica of Our Lady, a modern basilica and Marian

Bottles of holy water for sale at the shrine in Knock

shrine. **Knock Folk Museum**, beside the basilica, portrays life in 19th-century rural Ireland with reconstructions of a cottage and schoolroom. An Apparition section covers the background to the miracle.

🏛 Knock Shrine and Folk Museum

ⓘ 094 88100. ◯ May–Oct: daily; Nov–Apr: by appt. ▨ ▥

Croagh Patrick 6

Road map B3. Murrisk, Co Mayo. ⊟ from Westport.

IRELAND'S holy mountain, named after the national saint (see p273), is one of Mayo's best-known landmarks. From the bottom it seems cone-shaped, an impression dispelled by climbing to its flat peak. This quartzite, scree-clad mountain has a history of pagan worship from 3000 BC. However, in AD 441, St Patrick is said to have spent 40 days on the mountain fasting and praying for the Irish.

Since then, penitents, often barefoot, have made the pilgrimage to the summit in his honour, especially on Reek or Garland Sunday, the last in July. From the start of the trail at Campbell's Pub in Murrisk, where there is huge statue of the saint, it is a two-hour climb to the top, at 765 m (2,510 ft). Mass is celebrated in the modern chapel. There are also panoramic views over Clew Bay. Recently, there have been proposals to mine for gold and bauxite on the mountain.

Clare Island ❼

Road map A3. Co Mayo. 👥 *180.* ⛴
from Roonagh Quay, 6.5 km (4 miles)
W of Louisburgh. ℹ *Westport.*

CLARE ISLAND, set in Clew
Bay, is dominated by two
hills, and a square 15th-
century castle commands the
headland and harbour. In the
16th century the island was
the stronghold of Grace
O'Malley, pirate queen and
patriot, who held sway over
the western coast. Although,
according to Tudor state
papers, she was received at
Queen Elizabeth I's court, she
stood out against English rule
until her death in her seventies
in 1603. She is buried here in
a tiny Cistercian abbey decorated with medieval murals
and inscribed with her motto:
"Invincible on land and sea".

The island is dotted with Iron
Age huts and field systems as
well as promontory forts and
Bronze Age cooking sites *(see
p162)*. Clare is rich in bog
flora and fauna, making it
popular with walkers. Animal
lovers come to see the seals,
dolphins, falcons and otters.

ENVIRONS: The mainland coastal
village of **Louisburgh** offers
rugged Atlantic landscape,
sheltered coves, sea angling

The ferry to Inishbofin leaving Cleggan Harbour

and water sports. It is also
home to the **Granuaile Centre**
which celebrates the exploits
of Grace O'Malley (*Granuaile*
in Gaelic) and has displays on
Mayo folklore and archaeology.

🏛 **Granuaile Centre**
St Catherine's Church, Louisburgh.
【 *098 66195.* ◯ *May–Oct: daily.*
🖼 🕭

Inishbofin ❽

Road map A3. Co Galway. 👥 *200.*
⛴ *from Cleggan.* ℹ *Clifden.*

THE NAME Inishbofin means
"island of the white cow".
This mysterious, often mist-
swathed island was chosen
for its remoteness by the
exiled 7th-century St Colman,
English Abbot of Lindisfarne.
On the site of his original
monastery is a late medieval
church, graveyard and holy
well. At the sheltered harbour

entrance lies a ruined castle,
occupied in the 16th century
by Spanish pirate Don Bosco
in alliance with Grace O'Malley.
In 1653 it was captured by
Cromwellian forces and used
as a prison for Catholic priests.
Inishbofin was later owned
by a succession of absentee
landlords and now survives
on farming and lobster-fishing.

Surrounded by reefs and
islets, the island's landscape is
characterized by stone walls,
small abandoned cottages,
reed-fringed lakes and hay
meadows, where the corn-
crake *(see p16)* can be seen,
or heard. Inishbofin's beaches
offer bracing walks.

Clifden ❾

Road map A3. Co Galway. 👥 *800.*
🚏 ℹ *May–Sep: Market St (095
21163).* 🚌 *Tue.*

FRAMED by the grandeur of
the Twelve Bens mountain
range and with a striking
skyline dominated by two
church spires, this early 19th-
century market town passes
for the capital of the Connemara region and is a good
base for exploring. Clifden
was founded in 1812 by John
d'Arcy, a local landowner and
High Sheriff of Galway, to
create a pocket of respect-
ability within the lawlessness
of Connemara. The family
eventually went bankrupt
trying to bring prosperity and
order to the town. The Protestant church contains a copy
of the Cross of Cong *(see p65)*.

Today craft shops have
taken over much of the town.
In the centre is the Square, a
place for lively pubs such as
EJ Kings *(see p320)*. Nearby is
O'Grady's Seafood Restaurant
(see p313), one of the finest
in Galway. Connemara is
noted for its *sean-nos*

Clifden against a backdrop of the Twelve Bens mountains

CONNEMARA

This wild region in the west of Galway encompasses bogs, mountains and a rugged coastline. Major sights include the Connemara National Park and Kylemore Abbey *(see p200)*. For those without a car, coach tours are available from Galway and Clifden *(see p360)*.

Cottage in Connemara

KEY

▬▬	Major road
═══	Regional road
═══	Minor road
───	National Park boundary
⛴	Ferry to Inishbofin
ℹ	Tourist information
☀	Viewpoint

0 kilometres   10

0 miles   5

(unaccompanied singing), but in Clifden, general traditional music is more common.

Jutting out into **Clifden Bay** is a sand spit and beach, signposted from Clifden Square. South of Clifden, at the start of the Roundstone Road, is Owenglen Cascade where, in May, salmon leap on their way to spawn upstream.

ENVIRONS: The **Sky Road** is an 11-km (7-mile) circular route with stunning ocean views. The road goes northwest from Clifden and passes desolate scenery and the narrow inlet of Clifden Bay. Clifden Castle, John d'Arcy's Gothic Revival ruin, lies just off the Sky Road, as do several beaches.

The coastal road north from Clifden to **Cleggan**, via Claddaghduff, is spectacular, passing former smuggling coves. Cleggan, an attractive fishing village, nestles into the head of Cleggan Bay. From here boats leave for Inishbofin and Inishturk. **Cleggan Hill** has a ruined Napoleonic Martello tower at the top and a megalithic tomb at the foot.

To the south of Clifden, the coastal route to Roundstone skirts a mass of bogland pitted with tiny lakes. The **Alcock and Brown Memorial** overlooks the bog landing site of the first transatlantic flight made by Alcock and Brown in 1919. Nearby is Marconi's wireless station, which exchanged the first transatlantic radio messages with Nova Scotia in 1907. The **Ballyconneely** area has craggy islands and the beautiful **Coral Strand Beach**. The village of **Roundstone** is best seen during the summer regatta of traditional Galway hookers *(see p203)*.

A short drive to the east of Clifden is **Dan O'Hara's Homestead**. In a wild, rocky setting, this organic farm recreates the tough conditions of life in Connemara before the 1840s. The folksy air of Connemara is accentuated by pony and trap rides and traditional music.

🏛 Dan O'Hara's Homestead
Heritage Centre, Lettershea, off N59.
📞 095 21246. ⚪ end Mar–end Oct: daily. 🅿

View of the coast from the Sky Road

The imposing Kylemore Abbey on the shores of Kylemore Lough

Kylemore Abbey ⑩

Road map A3. Connemara, Co Galway. (*095 41113.* 🚌 *from Galway and Clifden.* ◯ *Mar–Oct: daily.* 🎫 🚻 *limited.*

SHELTERED BY THE SLOPES of the Twelve Bens, this lakeside castle is a romantic, battlemented Gothic Revival fantasy. It was built as a present for his wife by Mitchell Henry (1826–1911), who was a Manchester tycoon and later Galway MP. The Henrys also purchased a huge area of moorland, drained the boggy hillside and planted thousands of trees as a windbreak for their new orchards and exotic walled gardens. After the sudden deaths of his wife and daughter, Henry left Kylemore and the castle was sold.

It became an abbey when Benedictine nuns, fleeing from Ypres in Belgium during World War I, sought refuge here. The nuns now run the abbey as a select girls' boarding school. Visitors are restricted to the grounds, restaurant and craft shop where they can watch the abbey pottery being hand-decorated and fired. The cream earthenware pottery is painted with a fuchsia motif.

In the grounds, rhododendrons and fuchsias enhance lakeside walks. By the lakeshore stands a Neo-Gothic chapel, a miniature copy of Norwich Cathedral.

Connemara National Park ⑪

Road map A3. Letterfrack, Connemara, Co Galway. (*095 41054.* **Visitors' Centre** ◯ *May–Sep: daily.* 🎫 🚻

A COMBINATION of bogland, lakes and mountains makes up this National Park in the heart of Connemara. Within its more than 2,000 ha (5,000 acres) are four of the Twelve Bens, including Benbaun, the highest mountain in the range at 730 m (2,400 ft), and the peak of Diamond Hill. At the centre is the valley of Glanmore with the Polladirk River flowing through it.

Visitors come for some of the most spectacular landscape in the region and to glimpse the famous Connemara ponies.

Part of the land originally belonged to the Kylemore Abbey estate. In 1980 it became a National Park. There are traces of the land's previous uses all over the park: megalithic tombs, up to 4,000 years old, can be seen as well as old ridges marking former grazing areas and arable fields.

The park is open all year, while the Visitors' Centre near the entrance, just outside Letterfrack, is open only in the summer months. It has displays on how the landscape developed and was used and on local flora and fauna. There is also an audiovisual theatre and an indoor picnic area. Two signposted walks start from the Visitors' Centre. In summer there are guided walks, some led by botanists, and various children's activities. Climbing the Twelve Bens should be attempted only by experienced walkers equipped for all weather conditions.

CONNEMARA WILDLIFE

The blanket bogs and moorlands of Connemara are a botanist's paradise, especially for unusual bog and heathland plants. Birdlife is also varied with hooded crows, which can be recognized by their grey and black plumage, stonechats, peregrines and merlins – the smallest falcons in the British Isles. Red deer have been successfully reintroduced into the area and a herd can be seen in the National Park. Badgers, foxes, stoats and otters may also be spotted, as well as grey seals along the rocky coast.

The merlin *nests in old clumps of heather and feeds mainly on small birds.*

St Dabeoc's heath, *a pretty heather, grows nowhere else in Ireland or Great Britain.*

Cong ⑫

Road map B3. Co Mayo. 🚶 *200.*
🚌 ℹ️ *Galway (091 563081).*

THIS PICTURESQUE VILLAGE lies on the shores of Lough Corrib, just within County Mayo. Cong means isthmus – the village lies on the strip of land between Lough Corrib and Lough Mask. During the 1840s, as a famine relief project, a canal was built linking the two lakes, but the water drained through the porous limestone bed. Stone bridges and stone-clad locks are still in place along the dry canal.

Cong Abbey lies close to the main street. The Augustinian abbey was founded in the early 12th century by Turlough O'Connor, King of Connaught and High King of Ireland, on the site of a 6th-century monastery established by St Fechin. The abbey has doorways in a style transitional between Romanesque and Gothic, stone carvings and restored cloisters. The Cross of Cong, an ornate processional cross intended for the abbey, is now in Dublin's National Museum *(see pp64–5)*. The most fascinating remains are the Gothic chapter house, stone bridges and the monks' fishing-house overhanging the river – the monks devised a system so that a bell rang in the kitchen when a fish took the bait.

Carved 12th-century doorway of Cong Abbey

Just south of Cong is **Ashford Castle**, rebuilt in Gothic Revival style in 1870 by Lord Ardilaun of the Guinness family. One of Ireland's best hotels *(see p284)*, its grounds can be visited by boat from Galway and Oughterard. Cong was the setting for *The Quiet Man*, the 1950s' film starring John Wayne. "Quiet Man" tours cover locations near the castle.

Lough Corrib ⑬

Road map B3. Co Galway. 🚌 *from Galway and Cong.* 🚢 *from Oughterard and Wood Quay, Galway.* ℹ️ *Oughterard (091 552808).*

AN ANGLER'S PARADISE, Lough Corrib offers the chance to fish with local fishermen for brown trout, salmon, pike, perch and eels. Despite its proximity to Galway, the lake is a haven of tranquillity, dotted with uninhabited islands and framed by meadows, reed-beds and wooded shores. The waterside is home to swans and coots. On **Inchagoill**, one of the largest islands, stand the ruins of an early Christian monastic settlement and a Romanesque church.

The lake's atmosphere is best appreciated on a cruise. From Galway, the standard short cruise winds through the marshes to the site of an Iron Age fort, limestone

View over Lough Corrib from the shore northwest of Oughterard

quarries and the battlemented Menlo Castle. Longer cruises continue to Cong or include picnics on the islands.

ENVIRONS: On the banks of Lough Corrib, **Oughterard** is known as "the gateway to Connemara". The village has craft shops, thatched cottages and friendly pubs. It is also an important centre for golf, angling, hiking and pony trekking. Other country pursuits include riverside walks, a stroll to a waterfall west of the village and cycle rides.

About 4 km (2.5 miles) southeast of Oughterard (off the N59) is **Aughnanure Castle**. This well-restored six-storey tower house clings to a rocky island on the River Drimneen. The present castle, built by the O'Flaherty clan, is on the site of one dating from 1256. The clan controlled West Connaught from Lough Corrib to Galway and the coast in the 13th to 16th centuries. From this castle the feuding O'Flaherty chieftains held out against the British in the 16th century. In 1545 Donal O'Flaherty married the pirate Grace O'Malley *(see p198)*. The tower house has an unusual double bawn *(see p18)* and a murder hole from which missiles could be dropped on invaders.

♣ **Aughnanure Castle**
Oughterard. 🔲 *091 522214.*
⭕ *mid-Jun–mid-Sep: daily.* 💷
♿ *limited.*

Connemara ponies *roam semi-wild and are fabled to be from Arab stock that came ashore from Spanish Armada wrecks.*

Fuchsias *grow profusely in the hedgerows of Connemara, thriving in the mild climate.*

Galway ⑭

Sign with Claddagh ring design

GALWAY IS BOTH THE CENTRE for the Irish-speaking regions in the West and a lively university city. Under the Anglo-Normans, it flourished as a trading post. In 1396 it gained a Royal Charter and, for the next two centuries, was controlled by 14 merchant families, or "tribes". The city prospered under English influence, but this allegiance to the Crown cost Galway dear when, in 1652, Cromwell's forces wreaked havoc. After the Battle of the Boyne *(see p236)*, Galway fell into decline, unable to compete with east-coast trade. In recent years, as a developing centre for high-tech industry, the city's profile has been revived.

Inside The Quays seafood restaurant and pub

Houses on the banks of the Corrib

Exploring Galway

The centre of the city lies on the banks of the River Corrib, which flows down from Lough Corrib *(see p201)* widening out as it reaches Galway Bay. Urban renewal since the 1970s has led to extensive restoration of the narrow, winding streets of this once-walled city. Due to its compact size, Galway is easy to explore on foot, and a leisurely pace provides plenty of opportunity to stop off at its shops, pubs and historic sights.

Eyre Square

The square encloses a pleasant park lined with imposing, mainly 19th-century, buildings. On the northwest of the square is the **Browne Doorway**, a 17th-century entrance from a mansion in Abbeygate Street Lower. Beside it are two cannons from the Crimean War and a fountain adorned with a sculpture of a Galway hooker boat. The **Eyre Square Centre**, overlooking the park, is a modern shopping mall built to incorporate sections of the historic city walls. Walkways link Shoemakers and Penrice towers, two of the wall towers that used to ring the city in the 17th century.

Lynch family crest on Lynch's Castle

Latin Quarter

From Eyre Square, William Street and Shop Street are the main routes into the bustling "Latin Quarter". On the corner of Abbeygate Street Upper and Shop Street stands **Lynch's Castle**, now a bank, but still the grandest 16th-century town house in Galway. It was owned by the Lynch family, one of the 14 "tribes".

A side street leads to the **Collegiate Church of St Nicholas**, Galway's finest medieval building. The church, founded in 1320, was extended in the 15th and 16th centuries, but then damaged by the Cromwellians, who used it to stable horses. The west porch is from the 15th century and there are some finely carved gargoyles under the parapet.

Quay Street is lined with restaurants and pubs, including **The Quays** *(see p320)*. Tí Neachtain is a town house which belonged to "Humanity Dick", an 18th-century MP who promoted laws against cruelty to animals. Today, it too is a restaurant and pub *(see p320)*. Nearby are the Taibhdhearc and Druid theatres *(see p328)*.

North Galway

The **Cathedral of St Nicholas** (1965), made from local limestone and Connemara marble, stands on the west bank. From here you can see Wood Quay, where Lough Corrib cruises start *(see p201)*. **University College Galway**, further west,

Outside dining at one of the cosmopolitan cafés in Shop Street

GALWAY HOOKERS

Galway's traditional wooden sailing boats, featured on the city's coat of arms, were known as *pucans* and *gleotogs* – hookers in English. They have broad black hulls, thick masts and white or rust-coloured sails. Once common in the Claddagh district, they were also used along the Atlantic coast to ferry peat, cattle and beer. Hookers can be seen in action at the Cruinniú na mBád festival in Kinvarra *(see p204).*

Small Galway hooker sailing by the old quays and Spanish Arch

VISITORS' CHECKLIST

Road map B4. Co Galway. 52,000. ✈ Carnmore, 11 km (7 miles) NE of Galway. 🚆 Ceannt Station (091 564222). 🚌 Ceannt Station (091 562000). ℹ Victoria Place, Eyre Square (091 563081). 🛍 Sat. 🎭 Galway Arts Festival (late Jul); Galway Races (late Jul); Galway Oyster Festival (late Sep).

is a sprawling campus with a 1849 Gothic Revival quad. Salmon Weir Bridge links the two banks. Shoals of salmon rest under the bridge on their way upstream to spawn.

The Old Quays
The **Spanish Arch**, where the river opens out, was built in 1584 to protect the harbour, which was then outside the city walls. Here, Spanish traders unloaded their ships. The old quays are a tranquil spot for a stroll down the Long Walk to the docks.

The Claddagh
Beyond the Spanish Arch, on the west bank of the Corrib, lies the Claddagh. The name comes from *An Cladach*, meaning "flat, stony shore". From medieval times, this fiercely independent fishing community beyond the city walls was governed by a "king" or "mayor", the last of whom died in 1954. The only remnants of this once close-knit, Gaelic-speaking community

are friendly pubs and Claddagh rings, betrothal rings traditionally handed down from mother to daughter *(see p326).*

ENVIRONS: Just west of the city is **Salthill**, Galway's seaside resort. The beaches at Palmer's Rock and Grattan Road are particularly popular with families in summer. A bracing walk along the promenade is still a Galway tradition.

Spanish Arch on the site of the former docks

GALWAY CITY CENTRE

Browne Doorway ④
Cathedral of
  St Nicholas ①
The Claddagh ⑦
Collegiate Church of
  St Nicholas ②
Lynch's Castle ③
The Quays ⑤
Spanish Arch ⑥

KEY

🚆	Railway station
🚌	Coach station
🅿	Parking
ℹ	Tourist information
⌣	Weir

0 metres   200

0 yards   200

Mural in the centre of Kinvarra depicting a shopfront

Aran Islands **⑮**

See pp206–7.

Kinvarra **⑯**

Road map B4. Co Galway. 🚶 430.
🚌 ℹ️ *Galway (091 563081).*

ONE OF the most charming fishing villages on Galway Bay, Kinvarra's appeal lies in its sheltered, seaweed-clad harbour and traditional seafaring atmosphere. From medieval times, its fortunes were closely linked to Kilmacduagh, the powerful monastery and bishopric upon which the village depended.

The pier is bordered by a row of fishermen's cottages. Kinvarra remains a popular port of call for sailors of traditional Galway hookers *(see p203)* and is known for the Cruinniú na mBád (gathering of the boats) festival in August. Rambles include historical and nature trails. Bird-watchers may spot teal, curlews and oystercatchers by the shore.

ENVIRONS: North of Kinvarra, on a promontory on the shore of Galway Bay, lies **Dunguaire Castle**. It is perched just beyond some quaint thatched cottages and a stone bridge. The castle is named after the 7th-century King Guaire of Connaught, whose court here was renowned as the haunt of bards and balladeers. Although the medieval earthworks survive, the present castle was built in the 16th century, a quintessential tower house *(see p18)* with sophisticated machicolations. The banqueting hall is still used for "medieval banquets" with Celtic harp music and the poetry of Yeats.

🏰 **Dunguaire Castle**
📞 *091 37108.* ⬜ *mid-Apr–Sep: daily.* 🎦

Kilmacduagh **⑰**

Road map B4. Outside Gort on Corofin Rd, Co Galway. 🚌 *to Gort.* ⬜ *daily.*

THIS MONASTIC SETTLEMENT is in a remote location on the borders of Counties Clare and Galway, roughly 5 km (3 miles) southwest of Gort. The sense of isolation is accentuated by the stony moonscape of the Burren to the west *(see pp178–80).* Reputedly founded by St Colman MacDuagh in the early 7th century, Kilmacduagh owes more to the monastic revival which led to rebuilding from the 11th century onwards.

The centrepiece of the extensive site is a large, slightly leaning 11th- or 12th-century round tower and a roofless church, known as the cathedral or Teampall. The cathedral is a pre-Norman structure, which was later remodelled in Gothic style, with flamboyant tracery and fine tomb carvings. In the surrounding fields lie the remains of several other churches that once depended on the monastery. To the northeast of the Teampall is the late medieval Glebe or Abbot's House, a variant of a 14th- or 15th-century tower house *(see p18).*

Thoor Ballylee **⑱**

Road map B4. Gort, Co Galway.
📞 *091 631436.* 🚌 *to Gort.* ⬜ *Apr–Oct: daily.* 🎦 ♿ *limited.*

FOR MUCH of the 1920s, this beguiling tower house was a summer home to the poet WB Yeats *(see pp20–21).* Yeats was a regular visitor to nearby Coole Park, the home of his friend Lady Gregory (1852–1932), who was a cofounder of the Abbey Theatre *(see p86).*

On one visit Yeats came upon Ballylee Castle, a 14th-century de Burgo tower adjoining a cosy cottage with a walled garden and stream. In 1902, both the tower and the cottage became part of the Gregory estate and Yeats bought them in 1916. From 1919 onwards, his family divided their time between

Round tower and cathedral, the most impressive monastic remains at Kilmacduagh

Dublin and their Galway tower. Yeats used the name Thoor Ballylee as the address, using the Irish word for tower to "keep people from suspecting us of modern gothic and a deer park". His collection, *The Tower* (1928), includes several poems inspired by Thoor Ballylee.

Today, the audiovisual tour includes readings from Yeats's poetry, but the charm of a visit lies in the tower itself, with its spiral stone steps and views from the battlements over forest and farmland.

ENVIRONS: Just to the north of Gort is **Coole Park**, once the home of Lady Gregory. Although the house was demolished in the 1950s, the estate farm has been restored and the fine gardens survive. In particular, there is the "autograph tree", a spreading copper beech carved with the initials of George Bernard Shaw, JM Synge *(see pp20–21)*, Jack Yeats *(see p68)* and other famous visitors. In the farm buildings is an audiovisual display. The emphasis of the visitors' centre is on natural history: it is the start of two signposted walks, one around the gardens and the other through beech, hazel, birch and ash woodland to Coole Lake.

Coole Park
3 km (2 miles) NE of Gort. 091 631804. mid-Apr–mid-Jun: Tue–Sun; mid-Jun–end Aug: daily. limited.

Gentle hills and woodland by Coole Lake in Coole Park

Thoor Ballylee tower house, the summer home of WB Yeats

Portumna ⑲

Road map C4. Co Galway. 1,000. Galway (091 563081). Fri.

PORTUMNA is a historic market town with scattered sights, many of which are newly restored. Situated on Lough Derg, it is a convenient base for cruising the River Shannon *(see p177)* and has a modern marina. **Portumna Castle**, built in the early 17th century, was the main seat of the de Burgo family. Now partially restored, it has a symmetrical façade and some elaborate interior stonework. The façade surveys formal gardens. Near the castle is **Portumna Priory**. Most of the remains date from around 1414 when the priory was founded by the Dominicans, but traces can also be found of the Cistercian abbey that was previously on the site. The large de Burgo estate to the west of the town now forms **Portumna Forest Park**, with picnic sites and signposted woodland trails leading to Lough Derg.

Clonfert Cathedral ⑳

Road map C4. Clonfert, Co Galway. daily.

SITUATED near a bleak stretch of the Shannon bordering the boglands of the Midlands, Clonfert is one of the jewels of Irish-Romanesque architecture.

Human heads carved on the tympanum at Clonfert Cathedral

The tiny cathedral occupies the site of a monastery, which was founded by St Brendan in AD 563, and is believed to be the burial place of the saint.

Although a great scholar and enthusiastic founder of monasteries, St Brendan is best known as the "great navigator". His journeys are recounted in *Navigatio Sancti Brendani*, written in about 1050, which survives in medieval manuscripts including Flemish, Norse and French. The account seems to describe a voyage to Wales, the Orkneys, Iceland and conceivably the east coast of North America. His voyage and his boat *(see p182)*, have been re-created by modern explorers in an attempt to prove that St Brendan may have preceded Columbus by about 900 years.

The highlight of Clonfert is its intricately sculpted sandstone doorway. The round arch above the door is decorated with animal and human heads, geometrical shapes, foliage and symbolic motifs. The carvings on the triangular tympanum above the arch are of strange human heads. In the chancel, the 13th-century east windows are fine examples of late Irish-Romanesque art. The 15th-century chancel arch is adorned with sculptures of angels and a mermaid. Although Clonfert was built over several centuries and altered in the 17th century, the church has a profound sense of unity.

Aran Islands ⑮

Jaunting car on Inishmore

INISHMORE, INISHMAAN and Inisheer, the three Aran Islands, are formed from a limestone ridge. The largest, Inishmore, is 13 km (8 miles) long and 3 km (2 miles) wide. The attractions of these islands include the austere landscape crisscrossed with dry-stone walls, stunning coastal views and several large prehistoric stone forts. In the 5th century, St Enda brought Christianity to the islands, starting a long monastic tradition. Protected for centuries by their isolated position, the islands today are a bastion of traditional Irish culture. Farming, fishing and tourism are the main occupations of the islanders.

Looking over the cliff edge at Dún Aonghasa

Clochán na Carraige is a large, well-preserved beehive hut (see p19), probably built by early Christian settlers on the islands.

The Seven Churches
(Na Seacht dTeampaill)

Clochán na Carraige

Dún Eoghanachta

Dún Eoghanachta is a 1st-century BC circular stone fort with a single wall terraced on the inside.

Dun Aengus
(Dún Aonghasa)

KILMURVY
(Cill Mhuirbh)

I N I S H M O R E

Na Seacht dTeampaill
The so-called Seven Churches make up a monastic settlement dedicated to St Brecan. Built between the 9th and 15th centuries, some are probably domestic buildings.

★ Dún Aonghasa
This Iron or Bronze Age promontory fort (see p18), has four concentric stone walls. It is also protected by a chevaux de frise, a ring of razor-sharp, pointed stone stakes.

ARAN TRADITIONS

Colourful Aran costume

The islands are famous for their distinctive knitwear (see p324) and for the traditional Aran costume that is still worn: for women this consists of a red flannel skirt and crocheted shawl; for men it includes a sleeveless tweed jacket and a colourful knitted belt. From time to time you also see a *currach* or low rowing boat, the principal form of transport for centuries. Land-making, the ancient and arduous process of creating soil by covering bare rock with sand and seaweed, continues to this day.

Currach made from canvas coated in tar

FERRY ROUTES TO THE ARAN ISLANDS

THE WEST OF IRELAND

Rossaveal
Inverin
GALWAY
GALWAY BAY

Kilronan
INISHMORE
INISHMAAN
ARAN
ISLANDS
INISHEER
THE LOWER SHANNON
Doolin

VISITORS' CHECKLIST

Road map A4, B4. Co Galway. 1,500. from Connemara Airport, Inverin (091 593034). from Rossaveal: **Island Ferries** (091 561767), from Galway: **O'Brien Shipping** (091 567676), Aran Ferries; from Doolin: **Doolin Ferry Company** (065 74455) (summer only). Ferries depart at least once daily in winter, several times daily in summer; some go to all three main islands. Phone for details. Cars cannot be taken to the islands. From Kilronan, you can hire bicycles and jaunting cars, or go on minibus tours (099 61169). May–Sep: Kilronan, Inishmore (099 61263). **Aran Heritage Centre** Kilronan. 099 61355. Jun–Aug: 10am–7pm daily; Apr, May, Sep & Oct: 11am–5pm daily.

Kilmurvy Beach

The attractive sandy beach east of Kilmurvy offers safe swimming in a sheltered cove. The town itself is a quiet place to stay near a number of the island's most important sights.

Teampall Chiaráin, dedicated to St Ciaran, is a ruined 12th-century church with striking doorways. Nearby are several stones inscribed with crosses.

Teampall Chiaráin
Dún Eochla
KILRONAN (Cill Rónáin)
Dún Duchathair

I n i s
M ó r

Dún Eochla is a circular Bronze Age fort standing close to the highest point on Inishmore.

★ Kilronan

The Aran Islands' main port is a busy place, with jaunting cars (ponies and traps) and minibuses waiting by the pier to give island tours; bicycles can also be hired. Nearby, the fascinating Aran Heritage Centre is dedicated to the disappearing Aran way of life.

KEY

▬▬	Main road
▬▬	Minor road
---	Track
▦	Beach
✕	Airport
⚓	Ferry service
ℹ	Tourist information
☼	Viewpoint

0 kilometres   2

0 miles   1

★ Dún Duchathair

Built on a headland, this Iron Age construction is known as the Black Fort. It has dry-stone ramparts.

STAR SIGHTS

★ Kilronan

★ Dún Aonghasa

★ Dún Duchathair

Farmer on Inishmore, largest of the Aran Islands ▷

East wall and gatehouse at Roscommon Castle

Turoe Stone ㉑

Road map B4. Turoe, Bullaun, Loughrea, Co Galway. **(** 091 841580. ◯ Apr–Oct: daily; Nov–Mar: groups by appt. 🖾 🖾 🖵

THE TUROE STONE stands at the centre of a large area of parkland, the Turoe Pet Farm and Leisure Park, near the village of Bullaun (on the R350). The white granite boulder, which stands about 1 m (3 ft) high, dates back to the 3rd or 2nd century BC. Its top half is carved with curvilinear designs in a graceful Celtic style, known as La Tène, also found in Celtic parts of Europe, particularly Brittany. The lower half has a smooth section and a band of step-pattern carving. The stone was originally found at an Iron Age ring fort nearby, and is thought to have been used there in fertility rituals.

The park around the Turoe Stone is designed mainly for children. The Pet Farm has some small fields containing farm animals and a pond with several varieties of ducks and geese. There is also a wooded

The Celtic Turoe Stone carved with graceful swirling patterns

riverside walk (wear heavy shoes or walking boots as it's often muddy), a picnic area, tea rooms and a playground.

Roscommon ㉒

Road map C3. Co Roscommon. 🚶 3,500. 🚌 🚏 🛈 Jun–Sep: Harrison Hall (0903 26342). 🖾 Fri.

THE COUNTY CAPITAL is a busy market town with scattered sights. In Main Street is the former gaol, celebrated for having a woman as its last executioner. "Lady Betty", as she came to be known, was sentenced to death for the murder of her son in 1780, but negotiated a pardon by agreeing to become a hangwoman. She continued for 30 years.

South of the town centre, just off Abbey Street, is the **Dominican Friary**, founded in 1253 by Felim O'Conor, King of Connaught. Set in the north wall of the choir is a late 13th-century effigy of the founder.

Roscommon Castle, an Anglo-Norman fortress north of the town, was built in 1269 by Robert d'Ufford, Lord Justice of Ireland, and rebuilt 11 years later after being destroyed by the Irish led by Hugh O'Conor, King of Connaught. The rectangular castle has 16th-century mullioned windows.

Clonalis House ㉓

Road map B3. Castlerea, Co Roscommon. **(** 0907 20014. ◯ Jun–mid-Sep: Tue–Sun. 🖾 🖾 ground floor.

THIS VICTORIAN manor just outside Castlerea is the ancestral home of the O'Conors, the last High Kings of Ireland

and Kings of Connaught. This old Gaelic family can trace its heritage back 1,500 years. The ruins of their gabled 17th-century home are visible in the grounds. On the lawn lies the O'Conor inauguration stone, dating from 90 BC.

The interior includes a Venetian hallway, a library of many books and documents recording Irish history, a tiny private chapel and a gallery of family portraits spanning 500 years. In the billiard room is the harp once played by Turlough O'Carolan (1670–1738), blind harpist and last of the Gaelic bards *(see p22)*.

Strokestown Park House ㉔

Road map C3. Strokestown, Co Roscommon. 🏠 **House and Museum**. **(** 078 33013. ◯ Easter–Oct: Tue–Sun; Nov–Easter: by appt. 🖾 🖾 museum only.

STROKESTOWN PARK HOUSE, the greatest Palladian mansion in County Roscommon, was built in the 1730s for Thomas Mahon, an MP whose family was granted the lands by Charles II after the Restoration. It incorporates an earlier 17th-century tower house *(see p18)*. The design of the new house owes most to Richard Castle, architect of Russborough *(see p124)*. The galleried kitchen, panelled stairwell and groin-vaulted stables are undoubtedly his work, tailoring Palladian principles to the requirements of the Anglo-Irish gentry.

The house stayed in the family's hands until 1979, when major restoration began. In its heyday, the estate included ornamental parkland, a deer park, folly, mausoleum and the town of Roscommon itself. By 1979, the estate's original 12,000 ha (30,000 acres) had dwindled to 120 ha (300 acres), but recent replanting restores a sense of spaciousness. The original decor and furnishings of the house are intact.

Set in the stable yards, the **Famine Museum** commemorates the 1840s Famine. During the crisis, landlords divided into two camps: the charitable, some of whom started up Famine Relief schemes, and the callous, like the Mahons of Strokestown. Major Denis Mahon, landlord in the 1840s, was murdered after forcing two-thirds of the starving peasantry off his land by a combination of eviction and assisted passages in "coffin ships" to North America. The exhibition uses the Strokestown archives to tell the story of tenants and landlords during the Famine. A section deals with continuing famine and malnutrition worldwide.

Boyle ㉕

Road map C3. Co Roscommon.
👥 2,200. 🚌 ℹ️ Jun–mid-Sep:
The Courthouse, Market Street (079 62145). 🛒 Fri.

COUNTY ROSCOMMON'S most charming town, Boyle is blessed with fine Georgian and medieval architecture. **Boyle Abbey** is a well-preserved Cistercian abbey founded in 1161 as a sister house to Mellifont in County Louth (see p237). It survived raids by Anglo-Norman barons and Irish chieftains, as well as the 1539 suppression of the

THE GREAT FAMINE

The failure of the Irish potato crop in 1845, 1846 and 1848, due to potato blight, had disastrous consequences for the people of Ireland, many of whom relied on this staple crop. More than a million died of starvation and disease, and by 1856 over two and a half million had been forced to emigrate. The crisis was worsened by unsympathetic landlords who often continued collecting rents. The Famine had far-reaching effects: mass emigration became a way of life (see pp40–41) and many rural communities, particularly in the far west, were decimated.

Peasants queuing for soup during the Famine (1847)

monasteries. In 1659 it was turned into a castle. The abbey is still remarkably intact, with a church, cloisters, cellars, sacristy and even kitchens. The nave of the church has both Romanesque and Gothic arches and there are well-preserved 12th-century capitals. The visitors' centre is housed in the old gatehouse.

King House, a Palladian mansion near the centre of town, is the ancestral home of the Anglo-Irish King family, later Earls of Kingston. Inside is a contemporary art gallery, as well as displays covering various subjects, such as Georgian architecture and the mansion's restoration, the history of the surrounding area and the Connaught chieftains.

Carved capital in the nave at Boyle Abbey

🏛 **Boyle Abbey**
⭕ mid-May–Oct: daily. 🎟
🏛 **King House**
Main St. 📞 079 63242. ⭕ May–Sep: Tue–Sun; Apr & Oct: Sat & Sun. 🎟

ENVIRONS: Lough Key is often called the loveliest lake in Ireland. The island-studded lake and surrounding woodland make a glorious setting for the **Lough Key Forest Park**. The 320-ha (790-acre) park formed part of the Rockingham estate until 1957. In that year Rockingham House, a John Nash design, burnt down, but farm buildings and estate houses remain. The extensive woods were added by 18th-century landlords. Other features of the park include nature trails, an observation tower, a 17th-century ice house, a deer enclosure and, by the lake, a 17th-century gazebo known as the Temple. The park also has several ring forts (see p18). From the jetty, cruisers ply the Boyle River. A river bus visits Church and Trinity Islands, which both contain medieval ruins, and Castle Island, which has a 19th-century folly.

🎋 **Lough Key Forest Park**
N4 8 km (5 miles) E of Boyle.
⭕ daily. 🎟 Easter–Sep. ♿

The gatehouse and remains of the nave at Boyle Abbey

NORTHWEST IRELAND

DONEGAL · SLIGO · LEITRIM

Towering cliffs, *deserted golden beaches and rocky headlands abound along the rugged coast of Donegal, which incorporates some of Ireland's wildest scenery. To the south, Sligo is steeped in prehistory and Celtic myth, with its legacy of ancient monuments and natural beauty enriched by associations with the poet, WB Yeats. By contrast, Leitrim is a quiet county of unruffled lakes and waterways.*

In Celtic mythology Sligo was the power base of the warrior Queen Maeve of Connaught *(see p24)*, and the county's legacy of prehistoric sites shows that the area was heavily populated in Celtic times. Later, however, both County Sligo and neighbouring County Leitrim often seemed to be little affected by events taking place in the rest of Ireland. The Normans, for example, barely disturbed the rule of local Gaelic clans.

Donegal, on the other hand, was part of Ulster until 1921 and played an active role in that province's history. The O'Donnells held sway over most of Donegal in the Middle Ages, but they fled to Europe in 1607 following their ill-fated stand against the English alongside the O'Neills *(see p247)*. Protestant settlers moved on to land

confiscated from the two clans, but they left much of Donegal and its poor soil to the native Irish, who lived there in isolation from the rest of Ulster. This remote corner of the province remained largely Catholic and, at the time of Partition in 1921, Donegal was excluded from the new Protestant Northern Ireland.

County Donegal has little in common with its neighbours in the Republic, either geographically or historically. It is one of the most remote parts of Ireland, and it is no coincidence that Donegal boasts the country's largest number of Gaelic speakers.

While the beauty of Donegal lies mainly along the coast, Sligo's finest landscapes are found inland, around Lough Gill and among the sparsely populated Bricklieve Mountains.

The 19th-century interior of Hargadon's bar in Sligo town, with its original counter and stout jars

◁ View across to Falcarragh from Bloody Foreland in County Donegal

Exploring Northwest Ireland

THE SUPREME APPEAL of Donegal lies in the natural beauty of its coast, with windswept peninsulas, precipitous cliffs and a host of golden beaches. There is a scattering of small seaside resorts which make good bases, and Donegal town is well placed for exploring the southern part of the county. The cultural heartland of the Northwest lies in and around Sligo, the only sizeable town in the region, from where you can reach several prehistoric remains and other historic sights. Further south, lovely scenery surrounds Lough Gill and the more remote Lough Arrow. In Leitrim, a county of lakes and rivers, the main centre of activity is the lively boating resort of Carrick-on-Shannon.

Procession during the Mary of Dungloe beauty contest in July

SEE ALSO

- *Where to Stay* pp297–8

- *Restaurants, Cafés and Pubs* pp314–15 & p321

TORY ISLAND ❶

BLOODY FORELAND ❷

HORN HE

DUNFANAC

BUNBEG ●

❸

THE ROSSES

ARANMORE ISLAND

DERRYVEAG

MOUNTAIN

BURTONPORT

DUNGLOE

❿

R253

❶❶ ARDARA

BLUE STA MOUNTAI

❶❷ GLENCOLUMBKILLE

SLIEVE LEAGUE

❶❸

KILLYBEGS

❶❹

DONEGA

❶❺

ROSSNOWLAGH

❶❼

R231

BALLYSHANNO

❶❽

BUNDORAN ●

Lough Melvin

LISSADELL HOUSE ❶❾

❷⓿

DRUMCLIFF   N16   Enniski

❷❷ SLIGO   MANORHAMILTON

❷❶

PARKE'S CASTLE

OX MOUNTAINS   N59   N17   N4

/Ballina

Lough Allen

R280

KEY

▬	Major road
▬	Minor road
▬	Scenic route
∼	River
☀	Viewpoint

LOUGH ARROW ❷❸

BRICKLIEVE MOUNTAINS

CARRICK-ON-SHANNON ❷❹

0 kilometres   20

0 miles   10

GETTING AROUND

The N56, linking Letterkenny and Donegal, provides access to much of the Northwest's best scenery, with minor roads branching off it around the coast's rocky peninsulas. A few buses serve this route, but travelling around without a car is easier further south, with buses running daily from Donegal along the N15 to Sligo via Ballyshannon. The rail network barely reaches the Northwest, though there are daily trains between Sligo and Carrick-on-Shannon.

Thatched cottage near Malin Head on Inishowen Peninsula

SIGHTS AT A GLANCE

View from Carrowkeel Bronze Age cemetery above Lough Arrow

Quartzite cone of Errigal, the highest of the Derryveagh Mountains

Tory Island ❶

Road map C1. Co Donegal. 🏃 140.
🚢 from Magheraroarty Pier near
Gortahork (074 35061) and Bunbeg
(075 31991): daily in summer,
weather permitting in winter.

T HE TURBULENT Tory Sound
separates this windswept
island from the northwestern
corner of mainland Donegal.
Given that rough weather can
cut off the tiny island for days,
it is not surprising that Tory's
inhabitants have developed a
strong sense of independence.
Most of the islanders speak
Gaelic and they even have
their own monarch: the powers
of this non-hereditary position
are minimal, but the current
incumbent is heavily involved
in promoting the interests of
his "subjects" and in attracting
visitors to the island.

During the 1970s, the Irish
government tried to resettle
most of the islanders on the
mainland, but they refused to
move. Their campaign of
resistance was led by Tory's
school of Primitive artists. This
emerged after 1968, inspired
by a local man called James
Dixon who claimed he could
do better than a visiting
English painter, Derek Hill.
Since then, the school of artists
has drawn a growing number
of tourists; the new **Dixon
Gallery** opened recently in
the main village of West Town.

There are ruins of a monastery
founded by St Columba *(see
p32)* nearby, or else you can
explore the island's dramatic
cliffs and seabird rookeries.

🏛 Dixon Gallery
West Town. 📞 074 35011.
◻ May–Sep: daily.

Bloody Foreland ❷

Road map C1. Co Donegal. 🚌 to
Bunbeg from Letterkenny or Dungloe.

B LOODY FORELAND, which gets
its name from the rubescent
glow of the rocks at sunset,
boasts magnificent scenery.
The R257 road skirts the coast
around the headland, providing lovely views. The most
scenic viewpoint is on the

north coast and looks across
to the cliffs of nearby offshore
islands, including Tory. A short
distance further south, the tiny
village of **Bunbeg** has a pretty
harbour, but elsewhere the
rocky landscape is spoilt by a
blanket of holiday bungalows.

Derryveagh
Mountains ❸

Road map C1. Co Donegal.

T HE WILD BEAUTY of these
mountains provides one of
the high spots of a visit to
Donegal. Errigal Mountain, the
range's tallest peak at 751 m
(2,466 ft), attracts keen hikers,
but the cream of the mountain
scenery lies within **Glenveagh
National Park**. Covering
nearly 10,000 ha (25,000 acres),
this takes in the beautiful
valley occupied by Lough
Veagh, and Poisoned Glen, a
marshy valley enclosed by
dramatic cliffs. The park also
protects the largest herd of
red deer in the country.

Glenveagh Castle stands on
the southern shores of Lough
Veagh, near the visitors' centre.
This splendid granite building
was constructed in 1870 by
John Adair, notorious for his
eviction of many families from
the area after the Famine *(see
p211)*. The castle was given
to the nation in the 1970s by
its last owner, a wealthy art
dealer from Pennsylvania.

Minibuses whisk you up the
private road to the castle from
the visitors' centre. You can
go on a guided tour of the
sumptuous interior or just stroll

Glenveagh Castle overlooking Lough Veagh

Looking across to Dunfanaghy, gateway to the Horn Head peninsula

through the formal gardens and rhododendron woods. Trails weave all around the castle grounds; one path climbs steeply to reward you with a lovely view over Lough Veagh.

Glebe House and Gallery overlooks Lough Gartan 6 km (4 miles) south of the visitors' centre. This modest Regency mansion was the home of the painter, Derek Hill, who was also a keen collector. The house reveals his varied tastes, with William Morris wall-papers, Islamic ceramics and paintings by Tory Island artists. The gallery contains works

Fountain at Glenveagh

by Picasso, Renoir and Jack B Yeats among others.

The **Colmcille Heritage Centre**, a short distance south, uses stained glass and illuminated manuscripts to trace the life of St Columba (Colmcille in Gaelic), who was born in nearby Church Hill in AD 521 *(see p32)*. A flagstone in the village is said to mark the site of the saint's birthplace.

🍀 **Glenveagh National Park and Castle**
Off R251, 16 km (10 miles) N of Church Hill. 🄲 *074 37090.* **Park** *and* **Castle** ◯ *Easter–Oct: daily.* 📷 🎫 ♿ limited.
🏛 **Glebe House and Gallery**
🄲 *074 37071.* ◯ *Easter & May–Sep: Sat–Thu.* 📷 ♿ limited.
🏛 **Colmcille Heritage Centre**
🄲 *074 37306.* ◯ *Easter & May–Sep: daily.* 📷

Horn Head ❹

Road map C1. Co Donegal. 🚌 *to Dunfanaghy from Letterkenny.*
ℹ *The Workhouse, Dunfanaghy (074 36540).*

CARPETED IN HEATHER and rich in birdlife, Horn Head is the most scenic of the northern Donegal headlands. It rises 180 m (600 ft) straight out of the Atlantic and gives lovely views out to sea and inland towards the mountains. The appeal of the area is enhanced by **Dunfanaghy**, a delightful town with an air of affluence and Presbyterianism unusual in this area. The local beach, **Killahoey Strand**, offers excellent swimming.

Rosguill Peninsula ❺

Road map C1. Co Donegal.

ROSGUILL PENINSULA juts out into the Atlantic Ocean between Sheephaven and Mulroy bays. The simplest way to see it is to follow the 11-km (7-mile) Atlantic Drive, a circular route which skirts the clifftops at the tip of the headland.

Doe Castle, 5 km (3 miles) north of Creeslough village, is worth a visit as much for its setting on a promontory overlooking Sheephaven Bay as for its architectural or historical interest. Even so, it is still a substantial ruin – the remains of a castle erected in the 16th century by the MacSweeneys, a family of Scottish mercenaries.

Fanad Peninsula ❻

Road map C1. Co Donegal. 🚌 *to Rathmelton & Portsalon from Letterkenny.*

A PANORAMIC ROUTE winds between the hilly spine and rugged coast of this tranquil peninsula. The eastern side is by far the most enjoyable and begins at **Rathmelton,** a charming Plantation town founded in the 17th century. Elegant Georgian homes and handsome old warehouses flank its tree-lined Main Street.

Further north, **Portsalon** offers safe bathing and great views from nearby Saldanha Head. Near **Doaghbeg**, on the way to Fanad Head in the far north, the cliffs have been eroded into arches and other dramatic shapes.

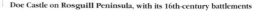
Doe Castle on Rosguill Peninsula, with its 16th-century battlements

A Tour of the Inishowen Peninsula ❼

INISHOWEN, THE LARGEST of Donegal's northern peninsulas, is an area laden with history, from early Christian relics to strategically positioned castles and forts. The most rugged scenery lies in the west and north, around the the steep rock-strewn landscape of the Gap of Mamore and the spectacular cape of Malin Head, the northern-most point in Ireland. Numerous beaches dot the coastline and cater for all tastes, from the remote Isle of Doagh to the busy family resort of Buncrana. From the shores, there are views to Donegal's Derryveagh Mountains in the west and the Northern Ireland coast in the east. The Inishowen Peninsula can be explored by car as a leisurely day trip.

Tower on Banba's Crown, Malin Head

Carndonagh Cross ④
This 7th-century early Christian cross is carved with human figures and interlacing lines.

Gap of Mamore ③
The road between Mamore Hill and the Urris Hills is 250 m (820 ft) above sea level and offers panoramic views.

Dunree Head ②
On the headland, Dunree Fort overlooks Lough Swilly. It was built in 1798 to counter the threat of French invasion. Since 1986, it has been a military museum.

Buncrana ①
Buncrana has 5 km (3 miles) of sandy beaches and two castles. Buncrana Castle was rebuilt in 1718 and the intact keep of O'Doherty Castle dates from Norman times.

KEY

▬	Tour route
═	Other roads
☀	Viewpoint

Shores of Lough Swilly near Dunree Fort

Grianán of Ailigh ⑦
At the neck of the Inishowen Peninsula, perched on a hilltop, stands this formidable circular stone fort. The solid structure that can be seen today is the result of extensive restoration in the 1870s.

Enjoying the views from the ramparts of the Grianán of Aileach

Malin Head ⑤

This traditional cottage makes a good stop for tea after enjoying the superb Atlantic views from Malin Head. At the highest point, Banba's Crown, stands a tower built in 1805 to monitor shipping.

Greencastle ⑥

A resort and fishing port, Greencastle is named after the overgrown castle ruins just outside town. Built in 1305 by Richard de Burgo, Earl of Ulster, the castle guarded the entrance to Lough Foyle.

0 kilometres   5

0 miles   5

Grianán of Ailigh ⑧

Road map C1. Co Donegal. 🚌 from Letterkenny or Londonderry.
ℹ️ Burt (077 68512).

DONEGAL'S most impressive and intriguing ancient monument stands just 10 km (6 miles) west of Londonderry (see pp250–51) at the entrance to the Inishowen Peninsula. Overlooking Lough Swilly and Lough Foyle, the circular stone structure, measuring 23 m (77 ft) in diameter, is believed to have been built as a pagan temple around the 5th century BC, although the site was probably a place of worship before this date. Later, Christians adopted the fort: St Patrick is said to have baptized Owen, founder of the O'Neill dynasty, here in AD 450. The fort became the royal residence of the O'Neills, but was damaged in the 12th century by the army of Murtagh O'Brien, King of Munster.

The fort was restored in the 1870s. Two doorways lead from the outside through 4-m (13-ft) thick defences into a grassy arena ringed by three terraces. The most memorable feature of the fort, however, is its magnificent vantage point, which affords stunning views in every direction.

At the foot of the hill stands an attractive church, dedicated to St Aengus and built in 1967. Its circular design echoes that of the Grianán.

Letterkenny ⑨

Road map C1. Co Donegal. 🚶 7,100.
🚌 ℹ️ Derry Rd (074 21160).

STRADDLING the river Swilly, with the Sperrin Mountains to the east and the Derryveagh Mountains (see pp216–17) to the west, Letterkenny is Donegal's largest town. It is also the region's main business centre, a role it took over from Londonderry after partition in 1921. The likeable town makes a good base from which to explore the northern coast of Donegal and, for anglers, is well placed for access to the waters of Lough Swilly.

Letterkenny has one of the longest main streets in Ireland, which is dominated by the 65-m (215-ft) steeple of **St Eunan's Cathedral**. A Neo-Gothic creation built in the late 19th century, it contains Celtic-style stonework, a rich marble altar and vivid stained-glass windows. The **County Museum** is small but has informative displays on local history and a collection of archaeological artifacts found in Donegal, some of them dating from the Iron Age.

Every August, the centre of Letterkenny is taken over for four days by the International Folk Festival, when traditional and folk musicians play in the bars and hotels, and dancing competitions are held.

🏛 County Museum

High Rd. 📞 074 24613. 🕐 Mon–Sat. 🔴 10 days at Christmas and public hols. ♿

The imposing spire of St Eunan's Cathedral in Letterkenny

Isolated cottage near Burtonport in the Rosses

The Rosses ❿

Road map C1. Co Donegal. 🚌 *to Dungloe or Burtonport from Letterkenny.* ℹ️ *Jun–Sep: Main St, Dungloe (075 21297).* ⛴ *to Aranmore from Burtonport (075 21532).*

A ROCKY HEADLAND dotted with more than 100 lakes, the Rosses is one of the most picturesque and unspoilt corners of Donegal. It is also a strong Gaeltacht area, with many people speaking Gaelic.

The hub of the Rosses, at the southern end of the headland, is **Dungloe**, a bustling market town and major angling centre.

ENVIRONS: There is a glorious sheltered beach 8 km (5 miles) west of Dungloe at **Maghery Bay**. From here you can also walk to nearby **Crohy Head**, known for its caves, arches and unusual cliff formations. From Burtonport, 8 km (5 miles)

north of Dungloe, car ferries sail daily to Donegal's largest island, **Aranmore**. This rugged place is ideal for clifftop walks, particularly in the northwest, and from the south coast you can enjoy fine views across to the Rosses. Most of Aranmore's population of 1,000 lives in Leabgarrow. The village's thriving pub culture is due partly to lax licensing laws.

Ardara ⓫

Road map C2. Co Donegal. 🚶 *700.* 🚌 *from Killybegs or Donegal.* ℹ️ *Easter–Sep: Heritage Centre, The Diamond (075 41704).*

T HE TOWN of Ardara is the weaving capital of Donegal and it has a proliferation of shops selling locally made tweeds and hand-knitted sweaters. Some larger stores put on displays of hand-loom

weaving. There is not much to Ardara otherwise, but it is a spruce place whose main street is lined with pubs much loved for their fiddle sessions.

ENVIRONS: There is superb scenery between Ardara and **Loughros Point**, 10 km (6 miles) west of the town: the drive along the narrow peninsula provides dramatic coastal views. Another picturesque route runs southwest from Ardara to Glencolumbkille, going over **Glengesh Pass**, a series of bends through a wild, deserted landscape.

Hand-loom worker in Ardara

Glencolumbkille ⓬

Road map B2. Co Donegal. 🚶 *260.* 🚌 *from Killybegs.* ℹ️ *Donegal (073 21148).*

G LENCOLUMBKILLE, a quiet, grassy valley scattered with brightly coloured cottages, feels very much like a backwater, in spite of the sizeable number of visitors who come here.

The "Glen of St Colmcille" is a popular place of pilgrimage due to its associations with the saint more commonly known as St Columba. Just north of the valley's main village of Cashel, on the way to Glen Head, there is a tiny church where St Columba worshipped: it is said that between prayers the saint slept on the two stone slabs still visible in one corner.

Another attraction here is the **Folk Village Museum**, which depicts rural Donegal lifestyles through the ages. It was started in the 1950s by a local priest called Father James

Old irons at the Folk Village Museum in Glencolumbkille

Slieve League, the highest sea cliffs in Europe

MacDyer. Concerned about the high rate of emigration from this poor region, he sought to provide jobs and a sense of regional pride, partly by encouraging people to set up craft cooperatives. The Folk Village shop sells local wares, and has a good stock of wine – made of anything from seaweed to fuchsias.

There is plenty to explore in the valley, which is littered with cairns, dolmens and other ancient monuments. The nearby coast is lovely too, the best walks taking you west across the grassy foreland of **Malinbeg**. Beyond the small resort of Malin More, steps drop down to an idyllic sandy cove hemmed in by cliffs.

🏛 **Folk Village Museum**
Cashel. **℃** 073 30017. **◯** Easter & May–Sep: daily. 🌀 🔲

Slieve League ⓭

Road map B2. Co Donegal. 🚌 *to Carrick from Glencolumbkille or Killybegs.*

THE HIGHEST cliff face in Europe, Slieve League is spectacular not just for its sheer elevation but also for its colour: at sunset the rock is streaked with changing shades of red, amber and ochre. The 8-km (5-mile) drive to the eastern end of Slieve League from **Carrick** is bumpy but well worth enduring. Beyond Teelin, the road becomes a

series of alarming switchbacks before reaching **Bunglass Point** and Amharc Mor, the "good view". From here, you can see the whole of Slieve League, its sheer cliffs rising dramatically out of the ocean.

Only experienced hikers should attempt the treacherous ledges of **One Man's Pass**. This is part of a trail which climbs westwards out of Teelin and up to the highest point of Slieve League – from where you can admire the Atlantic Ocean shimmering 598 m (1,972 ft) below. The path then continues on to Malinbeg, 16 km (10 miles) west. During the summer, for a less strenuous but safer and equally rewarding excursion, pay a boat-owner from Teelin to take you out to see Slieve League from the sea.

Killybegs ⓮

Road map C2. Co Donegal. 🚶 *1,700.* 🚌 *from Donegal.* ℹ️ *Donegal (073 21148).*

NARROW WINDING streets give Killybegs a timeless feel, which contrasts sharply with the industriousness of this small town. The sense of prosperity stems in part from the manufacture of the Donegal carpets for which the town is famous, and which adorn Dublin Castle *(see pp74–5)* and other palaces around the world.

Killybegs is one of Ireland's busiest fishing ports and the quays are well worth seeing when the trawlers arrive to off-load their catch: gulls squawk overhead and the smell of fish fills the air. Trawlermen come from far and wide – so do not be surprised if you hear Eastern European voices as you wander around the town.

Trawler crew in Killybegs relaxing after unloading their catch

Gaelic pub sign in Gaeltacht region

THE IRISH GAELTACHTS

The term "Gaeltacht" refers to Gaelic-speaking areas of Ireland. Up to the 16th century, virtually the entire population spoke the native tongue. British rule, however, undermined Irish culture, and the Famine *(see p211)* drained the country of many of its Gaelic-speakers. The use of the local language has fallen steadily since. Even so, in the Gaeltachts 75 per cent of the people still speak it, and road signs are exclusively in Irish – unlike in most other parts of Ireland.

The Donegal Gaeltacht stretches almost unbroken along the coast from Fanad Head to Slieve League and boasts the largest number of Irish-speakers in the country. Ireland's other principal Gaeltachts are in Galway and Kerry.

Donegal town, overlooked by the ruins of its 15th-century castle

Donegal **⑮**

Road map C2. Co Donegal. **🚶** 2,300.
🚌 ℹ Quay St (073 21148).

DONEGAL MEANS "Fort of the Foreigners", after the Vikings who built a garrison here. However, it was under the O'Donnells that the town began to take shape. The ruins of **Donegal Castle** in the town centre incorporate the gabled tower of a fortified house built by the family in the 15th century. The adjoining house and most other features are Jacobean – added by Sir Basil Brooke, who moved in after the O'Donnells were ousted by the English in 1607 (see pp36–7). The castle has recently been partly restored.

Brooke was also responsible for laying out the market square, which is known as the **Diamond**. An obelisk in the centre commemorates four Franciscans who wrote the Annals of the Four Masters in the 1630s. This manuscript traces the history of the Gaelic people from 40 days before the Great Flood up to the end of the 16th century. Part of it was written at **Donegal Abbey**, south of the market square along the River Eske. Built in 1474, little now remains of the abbey but a few Gothic windows and cloister arches. About 1.5 km (1 mile) further on is **Donegal Craft Village**, a showcase for the work of local craftspeople.

While there is not a huge amount to explore in Donegal town, it has some pleasant hotels (see p298) and makes a good base for exploring the southern part of the county.

♣ Donegal Castle
Tirchonaill St. **📞** 073 22405. **◯** mid-Jun–Sep: daily. **📷** **⟨** limited.
🏛 Donegal Craft Village
Ballyshannon Rd. **📞** 073 22053.
◯ May–Sep: daily. **⟨** limited.

Lough Derg **⑯**

Road map C2. Co Donegal. **⛴** Jun–mid-Aug (pilgrims only). **🚌** to Pettigo from Donegal.

PILGRIMS HAVE made their way to Lough Derg ever since St Patrick spent 40 days praying on one of the lake's islands in an attempt to rid Ireland of all evil spirits. The Pilgrimage of St Patrick's Purgatory began in around 1150 and still attracts thousands of Catholics every summer. Their destination is the tiny **Station Island**, close to Lough Derg's southern shore and reached by boat from a jetty 8 km (5 miles) north of the border village of Pettigo. The island is completely covered by a religious complex, which includes a basilica, built in 1921, and hostels for pilgrims.

The pilgrimage season runs from June to mid-August. People spend three days on the island, eating just one meal of dry bread and black tea per day. Although only pilgrims can visit Station Island, it is interesting to go to the jetty to savour the atmosphere and get a good view of the basilica near the shore.

Rossnowlagh **⑰**

Road map C2. Co Donegal. **🚶** 55.
🚌 from Bundoran & Donegal.
ℹ May–mid-Sep: Main St, Bundoran (072 41350).

Holiday-makers enjoying the fine sandy beach at Rossnowlagh

AT ROSSNOWLAGH, Atlantic waves break on to one of Ireland's finest beaches, drawing crowds of both bathers and surfers to this tiny place. Even so, the village remains far more peaceful than the resort of Bundoran, 14 km (9 miles) south. In addition, the cliffs at Rossnowlagh provide scope for exhilarating coastal walks. Away from the sea, you can visit the **Donegal Historical Society Museum**, housed in a striking Franciscan friary

Basilica on Station Island viewed from the shores of Lough Derg

Lissadell House dining room with Gore-Booth family portraits

Lissadell House ⑲

Road map B2. Carney, Co Sligo.
☎ 071 63150. **🚌** or **🚆** to Sligo.
○ Jun–mid-Sep: Mon–Sat. 🎫 ♿

A LATE GEORGIAN mansion built in the 1830s, Lissadell is famous more for its occupants than its architecture. It was once the home of the Gore-Booths who, unlike some of the Anglo-Irish gentry, contributed much to the region. During the Famine *(see p211)*, Sir Robert mortgaged the house to help feed his employees.

The most famous member of the Gore-Booth family was Sir Robert's granddaughter, Constance Markievicz (1868–1927). She was a leading revolutionary who took part in the 1916 Rising *(see pp42–3)* and was the first woman to be elected to the British House of Commons. WB Yeats, a regular visitor to the house, immortalized Constance and her sister, Eva, in one of his poems, describing them as "Two girls in silk kimonos, both beautiful, one a gazelle". The house is still in the hands of the Gore-Booth family.

Built in grey limestone, the exterior of Lissadell House is rather austere. The interior, on the other hand, has an appealing atmosphere of faded grandeur, with peeling paintwork and copious memorabilia of the building's former occupants. The finest rooms are the gallery (previously the music room) and the dining room, which is decorated with extraordinary full-length murals of the Gore-Booth family, their servants and their dog. Painted directly on to the wall, they were the work of Constance's husband, Count Casimir Markievicz.

Both the house and the overgrown estate are slowly being restored. There are plans, for example, to open up the woodland vistas to recreate the sweeping views down to the sea. You can already explore along paths skirting the lakeshore, and there is also a wildlife reserve which is a popular winter refuge for barnacle geese.

built in the 1950s. The tiny but fascinating collection includes displays of Stone Age flints, Irish musical instruments and other local artifacts.

Rossnowlagh never fails to make the news on 12 July, when it hosts the only parade to take place in the Republic by the Protestant organization, the Orange Order *(see p47)*.

🏛 Donegal Historical Society Museum
☎ 072 51267. **○** daily. **●** 25 Dec.

Ballyshannon ⑱

Road map C2. Co Donegal. **👥** 2,600.
🚌 from Bundoran & Donegal.

I N BALLYSHANNON, well-kept Georgian homes jostle for space along hilly streets on the banks of the River Erne, near where it flows into Donegal Bay. This is a bustling town, full of character and off the main tourist track – though it gets packed during August's festival of traditional music, which is one of the best of its kind in the country.

The festival apart, Ballyshannon is most famous as the birthplace of poet William Allingham (1824–89), who recalled his home town in the lines "Adieu to Ballyshanny and the winding banks of the Erne". He lies buried in the graveyard of St Anne's Church, off Main Street. There is a fine view over the river from here: you can see the small island of **Inis Saimer** where, according to legend, Greeks founded the first colony in Ireland after the Great Flood. Beyond, you can glimpse a large Irish Army base: Ballyshannon's position on a steeply rising bluff overlooking the River Erne has always made the town a strategic military site.

About 1.5 km (1 mile) northwest of town lie the scant ruins of **Assaroe Abbey**, founded by Cistercians in 1184. A graveyard with some ancient burial slabs and headstones remains. Nearby, two water wheels installed by the monks have been restored and incorporated into an interpretive centre called the **Water Wheels**. One wheel now drives a generator.

Mural of the family dog in Lissadell's dining room

🏛 Water Wheels
Assaroe Abbey. **☎** 072 51580.
○ Jun–Aug: daily; mid-Feb–May & Sep: Sun pm; Oct–mid-Feb: by appt.

A Tour of Yeats Country ⑳

Yeats tour sign

EVEN FOR PEOPLE unfamiliar with the poetry of WB Yeats, Sligo's engaging landscapes are reason enough to make a pilgrimage. This tour follows a route through varied scenery, taking you past sandy bays and dramatic limestone ridges, through forest and alongside rivers and lakes. The delightful Lough Gill lies at the heart of Yeats country, enclosed by wooded hills crisscrossed by walking trails. In summer, boats ply the length of the lough, or you can head to one of the northwest's best beaches, at Rosses Point.

Ben Bulben ⑤
The eerie silhouette of Ben Bulben rises abruptly out of the plain. You can climb to the top, but go with great care.

Lissadell House ④
Yeats was a close friend of the Gore-Booth sisters who lived at Lissadell. You can see the room where the poet slept as a guest (see p223).

Drumcliff ③
Although he died in France, in 1948 Yeats's body was laid to rest in Drumcliff churchyard. The ruins of an old monastic site include a fine High Cross.

TIPS FOR DRIVERS

Length: 88 km (55 miles).
Stopping-off points: Outside Sligo, the best choice of eating places is at Rosses Point, although there are good pubs in Drumcliff and Dromahair, and Parke's Castle has a café. Lough Gill provides most choice in terms of picnic spots.
Boat trips: Wild Rose Water Bus (071 64266 or 088 598869). (See also pp355–7.)

KEY

▬▬	Tour route
═══	Other roads
🖾	Boat trips
❈	Viewpoint

DONEGAL

Carney

Drumcliff Bay

Sligo Harbour

Drum

Drum

Rosses Point ②
Yeats and his brother used to spend their summers at this pretty resort. It stands at the entrance to Sligo Bay, and a steady flow of boats passes by.

GALWAY

Sligo ①
This town is a good place to begin a tour of Yeats country. It has many connections with the poet and his family, whose literary and artistic legacy has helped to inspire Sligo's thriving arts scene (see p226).

WB YEATS AND SLIGO

**WB Yeats
(1865–1939)**

As a schoolboy in London, Yeats *(see p21)* longed for his native Sligo, and as an adult he often returned here. He lovingly describes the county in his *Reveries over Childhood and Youth*, and the lake-studded landscape haunts his poetry. "In a sense", Yeats said, "Sligo has always been my home", and it is here that he wished to be buried. His gravestone in Drumcliff bears an epitaph he penned himself: "Cast a cold eye on life, on death. Horseman pass by."

Parke's Castle viewed from across the calm waters of Lough Gill

Glencar Lough ⑥

"There is a waterfall ... that all my childhood counted dear", wrote Yeats of the cataract which tumbles into Glencar Lough. A path leads down to it from the road.

Parke's Castle ⑦
This 17th-century fortified manor house commands a splendid view over the tranquil waters of Lough Gill. It is a starting point for boat trips around the lough.

Isle of Innisfree ⑧

"There midnight's all a glimmer, and noon a purple glow", is how Yeats once described Innisfree. There is not much to see on this tiny island but it is a romantic spot. In summer, a boatman ferries visitors here.

Dooney Rock ⑨
A steep path leads from the road to Dooney Rock, from where glorious views extend over the lough to Ben Bulben. Trails weave through the surrounding woods and by the lake.

0 kilometres   3
0 miles   2

Parke's Castle ㉑

Road map C2. 6 km (4 miles) N of Dromahair, Co Leitrim. 📞 *071 64149.* 🚍 or 🚆 *to Sligo.* ◯ *Easter–May: Tue–Sun; Jun–Oct: daily.* 🅿 👟 *ground floor only.* ✉

THIS FORTIFIED MANOR HOUSE dominates the eastern end of Lough Gill. It was built in 1609 by Captain Robert Parke, an English settler who later became MP for Leitrim. It has been beautifully restored by the Office of Public Works using 17th-century building methods and native Irish oak.

Parke's Castle was erected on the site of a 16th-century tower house belonging to the O'Rourkes, a powerful local clan, and stones from this earlier structure were used in the new building. The original foundations and part of the moat were incorporated, but otherwise Parke's Castle is the epitome of a Plantation manor house *(see p37).* It is protected by a large enclosure or bawn, whose sturdy wall includes a gatehouse and two turrets as well as the house itself.

Among the most distinctive architectural features of Parke's Castle are the diamond-shaped chimneys, mullioned windows and the parapets. There is also a curious stone hut, known as the "sweathouse", which was an early Irish sauna. Inside, an exhibition and audiovisual display cover Parke's Castle and various historic and prehistoric sites in the area, with photos and archaeological finds. There is also a working forge.

Boat trips around sights on Lough Gill that are associated with the poet, WB Yeats, leave from outside the castle walls.

Hargadon's bar, one of Sligo town's most famous watering holes

Sligo ㉒

Road map C2. Co Sligo. 🏃 20,000.
🚉 🚌 ℹ *Aras Reddan, Temple St
(071 61201).* ⛴ *Fri.*

THE PORT of Sligo sits at the mouth of the River Garavogue, sandwiched between the Atlantic and Lough Gill. The largest town in the northwest, it rose to prominence under the Normans, being well placed as a gateway between the provinces of Ulster and Connaught. The appearance of Sligo today is mainly the result of growth during the late 18th and 19th centuries.

Sligo is perfectly situated for touring the ravishing countryside nearby, and it is a also a good centre for traditional music. While the town itself can seem rather sombre, the quiet back streets are reasonably atmospheric.

Sligo's link with the Yeats family is the main source of the town's appeal. WB Yeats *(see pp224–5)*, Ireland's best-known poet, was born into a prominent local family. The Pollexfen warehouse, at the western end of Wine Street, has a rooftop turret from which the poet's grandfather would observe his merchant fleet moored in the docks.

The town's sole surviving medieval building is **Sligo Abbey**, founded in 1253. Some original features remain, such as the delicate lancet windows in the choir, but this ruined Dominican friary dates mainly from the 15th century. The best features are a beautifully carved altar and the cloisters.

A short distance west from the abbey is O'Connell Street, with the town's main shops

Bronze statue of WB Yeats

and Hargadon's bar – an old Sligo institution complete with a dark, wooden interior, snugs and a grocery counter. Near the junction with Wine Street, overlooking Hyde Bridge, is the Yeats Memorial Building. This houses the Yeats Society and the **Sligo Art Gallery**, which puts on shows by foreign and Irish artists. The Yeats International Summer School is held here too: Sligo's renown as the arts capital of northwest Ireland rests partly on this annual festival of readings and lectures on the poet's life and work.

The Yeatsian associations continue on the other side of the river. The first thing you see on crossing Hyde Bridge is a statue of the poet, engraved with lines from his own verse. From here, it is just a short walk east to **Sligo County Museum and Art Gallery**. The museum has a small selection of Yeatsian memorabilia, while the gallery includes evocative Sligo landscapes by WB Yeats's brother, Jack, and several portraits by his father, John B Yeats.

🏛 **Sligo Abbey**
Abbey St. ◯ *daily.* ✦ *mid-Jun–Sep.*
🏛 **Sligo Art Gallery**
Hyde Bridge. 📞 *071 45847.*
◯ *Mon–Sat (for exhibitions only).*
🏛 **Sligo County Museum and Art Gallery**
Stephen St. 📞 *071 42212.*
◯ *Apr–Oct: Mon–Sat (Apr–May & Oct: am only).*

ENVIRONS: In a most unlikely setting in the suburbs of Sligo, **Carrowmore Megalithic Cemetery** once boasted the country's largest collection of Stone Age tombs. Quarrying has destroyed many graves, but about 40 passage tombs *(see pp238–9)* and dolmens *(see p30)* survive. They lie scattered among abandoned gravel pits and quarries, with some in private gardens and even protruding from cottages.

Dwarfing these tombs from atop **Knocknarea** mountain is a huge, unexcavated cairn, which dates back about 5,000 years and is said to contain the tomb of the legendary Queen Maeve of Connaught *(see p24)*. You can climb the mountain in about an hour; the path starts 4 km (2.5 miles) west of Carrowmore.

Tobernalt, by Lough Gill 5 km (3 miles) south of Sligo, means "cliff well", after a nearby spring with alleged curative powers. It was a holy site in Celtic times and later became a Christian shrine. Priests came here to celebrate Mass in secret during the 18th century, when Catholic worship was illegal. The Mass rock, which is still visible next to an altar erected at the turn of the century, remains a place of pilgrimage.

Altar by the holy well at Tobernalt, overlooking Lough Gill in Sligo

Lough Arrow 🕲

Road map C3. Co Sligo. 🚌 to Ballinafad. 🛈 May–Oct: Boyle (079 62145).

Peaceful go to Lough Arrow to sail and fish for the local trout, and also simply to enjoy the glorious countryside. You can explore the lake by boat, but the views from the shore are the real joy of Lough Arrow. A full circuit of the lake is recommended, but for the most breathtaking views head for the southern end around **Ballinafad**. This small town lies in a gorgeous spot, enclosed to the north and south by the Bricklieve and Curlew Mountains.

The **Carrowkeel Passage Tomb Cemetery** occupies a remote and eerie spot in the Bricklieve Mountains to the north of Ballinafad. The best approach is up the single track road from Castlebaldwin, 5 km (3 miles) northeast of the site.

The 14 Neolithic passage graves, which are scattered around a hilltop overlooking Lough Arrow, are elaborate corbelled structures. One is comparable with Newgrange *(see pp238–9)*, except that the burial chamber inside this cairn is lit by the sun on the day of the summer solstice (21 June) as opposed to the winter solstice. On a nearby ridge are the remains of Stone Age huts, presumably those occupied by the farmers who buried their dead in the Carrowkeel passage graves.

Passage tomb in Carrowkeel cemetery above Lough Arrow

Carrick-on-Shannon 🕲

Road map C3. Co Leitrim. 🚶 1,900. 🚌 🚂 🛈 Apr–Sep: The Marina (078 20170).

The tiny capital of Leitrim, one of the least populated counties in Ireland, stands in a lovely spot on a tight bend of the River Shannon.

The town's location by the river and its proximity to the Grand Canal were crucial to Carrick's development. They are also the main reasons for its thriving tourist industry. There is a colourful, modern marina, which in summer fills up with private launches and boats available for hire.

Already a major boating centre, Carrick has benefited from the reopening of the Shannon-Erne Waterway, one end of which begins 6 km (4 miles) north at Leitrim. The channel was restored in a

cross-border joint venture billed as a symbol of peaceful cooperation between Northern Ireland and the Republic.

Away from the bustle of the marina, Carrick-on-Shannon is an old-fashioned place, with 19th-century churches and convents mixed in with more refined Georgian houses and shopfronts. The town's most curious building is the quaint **Costello Chapel** on Bridge Street. One of the smallest of its kind anywhere in the world, the chapel was built in 1877 by local businessman, Edward Costello, to house the tombs of himself and his wife.

Lough Rynn Estate 🕲

Road map C3. Mohill, Co Leitrim. 🕿 078 31427. 🚌 or 🚂 to Carrick-on-Shannon. ◯ April–mid-Sep: daily. 🎦 🛍 🛗

This vast estate, lying 3 km (2 miles) south of Mohill, was the ancestral seat of the Clements family, Earls of Leitrim. The baronial-style house, constructed in 1832 and full of hunting trophies and grandiose furniture, is of less interest than the grounds. These extend across 40 ha (100 acres) of land and more than 240 ha (600 acres) of lakes. There is a lot to explore, including ornamental gardens, water meadows, lush woodland and an arboretum with California redwoods and other exotic trees. The ruins of a 16th-century castle overlook one of the lakes, and you can also walk up to the remains of a Neolithic burial site.

SHANNON-ERNE WATERWAY

This labyrinthine system of rivers and lakes passes through unspoilt border country, linking Leitrim on the Shannon and Upper Lough Erne in Fermanagh. It follows the course of a canal which was completed and then abandoned in the 1860s. The channel was reopened in 1993, enabling the public to enjoy both the Victorian stonework (including 34 bridges) and the state-of-the-art technology used to operate the 16 locks.

Cruiser negotiating a lock on the Shannon-Erne Waterway

THE MIDLANDS

CAVAN · MONAGHAN · LOUTH · LONGFORD · WESTMEATH
MEATH · OFFALY · LAOIS

THE CRADLE *of Irish civilization and the Celts' spiritual home, the Midlands encompass some of Ireland's most sacred and symbolic sites. Much of the region is ignored, but the ragged landscapes of lush pastures, lakes and bogland reveal ancient Celtic crosses, gracious Norman abbeys and Gothic Revival castles.*

The fertile Boyne Valley in County Meath was settled during the Stone Age and became the most important centre of habitation in the country. The remains of ancient sites from this early civilization fill the area and include Newgrange, the finest Neolithic tomb in the country. In Celtic times, the focus shifted south to the Hill of Tara, the seat of the High Kings of Ireland and the Celts' spiritual and political capital. Tara's heyday came in the 3rd century AD, but it retained its importance until the Normans invaded in the 1100s.

Norman castles, such as the immense fortress at Trim in County Meath, attest to the shifting frontiers around the region of English influence known as the Pale *(see p124)*. By the end of the 16th century, this area incorporated nearly all the counties in the Midlands.

The Boyne Valley returned to prominence in 1690, when the Battle of the Boyne ended in a landmark Protestant victory over the Catholics *(see pp36–7)*.

Although part of the Republic since 1921, historically Monaghan and Cavan belong to Ulster, and the former retains strong links with the province. The rounded hills called drumlins, found in both counties, are typical of the border region between the Republic and Northern Ireland.

Grassland and bog dotted with lakes are most characteristic of the Midlands, but the Slieve Bloom Mountains and the Cooley Peninsula provide good walking country. In addition to Meath's ancient sites, the historical highlights of the region are monasteries like Fore Abbey and Clonmacnoise, this last ranking among Europe's greatest early Christian centres.

Carlingford village and harbour, with the hills of the Cooley Peninsula rising behind

◁ Temple Finghin round tower at Clonmacnoise monastery on the banks of the River Shannon

Exploring the Midlands

DROGHEDA IS THE OBVIOUS BASE from which to explore the Boyne Valley and neighbouring monastic sites, such as Monasterboice. Trim and Mullingar, to the southwest, are less convenient but make pleasanter places in which to stay. The northern counties of Monaghan, Cavan and Longford are quiet backwaters with a patchwork of lakes that attract many anglers. To the south, Offaly and Laois are dominated by dark expanses of bog, though there is a cluster of sights around the attractive Georgian town of Birr. For a break by the sea, head for the picturesque village of Carlingford on the Cooley Peninsula.

West doorway of Nuns' Church at Clonmacnoise

KEY

▬	Motorway
▬	Major road
▬	Minor road
▬	Scenic route
～	River
✹	Viewpoint

SEE ALSO

- *Where to Stay* p299

- *Restaurants, Cafés and Pubs*
  pp315–16 & p321

GETTING AROUND

In the Midlands, there is an extensive network of roads and rail lines fanning out across the country from Dublin. As a result, getting around on public transport is easier than in most other areas. The Dublin–Belfast railway serves Dundalk and Drogheda, while Mullingar and Longford town lie on the Dublin–Sligo route. The railway and N7 road between Dublin and Limerick give good access to Laois and Offaly. For motorists, roads in the Midlands are often flat and straight but also potholed.

Enniskillen
Sligo
R200
Shannon–Erne Waterway
DRUMLANE ②
Lough Oughter
CAVAN
N55
Sligo
CARRIGGLAS MANOR ③
R194
LONGFORD
TULLYNALLY CASTLE ④
Lough Derravaragh
Galway
Royal Canal
N4
N55
R390
MULLINGAR
Lough Ree
ATHLONE ⑱
N6
KILBEGGAN ⑰
CLONMACNOISE ⑲
N62
Grand Canal
TULLAMORE
⑳ **SHANNONBRIDGE BOG RAILWAY**
Shannon
N52
N80
R440
S L I E V E B L O O M M O U N T A I N S
BIRR ㉑
PORTLAOISE
㉒
N62
N7
Thurles
N7
Limerick
Cashel

Statue in Birr Castle's formal gardens

View of Trim across the River Boyne

SIGHTS AT A GLANCE

0 kilometres   20

0 miles   10

Rossmore Memorial drinking fountain in Monaghan

Monaghan ❶

Road map D2. Co Monaghan.
🏚 6,000. 🚌 ℹ️ Market House,
Market Square (047 81122).

THE SPRUCE AND THRIVING town of Monaghan is the urban highlight of the northern Midlands. Planted by James I in 1613 (see p37), it developed into a prosperous industrial centre, thanks mainly to the local manufacture of linen. A crannog (see p31) off Glen Road is the sole trace of the town's Celtic beginnings.

Monaghan centres on three almost contiguous squares. The main attraction in Market Square is the 18th-century **Market House**, a squat but charming building with the original oak beams still visible. It is now home to the tourist office. To the east lies Church Square, very much the heart of modern Monaghan and lined with dignified 19th-century buildings, such as the Classical-style courthouse. The third square, which is known as the Diamond, was the original marketplace. It contains the **Rossmore Memorial**, a large Victorian drinking fountain with an ornate stone canopy supported by marble columns.

Do not miss the excellent **County Museum**, just off Market Square, which tells the story of Monaghan's linen and lace-making industries. The pride of its historical collection is the Cross of Clogher, an ornate bronze altar cross which dates from around 1400.

The Gothic Revival Cathedral of St Macartan perches on a hilltop south of the town, from where you can enjoy a fine view over Monaghan.

🏛 County Museum
Hill St. 📞 047 82928. ⏰ Tue–Sat.
⏺ public hols. ♿ limited.

Drumlane ❷

Road map C3. 1 km (0.5 miles) S of Milltown, Co Cavan. 🚌 to Belturbet.

STANDING ALONE by the River Erne, the medieval church and round tower of Drumlane merit a visit as much for their delightful setting as for the ruins themselves. The abbey church, founded in the early 13th century but significantly altered about 200 years later, features fine Romanesque carvings. The nearby round tower has lost its cap but is unusual for the well-finished stonework, with carvings of birds on the north side.

Carrigglas Manor ❸

Road map C3. Co Longford. 📞 043 45165. 🚌 to Longford. ⏰ Jun–Sep: Thu–Mon (phone to arrange). 📷 🎟
♿ limited.

CARRIGGLAS MANOR has been the seat of the Lefroys, a family of Huguenot descent, ever since its construction in 1837. It has changed little in the intervening years and is a fine example of the Tudor Revival style. The Victorian atmosphere is still very much alive inside, where the rooms are decorated with pseudo-

Drawing room in Carrigglas Manor with original 19th-century features

Authentic Victorian kitchen in Tullynally Castle

Gothic panelling and ornate plasterwork ceilings. The stable block, by contrast, is a grand Neo-Classical building by James Gandon, the architect of Dublin's Custom House *(see p86)*. The manor is set in pleasant grounds consisting primarily of woodland.

ENVIRONS: Just 14 km (9 miles) south of Carrigglas Manor, **Ardagh** is considered the most attractive village in Longford, with pretty stone cottages gathered around a green.

Tullynally Castle ❹

Road map C3. Castle Pollard, Co Westmeath. 🕻 044 61159. 🚌 to Mullingar. **Castle** ☐ mid-Jun–Jul: daily (pm only). 🆚 🎫 obligatory. 🕭 **Grounds** ☐ May–Sep: daily (pm only). 🆚 🕭 limited.

THIS HUGE STRUCTURE, adorned with numerous turrets and battlements, is one of Ireland's largest castles. The original 17th-century tower house was given a Georgian gloss, but this was all but submerged under later Gothic Revival changes. The Pakenham family have lived at Tullynally since 1655. Thomas Pakenham, son of the present Earl of Longford, now manages the estate.

The imposing great hall leads to a fine panelled dining room hung with family portraits. Of equal interest are the Victorian kitchen and laundry room and the adjacent drying room, complete with its immense boiler.

The 8,000-volume library looks out on to rolling wooded parkland, much of which was landscaped in the 1760s. The grounds include Victorian terraces, walled kitchen and flower gardens, and two small lakes where black swans have recently been introduced.

Fore Abbey ❺

Road map C3. Fore, Castle Pollard, Co Westmeath. 🚌 to Castle Pollard. ☐ daily.

THE RUINS of Fore Abbey lie in glorious rolling country-side about 8 km (5 miles) east of Tullynally Castle. St Fechin set up a monastery here in 630, but what you see now are the remains of a large Benedictine priory founded around 1200. Located on the northern border of the Pale *(see p124)*, Fore Abbey was heavily fortified in the 15th century as protection against the native Irish.

The ruined church was part of the original Norman priory, but the cloister and refectory date from the 1400s. On the hill opposite lies St Fechin's Church, a Norman building said to mark the site of the first monastery. The tiny church nearby incorporates a 15th-century anchorite's cell.

Kells ❻

Road map D3. Co Meath. 🏃 3,500. 🚌 🛈 Mill St, Trim (046 37111).

SIGNPOSTED by its Irish name, Ceanannus Mór, this modest town provides an unlikely backdrop to the monastery for which it is so famous.

Kells Monastery was set up by St Columba in the 6th century, but its heyday came after 806, when monks fled here from Iona. They may have been the scribes who illuminated the superb *Book of Kells*, now kept at Trinity College, Dublin *(see p62)*.

Lying in the west of town, the monastery centres on an 18th-century church. This is a rather gloomy building, but the displays in the gallery that relate to Kells are worth seeing. A decapitated round tower stands guard outside, and you can also see several 9th-century High Crosses; the South Cross is in the best condition.

Just north of the enclosure is **St Columba's House**, a tiny steep-roofed stone oratory, similar to St Kevin's Kitchen at Glendalough *(see p132)*.

In Cross Street is the Market Cross, a High Cross that once marked the entrance to the monastery. It was used as a gallows during the uprising in 1798 *(see p39)*. The battle scene on the base is a subject rarely used in High Cross art.

Ruins of Fore Abbey, a medieval Benedictine priory

Thatched cottage in Carlingford on the mountainous Cooley Peninsula

Dundalk 7

Road map D3. Co Louth. 30,000. Jocelyn Street (042 35484). Thu.

DUNDALK once marked the northernmost point of the Pale, the area controlled by the English during the Middle Ages *(see p124)*. Now, lying midway between Dublin and Belfast, it is the last major town before the Northern Ireland border.

Dundalk is the gateway to the magnificent countryside of the Cooley Peninsula, but there is little worth stopping for in the town itself. However, the **County Museum**, which is housed in an 18th-century distillery, gives an insight into some of Louth's traditional industries such as beer-making.

County Museum
Jocleyn St. 042 27056. Tue–Sun. 25 & 26 Dec & 1 Jan.

Carlingford 8

Road map D3. Co Louth. 650. Holy Trinity Heritage Centre Churchyard Rd (042 73454). **Carlingford Adventure Centre** Tholsel St (042 73100).

THIS IS A PICTURESQUE fishing village, beautifully located between the mountains of the Cooley Peninsula and the waters of Carlingford Lough. The border with Northern Ireland runs right through the centre of this drowned river valley, and from the village you can look across to the Mountains of Mourne on the Ulster side *(see pp276–7)*. Carlingford is an interesting place to explore, with its

pretty whitewashed cottages and ancient buildings clustered along medieval alleyways. The ruins of **King John's Castle**, built by the Normans to protect the entrance to the lough, still dominate the village, and there are other impressive fortified buildings, including the Mint. The **Holy Trinity Heritage Centre**, which is housed in a medieval church, traces the history of the port from Anglo-Norman times.

Carlingford is the country's oyster capital, and its oyster festival in August draws a large crowd. The lough is a popular watersports centre too, and in summer you can go on cruises around the lough from the village quayside.

Detail from a tomb in Monasterboice graveyard

Carlingford is well placed for hikes around the Cooley Peninsula. The **Carlingford Adventure Centre** provides information for walkers and also organizes its own tours.

ENVIRONS: A scenic route weaves around the **Cooley Peninsula**, skirting the coast and then cutting right through the mountains. The section along the north coast is the most dramatic: just 3 km (1.5 miles) northwest of Carlingford, in the **Slieve Foye Forest Park**, a corkscrew road climbs to give a gorgeous panoramic view over the hills and lough.

The Tain Trail, which you can join at Carlingford, is a 30-km (19-mile) circuit through some of the peninsula's most rugged scenery, with cairns and other prehistoric sites scattered over the moorland. Keen hikers will be able to walk it in a day.

Monasterboice 9

Road map D3. Co Louth. to Drogheda. daily.

FOUNDED in the 5th century by an obscure disciple of St Patrick called St Buite, this monastic settlement is one of the most famous religious sites in the country. The ruins of the medieval monastery are enclosed within a graveyard in a lovely secluded spot north of Drogheda. The site includes a roofless round tower and two churches, but Monasterboice's greatest treasures are its 10th-century High Crosses.

Muiredach's High Cross is the finest of its kind in Ireland, and its sculpted biblical scenes are still remarkably fresh. They depict the life of Christ on the west face, while the east face, described in detail opposite, features mainly Old Testament scenes. The cross is named after an inscription on the base – "A prayer for Muiredach by whom this cross was made" – which is perhaps a reference to the abbot of Monasterboice. The 6.5-m (21-ft) West Cross, also known as the Tall Cross, is one of the largest in Ireland. The carving has not lasted as well as on Muiredach's Cross, but you can make out scenes from the Death of Christ. The North Cross, which is the least notable of the three, features a Crucifixion and a carved spiral pattern.

Round tower and West High Cross at Monasterboice

Ireland's High Crosses

HIGH CROSSES exist in Celtic parts of both Britain and Ireland. Yet in their profusion and craftsmanship, Irish High Crosses are exceptional. The distinctive ringed cross has become a symbol of Irish Christianity and is still imitated today. The beautiful High Crosses associated with medieval monasteries were carved between the 8th and 12th centuries. The early crosses bore only geometric motifs, but in the 9th to 10th centuries a new style emerged when sculpted scenes from the Bible were introduced. Referred to as "sermons in stone", these later versions may have been used to educate the masses. In essence, though, the High Cross was a status symbol for the monastery or a local patron.

Pillar stones *inscribed with crosses, like this 6th-century example at Riasc (see p150), were precursors of the High Cross.*

Capstone, showing St Anthony and St Paul meeting in the desert

Tenon

The High Cross at Ahenny *(see p191) is typical of 8th-century "ornamental" crosses. These were carved with interlacing patterns and spirals similar to those used in Celtic metalwork and jewellery.*

MUIREDACH'S CROSS

Each face of this 10th-century cross at Monasterboice features scenes from the Bible, including the east face seen here. The 5.5-m (18-ft) cross consists of three blocks of sandstone fitted together by means of tenons and sockets.

The Last Judgment shows Christ in Glory surrounded by a crowd of resurrected souls. The devil stands on his right clutching a pitchfork, ready to chase the damned souls into Hell.

Angle moulding

The ring served a functional as well as a decorative purpose, providing support for the head and arms of the stone cross.

Moses smites the rock to obtain water for the Israelites.

Adoration of the Magi

David struggling with Goliath

The Dysert O'Dea Cross (see p181) *dates from the 1100s and represents the late phase of High Cross art. It features the figures of Christ and a bishop carved in high relief.*

Socket

Base

Tenon

The Fall of Man *shows Adam and Eve beneath an apple-laden tree, with Cain slaying Abel alongside. Both scenes are frequently depicted on Irish High Crosses.*

Drogheda ⑩

Road map D3. Co Louth. 25,000.
West St (mid-Jun–mid-Sep: 041 37070). Sat.

Drogheda viewed from Millmount across the River Boyne

IN THE 14TH CENTURY, this historic Norman port near the mouth of the River Boyne was one of Ireland's most important towns. However, the place seems never to have recovered from the trauma of a vicious attack by Cromwell in 1649 *(see p37)*, in which 2,000 citizens were killed. Although it now looks rather dilapidated, the town has retained its original street plan and has a rich medieval heritage.

Little remains of Drogheda's medieval defences but **St Lawrence Gate**, a fine 13th-century barbican, has survived. Nearby, there are two churches called **St Peter's**. The one belonging to the Church of Ireland, built in 1753, is the more striking and has some splendid grave slabs. The Catholic church is worth visiting to see the embalmed head of Oliver Plunkett, an archbishop martyred in 1681.

South of the river you can climb Millmount, a Norman motte topped by a Martello tower. As well as providing a good view, this is the site of the **Millmount Museum**, which contains an interesting display of historical artifacts, as well as craft workshops.

🏛 **Millmount Museum**
Millmount Square. 041 33097.
Tue–Sun. 10 days at Christmas.

Newgrange and the Boyne Valley ⑪

Road map D3. Co Meath. to Drogheda. to Slane or Drogheda. Brú na Bóinne Interpretive Centre (041 24488).

KNOWN AS Brú na Bóinne, the "Palace of the Boyne", this river valley was the cradle of Irish civilization. The fertile soil supported a sophisticated society in Neolithic times. Much evidence survives, in the form of ring forts, passage graves and sacred enclosures. The most important Neolithic monuments in the valley are three passage graves: supreme among these is **Newgrange** *(see pp238–9)*, but **Dowth** and **Knowth** are significant too. The Boyne Valley also encompasses the Hill of Slane and the Hill of Tara *(see p240)*, both of which are major sites in Celtic mythology. Indeed, this whole region is rich in

River Boyne near the site of the Battle of the Boyne

THE BATTLE OF THE BOYNE

In 1688, the Catholic King of England, James II, was deposed from his throne, to be re-placed by his Protestant daughter, Mary, and her husband, William of Orange. Determined to win back the crown, James sought the support of Irish Catholics, and challenged William at Oldbridge by the River Boyne west of Drogheda. The Battle of the Boyne took place on 1 July 1690, with James's poorly trained force of 25,000 French and Irish Catholics facing William's hardened army of 36,000 French Huguenots, Dutch, English and Scots. The Protestants triumphed and James fled to France, after a battle that signalled the beginning of total Protestant power over Ireland. It ushered in the confiscation of Catholic lands and the suppression of Catholic interests, sealing the country's fate for the next 300 years.

William of Orange leading his troops at the Battle of the Boyne, 1 July 1690

associations with Ireland's prehistory. With monuments predating Egypt's pyramids, the Boyne Valley is marketed as the Irish "Valley of the Kings".

Newgrange and Knowth can only be seen on a tour run by **Brú na Bóinne Interpretive Centre** near Newgrange. The centre also has displays on the area's Stone Age heritage and a reconstruction of Newgrange.

⋔ Dowth
Off N51, 3 km (2 miles) E of Newgrange. ● *to the public.*
The passage grave at Dowth was plundered by Victorian souvenir hunters and has not been fully excavated. You cannot approach the tomb, but it can be seen from the road.

⋔ Knowth
1.5 km (1 mile) NW of Newgrange. ○ *as Newgrange (see pp238–9).*
Knowth outdoes Newgrange in several respects, above all in the quantity of its treasures, which form the greatest concentration of megalithic art in Europe. Also, the site was occupied for a much longer period – from Neolithic times right up until about 1400.

Unusually, Knowth has two passage tombs rather than one. These are closed during excavation work, which has been going on since 1962. However, while just a third of the site is open, you can see into several of the 17 satellite tombs. Some of the kerbstones, many of them finely carved, are also on display.

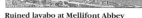
Ruined lavabo at Mellifont Abbey

Slane Castle in grounds landscaped by Capability Brown

Mellifont Abbey ⓬

Road map D3. Cullen, Co Louth. 🆑 041 26459. 🚌 *to Drogheda.* 🚆 *to Drogheda or Slane.* ○ *May–Oct: daily.* 🅿️

ON THE BANKS of the River Mattock, 10 km (6 miles) west of Drogheda, lies the first Cistercian monastery to have been built in Ireland. Mellifont was founded in 1142 on the orders of St Malachy, the Archbishop of Armagh. He was greatly influenced

Glazed medieval tiles at Mellifont Abbey

by St Bernard who, based at his monastery at Clairvaux in France, was behind the success of the Cistercian Order in Europe. The archbishop introduced not only Cisterican rigour to Mellifont, but also the formal style of monastic architecture used on the continent. His new monastery became a model for other Cistercian centres built in Ireland, retaining its supremacy over them until 1539, when the abbey was closed and turned into a fortified house. William of Orange used Mellifont as his headquarters during the Battle of the Boyne in 1690. The abbey is now a ruin, but it is still possible to appreciate the scale and ground plan of the original complex. Not much survives of the abbey church, but to the south of it, enclosed by what remains of the Romanesque cloister, is the most interesting building at Mellifont: a unique 13th-century lavabo where monks came to wash their hands in a fountain before meals. Four of the building's original eight sides survive, each with a graceful Romanesque arch. On the eastern side of the cloister stands the 14th-century chapter house. It has an impressive vaulted ceiling and a floor laid with glazed medieval tiles taken from the abbey church.

Slane ⓭

Road map D3. Co Meath. 🚶 *700.* 🚌

SLANE IS AN ATTRACTIVE estate village, centred on a quartet of Georgian houses. The Boyne flows through it and skirts the grounds of **Slane Castle**, set in glorious gardens laid out in the 18th century by Capability Brown. Sadly, the Gothic Revival castle has been closed since a fire in 1991.

Just to the north rises the **Hill of Slane** where, in 433, St Patrick is said to have lit a Paschal (Easter) fire as a challenge to the pagan High King of Tara *(see p240)*. The event is endowed with symbolic importance as the triumph of Christianity over paganism.

Newgrange

Tri-spiral carving on stone in chamber

THE ORIGINS of Newgrange, one of the most important passage graves in Europe, are steeped in mystery. According to Celtic lore, the legendary kings of Tara *(see p240)* were buried here, but Newgrange predates them. Built in around 3200 BC, the grave was left untouched by all invaders until it was rediscovered in 1699. When it was excavated in the 1960s, archaeologists discovered that on the winter solstice (21 December), rays of sun enter the tomb and light up the burial chamber – making it the world's oldest solar observatory. Newgrange is popular, especially in summer, but visits are by tour only, so the site itself does not get too crowded. Tours start at Brú na Bóinne Interpretive Centre and include nearby Knowth *(see pp236–7)*.

Basin Stone
The chiselled stones, found in each recess, would have once contained funerary offerings and the bones of the dead.

The chamber has three recesses or side chambers: the north recess is the one struck by sunlight on the winter solstice.

Chamber Ceiling
The burial chamber's intricate corbelled ceiling, which reaches a height of 6 m (20 ft) above the floor, has survived intact. The overlapping slabs form a conical hollow, topped by a single capstone.

CONSTRUCTION OF NEWGRANGE

The tomb at Newgrange was designed by people with clearly exceptional artistic and engineering skills, who had use of neither the wheel nor metal tools. About 200,000 tonnes of loose stones were transported to build the mound, or cairn, which protects the passage grave. Larger slabs were used to make the circle around the cairn (12 out of a probable 35 stones have survived), the kerb and the tomb itself. Many of the kerbstones and the slabs lining the passage, the chamber and its recesses are decorated with zigzags, spirals and other geometric motifs. The grave's corbelled ceiling consists of smaller, unadorned slabs and has proved completely waterproof for the last 5,000 years.

Mound

Entrance

Stone circle (existing stones shaded)

100 m
328 ft

Decorated stones (shaded)

Recesses   Passage   Entrance

25 m
82 ft

Plan of passage and burial chamber

Restoration of Newgrange
Located on a low ridge north of the Boyne, Newgrange took more than 70 years to build. Between 1962 and 1975 the passage grave and mound were restored as closely as possible to their original state.

The standing stones in the passage are slabs of slate which would have been collected locally.

Passage
At dawn on 21 December, a beam of sunlight shines through the roof box (a feature unique to Newgrange), travels along the 19-m (62-ft) passage and hits the central recess in the burial chamber.

The retaining wall around the front of the cairn was rebuilt using the white quartz and granite stones found scattered around the site during excavations.

Roof box

Entrance
The opening was originally blocked by the stone standing to its right. Newgrange's most elaborately carved kerbstone is in front, part of the kerb of huge slabs around the cairn.

Trim Castle set in water meadows beside the River Boyne

Hill of Tara 🎠

Road map D3. Nr Killmessan Village, Co Meath. 🛈 *046 25903 (early May–Sep).* 🚌 *to Navan.* ⭕ *daily.* 📷 *for Interpretative Centre.* 🛗

A SITE of mythical importance, Tara was the political and spiritual centre of Celtic Ireland and the seat of the High Kings until the 11th century. The spread of Christianity, which eroded the importance of Tara, is marked by a statue of St Patrick. The symbolism of the site was not lost on Daniel O'Connell *(see p40),* who chose Tara for a rally in 1843, attended by over one million people.

Tours from the Interpretative Centre point out a Stone Age passage grave and Iron Age hill forts, though to the untutored eye, these earthworks look like mere hollows and grassy mounds. Clearest is the Royal Enclosure, an oval fort, in the centre of which is Cormac's House containing the "stone of destiny" *(Lialh Fail),* an ancient fertility symbol and inauguration stone of the High Kings. However, all this is secondary to the poignant atmosphere and views over the Boyne Valley.

Trim 🎠

Road map D3. Co Meath. 🏚 *4,000.* 🚌 🛈 *Mill St (046 37111).* 🛒 *Fri.*

T RIM IS ONE of the most pleasing Midlands market towns. A Norman stronghold on the River Boyne, it marked a boundary of the Pale *(see p124).* Trim runs efficient heritage and genealogy centres

while the **Duchas Trim Folk Theatre** provides rousing summer entertainment. (This popular company is at present in search of new premises.) Equally engrossing is the Nun Run, a bizarre summer horse race with nuns as jockeys, which takes place near **Trim Castle**. The castle was founded in 1173 by Hugh de Lacy, a Norman knight, and is one of the largest medieval castles in Ireland. It makes a spectacular backdrop so is often used as a film set, most recently seen in Mel Gibson's *Braveheart* (1995). Over the river is **Talbot Castle**, an Augustinian abbey converted to a manor house in the 15th century. Just north of the abbey, **St Patrick's Cathedral** incorporates part of a medieval church with a 15th-century tower and sections of the original chancel.

Butterstream Gardens, on the edge of town, are the best in the county. A luxuriant herbaceous bed is the centrepiece, but equally pleasing are the exotic woodland, rose and white gardens. The design is enhanced by pergolas, pools and bridges.

🏰 **Trim Castle**
🛈 *046 37111.* ⭕ *daily.*
🌷 **Butterstream Gardens**
Kildalkey Rd. 🛈 *046 36017.*
⭕ *Apr–Sep: daily.* 📷

Mullingar 🎠

Road map C3. Co Westmeath.
🏚 *12,000.* 🚌 🚌 🛈 *Dublin Rd (044 48650).* 🛒 *Sat.*

T HE COUNTY TOWN of Westmeath is a prosperous but unremarkable market town encircled by the Royal Canal

Aerial view of Iron Age forts on the Hill of Tara

(see p99), which with its 46 locks links Dublin with the River Shannon. The cost of building the canal bankrupted its investors and it was never profitable. Although Mullingar's main appeal is as a base to explore the surrounding area, pubs such as Con's and the cheery Canton Casey's can make a pleasant interlude.

ENVIRONS: Recent restoration of the Dublin to Mullingar stretch of the Royal Canal has created attractive towpaths for walkers, and angling facilities.

Just off the Kilbeggan road from Mullingar stands **Belvedere House**, a romantic Palladian villa overlooking Lough Ennel. The house, built in 1740 by Richard Castle, and decorated with Rococo plasterwork, is being restored, but the wonderful gardens are open.

Shortly after the house was built, the first Earl of Belvedere accused his young wife of having an affair with his brother, and imprisoned her for 31 years in a neighbouring house. In 1755, the Earl built a Gothic folly – the Jealous Wall – to block the view of his second brother's more opulent mansion across the lake. The Jealous Wall remains, as does an octagonal gazebo and other follies.

Charming terraces, framed by urns and yews, descend to the lake; on the other side of the house is a picturesque walled garden, enclosed by an arboretum and rolling parkland.

🏛 Belvedere House
6.5 km (4 miles) S of Mullingar.
(044 40861. **House and Gardens**
○ Apr–Oct: daily. ⏳ 🅿 &

The Jealous Wall at Belvedere House, near Mullingar

Athlone Castle below the towers of the church of St Peter and St Paul

Kilbeggan ⑰

Road map C4. Co Westmeath.
🚶 600. 🚆

SITUATED BETWEEN Mullingar and Tullamore, this pleasant village has a small harbour on the Grand Canal. However, the main point of interest is **Locke's Distillery**. Founded in 1757, it claims to be the oldest licensed pot still distillery in the world. Unable to compete with Scotch whisky manufacturers, the company went bankrupt in 1954, but the aroma hung in the warehouses for years and was known as "the angel's share". The distillery was reopened as a museum in 1987. The building is authentic, a solid structure

Miniature whiskey bottles at Locke's Distillery in Kilbeggan

complete with water wheel and inside steam engine. A tour traces the process of Irish whiskey-making, from the mash tuns to the vast fermentation vats and creation of wash (rough beer) to the distillation and maturation stages. At the tasting stage, workers would sample the whiskey in the can pit room. Visitors can still taste whiskeys in the bar but, unlike the original workers, cannot bathe in the whiskey vats.

🏛 Locke's Distillery
Main Street. **(** 0506 32134.
○ daily. ⏳

Athlone ⑱

Road map C3. Co Westmeath.
🚶 15,000. 🚆 🚌 🛈 Market Square (0902 94630). 🚆 Fri.

THE TOWN owes its historical importance to its position by a natural ford on the River Shannon. **Athlone Castle** is a much altered 13th-century fortress, which was badly damaged in the Jacobite Wars *(see pp36–7)*. It lies in the shadow of the 19th-century church of St Peter and St Paul. The neighbouring streets offer several good pubs as well as docks lined with warehouses. Across the river from the castle, boats depart for Clonmacnoise *(see pp242–3)* or Lough Ree.

🏰 Athlone Castle
Market Square. **(** 0902 94630.
○ May–Oct: daily. ⏳ & limited.

ENVIRONS: The **Lough Ree Trail** starts 8 km (5 miles) northeast of Athlone, at Glasson. The route passes picturesque views and unspoilt countryside. The trail is a popular cycling tour.

Clonmacnoise ⑲

Detail on a grave slab

T HIS MEDIEVAL MONASTERY, in a remote spot by the River Shannon, was founded by St Ciaran in 545–548. Clonmacnoise lay at a crossroads of medieval routes, linking all parts of Ireland. Known for its scholarship and piety, it thrived from the 7th to the 12th century. Many kings of Tara and of Connaught were buried here. Plundered by the Vikings and Anglo-Normans, it fell to the English in 1552. Today, a group of stone churches (temples), a cathedral, two round towers and three High Crosses remain.

Last Circuit of Pilgrims at Clonmacnoise
This painting (1838), by George Petrie, shows pilgrims walking the traditional route three times around the site. Pilgrims still do this every year on 9 September, St Ciaran's Day.

The Pope's Shelter was where John Paul II conducted Mass during his visit in 1979.

Cross of the Scriptures
This copy of the original 9th-century cross (now in the museum) is decorated with biblical scenes, but the identity of most of the figures is uncertain.

VISITING CLONMACNOISE

The Visitors' Centre is housed in three buildings modelled on beehive huts *(see p19)*. The museum section contains early grave slabs and the three remaining High Crosses, replicas of which now stand in their original locations. The Nuns' Church, northeast of the main site, has a Romanesque doorway and chancel arch.

KEY

1 South Cross	**7** Cathedral
2 Temple Dowling	**8** North Cross
3 Temple Hurpan	**9** Cross of the Scriptures
4 Temple Melaghlin	**10** Round Tower
5 Temple Ciaran	**11** Temple Connor
6 Temple Kelly	**12** Temple Finghin

0 metres   50

0 yards   50

Pilgrim path to Nuns' Church

Entrance

Pope's Shelter

To Visitors' Centre

Whispering Door
*Above the cathedral's 15th-
century north doorway are
carvings of saints Francis,
Patrick and Dominic. The
acoustics of the doorway are
such that even a whisper is
carried inside the building.*

**The Shannonbridge Bog Railway
passing an area of cut bog**

Shannonbridge
Bog Railway ⑳

Road map C4. 5 km (3 miles) E of
Shannonbridge, Co Offaly. ▮ *0905
74114.* ▯ *to Athlone.* ◯ *Apr–Oct:
daily; Nov–Mar: groups by appt.* ▨ ▮

STARTING near Shannonbridge,
this guided tour by train is
run by the Irish Peat Board
(Bord na Móna). The 45-minute
tour covers 9 km (6 miles) of
bogland and gives a fascinating
insight into the history and
development of the Blackwater
raised bogs – an area of great
ecological importance, parts
of which are protected.

Tour guides describe the
transformation from lake to
marshy fen and thence to bog
(see p244), and explain that
in several hundred years the
bog will become fields and
woodland. They also point out
the area's distinctive flora and
fauna, from dragonflies to bog
cotton, bog asphodel and
sphagnum moss. The small
lakes and pools that punctuate
the bog provide excellent
habitats for wetland birds.

Bog oaks – old trees which
have been preserved in the
bog – are visible in the places
where the peat has been har-
vested. For centuries, peat has
been the main source of fuel
in rural Ireland, and visitors
can watch peat being cut by
hand using the traditional tool
known as a "slane". Modern
peat-harvesting machines in
use nearby supply the power
station at Shannonbridge.
There is a craft shop and also a
machinery museum close to
where the train ride begins.

The Round Tower *(see p18)* is
over 19 m (62 ft) high with its
doorway above ground level.

Temples Dowling, Hurpan and Melaghlin
*Built as a family crypt, Temple Hurpan was a 17th-century
addition to the early Romanesque Temple Dowling. The 13th-
century Temple Melaghlin has two fine round-headed windows.*

The Raised Bogs of the Midlands

PEATLAND OR BOG, which covers about 15 per cent of the Irish landscape, exists in two principal forms. Most extensive is the thin blanket bog found chiefly in the west, while the dome-shaped raised bogs are more characteristic of the Midlands – notably in an area known as the Bog of Allen.

Four-spotted chaser dragonfly

Although Irish boglands are some of the largest in Europe, the use of peat for domestic fuel and fertilizer has greatly reduced their extent. This has threatened not only the shape of the Irish landscape but also the survival of a unique habitat and the unusual plants and insects it supports.

Unspoilt expanse of the Bog of Allen

Peat cutters still gather turf (as peat is known locally) by hand in parts of Ireland. It is then set in stacks to dry. Peat makes a good fuel, because it is rich in partially decayed vegetation, laid down over thousands of years.

Fen plants / Birch and willow scrub / Moraine (glacial deposits)

8000 BC: *Shallow meltwater lakes that formed after the Ice Age gradually filled with mud. Reeds, sedges and other fen plants began to dominate in the marshy conditions which resulted.*

Fen plants (reeds and sedges) / Fen peat / Mud

6000 BC: *As the fen vegetation died, it sank to the lake bed but did not decompose fully in the waterlogged conditions, forming a layer of peat. This slowly built up and also spread outwards.*

Fen peat / Fresh sphagnum peat / Buried tree stumps

3000 BC: *As the peat built up and the lake slowly disappeared, plant life in the developing bog had to rely almost exclusively on rainwater, which is acid. Fen plants could not survive in these acidic conditions and gave way to bog mosses, mainly species of sphagnum. As these mosses died, they formed a layer of sphagnum peat on the surface of the bog which, over the centuries, attained a distinctive domed shape.*

Pine and alder trees / Raised bog / Tree stumps

Present day: *Few raised bogs are actively growing today. Those that remain contain a fascinating historical record of the landscape. The survival of ancient tree stumps shows how well plants are preserved in peat.*

Sphagnum moss

Birr ㉑

Road map 4C. Co Offaly. 🏛 *4,100*.
🚌 🛈 *May–Sep: Rosse Row (0509 20110)*.

BIRR, A GENTRIFIED estate town, grew up in the shadow of the castle where the Earls of Rosse have resided for almost four centuries. It is famous for its authentic Georgian layout, with houses displaying original fanlights, door panelling and iron railings. Two particularly elegant streets are Oxmantown Mall, designed by the 2nd Earl of Rosse, and John's Mall. Emmet Square may have sold its Georgian soul to commerce, but Dooly's Hotel is still a fine example of an old coaching inn. Foster's bar, in nearby Connaught Street, is one of many traditional shopfronts to have been restored in Birr.

🏯 Birr Castle
Rosse Row. 【 *0509 20056*.
Gardens ◯ *daily*. ● *25 Dec*. 📷 ⛭
Birr Castle was founded in 1620 by the Parsons, later Earls of Rosse, and is still the family seat. They have been most noted for their contribution to astronomy – a telescope, built by the 3rd Earl in 1845, was the largest in the world at the time. The 17-m (56-ft) wooden tube, supported by two walls, can be seen in the grounds and is currently being restored to its original condition.

The castle is closed to the general public, but the glory of Birr lies in its grounds. First landscaped in the 18th century, these are famous for their 9-m (30-ft) box hedges and for the exotic trees and shrubs that were gathered during foreign expeditions sponsored by the 6th Earl. The magnolias and maples are particularly striking. The gardens overlook the meeting of two rivers, and water greatly influenced the planning of the grounds. There is a charming riverside garden and a small suspension bridge.

Slieve Bloom Mountains ㉒

Road map D4. Co Offaly and Co Laois.
🚌 *to Mountmellick*. 🛈 *May–Sep: Rosse Row, Birr (0509 20110, 20029)*.

THIS LOW RANGE of mountains rises unexpectedly from the bogs and plains of Offaly and Laois, providing a welcome change in the predominantly flat Midlands. You can walk along the **Slieve Bloom Way**, a 30-km (19-mile) circular trail through an unspoilt landscape of open vistas, deep wooded glens and mountain streams. There are other marked paths too. Good starting points are **Cadamstown**, with an attractive old mill, and the pretty village of **Kinnitty** – both in the northern foothills.

An alcove in the front hall of Emo Court with a *trompe l'oeil* ceiling

Emo Court ㉓

Road map D4. 13 km (8 miles) NE of Portlaoise, Co Laois. 【 *0502 26573*.
🚌 *to Monasterevin or Portlaoise*.
House ◯ *mid-Jun–Sep: daily*.
Gardens ◯ *daily*. 📷 ⛭ *limited*.

EMO COURT, commissioned by the Earl of Portarlington in 1790, represents the only foray into domestic architecture by James Gandon, designer of the Custom House in Dublin *(see p86)*. The monumental Neo-Classical mansion has a splendid façade featuring an Ionic portico. Inside are a magnificent gilded rotunda and fine stuccowork ceilings.

Emo Court became the property of the Office of Public Works in 1994 but the previous owner, who restored the house, is still resident and is now working on the grounds. These are adorned with fine statuary and include a lakeside walk.

Rock of Dunamase ㉔

Road map D4. 5 km (3 miles) E of Portlaoise, Co Laois. 🚌 *to Portlaoise*.

THE ROCK OF DUNAMASE, which looms dramatically above the plains east of Portlaoise, has long been a military site. Originally crowned by an Iron Age ring fort, the 13th-century castle which succeeded it is now more prominent – though it was virtually destroyed by Cromwellian forces in 1650. You can reach the battered keep by climbing up banks and ditches through two gateways and a fortified courtyard.

Rock of Dunamase viewed from Stradbally to the east

NORTHERN IRELAND

LONDONDERRY · ANTRIM · TYRONE · FERMANAGH
ARMAGH · DOWN

ORTHERN IRELAND *has sights from every era of Ireland's history as well as magnificently varied coastal and lakeland scenery. In the past, it has received fewer visitors than the Republic as a result of the "Troubles". Following recent moves towards peace, there seems every chance that it will at last attract the attention it deserves.*

The province of Northern Ireland was created after partition of the island in 1921. Its six counties (plus Donegal, Monaghan and Cavan) were part of Ulster, one of Ireland's four traditional kingdoms. It was most probably in Ulster that Christianity first ousted the old Celtic pagan beliefs. In 432 St Patrick landed at Saul in County Down, later founding a church at Armagh, which is still the spiritual capital of Ireland.

The dominant political force in early Christian times was the Uí Néill clan. Their descendants, the O'Neills, put up fierce resistance to English conquest in the late 16th century. Hugh O'Neill, Earl of Tyrone, had some notable successes against the armies of Elizabeth I, but was defeated and in 1607 fled to Europe with other Irish lords from Ulster, in what became known as the "Flight of the Earls". Vacant estates were granted to individuals and companies, who planted them with English and Scottish Protestants *(see p37)*. Many Plantation towns, such as Londonderry, preserve their 17th-century layout around a central square or "diamond".

The arrival of new settlers meant that Irish Catholics were increasingly marginalized, thereby sowing the seeds of 400 years of conflict.

In the relative tranquillity of the 18th century, the Anglo-Irish nobility built stately homes, such as Mount Stewart House on the Ards Peninsula and Castle Coole near Enniskillen. Ulster also enjoyed prosperity in the 19th century through its ship-building, linen and rope-making industries.

Though densely populated and industrialized around Belfast, away from the capital the region is primarily agricultural. It also has areas of outstanding natural beauty, notably the rugged Antrim coastline around the Giant's Causeway, the Mountains of Mourne in County Down and the Erne lakeland in the west of the region.

Belfast's City Hall (1906), symbol of the city's civic pride

◁ **Carrick-a-rede Rope Bridge, an unusual tourist attraction on the Causeway Coast**

Exploring Northern Ireland

THE STARTING POINT for most visitors to the province is Belfast. The capital has grand Victorian buildings, good pubs and the excellent Ulster Museum. However, Northern Ireland's greatest attractions lie along its coast. These range from the extraordinary volcanic landscape of the Giant's Causeway to Carrickfergus, Ireland's best preserved Norman castle. There are also Victorian resorts, like Portstewart, tiny fishing villages and unspoilt sandy beaches, such as Benone Strand. Ramblers are drawn to the Mountains of Mourne, while anglers and boating enthusiasts can enjoy the lakeland of Lower Lough Erne.

Harbour and promenade at the seaside resort of Portstewart

0 kilometres   10

0 miles   5

CAUSEV
CO

BENONE STRAND   PORTSTE

②   ③   ④

Lough Foyle

MUSSENDEN
TEMPLE

COLE

A2

Letterkenny

①
LONDONDERRY

Roe

Foyle

A6

A5

B48   SPERRIN   MOUNTAINS

STRABANE

BEAGHMORE
STONE CIRCLES

⑬

ULSTER HISTORY PARK   ⑭

⑮   A505

COOKSTOWN   ⑫

Derg

ULSTER-AMERICAN
FOLK PARK

A29

OMAGH

A5

DUNGANNON   ㉒

A47

⑰   LOWER
LOUGH
ERNE

A32

Sligo

⑯

BELLEEK
POTTERY

A4

DEVENISH
ISLAND   ⑱

A32

⑲
ENNISKILLEN

ARMAG

MARBLE   ⑳
ARCH CAVES

A509

Upper Lough Erne

A34

FLORENCE   ㉑
COURT

Monaghan

GETTING AROUND

Belfast is the transport hub of Northern Ireland. From here the very limited train network runs northwest to Londonderry and south to Dublin. In most parts of the province you have to rely on buses, but fortunately, even in rural areas, these are fairly frequent and punctual. However, a car is essential if you want to go off the beaten track in search of ancient monuments or tour the coast at leisure. Depending on the security situation, you may still encounter temporary checkpoints set up by the army and police (see p343).

KEY

▬	Motorway
▬	Major road
═	Minor road
▬	Scenic route
～	River
☀	Viewpoint

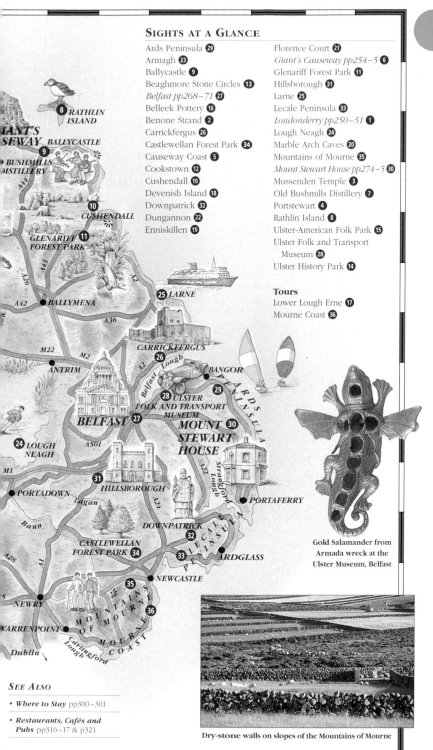

SIGHTS AT A GLANCE

Gold Salamander from Armada wreck at the Ulster Museum, Belfast

Dry-stone walls on slopes of the Mountains of Mourne

Londonderry ❶

Carving on Shipquay Gate

S T COLUMBA founded a monastery here beside the River Foyle in 546. He called the place Doire or "oak grove", later anglicized as Derry. In 1613, the city was selected as a major Plantation project *(see pp36–7)*, organized by London livery companies. As a result, it acquired the prefix London, though most people still call it Derry. When British troops shot dead 13 demonstrators in 1972, Derry hit the world's headlines. Today, with an end to the Troubles in sight, the city council has undertaken several admirable heritage projects.

★ Tower Museum
The excellent displays on local history in this new museum include one on the mapping of the area during the reign of Elizabeth I.

Shipquay Gate

The Craft Village was opened in 1992 as part of the city's plans to bring the centre back to life.

Butcher's Gate

The Diamond
The war memorial in the Diamond or main square was erected in 1927. It was originally made for the city of Sheffield in England.

Court House

Army post

Bishop's Gate

★ St Columb's Cathedral
The nave's wooden ceiling dates from 1862. The corbels are carved with the heads of former bishops and deans.

The Playhouse

New Gate

KEY

P	Parking
i	Tourist information
– – –	Suggested route

★ **Guildhall**
This stained-glass window shows St Columba. Others feature incidents from the siege of Derry, including the apprentice boys shutting the city gates in 1688.

Ferryquay Gate

To Craigavon Bridge and River Foyle

0 metres   100

0 yards   100

STAR SIGHTS

★ **Tower Museum**

★ **Guildhall**

★ **St Columb's Cathedral**

⛪ St Columb's Cathedral
St Columb's Court. ☎ 01504 267313.
🕐 Mon–Sat. 🔲 📷 ♿
Built between 1628 and 1633, in "Planters' Gothic" style, St Columb's was the first cathedral to be founded in the British Isles after the Reformation. The interior was extensively rebuilt in the 19th century. A small museum in the Chapter House contains relics from the siege of 1689 *(see pp36–7)*, including the 17th-century locks and keys of the city. In the vestibule is a hollow mortar cannonball that was fired into the city by James II's army. It carried terms for capitulation, but the reply of the Protestants within the walls was a defiant "No surrender", a phrase used by Loyalists to this day.

Lock of city gate in St Columb's Cathedral

🏛 Tower Museum
Union Hall Place. ☎ 01504 372411.
🕐 Jul & Aug: daily; Sep–Jun: Tue–Sat.
● 17 Mar, Good Fri, 25 & 26 Dec.
📷 🎟 by arrangement. ♿
Housed in O'Doherty Tower (a replica of the original 16th-century building on this site), the museum traces the history of the city from its foundation to the recent Troubles using multimedia displays. Upstairs, an exhibition about the 1688 Spanish Armada includes artifacts from ships wrecked in nearby Kinnagoe Bay.

⚓ Walls of Derry
Access from Magazine Street.
Among the best preserved city fortifications in Europe, the city walls rise to a height of 8 m (26 ft) and in places are 9 m (30 ft) wide. Completed in 1618 to defend the new merchant city from Gaelic chieftains in Donegal, the walls have never been breached, not even during the siege of 1689, when 7,000 out of a population of 20,000 perished from disease or starvation. Extensive restoration work means that it should soon be possible to walk right around the walls for the first time in decades. Just outside the old fortifications, beyond Butcher's Gate, is the Bogside, a Catholic area with a famous mural that announces "You are now entering free Derry".

🏛 Guildhall
Guildhall Square. ☎ 01504 377335.
🕐 Mon–Fri. 📷
Standing between the walled city and the River Foyle, this Neo-Gothic building was constructed in 1890, but a fire in 1908 and a bomb in 1972 both necessitated substantial repairs. Stained-glass windows – copies of the originals – recount the history of Derry. To the rear of the Guildhall is Derry Quay, from where Irish emigrants sailed to America in the 18th and 19th centuries.

ENVIRONS: Just off the B194, on the way to Muff, stands a memorial to American aviator Amelia Earhart, the first woman to complete a transatlantic solo flight. She had intended to fly to Paris, but in May 1932 landed in a field outside Derry. A sculpture marks the spot and the nearby **Earhart Centre** contains a small exhibition.

🏛 Earhart Centre
Ballyarnet. ☎ 01504 354040.
🕐 Mon–Fri.

The old walled city viewed across the River Foyle

Terraced houses behind the promenade at Portstewart

Benone Strand ❷

Road map D1. Co Londonderry.
ℹ *Jul & Aug: Benone Tourist Complex, 53 Benone Ave, Seacoast Rd, Magilligan (015047 50555).*

THE WIDE, golden sands of Ireland's longest beach, also known as Magilligan Strand, sweep along the Londonderry coastline for more than 10 km (6 miles). The magnificent beach has been granted EU Blue Flag status for its cleanliness. Marking the western extremity of the beach is **Magilligan Point** where a Martello tower, built during the Napoleonic wars, stands guard over the bottleneck entrance to Lough Foyle. To get to the point, renowned for its rare shellfish and sea birds, you have to drive over ramps below the watchtowers and listening devices of a huge army base. The experience is rather unsettling, but well worth the trouble.

Mussenden Temple ❸

Road map D1. Co Londonderry.
☏ *01265 848728.* **◻** *Jul–Aug: daily (pm only); Apr–Jun & Sep: Sat, Sun & public hols.* **♿** *limited.*

THE ODDEST SIGHT along the Londonderry coast is this small, domed rotunda perched precariously on a windswept headland outside the family resort of Castlerock. The temple was built in 1785 by Frederick Augustus Hervey, the eccentric Earl of Bristol and Protestant Bishop of Derry, as a memorial to his cousin Mrs Frideswide Mussenden. The design was based on the Temple of Vesta at Tivoli outside Rome.

The walls, made of basalt faced with sandstone, open out at the four points of the compass to three windows and an entrance. Originally designed for use as a library (or, as some stories go, an elaborate boudoir for the bishop's mistress), the structure is now maintained by the National Trust and remains in excellent condition.

The bishop allowed the local priest to say Mass for his Roman Catholic tenants in the basement. Today, this contains artifacts from the bishop's former residence, the nearby Downhill Castle, which was gutted by fire and is now little more than an impressive shell.

The surrounding area offers some good glen and cliff walks and there are some magnificent views of the Londonderry and Antrim coastline. Below the temple is Downhill Strand, where the bishop sponsored horseback races between his clergy.

Portstewart ❹

Road map D1. Co Londonderry.
🏠 *5,500.* **🚉** *to Coleraine or Portrush.*
🚌 **ℹ** *Jul & Aug: Town Hall, The Crescent (01265 832286).*

A POPULAR HOLIDAY destination for Victorian middle-class families, the resort still emits a sedate, old-fashioned air. Its long, crescent-shaped seafront promenade is sheltered by rocky headlands. Just west of town, and accessible by road or by a cliffside walk, stretches **Portstewart Strand**, a magnificent, long, sandy beach, protected by the National Trust.

On Ramore Head, just to the east, lies **Portrush**, a brasher resort with an abundance of souvenir shops and amusement arcades. The East Strand is backed by sand dunes and runs parallel with the world-class **Royal Portrush Golf Links**. You can stroll along the beach to White Rocks – limestone cliffs carved by the wind and waves into caves and arches.

To the south is the university town of **Coleraine**. The North West 200 *(see p26)*, the world's fastest motorcycle road race, is run between Portstewart, Coleraine and Portrush. The race is held in May in front of 100,000 people.

Mussenden Temple set on a cliff top on the Londonderry coast

Causeway Coast **⑤**

Road map D1. Co Antrim. **ℹ** *Giant's Causeway (012657 31855).* **Carrick-a-rede Rope Bridge** **📞** *012657 31159.* ☐ *Easter & May–Aug: daily; Sep: Sat & Sun.* 🅿 *for car park.*

THE RENOWN of the **Giant's Causeway** *(see pp254–5),* Ireland's only World Heritage Site, overshadows the other attractions of this stretch of North Antrim coast. When visiting the Causeway, it is worth investigating the sandy bays, craggy headlands and dramatic ruins that punctuate the rest of this inspirational coastline.

Approaching the Causeway from the west, you pass the eerie ruins of **Dunluce Castle** perched vulnerably on a steep crag – a storm once blew its kitchen into the sea. Dating back to the 13th century, it was the main fortress of the MacDonnells, chiefs of Antrim. Although the roof has gone, it is still well preserved, with its twin towers, gateway and some original cobbling intact.

Dunseverick Castle can be reached by road or a lengthy hike from the Causeway. It is a much earlier fortification than Dunluce and only one massive

The roofless ruins of 13th-century Dunluce Castle

wall remains. Once the capital of the kingdom of Dalriada, it was linked to Tara *(see p240)* by a great road and was the departure point for 5th-century Irish raids on Scotland.

Just past the attractive, sandy **White Park Bay**, a tight switchback road leads down to the picturesque harbour of **Ballintoy**, reminiscent – on a good day – of an Aegean fishing village. **Sheep Island**, a rocky outcrop just offshore, is a cormorant colony. Local boat owners run trips past it in the summer.

Just east of Ballintoy is one of the most unusual and scary tourist attractions in Ireland, the **Carrick-a-rede Rope Bridge**. The bridge hangs 25 m (80 ft) above the sea and wobbles and twists as soon as you stand on it. Made of planks strung between wires, it provides access to the salmon

fishery on the tiny island across the 20-m (65-ft) chasm. There are strong handrails and safety nets, but it's definitely not for those with vertigo. Further east along the coast lies **Kinbane Castle**. Little remains of this 16th-century ruin but the views from it are spectacular.

♠ Dunluce Castle
📞 *012657 31206.* ☐ *daily.* 🅿 🈲

Fishing boats moored in the shelter of Ballintoy harbour

Carrick-a-rede Rope Bridge

THE NORTH ANTRIM COASTLINE

KEY

═	Minor road	🅿	Parking
▬	Major road	ℹ	Tourist information

Giant's Causeway •   Dunseverick Castle   White Park Bay   Sheep Island   Carrick-a-rede Rope Bridge
B146   Ballintoy   Kinbane Castle
Dunluce Castle   Portballintrae   A2   B15
Bushmills   B17   Ballycastle
Portrush   A2   B62   B17   B66   B147   B17   A2
Portstewart   B67

0 kilometres   5
0 miles   3

Giant's Causeway ❻

THE SHEER STRANGENESS of this place and the bizarre regularity of its basalt columns has made the Giant's Causeway the subject of numerous legends. The most popular tells how the giant, Finn MacCool *(see pp24–5)*, laid the causeway to provide a path across the sea to his lady love, who lived on the island of Staffa in Scotland – where similar columns are found. The Giant's Causeway

Chimney stacks attracts many tourists, who are taken by the busload from the visitors' centre down to the shore. Nothing, however, can destroy the magic of this place, with its looming grey cliffs and shrieking gulls; paths along the coast allow you to escape the crowds.

Aird's Snout
This nose-shaped promontory juts out from the 120-m (395-ft) basalt cliffs that soar above the Giant's Causeway.

THE FORMATION OF THE CAUSEWAY

Wooded landscape — Hot lava — Valley

Lower basalts

Limestone

61 million years ago: In a series of massive volcanic eruptions molten lava poured from narrow fissures in the ground, filling in the valleys and burning the vegetation that grew there.

Tholeiitic basalt lava — Non-eroded surface

Inter-basaltic layer

60 million years ago: This layer of tholeiitic basalt lava cooled rapidly. In the process it shrank and cracked evenly into polygonal-shaped blocks, forming columnar jointing beneath the surface.

Steam and gas clouds

New lava flows

58 million years ago: New volcanic eruptions produced further lava flows. These had a slightly different chemical composition from earlier flows and, once cool, did not form such well defined columns.

Snow — Scree — Ice

Sea water

15,000 years ago: At the end of the Ice Age, when the land was still frozen, sea ice ground its way slowly past the high basalt cliffs, eroding the foreshore and helping to form the Giant's Causeway.

Inter-basaltic layer

Shape of the Columns
Most columns are hexagonal, but some have four, five, eight or even ten sides. They generally measure about 30 cm (12 in) across.

Giant's Causeway and the North Antrim Coast
Millions of years of geological activity can be witnessed in the eroded cliffs flanking the Causeway. The striking band of reddish rock is the inter-basaltic layer, which formed during a long period of temperate climatic conditions. The high iron content explains the rock's rich ochre colour.

VISITORS' CHECKLIST

Road Map D1. Co Antrim. 🚌 *to Portrush.* 🚌 *from Portrush, Bushmills or Coleraine.* **Visitors' Centre** *Causeway Head, 3 km (2 miles) N of Bushmills (012657 31855).* ⬭ *Mar–May: 10am–5pm daily; Jun–Oct: 10am–6pm (Jul & Aug: 7pm); Nov–Feb: 10am–4:30pm.* ♿ *limited.* 🎧 *on request.* ▭

Middle Causeway
This section of the Middle Causeway is known as the Honeycomb. Like other unusual rock formations along the coast, it was christened by local guides during Victorian times.

Road

Little Causeway

GIANT'S CAUSEWAY TODAY
It has been estimated that 37,000 basalt columns extend from the cliffs down into the sea. Close to the shore, they have been eroded to form the Grand, Middle and Little Causeways.

Plant debris is trapped between the lava flows.

Lower basalts

Grand Causeway

Wishing Chair
Myth has it that this rocky seat was made for Finn MacCool when he was a boy, and that wishes made here will come true.

Visitors exploring the Giant's Causeway at low tide ▷

Old Bushmills Distillery **7**

Road map D1. Bushmills, Co Antrim.
C *012657 31521.* **E** *from Giant's Causeway & Coleraine.* **O** *Apr–Oct: daily; Nov–Mar: Mon–Fri.* **E** *2 weeks at Christmas.* **E** **E** *obligatory.*

THE SMALL TOWN of Bushmills has an attractive square and an excellent river for salmon and trout fishing, but its main claim to fame is whiskey. The Old Bushmills plant on the outskirts of the town prides itself on being the oldest distillery in the world. Its Grant to Distil was given in 1608, though the spirit was probably made here at least 200 years before that.

In 1974 Bushmills joined the Irish Distillers Group based at the Jameson plant *(see p171)* in Midleton, but its products have retained their distinctive character. Most brands are a blend of many different whiskeys; Old Bushmills, in contrast, is made from a blend of a single malt and a single grain.

The tour of the distillery ends with a sampling session in the Potstill Bar in the former malt kilns, which are also home to a mini-museum with old distilling equipment on display.

Whiskey barrel at Bushmills Distillery

Murlough Bay, on the coast facing Scotland to the east of Ballycastle

Rathlin Island **8**

Road map D1. Co Antrim. **A** *120.* **E** *daily from Ballycastle (012657 63915).* **i** *Ballycastle (012657 62024).*

RATHLIN IS SHAPED rather like a boomerang – 11 km (7 miles) in length and at no point more than 1.6 km (1 mile) wide. The island is just a 50-minute boat ride from Ballycastle. About 30 families remain on Rathlin Island, making a living from fishing, farming and a little tourism. Facilities are limited, amounting to just a café, a pub and a guesthouse. The fierce, salty Atlantic winds ensure that the landscape on Rathlin is virtually treeless.

High white cliffs encircle much of the island, and at craggy **Bull Point** on the westerly tip, tens of thousands of seabirds, including kittiwakes, puffins and razorbills, make their home. A local minibus service will take visitors to view the birds. At the opposite end of the island is **Bruce's Cave**, where, in 1306, Robert Bruce, King of Scotland, supposedly watched a spider climbing a thread. The spider's perseverance inspired the dejected Bruce to return and win back his kingdom.

Ballycastle **9**

Road map D1. Co Antrim. **A** *4,000.* **E** **i** *Sheskburn House, 7 Mary St (012657 62024).* **E** *Apple Fair (last Tue in Oct).*

A MEDIUM-SIZED resort town, Ballycastle boasts an attractive harbour and a central sandy beach. Near the harbour is a memorial to Guglielmo Marconi, whose assistant sent the first wireless message across water from here to Rathlin Island in 1898.

Ballycastle's annual Oul' Lammas Fair, held in late August, is one of the oldest traditional fairs in Ireland. It features noisy livestock sales and stalls selling yellowman (honeycomb toffee) and dulce (dried, heavily salted seaweed).

On the outskirts of town, the ruined 15th-century **Bonamargy Friary** houses the remains of Sorley Boy MacDonnell, former chieftain of this part of Antrim. Sections of the church, gatehouse and cloisters are well preserved.

IRISH WHISKEY

The word whiskey comes from the Gaelic *uisce beatha*, meaning water of life. Distillation was probably introduced to Ireland by monks from Asia over 1,000 years ago. Small-scale production became part of the Irish way of life, but in the 17th century, the English introduced a licensing system and started to close down stills. In the 19th century, post-famine poverty and the Temperance movement combined to lower demand. The result was that Scotch whisky (with no "e") stole an export march on the Irish, but in recent years, thanks to lower production costs, improved marketing and the rise in popularity of Irish coffee, sales have been increasing.

Poster showing the Old Bushmills Distillery beside the River Bush

ENVIRONS: Off the A2, 5 km (3 miles) east of town, a narrow scenic road starts to wind its way along the coast to Cushendall. First stop is **Fair Head**, where a poorly marked path meanders across heathery marshland to towering cliffs 200 m (650 ft) above the sea. From here there are stunning views of Rathlin and the islands off the Scottish coast.

To the lee side of the headland lies **Murlough Bay**, the prettiest inlet along the coast. This can be reached by road. Further to the southeast stands **Torr Head**, a peninsula that reaches to within 21 km (13 miles) of the Mull of Kintyre making it the closest point in Ireland to Scotland.

Cushendall ⑩

Road map D1. Co Antrim. 🚶 *1,400.*
🚌 ℹ️ *Jul & Aug: 4b Mill St (012667 71180).*

THREE OF THE NINE Glens of Antrim converge towards Cushendall, earning it the unofficial title of "Capital of the Glens". This attractive village has brightly painted houses and a distinctive tower made of local red sandstone,

Carnlough harbour, a popular stop south of Cushendall

known as the Curfew Tower. It was erected in the early 19th century as a lock-up for local thieves and idlers.

ENVIRONS: About 1.5 km (1 mile) north of the village stands **Layde Old Church**. It can be reached by a pretty walk along the cliffs. Founded by the Franciscans, it was a parish church from 1306 to 1790 and contains many monuments to the local chieftains, the MacDonnells.

Just over 3 km (2 miles) west of Cushendall, on the slopes of Tievebulliagh mountain, lies **Ossian's Grave**, named after the legendary warrior-poet and son of the giant Finn MacCool *(see pp24–5)*.

It is in fact a Neolithic court tomb: the area was a major centre of Stone Age tool-making and axeheads made of Tievebulliagh's hard porcellanite rock have been found at a wide range of sites all over the British Isles.

Other attractive villages further south along the coast road include **Carnlough**, which has a fine sandy beach and a delightful harbour, and **Ballygally**, whose 1625 castle is now a hotel *(see p300).*

Glenariff Forest Park ⑪

Road map D1. Co Antrim.
📞 *012667 58232.* ⭕ *daily.* 🅿️ *for car park.* ♿ *limited.*

NINE RIVERS have carved deep valleys through the Antrim Mountains to the sea. Celebrated in song and verse, the Glens of Antrim used to be the wildest and most remote part of Ulster. This region was not "planted" with English and Scots settlers in the 17th century and was the last place in Northern Ireland where Gaelic was spoken.

Today the Antrim coast road brings all the glens within easy reach of the tourist. Glenariff Forest Park contains some of the most spectacular scenery. The main scenic path runs through thick woodland and wildflower meadows and round the sheer sides of a gorge, past three waterfalls. There are also optional trails to distant mountain viewpoints. William Makepeace Thackeray, the 19th-century English novelist, called the landscape "Switzerland in miniature".

Glenariff Forest Park

Stone circle and stone rows at Beaghmore

Cookstown ⑫

Road map D2. Co Tyrone. 🚶 11,000.
🚌 ℹ️ Easter–Oct: 48 Molesworth St
(016487 66727). 🛒 Sat; Cattle
Market: Mon, Wed, Fri.

COOKSTOWN STICKS in the
memory for its grand
central thoroughfare –
2 km (1.25 miles) long
and perfectly straight.
The road is about
40 m (130 ft)
wide and, as you
look to the north,
it frames the
bulky outline of Slieve
Gallion, the highest of
the Sperrin Mountains.
A 17th-century
Plantation town (see
pp36–7), Cookstown
takes its name from its
founder Alan Cook.

ENVIRONS: The countryside
around Cookstown is rich in
Neolithic and early Christian
monuments. To the east, on a
desolate stretch of Lough

Neagh shoreline, the **Ardboe
Cross** stands on the site of a
6th-century monastery.
Although eroded, the 10th-
century cross is one of the best
examples of a High Cross (see
p235) in Ulster: its 22 sculpted
panels depict Old Testament
scenes on the east side and
New Testament ones on
the west. The **Wellbrook
Beetling Mill**, west of
Cookstown, is a relic
of Ulster's old linen
industry. "Beetling"
was the process of
hammering the cloth
to give it a sheen. Set
amid trees beside the
Ballinderry River, the mill
dates from 1768 and is
now a popular tourist
attraction. The National
Trust has restored the
whitewashed two-storey
building and its water
wheel. Inside, working
displays demonstrate just how
loud "beetling" could be. From
the mill, there are pleasant
walks along the river banks.

**Ardboe
Cross**

🏛 Ardboe Cross
Off B73, 16 km (10 miles) E of
Cookstown.

🏚 Wellbrook Beetling Mill
Off A505, 6.5 km (4 miles) W of
Cookstown. 📞 016487 51735. 🕐 Jul
& Aug: Wed–Mon (pm only); Apr–Jun
& Sep: Sat, Sun & public hols. 🅿️

Beaghmore Stone Circles ⑬

Road map D2. Co Tyrone. Off A505,
14 km (9 miles) NW of Cookstown.

ON A STRETCH of open
moorland in the foothills
of the Sperrin Mountains lies
a vast collection of stone
monuments, dating from
between 2000 and 1200 BC.
There are seven stone circles,
several stone rows and a
number of less prominent
features, possibly collapsed
field walls of an earlier
period. Their exact purpose
remains unknown, though in
some cases their alignment
correlates with movements of
the sun, moon and stars.
Three of the rows, for
example, are clearly aligned
with the point where the sun
rises at the summer solstice.
The individual circle stones
are small – none is more than
1.20 m (4 ft) in height – but
their sheer numbers make
them a truly impressive sight.
As well as the circles and
rows, there are a dozen
round cairns (burial mounds).
Up until 1945, the whole
complex, one of Ulster's
major archaeological finds,
had lain buried beneath a
thick layer of peat.

ULSTER'S HISTORIC LINEN INDUSTRY

The rise in Ulster's importance as a linen
producer was spurred on by the arrival from
France of refugee Huguenot
weavers at the end of the 17th
century. Linen remained a
flourishing industry for a
further two centuries, but
today it is produced only
in small quantities for the
luxury goods market.
Hundreds of abandoned
mills dot the former "Linen
Triangle" bounded by Belfast,
Armagh and Dungannon.
One of the reasons why the

**18th-century print, showing flax
being prepared for spinning**

material diminished in popularity was the
expensive production process: after cutting,
the flax had to be retted, or soaked,
in large artificial ponds so that
scutching – the separation
of the fibres – could begin.
After combing, the linen
was spun and woven
before being bleached
in the sun, typically in
fields along river banks.
The final stage was "beetling",
the process whereby the
cloth was hammered to
give it a sheen.

Copy of Iron Age Celtic stone head at the Ulster History Park

Ulster History Park ⑭

Road map C2. Co Tyrone. 📞 01662 648188. 🚌 from Omagh. ◯ Apr–Sep: daily; Oct–Mar: Mon–Fri. ● 1 Jan, 23–29 Dec. 🗎 🗐 ♿

N ESTLING AT THE EDGE of the Sperrin Mountains, the Ulster History Park is filled with full-scale models of structures built by successive waves of settlers in Ireland. They range from a Mesolithic hunter/gatherer's hut covered with animal pelts, dating from 7000 BC, to a 17th-century Plantation village *(see pp36–7)*. There are also megalithic burial tombs, a crannog *(see p31)* from the early Christian period and a Norman motte and bailey (a wooden fortress built on a high mound). An exhibition centre helps put the exhibits in perspective.

Ulster-American Folk Park ⑮

Road map C2. Co Tyrone. 📞 01662 243292. 🚌 from Omagh. ◯ Easter–Sep: daily; Oct–Easter: Mon–Fri exc public hols. 🗎 ♿

O NE OF THE BEST open-air museums of its kind, the Folk Park grew up around the restored boyhood home of Judge Thomas Mellon (founder of the Pittsburgh banking dynasty). The Park's permanent exhibition, called "Emigrants", examines why two million people left Ulster for America during the 18th and 19th centuries. It also shows what became of them, following stories of both fortune and failure, including the grim lives of indentured servants and the 15,000 Irish vagrants and convicts transported to North America in the mid-18th century.

The park has more than 30 historic buildings, some of them original, some replicas. There are settler homesteads (including that of John Joseph Hughes, the first Catholic Archbishop of New York), churches, a schoolhouse and a forge, some with craft displays, all with costumed interpretative guides. There's also an Ulster streetscape, a reconstructed emigrant ship and a Pennsylvania farmstead,

complete with log barn, corn crib and smokehouse. The six-roomed farmhouse is based on one built by Thomas Mellon and his father in the early years of their new life in America.

A fully stocked library and database allow visitors to trace their family roots. Popular American festivals such as Independence Day and Hallowe'en are celebrated at the park and there is an Appalachian-Bluegrass music festival in early September.

Belleek Pottery ⑯

Road map C2. Belleek, Co Fermanagh. 📞 013656 58501. 🚌 ◯ Mar–Aug: daily; Sep–Nov: Mon–Sat; Dec–Feb: Mon–Fri. ● 17 Mar & 10 days at Christmas. 🗐 ♿

Worker at the Belleek factory making a Parian ware figurine

T HE LITTLE BORDER VILLAGE of Belleek would attract few visitors other than anglers were it not for the world-famous Belleek Pottery, founded in 1857. The company's pearly coloured china is known as Parian ware. Developed in the 19th century, it was supposed to resemble the famous Parian marble of Ancient Greece.

Belleek is now best known for its ornamental pieces of fragile lattice work decorated with pastel-coloured flowers. These are especially popular in the USA. Several elaborate showpieces stand on display in the visitors' centre and small museum. There's also a 20-minute video presentation on the company's history, a gift shop and ample parking space for tour buses.

Pennsylvania log farmhouse at the Ulster-American Folk Park

A Tour of Lower Lough Erne ⑰

THE AREA AROUND Lower Lough Erne boasts a rich combination of both natural and historic sights. From pre-Christian times, settlers sought the security offered by the lough's forests and inlets. Monasteries were founded on several of its many islands in the Middle Ages, and a ring of castles recalls the Plantation era *(see p37)*. The lake is a haven for water birds such as ducks, grebes and kingfishers, and the trout-rich waters attract many anglers. Lough Erne is a delight to explore by land or by boat. In summer, ferries serve several islands, and cruisers are available for hire.

Kingfisher

View across Lower Lough Erne

Belleek ⑦
Northern Ireland's most westerly village, Belleek is famous for its pottery *(see p261)*. There is also a new museum, ExplorErne, which covers most aspects of the region.

Castle Caldwell Forest Park ⑥
The park's wooded peninsulas are a sanctuary for birds, and you can watch waterfowl from hides on the shore. You may see great crested grebes, the common scoter duck and perhaps even otters.

Boa Island ⑤
Two curious double-faced figures stand in Caldragh cemetery, a Christian graveyard on Boa Island. While little is known about the stone idols, they are certainly pre-Christian.

B136

⑤

A

Lusty Br

← BALLYSHANNON
R230

A47
Erne

⑦

A46

B52

SLIGO

⑥

LOWER   LOUC

Cliffs of Magho ☼

⑧

Lough Navar Forest Drive ⑧
An 11-km (7-mile) drive through pine forest leads to a viewpoint atop the Cliffs of Magho, with a magnificent panorama over Lough Erne and beyond. Trails weave through the woods.

Tully Castle ⑨
A delightful 17th-century-st
herb garden has recently been planted alongside th
fortified Plantation house, whose protective enclosu
or bawn, is still visible.

TIPS FOR DRIVERS

Length: 110 km (68 miles).
Stopping-off points: Outside Enniskillen, the best places to eat are the pubs in Kesh and Belleek; in summer, a café opens in Castle Archdale Country Park. There are good picnic places all along the route of this tour, including at the Cliffs of Magho viewpoint. (See also pp355–7.)

KEY

▬ Tour route

═ Other roads

⛴ Boats to islands

☼ Viewpoint

White Island ④
The Romanesque church on White Island has bizarre pagan-looking figures set into one wall. Of uncertain origin, they probably adorned an earlier monastery on this site. Ferries to the island leave from Castle Archdale Marina in summer.

Boats moored at Castle Archdale Marina

Castle Archdale Country Park ③
With a marina and caravan site, the park is busy in summer. Trails through the woods enable you to escape the crowds, and you may see red deer and other animals.

Devenish Island ②
Site of Lower Lough Erne's most important monastery, this island can be reached in summer by ferry or water-bus from Enniskillen.

Enniskillen ①
Dominated by its famous castle, Enniskillen (see p264) is the main cruiser base on the Erne. It overlooks the river flowing between the upper and lower loughs.

Monea Castle ⑩
Occupying a rocky bank in a remote spot away from the lake, this is the best-preserved Plantation castle in Fermanagh. Built around 1618, it has striking barrel towers.

0 kilometres   4

0 miles   2

Beautifully constructed round tower on Devenish Island

Devenish Island ⑱

Road map C2. Co Fermanagh.
🚢 from Trory Point, 5 km (3 miles) N of Enniskillen (01365 343700): Apr–Sep: Tue–Sat & Sun pm; from Enniskillen (01365 322882): May–Jun: Sun pm; Jul–Aug: daily; Sep: Tue, Sat & Sun. 🎫 for museum and tower.

S⊤ MOLAISE, who had 1,500 scholars under his tutelage, founded a monastery on this tiny windswept island in the 6th century. Although raided by Vikings in the 9th century and burnt in 1157, it remained an important religious centre up to the early 17th century.

Several fine buildings from the medieval monastery have survived, including **Teampall Mor** near the jetty. Built in 1225, this church displays the transition between Romanesque and Gothic styles. On the highest ground stands **St Mary's Priory**, an Augustinian church that was erected in the 15th century. An intricately carved stone cross close by dates from the same period.

The most spectacular sight on Devenish Island, however, is the 12th-century round tower, which stands some 25 m (82 ft) high. It is perfectly preserved, and the five floors can be reached by internal ladders. Supporting the roof is an elaborate cornice with a human face carved above each of the four windows; this is a unique feature in an Irish round tower. A small museum covers both the history and architecture of the island, and contains a collection of stone carvings and other antiquities discovered at the site.

Enniskillen ⑲

Road map C2. Co Fermanagh.
🏃 *14,000.* 🚌 ℹ️ *Wellington Road
(01365 323110).* 🛒 *Thu.*

T HE BUSY tourist centre of
Enniskillen occupies an
island between Upper and
Lower Lough Erne. The town
gained fame for the wrong
reason in 1987, when 11
people died in an IRA bomb
attack, but it deserves a visit
for its setting and sights.

At the west end of town
stands **Enniskillen Castle**,
which dates back to the 15th
century. It houses a heritage
centre and the Inniskilling
Regimental Museum. Its most
stunning feature, however, is
the Watergate, a fairy-tale twin-
turreted tower, best admired
from the far bank of the river.
Further west, **Portora Royal
School**, founded in 1618,
counts among its old boys the
playwrights Oscar Wilde and
Samuel Beckett *(see pp20–21)*.

The **Cole Monument**
stands on a little hill in a
pretty Victorian park on the
east side of town. It is a tall
Doric column with an internal

Enniskillen Castle seen from across the River Erne

spiral staircase that can be
climbed for magnificent views
of the lake country.

⚜ Enniskillen Castle
🅲 *01365 325000.* ⬜ *Jul & Aug:
daily (Sat–Mon pm only); May–Jun &
Sep: Mon–Sat; Oct–Apr: Mon–Fri.* 📷
⬤ *1 Jan, 25 & 26 Dec.* 🚻 *limited.*

ENVIRONS: Just outside town,
set in a park with mature oak
woodland overlooking a lake,
is **Castle Coole**, one of the
finest Neo-Classical homes in
Ireland. It has a long Portland
stone façade, with a central
portico and small pavilions at
each end. The stone was
shipped from Dorset to
Ballyshannon in County
Donegal. Many of the fixtures
and fittings were also brought
from England. The first Earl of
Belmore, who commissioned
the house in the 1790s, was
almost bankrupted by the
cost of it. The original design
was by Irish architect Richard
Johnston, but the Earl then
commissioned a second set of
drawings by the fashionable
English architect James Wyatt.
The extravagant Earl died,
deep in debt, in 1802 and it
was left to his son to complete
the decorating and furnishing
during the 1820s.

The glory of Castle Coole is
that almost all the house's
original furniture is still in
place. Family portraits from
the 18th century line the walls
of the dining room. In the
lavish State Bedroom there is
a bed made specially for King
George IV on the occasion of
his visit to Ireland in 1821,
though in the end he never
came here to sleep in it. One
of the finest rooms is the oval
saloon (or ballroom) at the
back of the house. The heavy
curtains and richly gilded
Regency furniture may not be
to everyone's taste, but the
spacious oak-floored room
produces a magnificent effect
of unostentatious luxury.

⌷ Castle Coole
Off A4, 1.6 km (1 mile) SE of Enniskillen.
🅲 *01365 322690.* ⬜ *May–Aug:
Fri–Wed (pm only); Apr & Sep: Sat &
Sun (pm only).* 📷 🚻

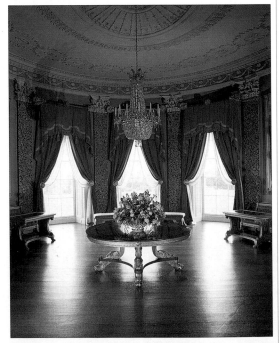

The saloon at Castle Coole, with original Regency furnishings

Marble Arch Caves ⑳

Road map C2. Marlbank Scenic Loop, Florence Court, Co Fermanagh. ℂ *01365 348855.* ◯ *Apr–Sep: daily (phone first as weather can cause sudden closure).* 🎫 🎥 *obligatory.*

THE CAVES are cut by three streams which flow down the slopes of Cuilcagh Mountain, unite underground and emerge as the Cladagh River. Tours lasting 75 minutes consist of a boat ride into the depths of the cave complex and a guided walk that leads past stalagmites, calcite cascades and other curious limestone formations. The 9-m (30-ft) "Marble Arch" itself stands outside the cave system in the glen where the river gushes out from below ground.

The caves are very popular, so it's best to book ahead. It is also advisable to ring to check the local weather conditions before setting out; the caves may be closed because of rain. Whatever the weather, bring a sweater and sensible walking shoes.

Florence Court ㉑

Road map C2. Co Fermanagh. ℂ *01365 348249.* 🚌 *from Enniskillen (Jul & Aug).* **House** ◯ *Jun–Aug: Wed–Mon (pm only); Apr–May & Sep: Sat, Sun & public hols.* 🎫 ♿ **Grounds** ◯ *daily.* 🎫 *for car park.*

THIS THREE-STOREY Palladian mansion was built for the Cole family in the mid-18th century. The arcades and pavilions, which are of a later date than the main house, were probably added around 1770 by William Cole, first Earl of Enniskillen. The house features flamboyant Rococo

Boat trip through Marble Arch Caves

plasterwork said to be by the Dublin stuccodore Robert West. Sadly, however, hardly any of what you see today is original as most of the central block was seriously damaged by fire in 1955. The furniture was lost, but the plasterwork was painstakingly recreated from photographs. The finest examples are in the dining room, the staircase and the small Venetian room.

Perhaps more spectacular are the grounds, which occupy a natural amphitheatre set between hills and mountains. The area is fairly wild and there are many enjoyable walks and nature trails around the house. One woodland trail leads to the famous Florence Court yew tree, whose descendants are to be found all over Ireland. Closer to the house is a walled garden where pink and white roses make an attractive sight in early summer.

Dungannon ㉒

Road map D2. Co Tyrone. 🚶 *9,500.* 🚌 🛈 *Apr–Sep: Killymaddy Tourist Centre, Ballygawly Rd, 8 km (5 miles) W of town (01868 767259).* 🛒 *Thu.*

DUNGANNON'S HILLY location made an ideal site for the seat of government of the O'Neill dynasty from the 14th century until Plantation *(see pp36–7)*, when their castle was razed. The town's **Royal School** claims to be the oldest school in Northern Ireland. Opened in 1614, it moved to its present site on Northland Row in 1789.

Once a major linen centre, this busy market town's best-known factory is now **Tyrone Crystal**, the largest concern of its kind in Northern Ireland. Tours of its modern complex cover all stages of production, including glass-blowing.

🏭 Tyrone Crystal
Coalisland Road. ℂ *01868 725335.* ◯ *Mon–Sat.* ● *10 days at Christmas.* 🎫 🎥 ♿

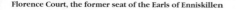

Florence Court, the former seat of the Earls of Enniskillen

View of Armagh dominated by St Patrick's Roman Catholic Cathedral

Armagh ㉓

Road map D2. Co Armagh.
🚶 *14,400.* 🚌 ℹ️ *40 English St
(01861 521800).* 🚆 *Tue & Fri.*

ONE OF IRELAND'S oldest cities,
Armagh dates back to the
age of St Patrick *(see p273)* and
the advent of Christianity. The
narrow streets in the city centre
follow the ditches that once
ringed the church, founded by
the saint in 455. Two cathedrals, both called **St Patrick's**,
sit on opposing hills. The more
visually striking is the
huge Roman Catholic
one, a twin-spired Neo-
Gothic building
with seemingly
every inch of
wall covered in
mosaic. The
older
Protestant Cathedral
dates back to med-
ieval times. It
boasts the bones of
Brian Boru, the King of Ireland
who defeated the Vikings in
1014 *(see pp32–3)*, and an
11th-century High Cross.

Armagh's gorgeous oval, tree-
lined Mall, where cricket is
played in summer, is surrounded by dignified Georgian
buildings. One of these houses
the small **Armagh County
Museum**, which has a good
exhibition on local history. Off
the Mall, **St Patrick's Trian** is
a heritage centre telling the
story of the city. It also has a
"Land of Lilliput" fantasy
centre for children, based on
Gulliver's Travels by Jonathan
Swift *(see p80)*. Ireland's only
planetarium is on College Hill
in the **Observatory Grounds**,
from where there are splendid
views over the city.

**Skull of Barbary ape
from Navan Fort**

🏛 **Armagh County Museum**
The Mall East. ☎ *01861 523070.*
🔲 *Mon–Sat.* ⬤ *some public hols.*
✍ *by arrangement.*
🏛 **St Patrick's Trian**
40 English St. ☎ *01861 521801.*
🔲 *daily.* ⬤ *some public hols.* 🅿️ ♿
🌱 **Observatory Grounds**
College Hill. ☎ *01861 522928.*
🔲 *daily.* **Planetarium** ☎ *01861
523689.* 🔲 *daily (Sep–Nov: Mon–Sat).*

ENVIRONS: To the west of
Armagh stands **Navan Fort**, a
large earthwork on the summit
of a hill. In legend, Navan was
Emain Macha,
ceremonial and
spiritual capital
of ancient Ulster,
associated with
tales of the warrior
Cuchulainn *(see p24)*.
The site may have been in
use as much as 4,000
years ago, but seems
to have been most
active around 100 BC
when a huge timber building,
40 m (130 ft) across, was
erected over a giant cairn. The
whole thing was then burnt
and the remains covered with
soil. Archaeological evidence
indicates that this was not an
act of war, but a solemn ritual
performed by the inhabitants
of Emain Macha themselves.

Below the fort, the grass-
roofed **Navan Centre**, built
to blend in with the landscape,
interprets the archaeology and
mythology of the site through
interactive displays and a 25-
minute film. The most unexpected exhibit is the skull of a
Barbary ape, found in the remains of a Bronze Age house.
The animal must have been
brought from Spain or North
Africa, evidence that by 500
BC Emain Macha had already
become an important place
with far-flung trading links.

🏛 **Navan Centre**
On A28 4 km (2.5 miles) W of Armagh.
☎ *01861 525550.* 🔲 *daily.*
⬤ *5 days at Christmas.* 🅿️ ♿

Lough Neagh ㉔

Road map D2. Co Armagh, Co
Tyrone, Co Londonderry, Co Antrim.

LEGEND HAS IT that the giant
Finn MacCool *(see pp24–5)*
created Lough Neagh by
picking up a piece of turf and
hurling it into the Irish Sea, thus
forming the Isle of Man in the
process. At 400 sq km (153 sq
miles), the lake is the largest
in Britain. Most of it is bordered
by sedgy marshland, so few
roads run along the shore.
The best recreational areas lie
in the south: Oxford Island,
actually a peninsula, has
walking trails, bird lookouts
and the informative **Lough
Neagh Discovery Centre**. In
the southwest corner of the
Lough Neagh basin, a narrow-
gauge railway runs through
the bogs of **Peatlands Park**.

Navan Fort, the site of Emain Macha, legendary capital of Ulster

Hide for birdwatchers at Oxford Island on the southern shore of Lough Neagh

Salmon and trout are found in the rivers that flow from Lough Neagh, while the lake itself is famous for its eels. One of the world's largest eel fisheries is at **Toome** on the north shore.

🏛 Lough Neagh Discovery Centre
Oxford Island. Exit 10 off M1.
(01762 322205. **◯** Apr–Sep: daily; Oct–Mar: Wed–Sun. **●** 25, 26 Dec. **⚼ 🛡**

♣ Peatlands Park
Exit 13 off M1. **(** 01762 851102. **◯** Jun–Aug: daily; Easter–May & Sep: Sat, Sun & public hols.

Larne ㉕

Road map D1. Co Antrim. **🏘** 18,000. **🚉 🚌 ℹ** Narrow Gauge Rd (01574 260088) & at Ferry Terminal (01574 270517).

INDUSTRIAL LARNE is the arrival point for ferries from Scotland (see pp352–4). The town is not the finest introduction to Ulster scenery, but it lies on the threshold of the magnificent Antrim coastline (see p259).

The sheltered waters of Larne Lough have been a landing point since Mesolithic times – flint flakes found here provide some of the earliest evidence of human presence on the island – nearly 9,000 years ago. Since then, Norsemen used the lough as a base in the 10th century, Edward Bruce landed his Scottish troops in the area in 1315, and in 1914 the Ulster Volunteer Force landed a huge cache of German arms here during its campaign against Home Rule (see pp42–3).

Carrickfergus ㉖

Road map E2. Co Antrim. **🏘** 35,000. **🚉 🚌 ℹ** Antrim St (01960 366455). **🛒** Thu.

CARRICKFERGUS grew up around the massive castle begun in 1180 by John de Courcy to guard the entrance to Belfast Lough. De Courcy was the leader of the Anglo-Norman force which invaded Ulster following Strongbow's conquest of Leinster in the south (see pp34–5).

Carrickfergus Castle was shaped to fit the crag on which it stands overlooking the harbour. The finest and best-preserved Norman castle in Ireland, it even has its original portcullis (see pp34–5). Naturally, many changes and adaptations have been made since the 12th century, including wide ramparts to accommodate the castle's cannons. Arms and armour are on display in the large rectangular keep, while life-size model soldiers are posed along the ramparts.

In continuous use up to 1928, the castle has changed hands several times over the years. The Scots, under Edward Bruce, took it in 1315, holding it for three years. In the 17th century James II's army was in control of the castle from 1688 until General Schomberg took it for William III in 1690. William himself stayed at the castle before the Battle of the Boyne (see p236) in July 1690.

The history of the town is recreated in a series of audio-visual displays at **Knight Ride**. The exhibition is literally a ride through history as you are transported from scene to scene in small cable cars. This appeals principally to children, who also enjoy the gorier episodes from the history of Carrickfergus.

♠ Carrickfergus Castle
(01960 351273. **◯** daily (Sun pm). **●** 25 Dec. **⚼ ♿**

🏛 Knight Ride
Antrim St. **(** 01960 366455. **◯** daily (Sun pm). **●** 25 Dec. **⚼**

The massive Norman keep of Carrickfergus Castle

Belfast ㉗

BELFAST WAS THE ONLY CITY in Ireland to experience the full force of the Industrial Revolution. Its ship-building, linen, rope-making and tobacco industries caused the population to rise to almost 400,000 by the end of World War I. The

Red Hand of Ulster, Linen Hall Library wealth it enjoyed is still evident in its imposing banks, churches and other public buildings. The Troubles and the decline of traditional industries have since damaged economic life, but Belfast remains a handsome city and most visitors are agreeably surprised by the genuine friendliness of the "Big Smoke".

Mosaic in St Anne's Cathedral, showing St Patrick's journey to Ireland

Interior of the Grand Opera House

🏛 City Hall

Donegall Square. █ 01232 320202 ext 2618. ☑ usually Wed (must be booked in advance).

Most of Belfast's main streets (and many major bus routes) radiate out from the hub of Donegall Square. In the centre of the square stands the vast rectangular Portland stone bulk of the 1906 City Hall. It has an elaborate tower at each corner and a central copper dome that rises to a height of 53 m (173 ft). Highlight of the tour of the interior is the sumptuous oak-panelled council chamber.

Statues around the building include a glum-looking Queen Victoria outside the main entrance and, on the east side, Sir Edward Harland, founder of the Harland and Wolff shipyard, which built the *Titanic*. A memorial to those who died when the *Titanic* sank in 1912 stands close by.

Detail of *Titanic* Memorial outside City Hall

🎭 Grand Opera House

Great Victoria St. █ 01232 240411. Designed by Frank Matcham, the renowned theatre-architect, this exuberant late-Victorian building opened its doors in 1894. The sumptuous interior, with its gilt, red plush and intricate plasterwork, was restored to its full glory in 1980. On occasions, bombings of the adjacent Europa Hotel disrupted business at the theatre, but it survives as a major venue for plays and concerts. In 1984, Belfast-born singer Van Morrison recorded a famous live album here.

⛪ St Anne's Cathedral

Donegall St. █ 01232 328332. The Neo-Romanesque façade of this Protestant cathedral, consecrated in 1904, fails to make much of an impression. The interior is far more attractive, especially the vast, colourful mosaics executed by the two Misses Martin in the 1920s. The one covering the baptistry ceiling contains over 150,000 pieces. The wide nave is paved with Canadian maple and the aisles with Irish marble. Lord Carson (1854–1935), implacable leader of the campaign against Home Rule (see *p42*), is buried in the south aisle.

SIGHTS AT A GLANCE

0 metres	500
0 yards	500

VISITORS' CHECKLIST

Road map D2. Co Antrim.
🚶 *305,000.* ✈ *Belfast City Airport, 6.5 km (4 miles) E; Belfast International, 29 km (18 miles) NW.* 🚉 *Central Station, East Bridge St (01232 899411); Great Victoria St Station.* 🚌 *Europa Buscentre, Great Victoria St & Oxford St (01232 333000).* ℹ *59 North St (01232 231221).* 🎪 *Royal Ulster Agricultural Show & Lord Mayor's Show (May); Belfast Festival at Queen's (Nov).*

if only for the delightful coffee shop and the vast selection of newspapers and periodicals. Above the library door you will see the Red Hand of Ulster, the emblem of the province. It is the subject of a gory legend about two Celtic heroes racing to see who would touch the land of Ulster first. In his determination to win, one cut off his own hand and threw it to the shore.

🍺 The Entries

The Entries are a series of narrow alleys between Ann Street and High Street. They feature some of the best pubs in the city, including White's Tavern *(see p321)*, reputedly the oldest bar in Belfast. The Globe in Joy's Entry and the Morning Star on Pottinger's

Entry both serve excellent lunches. In 1791, the United Irishmen, a radical movement inspired by the new ideas of the French Revolution, was founded in a tavern on Crown Entry. Its most famous member was Wolfe Tone *(see pp38–9)*.

🍺 Crown Liquor Saloon

Great Victoria St. 📞 *01232 249476.* 🕐 *daily.*
Even teetotallers should make a detour to the multi-coloured tiled façade of this flamboyant Victorian drinking palace. The Crown, which dates back to the 1880s, is the only pub owned by the National Trust. The lovingly restored interior features stained and painted glass, lots of marbling and mosaics and a splendid ceiling with scrolled plasterwork. The wooden snugs facing the long bar have their original gas lamps: the perfect place for a pint of Guinness or Bass and some Strangford Lough oysters.

🍺 Linen Hall Library

17 Donegall Square North.
📞 *01232 321707.* 🕐 *Mon–Sat.*
Founded as the Belfast Society for Promoting Knowledge in 1788, the library has thousands of rare, old books in its dark wooden stacks. There is also extensive documentation of political events in Ireland since 1968 and a vast database of genealogical information. Even if you have no special reason for visiting the library, it is still well worth going inside,

KEY

🚉	Railway station
🚌	Coach station
⛴	Ferry port
P	Parking
ℹ	Tourist information
✝	Church

The ornate Victorian interior of the Crown Liquor Saloon

Exploring Belfast

AWAY FROM THE CITY CENTRE, Belfast has many pleasant suburbs unaffected by the civil strife of recent times. The area around Queen's University to the south of the city has two major attractions in the Ulster Museum and the Botanic Gardens. To the north, there are splendid views to be enjoyed from the heights of Cave Hill, while visitors interested in Belfast's industrial heritage will be keen to see both the old docks and the Harland and Wolff working shipyards.

Interior of the Victorian Palm House at the Botanic Gardens

🏛 Ulster Museum
Botanic Gardens. **🕻** 01232 383000.
◗ daily (Sat & Sun: pm only).
● public hols. 🗹 🛦

This four-floor bunker of a museum covers all aspects of Ulster, from local history, archaeology, antiquities and art to geology, natural history and technology. Especially prized treasures include gold and silver jewellery recovered from the *Girona*, a Spanish Armada ship that sank off the Giant's Causeway in 1588 *(see p249)*. One of the most interesting exhibits is of Belfast industry, featuring some crude turn-of-the-century textile machinery.

In the top-floor gallery is a collection of paintings mostly by British and Irish artists, including a large number by Belfast-born Sir John Lavery (1856–1941).

In addition to the Irish collections, there are exhibits ranging from ancient Egyptian mummies to dinosaurs. The museum also mounts frequent temporary exhibitions on a wide variety of themes.

🌿 Botanic Gardens
Stranmillis Rd. **🕻** 01232 324902.
◗ daily.

Backing on to the university, the Botanic Gardens provide a quiet refuge from the bustle of campus. The 1839 Palm House is a superb example of curvilinear glass and cast-iron work. The Tropical Ravine, or Fernery, is another fine piece of Victorian garden architecture. Visitors can look down from the balcony to a sunken glen of exotic plants.

🎓 Queen's University
University Rd. **🕻** 01232 245133.

A 15-minute stroll south from Donegall Square, through the lively entertainment district known as the Golden Mile, leads to Northern Ireland's most prestigious university. The main building, designed in Tudor-style red and yellow brick by Charles Lanyon in 1849, bears similarities to Magdalene College, Oxford. A towered gateway leads to a colonnaded quadrangle.

Weighing Room, Hurst Park (1924) by Sir John Lavery, Ulster Museum

---

THE POLITICAL MURALS OF WEST BELFAST

Republican mural in the Falls Road

Ever since the onset of the "Troubles" in 1968, popular art has played a conspicuous role in proclaiming the loyalties of Belfast's two most intransigent working-class communities, on the Protestant Shankill Road and the Catholic Falls Road. The gable walls of dozens of houses in these areas have been decorated with vivid murals expressing local political and paramilitary affiliations. Likewise, kerbstones on certain streets are painted either in the red, white and blue of the United Kingdom or the green, white and gold of Ireland. Whatever the outcome of the current peace process, many are likely to remain. Some tourists make the journey out to West Belfast just to see the murals. The simplest way to do this is to take a taxi from the centre; cabs that go to the Falls Road leave from Castle Street, while those for the Shankill Road leave from North Street.

Protestant Loyalist mural

♛ Albert Memorial Clock Tower

Queen's Square.

One of Belfast's best-known monuments, the clock tower, was designed by WJ Barre. Prince Albert, Queen Victoria's consort, had no personal connection with Belfast, but memorials to him were built in many British cities in the decade following his death in 1861. Today, the tower arouses most interest for the fact that it leans slightly as a result of subsidence. Beyond it, facing the river, stands the Custom House (1854) by Charles Lanyon, architect of Queen's University.

Belfast cityscape showing the giant cranes, Samson and Goliath

♛ Lagan Weir Lookout

Donegall Quay. ☎ 01232 315444. ⬜ daily (Sat & Sun: pm only). ♿

Belfast's once thriving harbour area, five minutes' walk from Donegall Square, can best be viewed from the footbridge alongside the new Lagan Weir development. Five computer-controlled steel gates, unveiled in 1994, maintain a fixed water level, getting rid of the smelly mudbanks produced by varying tide levels and creating possibilities for angling and watersports along the river. The Visitors' Centre, on the footbridge, explains how it all works and tells some good tales of modern Belfast folklore. At night, the weir is lit by gas-filter blue light that shimmers across the water.

Unfortunately, the new Cross-Harbour Road and Rail Link bridge partly obscures the view across to the giant yellow cranes – appropriately named Samson and Goliath – of the once-mighty Harland and Wolff shipyards.

The unmistakeable profile of Cave Hill above the roofs of Belfast

ENVIRONS: The best place for an overall view of Belfast and Belfast Lough is the 360-m (1,118-ft) summit of Cave Hill, the most distinctively shaped of the hills encircling the city.

♛ Cave Hill

Antrim Rd, 6.5 km (4 miles) N of city centre. **Heritage Centre** ☎ 01232 776925. ⬜ daily. ● 25 Dec. ♿ **Zoo** ☎ 01232 774625. ⬜ daily. ● 25 Dec. ♨ ♿

It was on Cave Hill, next to the remains of MacArt's Fort (named after an Iron Age chieftain), that Wolfe Tone (see p39) and the northern leaders of the United Irishmen met in 1795 to pledge themselves to rebellion. The five artificial caves near the fort were carved out during the Neolithic period.

On the thickly wooded, eastern slopes of the hill stands the baronial pile of Belfast Castle, built in 1870. Previously home to the Earl of Shaftesbury, the castle now belongs to the city and houses two restaurants and a new heritage centre that interprets the area's history. A little further along the road past the castle is Belfast Zoo, which makes the most of its steep woodland setting.

⛰ Giant's Ring

Off B23, 5 km (3 miles) S of city centre.

Little is known about this awe-inspiring prehistoric enclosure almost 200 m (660 ft) in diameter. It is surrounded by a grassy bank averaging almost 6 m (20 ft) in width and 4.5 m (15 ft) in height. Bones from a Stone Age burial were found under the dolmen in the centre. During the 18th century the ring was a popular venue for horse races.

♛ Stormont

Newtownards Rd, 8 km (5 miles) SE of city centre. ● to the public. ♿ by arrangement only.

Built between 1928 and 1932, at a cost of £1,250,000, Stormont was designed to house the Northern Ireland Parliament. The huge Anglo-Palladian mass of Portland stone and Mourne granite stands at the end of a majestic avenue, 1.6 km (1 mile) long, bordered by parkland. A statue of Lord Carson (see p42) stands near the front entrance.

Since the parliament was disbanded in 1972, the building has been used as government offices. Its future depends very much on the outcome of the ongoing peace process. The debating chamber was badly damaged in a fire in 1994.

Stormont in its parkland setting outside Belfast

Ulster Folk and Transport Museum ㉘

Road map E2. Cultra, near Holywood, Co Down. 📞 *01232 428428.* 🚌 🚃 ○ *daily.* ● *24–26 Dec.* 🎫 *(free for the disabled).* ♿

DOZENS of old buildings, including flax-, corn- and sawmills, have been plucked from the Ulster countryside and re-erected in this absorbing folk park. Demonstrations of traditional crafts, industries and farming methods are given all year round.

The A2 road splits the folk museum from the transport section. This is dominated by a hangar that houses the Irish Railway Collection. The smaller Transport Gallery exhibits machinery made in Ulster, including a saloon carriage from the tram service that ran from Portrush to Giant's Causeway *(see pp254–5)*. Of particular note is a test model of the spectacularly unsuccessful De Lorean car, made in the early 1980s with a huge government subsidy. There's also a popular exhibit on another ill-fated construction – the *Titanic*. It's best to allow half a day to take in most of the attractions.

1883 tram carriage at the Ulster Folk and Transport Museum

Ards Peninsula ㉙

Road map E2. Co Down. 🚌 🚃 *to Bangor.* ℹ *34 Quay St, Bangor (01247 270069).*

THE PENINSULA – and some of Northern Ireland's finest scenery – begins east of Belfast at **Bangor**. This resort town has a modern marina and some well-known yacht clubs. A little way south is **Donaghadee**, from where boats sail to the three **Copeland Islands**. These are now populated only

Scrabo Tower, a prominent landmark of the Ards Peninsula

by seabirds, as the last human residents left in the 1940s. **Ballycopeland Windmill** (1784), Northern Ireland's only working windmill, stands on a small hill a little further south, near the town of Millisle.

Just across the peninsula is **Newtownards**, on the even more stunning Strangford Lough side. On a hill above the town is the pleasantly shaded **Scrabo Country Park**. In the park stands **Scrabo Tower**, built in 1857 as a memorial to the third Marquess of Londonderry. The tower's 122 steps lead to a great view of Strangford Lough.

Past the grounds of **Mount Stewart House** *(see pp274–5)* is the hamlet of Greyabbey, with its antique shops and Cistercian abbey ruins. Founded in 1193, **Grey Abbey** was used as a parish church until the 17th century. It is idyllically set in lush meadows by a stream and some of its features, particularly the finely carved west doorway, are well preserved.

On the tip of the peninsula, **Portaferry** overlooks the Strangford Narrows (stunning at sunset) across from the Lecale Peninsula *(see p276)*.

Portaferry's large aquarium, **Exploris**, displays the surprising diversity of marine life in the Irish Sea and Strangford Lough.

🏭 **Ballycopeland Windmill**
On B172 1.6 km (1 mile) W of Millisle. 📞 *01247 861413.* ○ *Easter–Sep: Tue–Sun & public hols.* 🎫
🏭 **Scrabo Country Park**
Near Newtownards. 📞 *01247 811491.* ○ *daily.* **Tower** ○ *Jun–Oct: Sat–Thu; Nov–May: public hols.*
🏛 **Grey Abbey**
Greyabbey village. ○ *Apr–Sep: Tue–Sun.* 🎫 ♿
🐠 **Exploris**
Castle Street, Portaferry. 📞 *012477 28062.* ○ *daily.* ● *25 Dec.* 🎫 ♿

Ballycopeland Windmill, which dates back to 1784

Mount Stewart House ㉚

See pp274–5.

Hillsborough ㉛

Road map D2. Co Down. 2,400. *The Square (01846 682477).*

DOTTED WITH antique shops and restaurants, this show-piece Georgian town lies less than 16 km (10 miles) from Belfast. Its most impressive building is the massive **Hillsborough Castle**, where visiting dignitaries to Northern Ireland stay. Though not open to the public, its elaborate wrought-iron gates and coat of arms are worth seeing.

Across from the 18th-century Market House in the town square, and next to the pleasant Forest Park, is **Hillsborough Fort**. An artillery fort dating from 1650, it was remodelled in the 18th century for feasts held by the descendants of Arthur Hill, founder of the town.

♣ Hillsborough Fort
Access from town square or car park at Forest Park. (01846 683285. Tue–Sun (pm).

Downpatrick ㉜

Road map E2. Co Down. 10,300. 74 Market St (01396 612233). Sat.

WERE IT NOT for its strong links with St Patrick, Downpatrick would attract few visitors. The Protestant **Down Cathedral**, high on the Hill of Down, dates in its present form from the early 19th century – many previous incarnations have been razed to the ground. In the churchyard is a well-worn 10th-century cross and the reputed burial place of St Patrick, marked by a granite slab (placed here this century) with the inscription "Patric".

Down County Museum, which is housed in the 18th-century Old County Gaol, features refurbished cells and exhibits relating to St Patrick, while close by is the **Mound of Down**, a large Norman motte and bailey.

Terraced houses in the town of Hillsborough

⛫ Down County Museum
The Mall. (01396 615218. Jun–Aug: daily (Sat & Sun: pm only); Sep–May: Tue–Sat (Sat: pm only). 25 & 26 Dec.

ENVIRONS: There are several sights associated with St Patrick on the outskirts of Downpatrick. **Struell Wells**, believed to be a former pagan place of worship that the saint blessed, has a ruined church, 17th-century bath houses and good potential for a picnic. Further out and to the north at **Saul**, where St Patrick landed and began his Irish mission in 432, is a small memorial church.

The nearby hill of **Slieve Patrick** is an important place of pilgrimage and has a granite figure of the saint at its summit. An open-air mass is celebrated here every June.

Not far from the banks of the River Quoile is the Cistercian **Inch Abbey**, founded by John de Courcy in about 1180. Its attractive marshland setting is probably more memorable than its scant remains, but it's worth a visit nonetheless.

🔒 Inch Abbey
5 km (3 miles) NW of Downpatrick. Apr–Sep: Tue–Sun.

THE LIFE OF ST PATRICK

Little hard information is known about St Patrick, the patron saint of Ireland, but he was probably not the first missionary to visit the country – a certain Palladius was sent by Pope Celestine in 431. Most stories tell that Patrick was kidnapped from Britain by pirates and brought to Ireland to tend sheep. From here he escaped to France to study Christianity. In 432, he sailed to Saul in County Down, where he quickly converted the local chieftain. He then travelled throughout the island convincing many other Celtic tribes of the truth of the new religion. The fact that Ireland has no snakes is explained by a legend that St Patrick drove them all into the sea.

19th-century engraving showing St Patrick banishing all snakes from Ireland

Mount Stewart House ⊛

THIS GRAND 19TH-CENTURY HOUSE has a splendid interior, but it is the magnificent gardens which are the main attraction. These were planted only in the 1920s, but the exotic plants and trees have thrived in the area's subtropical microclimate. Now owned by the National Trust, Mount Stewart used to belong to the London-derry family,

Lord Castlereagh (1769–1822)

the most famous of whom was Lord Castlereagh, British Foreign Secretary from 1812 until his death in 1822.

The Sunk Garden comprises symmetrical beds which in summer are full of rich blue, yellow and orange flowers, complemented by purple foliage.

Stone pergola

★ **Shamrock Garden**
A yew hedge in the shape of a shamrock encloses this topiary Irish harp and a striking flower-bed designed in the form of a red hand, emblem of Ulster.

The Music Room has a beautiful inlaid floor of mahogany and oak.

Italian Garden
The flowers in the Italian Garden, the largest of the formal gardens, are planted so that strong oranges and reds on the east side contrast with the softer pinks, whites and blues on the west.

Fountain

THE TEMPLE OF THE WINDS

This banqueting pavilion looks over Strangford Lough to the east of the house. It was built in 1785 by James "Athenian" Stuart, a renowned pioneer of Neo-Classical architecture, who took his inspiration from the Tower of the Winds in Athens. Restored in the 1960s and now being worked on once more, the building's finest features are the spiral staircase and the upper room's plasterwork ceiling and exquisite inlaid floor.

The Spanish Garden is framed by a neat arcade of clipped cypress trees.

★ Hambletonian by George Stubbs
This picture of the celebrated racehorse at Newmarket, painted in 1799, hangs halfway up the main staircase.

VISITORS' CHECKLIST

Road map E2. 3 km (2 miles) N of Greyabbey, Co Down. 012477 88387. to Newtownards from Belfast. **House** Apr & Oct: 1–6pm Sat & Sun; May–Sep: 1–6pm Wed–Mon. **Temple** as house but 2–5pm. **Gardens** Mar: 2–5pm Sun; Apr–Sep: 11am–6pm daily; Oct: 11am–6pm Sat & Sun. in house.

Entrance

The Dining Room contains 22 chairs used at the Congress of Vienna (1815) and given to Lord Castlereagh in recognition of his role in the talks.

Entrance Hall
The most austere room in the house, this hall features Ionic stone pillars which have been painted to resemble green marble. It is lit by an impressive glass dome.

The Chapel, converted from a sitting room in 1884, is still used by the Londonderry family.

STAR FEATURES

★ **Dodo Terrace**

★ **Shamrock Garden**

★ **Hambletonian by George Stubbs**

★ Dodo Terrace
The stone dodos and ark on this terrace relate to the Ark Club, a social circle set up by Lady Londonderry in London during World War I. Each member was given an animal nickname.

Lady Bangor's Gothic boudoir in Castle Ward on the Lecale Peninsula

Lecale Peninsula ㉝

Road map E2. Co Down. 🚌 *to Ardglass.* ℹ️ *Downpatrick (01396 612233).*

A GOOD WAY to get to this part of County Down is to take the short but scenic car ferry from Portaferry on the Ards Peninsula to Strangford. Just outside this tiny port is **Castle Ward**, the intriguing estate of Lord and Lady Bangor, who seemed to argue about everything – including the design of their mansion, built in the 1760s. His choice, Palladian, can be seen at the front, while her favourite Gothic style influences the garden façade. Likewise, the interior is a mix of Classical and Gothic fantasy. Look out for Lady Bangor's cluttered boudoir, with its extravagant fan-vaulted ceiling based on Henry VIII's chapel in Westminster Abbey. Around the extensive grounds are fine gardens, gentle walking trails and a lakeside farmyard with a working corn mill.

About 4 km (2.5 miles) south of Strangford, the A2 passes **Kilclief Castle**, which dates from the 15th century and is one of the oldest tower houses *(see p18)* in Ireland. The road continues to **Ardglass**, now a small fishing village but once Ulster's busiest harbour. A cluster of castles was erected between the 14th and 16th centuries to protect the port, of which six remain. Only one of these is open to the public,

Jordan's Castle. The finest view in the area is from **St John's Point**, 6 km (3.5 miles) southwest of Ardglass, which provides a sweeping panorama over Dundrum Bay.

🏛 **Castle Ward**
On A25, 2.5 km (1.5 miles) W of Strangford. 📞 *01396 881204.* **House** ⬜ *May–Aug: Fri–Wed (pm only); Apr, Sep & Oct: Sat, Sun & public hols.* 🎟 ♿ **Grounds** ⬜ *daily.* 🅿 *for car park.*
♜ **Jordan's Castle**
Ardglass. ⬜ *May–Aug: Tue–Sun.* 🎟

Castlewellan Forest Park ㉞

Road map D2. Main St, Castlewellan, Co Down. 📞 *013967 78664.* ⬜ *daily.* 🅿 *for car park.*

T HE OUTSTANDING FEATURE of Castlewellan Forest Park, in the foothills of the Mourne Mountains, is its magnificent arboretum. This has grown far beyond the

original walled garden, begun in 1740, and now comprises hothouses, dwarf conifer beds and a rhododendron wood.

Elsewhere in the park are a 19th-century Scottish baronial-style castle (now a conference centre), a lake and pleasant woodlands; these are at their most colourful in autumn.

Mountains of Mourne ㉟

Road map D2. Co Down. 🚌 *to Newry.* 🚌 *to Newcastle.* ℹ️ *10 Central Promenade, Newcastle (013967 22222).*

T HESE MOUNTAINS occupy just a small corner of County Down, with no more than a dozen peaks surpassing 600 m (2,000 ft), and yet they attract thousands of visitors each year.

Only one road of any size, the B27 between Kilkeel and Hilltown, crosses the Mournes, making this ideal territory for walkers. A popular but tough trail runs from **Newcastle**, the main gateway to the area, up to the peak of **Slieve Donard**: at 848 m (2,796 ft), this is the highest mountain in the range. Part of the route follows the **Mourne Wall**, which was erected in 1904–22 to enclose the catchment area of the two reservoirs in the **Silent Valley**.

Over 20 other short hikes are described in the *St Patrick's Vale Walks* booklet, available from local tourist offices. These range from easy strolls around Rostrevor Forest to rather more arduous treks up Slieve Muck and other Mourne peaks.

Some 35 km (22 miles) north of Newcastle, but still within the Mountains of Mourne, the **Legananny Dolmen** *(see p30)* is one of the finest and most photographed ancient sights in the country.

Rounded peaks of the Mountains of Mourne

A Tour of the Mourne Coast ㊱

NEWCASTLE, where, in the words of the 19th-century songwriter Percy French, "the Mountains of Mourne sweep down to the sea", makes a good base from which to explore this area. Driving up and down the dipping roads of the Mournes is one of the highlights of a trip to Northern Ireland. Along the coast, the road skirts between the foothills and the Irish Sea, providing lovely views and linking a variety of fishing villages and historic castles. Heading inland, you pass through an emptier landscape of moorland, purple with heather. The Silent Valley, with a visitors' centre and well-marked paths, is the only area to have been developed especially for tourists.

Tollymore Forest Park ③
This attractive park is dotted with follies like the Gothic Gate that formed part of the original 18th-century estate.

Dundrum ②
The town is overlooked by the ruins of a Norman castle, and from the nearby bay you can see the mountains rising in the distance.

Spelga Dam ④
There are stunning views north from the Spelga Dam over the Mourne foothills.

Newcastle ①
A popular resort since the early 19th century, Newcastle has a promenade overlooking a sweeping, sandy beach.

Rostrevor with Slieve Martin behind

Silent Valley ⑦
The valley is closed to traffic, but you can walk to the top of Ben Crom Mountain from the car park, or in summer go by bus.

Rostrevor ⑤
This tranquil and leafy Victorian resort nestles below the peak of Slieve Martin, on the shores of Carlingford Lough.

Green Castle ⑥
Erected in the 13th century, Green Castle lies at the end of a single track road on a rocky outcrop at the entrance to Carlingford Lough.

TIPS FOR DRIVERS

Length: 85 km (53 miles).
Stopping-off points: Newcastle has the biggest choice of pubs and restaurants. Dundrum, Annalong, Kilkeel and Rostrevor all have pubs, and a café opens in the Silent Valley in summer. The Spelga Dam and Tollymore Forest Park are good picnic spots. (See also pp355–7.)

Map labels: BELFAST · Slieve Donard · Slieve Muck · MOUNTAINS OF MOURNE · Annalong · Slieve Martin · NEWRY · Carlingford Lough · Kilkeel · B180 · B27 · B25 · A2

0 kilometres 5
0 miles 3

KEY

— Tour route
= Other roads
☆ Viewpoint

TRAVELLERS' NEEDS

WHERE TO STAY

WHETHER YOU ARE STAYING in exclusive luxury or modest self-catering accommodation, one thing you can be certain of in Ireland is that you'll receive a warm welcome. The Irish are renowned for their friendliness. Even in big corporate hotels, where you might expect the reception to be more impersonal, the staff go out of their way to be hospitable. The choice is enormous: you can stay in an elegant 18th-century country house, a luxurious (or slightly run-down) castle, a Victorian town house, an old-fashioned commercial hotel, a cosy village inn, or

Waterford Castle doorman

on a working farm. For the hardier visitor there are good hostels, plenty of caravan and camping sites, or even your own horse-drawn caravan. We give details here on the various types of accommodation available, tourist board gradings and the choices for self-catering. Our listings on pages 286–301 recommend over 200 hotels around the country – all places of quality, ranging from simple bed-and-breakfast to unashamed luxury accommodation. Bord Fáilte (the Irish Tourist Board) and the Northern Ireland Tourist Board both publish comprehensive guides.

Entrance hall of the Delphi Lodge *(see p296)* in Connemara

HOTELS

AT THE TOP of the price range there are a handful of expensive, luxury hotels in castles and stately country houses. Magnificently furnished and run, they offer maximum comfort, delicious food and a wide range of sports facilities – either owned by the hotel or available close by. Salmon-fishing, foxhunting and shooting can be arranged as well as riding, golf, sailing and cycling.

If your priority is a full range of indoor facilities, such as a gym, sauna and swimming pool, the modern hotel chains will best cater to your needs. **Jury's**, **Great Southern Hotels** and **Irish Welcome** offer this standard of accommodation in the Republic, as do **Hastings Hotels** and Irish Welcome in Northern Ireland. However,

these establishments can lack the charm and individuality of privately run hotels.

Coastal resort hotels usually offer a range of sports activities or can advise you on the best places to go. In smaller towns, the main hotel is often the social centre of the area with a lively public bar, popular with locals and guests alike.

The shamrock symbols of both the Northern Ireland Tourist Board and Bord Fáilte are displayed by hotels (and other forms of accommodation) that have been inspected and officially approved.

COUNTRY HOUSE ACCOMMODATION

VISITORS WISHING to stay in a period country home and sample authentic Irish country life can contact a specialist

organization called **Hidden Ireland**. However, this type of accommodation may not suit everybody for, as the organization emphasizes, the houses they offer are not guesthouses, hotels or bed-and-breakfast establishments, but something quite different. You should therefore not expect the same facilities and service usually found in a hotel, such as a swimming pool, lifts, televisions, porters or room service. Instead, the experience is a very intimate one; guests dine together with their host and hostess as if at a private dinner party. Many of the houses have been in the same family for hundreds of years and the history attached to them can be fascinating. Prices reflect the type of house and the standard of accommodation, but all offer

The entrance to the Shelbourne Hotel in Dublin *(see p287)*

Bar at the Hunter's Hotel *(see p290)* in Rathnew, County Wicklow

excellent value for money and a first-hand experience of an aspect of the Irish way of life.

In addition to the houses that are part of the Hidden Ireland group, there are many other private residences that also take paying guests. Local tourist boards throughout Ireland can supply listings and will make reservations with those residences which they have officially approved.

GUESTHOUSES

MOST GUESTHOUSES are found in cities and large towns. They are usually converted family homes and have an atmosphere all of their own. Most offer a good-value evening meal and all give you a delicious full Irish breakfast *(see p304)*. Top-of-the-range guesthouses can be just as good, and sometimes even better, than hotels. You will see a much more personal side of a town or city while staying at a guesthouse. If you are looking for anonymity, however, a guesthouse may not suit you – both the proprietor and your fellow guests are likely to try and draw you into conversation.

There are plenty of good guesthouses to choose from in the Dublin area and the prices are usually extremely reasonable. The **Irish Hotel Federation** publishes a useful booklet with guesthouse listings that cover the whole of Ireland including Dublin. The Northern Ireland Tourist Board publishes its own

similar booklet, called *Where to Stay in Northern Ireland*. This includes a comprehensive list of approved guesthouses which is updated annually. However, it is hard to beat personal recommendations you might receive from fellow guests.

Bedroom at Enniscoe House *(see p295)*, Crossmolina in County Mayo

PRICES

ROOM RATES advertised in both Northern Ireland and the Republic are inclusive of tax and service. In general, prices in the Republic are marginally cheaper than

in the North. Hotel rates can vary by as much as 40 per cent depending on the time of year; country house rates also vary a great deal according to the season. Guesthouse prices are influenced more by their location in relation to tourist sights and public transport.

For those on a tight budget, farmhouse accommodation represents excellent value for money, though the cheapest option is self-catering in a rented cottage *(see p282)*.

TIPPING

TIPPING IN IRELAND is a matter of personal discretion but is not common practice, even at the larger hotels. Tasks performed by staff are considered part of the service. Tipping is not expected, for example, for carrying bags to your room or for serving drinks. However, it is usual to tip the waiting staff in hotel restaurants: the standard tip is around 10 per cent and anything over 15 per cent of the bill would be considered generous.

BOOKING

IT IS WISE to reserve your accommodation during the peak season and public holidays *(see p49)*, particularly if your visit coincides with a local festival or major sporting event *(see pp26–7)*. Bord Fáilte can offer advice and make reservations through its nationwide accommodation service; the Northern Ireland Tourist Board runs a similar service. Central reservation facilities are available at the hotel chains that have been listed here.

Façade of the Londonderry Arms *(see p300)* in Carnlough, County Antrim

A bed-and-breakfast on the River Corrib in Galway

BED-AND-BREAKFAST ACCOMMODATION

IRELAND has the reputation for the best B&Bs in Europe. You will never be far from a place to stay, even in the remotest spots. Your welcome will always be friendly and the food and company excellent. Even if the house is no architectural beauty, the comfort and atmosphere will more than compensate. Not all bedrooms have bathrooms *en suite*. When one is available, you may have to pay a little extra, but considering the generally cheap rates, the surcharge is negligible.

The Irish swear by their B&Bs and many stay in them by choice rather than suffer the impersonality and prices of the mainstream hotels; frequent visitors to Ireland agree. The **Town and Seaside House Association** will provide details of bed-and-breakfast accommodation in Northern Ireland, while the **Town and Country Homes Association** covers the Republic.

FARMHOUSE ACCOMMODATION

FARMHOUSE HOLIDAYS are a popular tradition in Ireland. **Irish Farmhouse Holidays Ltd** has a list of farmhouses in the Republic that take paying guests. You can stay for one night or longer and they make an excellent base for touring the countryside. As with most things in Ireland, it is the hospitality and friendliness of the people that makes staying on a farm so memorable. You get a feel of rural Ireland with its rich agricultural heritage, and the families are determined you will enjoy every moment of your stay.

SELF-CATERING

SELF-CATERING HOLIDAYS are an increasingly popular option in Ireland and there are properties to rent all over the country. You are likely to have more choice in the south and west as these areas have traditionally attracted the majority of tourists. Bord Fáilte has a small self-catering section in its general accommodation guide, but local tourist offices have lists of apartments and houses to let in their area. It is also worth looking for adverts in the newspapers, both local and international. Accommodation can range from quaint, stone cottages, converted barns and stable yards to more modern, purpose-built bungalows. All will generally have adequate facilities, with simple but comfortable furnishings, modern kitchen equipment and televisions.

An organization called **Rent an Irish Cottage** runs a popular form of self-catering. Its cottages are built in traditional style with whitewashed walls inside and out, and painted roofs and windows; the decor is also traditional – simple and attractive. Locations are generally superb; the only possible criticism is, if you wanted to be "away from it all", they are built in clusters of about ten, so there isn't a great deal of privacy.

At the other end of the scale, you could rent a castle or country house, furnished with paintings and antiques. In some cases, the properties are fully staffed. A company called **Elegant Ireland** has a selection of such properties.

CAMPING AND CARAVANNING

A LIST of fully inspected caravan and camping parks is given in the Bord Fáilte accommodation guide. Many of the camping sites and caravan parks offer additional facilities – these might include a shop, restaurant or café/snack bar, an indoor games room, laundry, tennis court and pitch-and-putt course. The standard

A farmhouse in Clonakilty, County Cork

Traditional painted horse-drawn caravan from Slattery's in Tralee

and condition of these facilities will vary but you can be reliably guided by the tourist board's star ratings: four-star parks have an extensive range of facilities with a high standard of management; three-star parks have good facilities and management; two-star parks offer limited facilities and good management and the one-star parks have the minimum facilities required for registration with Bord Fáilte. A complete list of approved camping sites in the North is produced by the Northern Ireland Tourist Board.

If you want to experience the Irish countryside at a more leisurely pace, it is possible to hire a traditional horse-drawn caravan. Two of the best companies specializing in this type of holiday are **Kilvahan Caravans**, based at Portlaoise in the Midlands, and **Slattery's Travel Agency** in Tralee, County Kerry.

YOUTH HOSTELS

THERE ARE 40 youth hostels registered with **An Óige** (the Irish Youth Hostel Association), set in some wonderfully scenic areas of Ireland in buildings ranging from castles to military barracks. Accommodation is generally provided in simple dormitories with comfortable beds and basic cooking facilities. You can only use these hostels if you are a member of An Óige or another youth organization affiliated to the International Youth Hostel Federation. Charges vary according to standard, location and season. Northern Ireland is covered by the **Youth Hostel Association of Northern Ireland**, which is also affiliated to the international body and has over 30 registered hostels.

There are many independent hostels and places, such as universities, that offer similar inexpensive accommodation. Tourist boards have listings of those they recommend.

DISABLED TRAVELLERS

A FACT SHEET for disabled visitors is produced by Bord Fáilte and in their main accommodation guide there is a symbol for wheelchair accessibility. A similar symbol is used in the accommodation listings in this book *(see pp286–301)*. The National Rehabilitation Board *(see p340)* publishes two free guides *Accommodation for Disabled Persons* and *Dublin: A Guide for Disabled Persons*, both in conjunction with the tourist board. The annual publication *Holidays in the British Isles* caters specifically for the disabled traveller and covers Northern Ireland. There is also a guide, with comprehensive listings, available from the Northern Ireland Tourist Board entitled *Accessible Accommodation*.

Bord Fáilte sign for approved accommodation

Typical bed-and-bed-breakfast sign in Pettigo, County Donegal

Ireland's Best: Hotels

THE HOTELS featured here are a selection from our lists of recommended places to stay on pages 286–301. They give an indication of the very best that Ireland has to offer, ranging from private establishments which are members of the Hidden Ireland group *(see p280)* to the efficiency and luxury of five-star hotels or the romance of historic castles. All are impressive places, both for their setting and the buildings themselves.

St Ernan's House
This elegant, pink Regency country house is situated on its own private island not far from Donegal.
(See p298.)

Delphi Lodge
The atmosphere at this comfortable, well-run fishing lodge is extremely relaxing. The River Delphi and nearby loughs provide plenty of sport. (See p296.)

NORTHWEST IRELAND

THE WEST OF IRELAND

Ashford Castle
This huge Gothic-style edifice is set on the shores of Lough Corrib. The standard of service is impeccable and the food is excellent.
(See p296.)

THE LOWER SHANNON

Adare Manor
Set in a large estate beside one of the prettiest villages in the country, this luxurious hotel occupies a magnificent Victorian Gothic mansion.
(See p294.)

CORK AND KERRY

Bantry House
The spacious library in this 18th-century house looks out on to the gardens. Many of the bedrooms enjoy superb views of Bantry Bay. (See pp160–61 and p291.)

Streeve House
This 18th-century dower house is a member of the Hidden Ireland group. A stay here gives access to the stunning gardens of Drenagh House, which include the hidden Moon Garden. (See p301.)

NORTHERN IRELAND

THE IDLANDS

Hunter's Hotel
Cobbled courtyards, paddocks and a magnificent garden are only a few of the attractions of this friendly and comfortable inn. The building dates back to 1720, and is owned and run by the fourth generation of the Hunter family. (See p290.)

SOUTHEAST IRELAND

Roundwood House
This fine, small Palladian house is set in chestnut and beech woods. The Slieve Bloom Mountains are close by and you can fish and play golf locally. The lovely rooms are filled with antiques, books and pictures and the atmosphere is one of relaxed informality. (See p299.)

| 0 kilometres | 50 |
| 0 miles | 25 |

Waterford Castle
The ultimate in "getting away from it all", this 15th-century castle sits on a beautifully located island in the estuary of the River Suir. The hotel is reachable only by its own private ferry. (See p291.)

Choosing a Hotel

THESE HOTELS have been selected across a wide price range for their good value, facilities and location; they are listed by region, starting with Dublin. Use the colour-coded thumb tabs, which indicate the regions covered on each page, to guide you to the relevant section of the chart. For Dublin map references see pages 110–11; for road map references see the inside back cover.

DUBLIN

Hotel	Price	Credit Cards	Children's Facilities	Parking Facilities	Restaurant	Public Bar
SOUTHEAST DUBLIN: *Fitzwilliam* 41 Fitzwilliam St Upper, Dublin 2. **Map** E5. 01 6600448. FAX 01 6767488. A friendly, unpretentious guesthouse in an attractive Georgian street, with simple, elegant decor and comfortable bedrooms. TV *Rooms: 12*	£££	MC V AE DC	●	■		
SOUTHEAST DUBLIN: *Georgian House* 18 Baggot St Lower, Dublin 2. **Map** F5. 01 6618832. FAX 01 6618834. A short walk from St Stephen's Green, this small hotel is a good base for exploring Dublin. The bedrooms are large and comfortable and there's a good seafood restaurant in the basement. TV *Rooms: 47*	£££	MC V AE DC	●	■	●	■
SOUTHEAST DUBLIN: *Harcourt* 60 Harcourt St, Dublin 2. **Map** D5. 01 4783677. FAX 01 4752013. Just off St Stephen's Green, this hotel is close to many of the city's main sights. The bedrooms are modern and well-equipped, there is a popular bar, a restaurant for evening meals and a nightclub. TV *Rooms: 40*	£££	MC V AE	●		●	■
SOUTHEAST DUBLIN: *Kilronan House* 70 Adelaide Rd, Dublin 2. 01 4755266. FAX 01 4782841. A reasonably priced, small guesthouse in a quiet street in the centre. Charming owners and delicious breakfasts. TV *Rooms: 11*	£££	MC V	●	■		
SOUTHEAST DUBLIN: *Leeson Court* 26 Leeson St Lower, Dublin 2. **Map** E5. 01 6763380. FAX 01 6618273. Spread across two Georgian houses, this cheerfully decorated hotel has a relaxed, informal atmosphere and the service is good. St Stephen's Green is only a few minutes' walk away. TV *Rooms: 20*	£££	MC V AE DC	●	■	●	■
SOUTHEAST DUBLIN: *Buswells* 25 Molesworth St, Dublin 2. **Map** E4. 01 6764013. FAX 01 6762090. A short walk from Grafton Street, this old family favourite has recently been sold and given a thorough refurbishment. TV *Rooms: 65*	££££	MC V AE DC	●	■	●	■
SOUTHEAST DUBLIN: *The Grey Door Hotel* 22–23 Pembroke St Upper, Dublin 2. 01 6763286. FAX 01 6763287. This centrally located Georgian house has immaculately decorated, well-equipped rooms and an excellent restaurant. TV *Rooms: 7*	££££	MC V AE DC	●		●	
SOUTHEAST DUBLIN: *Longfields* 10 Fitzwilliam St Lower, Dublin 2. **Map** F5. 01 6761367. FAX 01 6761542. Two Georgian town houses have been knocked together to create this stylish hotel with an attractive sitting room and smart, pretty bedrooms. There is a very good restaurant in the basement. TV *Rooms: 28*	££££	MC V AE DC	●		●	■
SOUTHEAST DUBLIN: *Russell Court* 21–25 Harcourt St, Dublin 2. **Map** D5. 01 4784066. FAX 01 4781576. Jolly, welcoming hotel with young staff and a lively atmosphere in the evenings. There's a choice of bars and a more formal restaurant. Bedrooms are neat and well-equipped. TV *Rooms: 42*	££££	MC V AE DC	●	■	●	■
SOUTHEAST DUBLIN: *Stephen's Hall* 14–17 Leeson St Lower, Dublin 2. **Map** E5. 01 6610585. FAX 01 6610606. All the rooms are suites and represent good value for families who want smart, comfortable accommodation in the centre of the city near St Stephen's Green. Cooking facilities are available. TV *Rooms: 37*	££££	MC V AE DC	●	■	●	
SOUTHEAST DUBLIN: *Temple Bar* Fleet St, Temple Bar, Dublin 2. **Map** D3. 01 6773333. FAX 01 6773088. This new hotel, situated in a trendy area of Dublin, is a popular meeting place with its theme bar "Buskers" attracting a lively crowd. Bedrooms are comfortable but lack character. TV *Rooms: 108*	££££	MC V AE DC	●		●	■

Price categories are for a standard double room (not per person) for one night, including tax, service charges and breakfast. ⓔ under IR£50 ⓔⓔ IR£50–100 ⓔⓔⓔ IR£100–150 ⓔⓔⓔⓔ IR£150–200 ⓔⓔⓔⓔⓔ over IR£200	**CHILDREN'S FACILITIES** Cots and high chairs are available and some hotels will also provide a baby-sitting service. **PARKING FACILITIES** Parking provided by the hotel in either a private car park or a private garage close by. **RESTAURANT** The hotel has a restaurant for residents which also welcomes non-residents – usually only for evening meals. **PUBLIC BAR** The hotel has a bar that is open to non-residents and residents alike.	

	CREDIT CARDS	CHILDREN'S FACILITIES	PARKING FACILITIES	RESTAURANT	PUBLIC BAR
SOUTHEAST DUBLIN: *Mont Clare* ⓔⓔⓔⓔ Merrion Square, Dublin 2. **Map** F4. 【 *01 6616799*. ℻ *01 6615663*. Not as grand as the Davenport opposite, but with the same club-like feel. A busy, traditional pub takes up most of the ground floor. 🛏 TV *Rooms: 80*	MC V AE DC	●	■	●	■
SOUTHEAST DUBLIN: *Conrad Hotel* ⓔⓔⓔⓔⓔ Earlsfort Terrace, Dublin 2. **Map** D5. 【 *01 6765555*. ℻ *01 6765424*. This international-style hotel, by St Stephen's Green, is geared to business people for whom there are excellent facilities. A jolly pub with a large terrace is the only concession to traditional Dublin. 🛏 TV 🚹 *Rooms: 191*	MC V AE DC	●	■	●	■
SOUTHEAST DUBLIN: *Davenport* ⓔⓔⓔⓔⓔ Merrion Square, Dublin 2. **Map** F4. 【 *01 6616800*. ℻ *01 6615663*. The grand proportions of the Neo-Classical façade are carried through into the lobby – a vast, marble-floored atrium. Opened in 1994, it is elegant but rather like a gentleman's club. 🛏 TV 🚹 *Rooms: 120*	MC V AE DC	●	■		
SOUTHEAST DUBLIN: *Shelbourne Hotel* ⓔⓔⓔⓔⓔ 27 St Stephen's Green, Dublin 2. **Map** D4. 【 *01 6766471*. ℻ *01 6616006*. The Shelbourne has been the city's most distinguished hotel since it opened in the 19th century. Although it has every facility for the business traveller, it manages to retain a personal atmosphere. 🛏 TV 🚹 *Rooms: 164*	MC V AE DC	●	■	●	■
SOUTHEAST DUBLIN: *Westbury Hotel* ⓔⓔⓔⓔⓔ Grafton St, Dublin 2. **Map** D4. 【 *01 6791122*. ℻ *01 6797078*. You couldn't get much closer to the centre of things than here, only seconds from Dublin's major shopping street. It is a smart, ritzy hotel with lots of shiny floors and heavily co-ordinated bedrooms. 🛏 TV 🚹 *Rooms: 203*	MC V AE DC	●	■	●	■
SOUTHWEST DUBLIN: *Avalon House* ⓔ 55 Aungier St, Dublin 2. **Map** C4. 【 *01 4750001*. ℻ *01 4750303*. This cheap and cheerful budget accommodation is centrally located and has clean bedrooms and a self-service restaurant. *Rooms: 38*	MC V AE			●	
SOUTHWEST DUBLIN: *Blooms* ⓔⓔ Anglesea St, Temple Bar, Dublin 2. **Map** D3. 【 *01 6715622*. ℻ *01 6715997*. Situated near Trinity College in the heart of Dublin, this modern hotel is very convenient for exploring the city, but its reception areas are slightly limited. 🛏 TV *Rooms: 97*	MC V AE DC	●		●	■
SOUTHWEST DUBLIN: *Jury's Christchurch Inn* ⓔⓔ Christchurch Place, Dublin 8. **Map** B4. 【 *01 4750111*. ℻ *01 4540012*. The Jury's group "inns" offer spruce modern facilities. This "inn", 15 minutes from St Stephen's Green, has a good bar and restaurant, and neat, well-equipped rooms at reasonable prices. 🛏 TV 🚹 *Rooms: 182*	MC V AE DC	●		●	■
SOUTHWEST DUBLIN: *Central* ⓔⓔⓔ 1–5 Exchequer St, Dublin 2. **Map** D5. 【 *01 6797302*. ℻ *01 6797303*. As its name suggests, one of the great advantages of this hotel is its position. Molly Malone's Tavern, on the ground floor, offers music most nights, so choose your neat, functional bedroom carefully. 🛏 TV *Rooms: 70*	MC V AE DC	●		●	■
SOUTHWEST DUBLIN: *Grafton Plaza* ⓔⓔⓔ Johnson's Place, Dublin 2. **Map** D4. 【 *01 4750888*. ℻ *01 4750908*. This newly constructed hotel, with a Georgian façade is neat and tastefully decorated throughout. Only a few minutes' walk from Grafton Street, it makes an excellent city base. 🛏 TV 🚹 *Rooms: 75*	MC V AE DC	●		●	■
SOUTHWEST DUBLIN: *Clarence* ⓔⓔⓔⓔ 6–8 Wellington Quay, Dublin 2. **Map** C3. 【 *01 6709000*. ℻ *01 6707800*. The hotel is owned by the rock band U2 and has been completely refurbished. A stylish restaurant sets the standard for the rest of the hotel – one of the trendiest places to stay in town. 🛏 TV 🚹 *Rooms: 50*	MC V AE DC	●		●	■

Price categories are for a standard double room (not per person) for one night, including tax, service charges and breakfast.
£ under IR£50
££ IR£50–100
£££ IR£100–150
££££ IR£150–200
£££££ over IR£200

CHILDREN'S FACILITIES
Cots and high chairs are available and some hotels will also provide a baby-sitting service.
PARKING FACILITIES
Parking provided by the hotel in either a private car park or a private garage close by.
RESTAURANT
The hotel has a restaurant for residents which also welcomes non-residents – usually only for evening meals.
PUBLIC BAR
The hotel has a bar that is open to non-residents and residents alike.

	CREDIT CARDS	CHILDREN'S FACILITIES	PARKING FACILITIES	RESTAURANT	PUBLIC BAR
NORTH OF THE LIFFEY: *Isaacs* **££** Frenchman's Lane, Store St, Dublin 1. **Map** E2. 01 855 0067. FAX 01 836 5390. Recently developed alongside an older hostel of the same name, the hotel is reasonably priced, well-run and centrally located. *Rooms: 57*	MC V	●		●	
NORTH OF THE LIFFEY: *Royal Dublin* **££** 40 O'Connell St Upper, Dublin 1. **Map** D1. 01 8733666. FAX 01 8733120. Modern hotel in one of Dublin's most famous streets. It has well-equipped rooms and is smart, though lacking in atmosphere. *Rooms: 117*	MC V AE DC	●	■	●	■
NORTH OF THE LIFFEY: *Gresham Hotel* **£££** 23 O'Connell St Upper, Dublin 1. **Map** D1. 01 8746881. FAX 01 8787175. One of Dublin's oldest and best known hotels. It is a popular rendezvous spot so the public areas are always busy. The bedrooms are comfortable and there is ample safe parking. *Rooms: 200*	MC V AE DC	●	■	●	■
BALGRIFFIN: *Belcamp Hutchinson* **££** Malahide Rd, Balgriffin, Dublin 17. 01 8460843. FAX 01 8485703. Poorly located for central Dublin but only ten minutes from the airport, a comfortable, pleasant place to stay with good food. *Rooms: 5*	MC V		■		
BALLSBRIDGE: *Anglesea Town House* **££** 63 Anglesea Rd, Dublin 4. 01 6683877. FAX 01 6683461. This Edwardian house is beautifully decorated and furnished. It has a lovely drawing room, very comfortable bedrooms and offers a superb breakfast – all within ten minutes' drive of the centre. *Rooms: 7*	MC V AE	●	■		
BALLSBRIDGE: *Ariel House* **££** 52 Lansdowne Rd, Ballsbridge, Dublin 4. 01 6685512. FAX 01 6685845. Near Lansdowne Road Station, this Victorian house is elegantly decorated, with comfortable bedrooms and good breakfasts. *Rooms: 28*	MC V		■		
BALLSBRIDGE: *Glenogra Guesthouse* **££** 64 Merrion Rd, Ballsbridge, Dublin 4. 01 6683661. FAX 01 6683698. Attractive, stylish guesthouse convenient for both Dun Laoghaire and the centre. The bedrooms are charming and very comfortable. *Rooms: 10*	MC V AE	●	■		
BALLSBRIDGE: *Mount Herbert Hotel* **££** 7 Herbert Rd, Landsdown Rd, Ballsbridge, Dublin 4. 01 6684321. FAX 01 6607077. A Victorian hotel close to Lansdowne Road stadium. The rooms are light with modern furnishings and it is reasonably priced. *Rooms: 140*	MC V AE DC	●	■	●	
BALLSBRIDGE: *Hibernian* **£££** Eastmoreland Place, Ballsbridge, Dublin 4. 01 6687666. FAX 01 6602655. Tucked away in a quiet street but close to the centre, this impressive turn-of-the-century building opened as a smart, comfortable hotel in 1993. Elegant, luxurious rooms. *Rooms: 41*	MC V AE DC	●	■	●	
BALLSBRIDGE: *Herbert Park Hotel* **££££** Ballsbridge, Dublin 4. 01 6672200. FAX 01 6672595. A new hotel adjoining Herbert Park and close to the Royal Dublin Showground. Public areas are light and spacious with modern furnishings. *Rooms: 148*	MC V AE DC	●	■	●	■
BALLSBRIDGE: *Jury's Hotel & The Towers at Jury's* **££££** Pembroke Rd, Ballsbridge, Dublin 4. 01 6605000. FAX 01 6605540. A modern hotel, popular with business people and tourists, a short distance from the centre with all the facilities you'd expect from a five-star hotel. The Towers is an exclusive wing with de luxe bedrooms. *Rooms: 390*	MC V AE DC	●	■	●	■
BALLSBRIDGE: *Berkeley Court Hotel* **£££££** Lansdowne Rd, Dublin 4. 01 6601711. FAX 01 6617238. The very smart lobby area sets the standard for this luxury hotel, which is well located for Lansdowne Road stadium. *Rooms: 198*	MC V AE DC	●	■	●	■

BOOTERSTOWN: *Doyle Tara* ⓔⓔⓔ MC V AE DC
Merrion Rd, Dublin 4. 【 *01 2694666.* FAX *01 2691027.*
Conveniently situated for Dun Laoghaire, the hotel has recently undergone
refurbishment with a number of new rooms added. 🛏 TV ♿ *Rooms: 113*

DONNYBROOK: *Morehampton Townhouse* ⓔⓔ MC V
46 Morehampton Rd, Donnybrook, Dublin 4. 【 *01 6602106.* FAX *01 6602566.*
Attractively decorated Victorian town house, ten minutes' drive from the
centre, with great hospitality and delicious breakfasts. 🛏 TV *Rooms: 7*

RATHMINES: *Clara House* ⓔⓔ MC V
23 Leinster Rd, Rathmines, Dublin 6. 【 *01 4975904.* FAX *01 4975904.*
In an attractive area, ten minutes' walk from the centre, this Georgian
house is a comfortable B&B with a friendly atmosphere. 🛏 TV *Rooms: 13*

SOUTHEAST IRELAND

BAGENALSTOWN: *Lorum Old Rectory* ⓔⓔ MC V
Co Carlow. **Road map** D4. 【 *0503 75282.* FAX *0503 75455.*
Set beneath the Blackstairs Mountains with a cosy atmosphere and log fires
and an inspired five-course dinner. Member of Hidden Ireland. 🛏 *Rooms: 5*

BALLYMACARBRY: *Clonanav Farm Guesthouse* ⓔⓔ MC V AE
Clonmel, Co Waterford. **Road map** C5. 【 *052 36141.* FAX *052 36141.*
A friendly welcome and lots of outdoor activities on offer at this bungalow
farmhouse; there's an evening meal and a full breakfast. 🛏 *Rooms: 10*

BALLYMURN: *Ballinkeele House* ⓔⓔ MC V
Enniscorthy, Co Wexford. **Road map** D5. 【 *053 38105.* FAX *053 38468.*
The comfortable rooms overlook its parkland setting. Delicious dinners are
served in the original dining room. Member of Hidden Ireland. 🛏 *Rooms: 5*

BLESSINGTON: *Tulfarris House & Country Club* ⓔⓔ MC V AE DC
Blessington Lakes, Co Wicklow. **Road map** D4. 【 *045 864574.* FAX *045 864423.*
In a lovely position overlooking Poulaphouca Lake, the hotel offers stylish
comfort and the many facilities of the Country Club. 🛏 TV 🏊 *Rooms: 22*

CAPPOQUIN: *Richmond House* ⓔⓔ MC V AE DC
Co Waterford. **Road map** C5. 【 *058 54278.* FAX *058 54988.*
A delightful 18th-century, Georgian country house, charmingly decorated
and furnished with antiques, set in peaceful parkland. 🛏 *Rooms: 9*

CASTLEDERMOT: *Kilkea Lodge* ⓔⓔ AE
Co Kildare. **Road map** D4. 【 *0503 45112.* FAX *0503 45112.*
A member of Hidden Ireland, this attractive house is popular with racegoers
as the Curragh, Punchestown and Naas are within easy reach. 🛏 *Rooms: 7*

CLONEA: *Clonea Strand Hotel* ⓔⓔ MC V
Dungarvan, Co Waterford. **Road map** C5. 【 *058 42416.* FAX *058 42880.*
A large, modern resort hotel without huge charm but located next to a
lovely beach and with lots of facilities – great for families. 🛏 TV *Rooms: 59*

DUNMORE EAST: *Church Villa* ⓔ
Co Waterford. **Road map** D5. 【 *051 383390.*
Situated in the village, this attractive house offers excellent-value, simple
B&B. Very friendly owners and neat, comfortable bedrooms. 🛏 *Rooms: 5*

ENNISCORTHY: *Salville House* ⓔ
Enniscorthy, Co Wexford. **Road map** D5. 【 *054 35252.* FAX *054 35252.*
Very spacious rooms with huge windows give fine views over the
wooded countryside. Delicious breakfasts. Dinner available if pre-booked.
🛏 *Rooms: 4*

ENNISKERRY: *Enniscree Lodge* ⓔⓔ MC V AE DC
Glencree Valley, Enniskerry, Co Wicklow. **Road map** D4.
【 *01 2863542.* FAX *01 2866037.*
Set in a wonderful position with stunning views from most of the rooms,
it's a friendly place with country-style furnishings. 🛏 TV *Rooms: 10*

INISTIOGE: *Cullintra House* ⓔ
The Rower, Inistioge, Co Kilkenny. **Road map** D5. 【 *051 423614.* FAX *051 423614.*
An attractive farmhouse set in woods and farmland, very cosy and almost
idyllically bucolic, with open fires and a relaxed atmosphere. Member of
Hidden Ireland. 🛏 *Rooms: 6*

Price categories are for a standard double room (not per person) for one night, including tax, service charges and breakfast.
£ under IR£50
££ IR£50–100
£££ IR£100–150
££££ IR£150–200
£££££ over IR£200

CHILDREN'S FACILITIES
Cots and high chairs are available and some hotels will also provide a baby-sitting service.

PARKING FACILITIES
Parking provided by the hotel in either a private car park or a private garage close by.

RESTAURANT
The hotel has a restaurant for residents which also welcomes non-residents – usually only for evening meals.

PUBLIC BAR
The hotel has a bar that is open to non-residents and residents alike.

	Credit Cards	Children's Facilities	Parking Facilities	Restaurant	Public Bar
KILBRIDE: *The Manor* ££ Nr Blessington, Co Wicklow. **Road map** D4. (01 4582105. FAX 01 4582607. A member of the Hidden Ireland group, The Manor has large comfortable rooms, log fires and is surrounded by over 16 ha (40 acres) of gardens complete with a lake full of trout. Open April to end of September. **Rooms: 5**	MC V AE	●	■		
KILKENNY: *Butler House* ££ 16 Patrick St, Kilkenny, Co Kilkenny. **Road map** C4. (056 65707. FAX 056 65626. The former dower house of Kilkenny Castle right in the heart of town, it has been restored by the Civic Trust. The 18th-century building has fine proportions and is stylishly decorated throughout. **Rooms: 14**	MC V AE DC	●	■	●	
KILKENNY: *Lacken House* ££ Dublin Rd, Kilkenny, Co Kilkenny. **Road map** C4. (056 61085. FAX 056 62435. Within easy reach of the centre, this Victorian house is a very comfortable place to stay with a highly regarded restaurant. **Rooms: 9**	MC V AE DC	●	■	●	■
RATHASPECK: *Rathaspeck Manor* £ Co Wexford. **Road map** D5. (053 42661/45148. This 300-year-old Georgian manor has an 18-hole, par three golf course and a tennis court. Offering B&B only, the bedrooms are large and comfortable and the breakfast excellent. **Rooms: 7**			■		
RATHNEW: *Hunter's Hotel* ££ Co Wicklow. **Road map** D4. (0404 40106. FAX 0404 40338. This inn on the old Dublin coaching road dates back to 1720 and is run by the fourth generation of the Hunter family. Comfortable and relaxing if a little eccentric, it's a great place to stay and the food is delicious. **Rooms: 16**	MC V AE DC	●	■	●	
RATHNEW: *Tinakilly House, Hotel and Restaurant* £££ Co Wicklow. **Road map** D4. (0404 69274. FAX 0404 67806. The many outstanding features of this Victorian house include lovely views over the coast and large, attractive gardens. Comfort is assured with a mix of antiques and modern facilities. **Rooms: 41**	MC V AE DC	●	■	●	■
ROSSLARE: *Kelly's Resort Hotel* ££ Co Wexford. **Road map** D5. (053 32114. FAX 053 32222. This hotel on the beach is ideal for families who don't mind any lack of character but want lots of leisure and sports facilities. **Rooms: 99**	MC V AE	●	■	●	■
STRAFFAN: *Kildare Hotel & Country Club* £££££ Co Kildare. **Road map** D4. (01 6273333. FAX 01 6017299. Parts of this exclusive hotel building date back to the 17th century. As well as luxurious bedrooms and a grand drawing room, it boasts a one-star Michelin restaurant, The Byerley Turk. Excellent facilities include a championship golf course and extensive fishing. **Rooms: 43**	MC V AE DC	●	■	●	■
TACUMSHANE: *Furziestown House* £ Co Wexford. **Road map** D5. (053 31376. An attractive, peaceful spot, with access to local beaches and lakes, it offers cosy farmhouse rooms at very reasonable prices. **Rooms: 3**		●	■		
THOMASTOWN: *Mount Juliet Estate* ££££ Co Kilkenny. **Road map** D5. (056 24455. FAX 056 24522. One of Ireland's luxury hotels but retaining the character and style of a grand family house. Set in an estate of over 450 ha (1,100 acres) with lots of sports facilities including an 18-hole golf course. **Rooms: 64**	MC V AE DC	●	■	●	■
WATERFORD: *Foxmount Farm* £ Passage East Rd, off Dumore Rd, Waterford, Co Waterford. **Road map** D5. (051 874308. FAX 051 854906. An attractive, 17th-century house, full of antiques and personality. The atmosphere is homely and you can bring your own wine to dinner. **Rooms: 6**		●	■		

WATERFORD: *Waterford Castle Hotel* £££££
The Island, Ballinakill, Waterford, Co Waterford. **Road map** D5.
[051 878203. FAX 051 879316.
Guests are ferried across the river to this romantically sited, 15th-century castle. Log fires blaze in lofty rooms and both the large suites and the smaller cosy bedrooms are truly luxurious. **Rooms:** 19
Cards: MC V AE DC

WEXFORD: *Newbay Country House* ££
Newbay, Wexford, Co Wexford. **Road map** D5. [053 42779. FAX 053 46318.
This country house hotel is a member of Hidden Ireland. Part Georgian and part early Victorian, the house is very comfortable and relaxing with peat fires and interesting antiques. **Rooms:** 6
Cards: MC V

WEXFORD: *White's Hotel* ££
George St, Wexford, Co Wexford. **Road map** D5. [053 22311. FAX 053 46000.
Centrally located, this former coaching inn is neat and reasonably comfortable with a choice of formal or country-style restaurant. There is also a fitness and leisure centre with gym and solarium. **Rooms:** 82
Cards: MC V AE DC

WICKLOW: *The Old Rectory Country House* ££
Co Wicklow. **Road map** D4. [0404 67048. FAX 0404 69181.
A pretty house offering great comfort and good cooking. Guests can walk to the harbour and town centre. **Rooms:** 8
Cards: MC V AE

CORK AND KERRY

BALLINADEE: *Glebe Country House* £
Bandon, Co Cork. **Road map** B6. [021 778294. FAX 021 778456.
Only ten minutes from Kinsale with lots of sports opportunities close by, this attractive Georgian rectory is beautifully furnished and makes a great base for the area. Book by noon if you want dinner. **Rooms:** 4
Cards: MC V

BALLYLICKEY: *Ballylickey Manor House* £££
Bantry Bay, Co Cork. **Road map** B6. [027 50071. FAX 027 50124.
A 17th-century shooting lodge which has been completely refurbished over recent years. It's an attractive place to stay with lovely, comfortable rooms and delicious food. **Rooms:** 11
Cards: MC V AE

BANTEER: *Clonmeen Lodge* ££
Co Cork. **Road map** B5. [029 56238. FAX 029 56294.
A popular countryside spot, situated on the banks of the River Blackwater. There are lots of lovely riding trails and walks and a very friendly, relaxed atmosphere. Breakfast is served whenever you wake up. **Rooms:** 6
Cards: MC V AE DC

BANTRY: *Bantry House* £££
Co Cork. **Road map** B6. [027 50047. FAX 027 50795.
An outstanding, 18th-century, stately home *(see pp160–61)*, open to the public since 1946 and a Member of the Hidden Ireland Group. It has a fine collection of pictures, furniture and works of art. The comfortable bedrooms with *en suite* bathrooms are in the east and west wings. **Rooms:** 9
Cards: MC V AE DC

CARAGH LAKE: *Caragh Lodge* ££
Co Kerry. **Road map** A5. [066 69115. FAX 066 69316.
Colonial-style fishing lodge in magnificent, award-winning gardens bordering the lake. All rooms are neatly decorated and furnished with antique and period furniture. Open Easter to mid-October. **Rooms:** 10
Cards: MC V

CARAGH LAKE: *Ard-na-Sidhe* £££
Co Kerry. **Road map** A5. [066 69105. FAX 066 69282.
This attractive Victorian mansion enjoys a wonderfully peaceful setting beside the lake. The ambience is somewhat old-fashioned, reinforced by the neat period furnishings. Open May to September. **Rooms:** 20
Cards: MC V AE DC

CLONAKILTY: *O'Donovan's Hotel* £
Co Cork. **Road map** B6. [023 33250. FAX 023 33250.
A traditional, centrally located, family-run hotel in the old commercial mould. The decor and furnishings are unremarkable but the place is friendly. There are two restaurants and occasionally Irish music in the bar. **Rooms:** 30
Cards: MC V AE DC

CORK: *Jury's Cork Inn* £
Anderson's Quay, Cork, Co Cork. **Road map** C5.
[021 276444. FAX 021 276144.
A fixed room-rate hotel with modern, attractive furnishings and good facilities for reasonable prices – particularly good for families. **Rooms:** 133
Cards: MC V AE DC

For key to symbols see back flap

Price categories are for a standard double room (not per person) for one night, including tax, service charges and breakfast.
£ under IR£50
££ IR£50–100
£££ IR£100–150
££££ IR£150–200
£££££ over IR£200

CHILDREN'S FACILITIES
Cots and high chairs are available and some hotels will also provide a baby-sitting service.

PARKING FACILITIES
Parking provided by the hotel in either a private car park or a private garage close by.

RESTAURANT
The hotel has a restaurant for residents which also welcomes non-residents – usually only for evening meals.

PUBLIC BAR
The hotel has a bar that is open to non-residents and residents alike.

	Credit Cards	Children's Facilities	Parking Facilities	Restaurant	Public Bar
CORK: *Lotamore House* (£) Tivoli, Cork, Co Cork. **Road map** C5. 021 822344. FAX 021 822219. This Georgian manor converted into a guesthouse is surrounded by lovely grounds with good views of the harbour and Blackrock Castle. Five minutes' drive from the city centre. *Rooms: 20*	MC V AE	●	■		
CORK: *Seven North Mall* (££) 7 North Mall, Cork, Co Cork. **Road map** C5. 021 397191. FAX 021 300811. This smart 18th-century house overlooks the River Lee and is a convenient base for exploring the city and surrounding areas, or simply for relaxing among the pleasant interiors. *Rooms: 7*	MC V		■		
COURTMACSHERRY: *Travara Lodge* (£) Courtmacsherry, Co Cork. **Road map** C5. 023 46493. FAX 023 46045. Sea views from some of the rooms in this comfortable, well-fitted house. Simple and extremely tasty food served in the small restaurant. *Rooms: 5*	MC V AE	●	■	●	
DINGLE: *Benners Hotel* (££) Main St, Dingle, Co Kerry. **Road map** A5. 066 51638. FAX 066 51412. American-owned hotel right in the centre of town. The old building has been converted to provide an efficient hotel with a choice of bars, a restaurant and comfortable bedrooms. *Rooms: 48*	MC V AE DC	●	■	●	■
DINGLE: *Doyle's Seafood Bar and Townhouse* (££) John St, Dingle, Co Kerry. **Road map** A5. 066 51174. FAX 066 51816. Famous for its delicious seafood, Doyle's also provides first-class accommodation. Smart and stylish bedrooms with luxurious bathrooms and an attractive sitting room. Informal, relaxed atmosphere. *Rooms: 8*	MC V AE	●		●	■
INISHANNON: *Inishannon House* (£££) Co Cork. **Road map** B6. 021 775121. FAX 021 775609. This 18th-century house is very romantic with lovely gardens and parkland leading down to the River Bandon. The bedrooms are individual both in shape and decor and look out over the river or the garden. *Rooms: 13*	MC V AE DC	●	■	●	
KANTURK: *Assolas Country House* (£££) Co Cork. **Road map** B5. 029 50015. FAX 029 50795. An elegant, 17th-century house, run like a glorified family home with cosy decor and an excellent restaurant. Open April to November. *Rooms: 9*	MC V	●	■	●	
KENMARE: *Park Hotel* (£££££) Co Kerry. **Road map** B5. 064 41200. FAX 064 41402. Built in 1897 in a stunning setting by Kenmare Bay, the Park is rated one of Ireland's finest hotels, luxurious with an individual style and lots of original touches. The facilities include an 18-hole golf course. Open Easter to October and for Christmas and New Year. *Rooms: 49*	MC V AE DC	●	■	●	
KENMARE: *Sheen Falls Lodge* (£££££) Co Kerry. **Road map** B5. 064 41600. FAX 064 41386. The new hotel blends in well with the original 17th-century house. Luxurious, spacious bedrooms with great views over the falls or the huge grounds. Closed January to mid-February. *Rooms: 40*	MC V AE DC	●	■	●	■
KILLARNEY: *Royal Hotel* (££) College St, Killarney, Co Kerry. **Road map** B5. 064 31853. FAX 064 34001. A short walk from the centre of town, this traditional hotel is a smart, comfortable place to stay. *Rooms: 49*	MC V AE DC	●		●	■
KILLARNEY: *Dunloe Castle* (£££) Co Kerry. **Road map** B5. 064 44111. FAX 064 44583. A member of the Historic Castles and Gardens Association. The modern buildings are in lovely grounds by the ruins of the 13th-century castle. Excellent facilities. Open April to September. *Rooms: 120*	MC V AE DC	●	■	●	■

KILLARNEY: *Hotel Europe*   £££   MC V AE DC
Co Kerry. **Road map** B5. 📞 064 31900. FAX 064 32118.
Huge five-star resort hotel with stunning views of the Lakes of Killarney and the mountains, with every facility from beauty salon to Olympic-size pool and lots of outdoor sports. Open April to October. **Rooms:** 205

KILLARNEY: *Killarney Park Hotel*   ££££   MC V AE DC
Kenmare Place, Killarney, Co Kerry. **Road map** B5. 📞 064 35555. FAX 064 35266.
This modern hotel is conveniently located in the centre of town. It has been extremely well built and is tastefully decorated. **Rooms:** 67

KILLEAGH: *Ballymakeigh House*   ££   MC V
Youghal, Co Cork. **Road map** C5. 📞 024 95184. FAX 024 95370.
This attractive 18th-century farmhouse is a comfortable, reasonably priced base to explore the area. Cosy bedrooms and good food. **Rooms:** 5

KINSALE: *Old Presbytery*   £   MC V
43 Cork St, Kinsale, Co Cork. **Road map** B6. 📞 021 772027. FAX 021 772160.
A comfortable, relaxing place to stay in a quiet street in the town centre. Bedrooms are simple but stylish, furnished mainly with Victorian pieces. **Rooms:** 6

KINSALE: *The Blue Haven*   ££   MC V AE DC
3–4 Pearse St, Kinsale, Co Cork. **Road map** B6. 📞 021 772209. FAX 021 774268.
Attractive, small hotel right in the centre of Kinsale, built on the site of the old fish market. It is smart throughout, after a recent refurbishment, and has a very popular restaurant. **Rooms:** 18

KINSALE: *Old Bank House*   ££   MC V AE
11 Pearse St, Kinsale, Co Cork. **Road map** B6. 📞 021 774075. FAX 021 774296.
Right in the centre of town, the Old Bank House used to be a branch of the Munster and Leinster Bank. A listed Georgian building, it has finely proportioned, comfortable rooms and excellent staff. **Rooms:** 9

KINSALE: *Scilly House*   £££   MC V AE
Co Cork. **Road map** B6. 📞 021 772413. FAX 021 774629.
Very attractive old house overlooking Kinsale Bay and the harbour. The charming bedrooms and reception rooms are full of interesting and original furniture. Open April to October. **Rooms:** 7

MALLOW: *Longueville House*   £££   MC V AE DC
Co Cork. **Road map** B5. 📞 022 47156. FAX 022 47459.
The main part of the house is Georgian; the rooms are elegant and individually decorated, many with huge old-style beds. The hotel's Presidents' Restaurant has won a number of awards. **Rooms:** 21

PARKNASILLA: *Great Southern Hotel*   £££   MC V AE DC
Co Kerry. **Road map** A6. 📞 064 45122. FAX 064 45323.
Sitting in acres of sub-tropical gardens, the main building is Victorian. Leisure and conference facilities have been added, including a 9-hole golf course. All the rooms are smartly co-ordinated. **Rooms:** 84

SHANAGARRY: *Ballymaloe House*   £££   MC V AE DC
Midleton, Co Cork. **Road map** C6. 📞 021 652531. FAX 021 652021.
The house is charming with plenty of places to relax and lots for children to do. The farm provides the food, supplemented by local seafood, for the restaurant – one of Ireland's best. **Rooms:** 33

TAHILLA: *Tahilla Cove Country House*   ££   MC V AE DC
Nr Sneem Co Kerry. **Road map** A6. 📞 064 45204. FAX 064 45104.
A friendly guesthouse spread over two houses and set in lovely gardens. Views from the rooms are either of the sea or mountains. The bar is open to non-residents and is a great focus of hospitality. **Rooms:** 9

WATERVILLE: *The Smugglers' Inn*   £   MC V AE DC
Cliff Rd, Waterville, Co Kerry. **Road map** A6. 📞 066 74330. FAX 066 74422.
A 100-year-old, modernized, whitewashed inn on the Ring of Kerry. It is an unpretentious, jolly place with comfortable bedrooms, friendly bar and good restaurant. **Rooms:** 12

YOUGHAL: *Aherne's Seafood Restaurant*   ££   MC V AE DC
163 North Main St, Youghal, Co Kerry. **Road map** C5. 📞 024 92424. FAX 024 93633.
Run by the Fitzgibbon family, this well-known fish restaurant also has smart, comfortable bedrooms. **Rooms:** 12

Price categories are for a standard double room (not per person) for one night, including tax, service charges and breakfast.
€ under IR£50
€€ IR£50–100
€€€ IR£100–150
€€€€ IR£150–200
€€€€€ over IR£200

CHILDREN'S FACILITIES
Cots and high chairs are available and some hotels will also provide a baby-sitting service.
PARKING FACILITIES
Parking provided by the hotel in either a private car park or a private garage close by.
RESTAURANT
The hotel has a restaurant for residents which also welcomes non-residents – usually only for evening meals.
PUBLIC BAR
The hotel has a bar that is open to non-residents and residents alike.

THE LOWER SHANNON

Hotel		Credit Cards	Children's Facilities	Parking Facilities	Restaurant	Public Bar
ADARE: *Dunraven Arms* — Co Limerick. Road map B5. 061 396633. FAX 061 396541. Set in the extremely pretty village of Adare, this inn was established in 1792 and is a great touring base for the southwest. The bedrooms are luxurious and the restaurant is outstanding. TV **Rooms:** 78	€€€	MC V AE DC	●	■	●	■
ADARE: *Adare Manor* — Co Limerick. Road map B5. 061 396566. FAX 061 396124. This huge, Victorian-Gothic mansion was the former seat of the Earls of Dunraven. It was built in 1720 but was elaborated and enlarged in the 19th century. It's both tasteful and luxurious throughout. TV **Rooms:** 63	€€€€	MC V AE DC	●	■	●	■
AGLISH: *Ballycormac House* — Borrisokane, Co Tipperary. Road map C4. 067 21129. FAX 067 21200. Located in a quiet rural setting this cosy, 300-year-old house has a relaxed, informal atmosphere with lots of activities on offer, including riding and golf. Dinner is by reservation only. **Rooms:** 5	€€	MC V	●	■		
AHERLOW: *Aherlow House* — Glen of Aherlow, Co Tipperary. Road map C5. 062 56153. FAX 062 56212. In a wonderful setting in the middle of a coniferous forest with a view of the mountains, this comfortable and welcoming hunting lodge is a delight to stay in. TV **Rooms:** 30	€€	MC V AE DC	●	■	●	■
BALLYVAUGHAN: *Hylands* — Co Clare. Road map B4. 065 77037. FAX 065 77131. Dating back to the 18th century, this family run hotel is traditional in style, with simple but pretty bedrooms. Irish music in the bar. TV **Rooms:** 30	€€	MC V AE DC	●	■	●	■
BALLYVAUGHAN: *Gregans Castle* — Co Clare. Road map B4. 065 77005. FAX 065 77111. This is a marvellous hotel in the middle of the Burren, with views towards Galway Bay. Very comfortable. Open April to October. **Rooms:** 22	€€€	MC V	●	■	●	■
CASHEL: *Ballyowen House* — Co Tipperary. Road map C5. 062 61265. Situated about 6 km (4 miles) north of Cashel, this secluded 1750 manor house offers spacious, antique-filled rooms. The large estate is home to some wonderful old trees. Open May to September. **Rooms:** 3	€€			■		
CASHEL: *Cashel Palace* — Main St, Cashel, Co Tipperary. Road map C5. 062 62707. FAX 062 61521. Beautiful Palladian house originally built as an archbishop's palace in the 1730s. Right in the centre of town but surrounded by a peaceful garden, it is an extremely civilized place to stay. TV **Rooms:** 13	€€€€	MC V AE DC	●	■	●	■
CLARECASTLE: *Carnelly House* — Co Clare. Road map B4. 065 28442. FAX 065 29222. A lovely Queen Anne house designed by Francis Bindon and set in delightful grounds. A member of Hidden Ireland, it is elegantly and tastefully furnished and has a relaxed atmosphere. **Rooms:** 5	€€€€	MC V AE DC		■		
CLONMEL: *Clonmel Arms Hotel* — Sarsfield St, Clonmel, Co Tipperary. Road map C5. 052 21233. FAX 052 21526. A predictable but comfortable central hotel. The bars and restaurants are popular with the locals. Particularly helpful staff. TV **Rooms:** 31	€€	MC V AE DC	●	■	●	■
FEAKLE: *Smyths Village Hotel* — Co Clare. Road map B4. 061 924002. FAX 061 924244. A complex made up of modern cottages and a restaurant. Set in lovely countryside, it is a simple, cheap and jolly place to stay. TV **Rooms:** 12	€€	MC V AE DC	●	■	●	■

CASHEL HOUSE?

£££ | MC V AE
4173. FAX 068 34364.
...use, you can stay here, either as
...ne 1780s, this magnificent building is
...ber of Hidden Ireland. **Rooms: 9**

£ | 065 37606. FAX 065 37192.
...se and a useful base for exploring
...it is pristine and comfortable. Dinner
is available only if pre-booked. **Rooms: 6**

LIMERICK: *Woodfield House* ££ | MC V AE DC
Ennis Rd, Limerick, Co Limerick. **Road map** B4. 061 453022. FAX 061 326755.
Located just out of town, this traditional hotel has been recently
refurbished but still retains its friendly, informal family atmosphere.
Smart, well-equipped bedrooms. **TV Rooms: 22**

LIMERICK: *Jury's Hotel* £££ | MC V AE DC
Ennis Rd, Limerick, Co Limerick. **Road map** B4.
061 327777. FAX 061 326400.
Reliable part of the Jury's chain with good quality furnishings and
dependable service. Lovely location in 2 ha (5 acres) of garden
on the banks of the River Shannon. **TV Rooms: 95**

LISDOONVARNA: *Sheedy's Spa View and Orchid Restaurant* ££ | MC V AE DC
Co Clare. **Road map** B4. 065 74026. FAX 065 74555.
This house has been in the Sheedy family for five generations and
has now been converted into a very comfortable, efficient hotel by
the present owners. **Rooms: 11**

LISMACUE: *Lismacue House* ££ | MC V AE
Bansha, Co Tipperary. **Road map** C5. 062 54106. FAX 062 54126.
The house is part of the Hidden Ireland group. It's a classically beautiful,
Irish country house built at the beginning of the 19th century; it has
particularly fine reception rooms and comfortable bedrooms. **Rooms: 5**

NEWMARKET-ON-FERGUS: *Dromoland Castle* £££££ | MC V AE DC
Co Clare. **Road map** B4. 061 368144. FAX 061 363355.
Sister hotel to Ashford Castle in Cong, you can expect a high standard
of luxury here, too. The castle dates back to the 16th century and has a
fascinating history. The grounds cover 150 ha (370 acres). **TV Rooms: 74**

THE WEST OF IRELAND

BALLINA: *Mount Falcon* ££ | MC V AE DC
Co Mayo. **Road map** B2. 096 70811. FAX 096 71517.
This 19th-century castle, surrounded by over 40 ha (100 acres) of woods
and parkland, is a peaceful, friendly place to stay. Bedrooms are light and
spacious. There's fishing on local loughs and the River Moy. **Rooms: 9**

BALLYNAHINCH: *Ballynahinch Castle* £££ | MC V AE DC
Recess, Connemara, Co Galway. **Road map** A3. 095 31006. FAX 095 31085.
A magnificent castle, once owned by a maharajah, in a superb
location. The hotel is well-run, and has a friendly feel. There is an
excellent restaurant and lots of sporting possibilities. **TV Rooms: 28**

CASHEL BAY: *Zetland House* £££ | MC V AE DC
Connemara, Co Galway. **Road map** A3. 095 31111. FAX 095 31117.
A professionally run, stylishly decorated, 19th-century shooting lodge.
Set on the edge of Cashel Bay in lovely gardens, most of the bedrooms
and the dining room share the superb views. **Rooms: 19**

CASHEL BAY: *Cashel House* ££££ | MC V AE DC
Connemara, Co Galway. **Road map** A3. 095 31001. FAX 095 31077.
In a stunning position at the head of Cashel Bay, this is a great place to
stay. Extremely comfortable, relaxing rooms, full of interesting antiques.
Very welcoming hosts. **TV Rooms: 32**

CLIFDEN: *Erriseask House* ££ | MC V AE DC
Ballyconneely, Connemara, Co Galway. **Road map** A3. 095 23553. FAX 095 23639.
This modern farmhouse is stylishly decorated, with light, comfortable
bedrooms. It's set in a beautiful spot, only a short walk away from the sea
and the food is superb. Open late March to late October. **Rooms: 14**

Price categories are for a standard double room (not per person) for one night, including tax, service charges and breakfast.
£ under IR£50
££ IR£50–100
£££ IR£100–150
££££ IR£150–200
£££££ over IR£200

CHILDREN'S FACILITIES
Cots and high chairs are available and some hotels will also provide a baby-sitting service.
PARKING FACILITIES
Parking provided by the hotel in either a private car park or a private garage close by.
RESTAURANT
The hotel has a restaurant for residents which also welcomes non-residents – usually only for evening meals.
PUBLIC BAR
The hotel has a bar that is open to non-residents and residents alike.

	CREDIT CARDS	CHILDREN'S FACILITIES	PARKING FACILITIES	RESTAURANT	PUBLIC BAR
CLIFDEN: *Hotel Ardagh* £££ Connemara, Co Galway. **Road map** A3. 095 21384. FAX 095 21314. Many rooms at this modern, chalet-style hotel look out onto Ardbear Bay. The gardens are beautiful. Open April to October. **Rooms:** 21	MC V AE DC	●	▨	●	▨
CLIFDEN: *Rock Glen Manor House* £££ Connemara, Co Galway. **Road map** A3. 095 21035. FAX 095 21737. This traditional hotel used to be a shooting lodge for Clifden Castle. Comfortable rooms and reliable, friendly service. **Rooms:** 29	MC V AE DC	●	▨	●	
CONG: *Ashford Castle* £££££ Co Mayo. **Road map** B3. 092 46003. FAX 092 46260. A mixture of 13th-century and Gothic Revival, this magnificent castle is set on the shore of Lough Corrib. Rich wall-to-wall carpeting kills a lot of the historical atmosphere, but it is undoubtedly luxurious. **Rooms:** 83	MC V AE DC	●	▨		
CROSSMOLINA: *Enniscoe House* ££ Castlehill, Nr Crossmolina, Ballina, Co Mayo. **Road map** B2. 096 31112. FAX 096 31773. This fine Georgian house, set in magnificent grounds which lead down to Lough Conn, is full of beautiful antiques and has a relaxed, lived-in feel with attractive bedrooms and good food. Member of Hidden Ireland. **Rooms:** 6	MC V AE	●	▨		
GALWAY: *Ardilaun House* ££ Taylor's Hill, Galway, Co Galway. **Road map** B4. 091 521433. FAX 091 521546. A short distance from the city centre and quite close to Salthill, this hotel is popular with business people and tourists. Smart decor, friendly, efficient service and comfortable rooms. **Rooms:** 89	MC V AE DC	●	▨	●	
GALWAY: *Brennan's Yard Hotel* ££ Lower Merchant's Rd, Galway, Co Galway. **Road map** B4. 091 568166. FAX 091 568262. Converted from a stone warehouse, and now decked with designer fabrics and Irish art, it offers comfortable rooms with city views. **Rooms:** 24	MC V AE DC	●	▨	●	▨
GALWAY: *Great Southern Hotel* ££££ Eyre Sq, Galway, Co Galway. **Road map** B4. 091 564041. FAX 091 566704. The rooftop swimming pool is an unusual feature of this large and rambling Victorian hotel in the heart of the city. The rooms are comfortable and there are plenty of facilities. **Rooms:** 116	MC V AE DC	●	▨	●	▨
KNOCKFERRY: *Knockferry Lodge* £ Roscahill, Co Galway. **Road map** B3. 091 550122. FAX 091 550328. Situated in a tranquil spot on the western shore of Lough Corrib, the prices reflect the simple accommodation with plain decor and furnishings. The atmosphere is very friendly and the food good. **Rooms:** 12	MC V AE DC		▨		
LEENANE: *Delphi Lodge* ££ Co Galway. **Road map** B3. 095 42211. FAX 095 42296. A sporting lodge in a lovely setting surrounded by mountains. Informal atmosphere with plenty of fishing on the loughs and River Delphi. A member of Hidden Ireland. Open February to November. **Rooms:** 12	MC V		▨		
LETTERFRACK: *Rosleague Manor House* ££ Connemara, Co Galway. **Road map** A3. 091 41101. FAX 091 41168. A substantial Georgian house overlooking Ballinakill Bay and well situated for the Connemara National Park with only a short walk to the sea. Comfortable and relaxed with an excellent restaurant. **Rooms:** 20	MC V AE	●	▨	●	▨
MOYARD: *Crocnaraw Country House* ££ Connemara, Co Galway. **Road map** A3. 095 41068. Beautifully furnished Georgian house on Ballinakill Bay with award-winning gardens. Relaxed atmosphere and comfortable bedrooms. **Rooms:** 8	MC V AE	●	▨	●	

NEWPORT: *Newport House* £££ MC V AE DC
Co Mayo. **Road map** B3. 098 41222. FAX 098 41613.
A stay at this historic, creeper-covered Georgian house is extremely comfortable and civilized. It stands beside the River Newport, renowned as a great fishing centre. *Rooms: 18*

OUGHTERARD: *Currarevagh House* ££
Connemara, Co Galway. **Road map** B3. 091 552312. FAX 091 552731.
In an isolated, peaceful spot on the shores of Lough Corrib and surrounded by woods, parkland and gardens, this Victorian country house is traditionally run with a cosy, slightly old-fashioned atmosphere. *Rooms: 15*

OUGHTERARD: *Ross Lake House* ££ MC V AE DC
Rosscahill, Oughterard, Co Galway. **Road map** B3.
091 550109. FAX 091 550184.
This 18th-century house, surrounded by gardens is neatly decorated throughout and feels spruce and efficient. Fishing is available in nearby loughs and you can play tennis in the hotel grounds. *Rooms: 13*

PONTOON: *Healy's* ££ MC V
Foxford, Co Mayo. **Road map** B3. 094 56443. FAX 094 56572.
In a stunning position on the shores of Lough Conn and Lough Cullen, this traditional old stone house is a great spot for bird-watchers. Simple, neat bedrooms and good Irish cooking. TV *Rooms: 10*

RENVYLE: *Renvyle House* ££ MC V AE DC
Connemara, Co Galway. **Road map** A3. 095 43511. FAX 095 43515.
A very relaxed, family hotel on the edge of the Atlantic, it offers lots of sporting activities as well as comfort and good food. Beams and polished wooden floors with rugs give atmosphere and style. TV *Rooms: 65*

ROSTURK: *Rosturk Woods* £
Mulrany, Westport, Co Mayo. **Road map** B3. 098 36264. FAX 098 36264.
In a wonderfully quiet spot by the sea, 11 km (7 miles) from Newport, this stylishly furnished guesthouse is an extremely attractive and comfortable place to stay. *Rooms: 4*

WESTPORT: *Olde Railway* ££ M CV AE DC
The Mall, Westport, Co Mayo. **Road map** B3. 098 25166. FAX 098 25090.
Situated in the centre of town, this traditional hotel is comfortable and reliable and has recently been attractively refurbished. It makes an excellent base for the area. TV *Rooms: 24*

NORTHWEST IRELAND

ARDARA: *Woodhill House* ££ MC V AE DC
Co Donegal. **Road map** C2. 075 41112. FAX 075 41516.
The house dates back to the 17th century but is predominantly Victorian in appearance. The reasonably comfortable rooms are good value and it is a good base for exploring the surrounding area. *Rooms: 9*

BALLYMOTE: *Temple House* ££ MC V AE
Co Sligo. **Road map** B3. 071 83329. FAX 071 83808.
Lovely Georgian house, owned by the Perceval family since 1665, set in 420 ha (1,000 acres) of parkland. Comfortable sitting rooms, large bedrooms and good food. Member of Hidden Ireland. *Rooms: 5*

BRUCKLESS: *Bruckless House* ££ MC V AE
Co Donegal. **Road map** C2. 073 37071. FAX 073 37070.
Set in 7 ha (17 acres) of attractive grounds on the shores of Bruckless Bay, this 18th-century farmhouse is a comfortable and relaxing place to stay with friendly hosts and good food. *Rooms: 4*

CASTLEBALDWIN: *Cromleach Lodge Country House* £££ MC V AE DC
Ballindoon, Boyle, Co Sligo. **Road map** C3. 071 65155. FAX 071 65455.
Its superb position in the hills above Lough Arrow provides all the spacious bedrooms in this house with magnificent views. The lodge has an excellent restaurant and a high standard of comfort. TV *Rooms: 10*

COLLOONEY: *Markree Castle* £££ MC V AE DC
Co Sligo. **Road map** C2. 071 67800. FAX 071 67840.
The castle has been in the Cooper family since 1640 but it has only recently been restored and turned into a hotel. It has stately rooms and lovely grounds and the atmosphere is very civilized and relaxing. TV *Rooms: 30*

Price categories are for a standard double room (not per person) for one night, including tax, service charges and breakfast.
£ under IR£50
££ IR£50–100
£££ IR£100–150
££££ IR£150–200
£££££ over IR£200

CHILDREN'S FACILITIES
Cots and high chairs are available and some hotels will also provide a baby-sitting service.

PARKING FACILITIES
Parking provided by the hotel in either a private car park or a private garage close by.

RESTAURANT
The hotel has a restaurant for residents which also welcomes non-residents – usually only for evening meals.

PUBLIC BAR
The hotel has a bar that is open to non-residents and residents alike.

	Credit Cards	Children's Facilities	Parking Facilities	Restaurant	Public Bar
DONEGAL: *St Ernan's House* £££ — Co Donegal. Road map C2. 073 21065. FAX 073 22098. Situated on a small island, linked to the mainland by a causeway, this attractive, pink-painted, 19th-century house is elegantly furnished but retains a relaxed, informal atmosphere. TV *Rooms: 12*	MC V		■	●	
DRUMCLIFF: *Urlar House* £ — Co Sligo. Road map C2. 071 63110. In a peaceful, secluded position in the shadow of Ben Bulben, this attractive farmhouse offers good, simple accommodation and makes a perfect base for exploring Yeats Country. *Rooms: 6*	AE	●	■		
DUNKINEELY: *Castle Murray House* £ — St John's Point, Co Donegal. Road map C2. 073 37022. FAX 073 37330. Stunningly located on a cliff with views down the Donegal coast, this small hotel is a wonderful place to stay. The decor is simple but smart and the restaurant offers a delicious menu. TV *Rooms: 10*	MC V		■	●	
LETTERKENNY: *Castle Grove Country House* ££ — Co Donegal. Road map C1. 074 51118. FAX 074 51384. Approached down a long avenue through lovely parkland, this 17th-century house looks out on to Lough Swilly and is a peaceful and relaxing place to stay. TV *Rooms: 15*	MC V AE DC	●	■	●	
LOUGH ESKE: *Ardnamona House* ££ — Co Donegal. Road map C2. 073 22650. FAX 073 22819. A member of Hidden Ireland, this Edwardian house is in a beautiful spot, surrounded by famous gardens and backed by the Blue Stack Mountains. Comfortable rooms and a hospitable, informal atmosphere. *Rooms: 5*	MC V DC	●	■		
LOUGH ESKE: *Harvey's Point* £££ — Donegal Town, Co Donegal. Road map C2. 073 22208. FAX 073 22352. Swiss-style hotel on the banks of Lough Eske. Neat, modern furnishings, excellent restaurant and lots of sports facilities. Most rooms overlook the lough. TV & *Rooms: 32*	MC V AE DC		■	●	■
MOHILL: *Glebe House* £ — Ballinamore Rd, Mohill, Co Leitrim. Road map C3. 078 31086. FAX 078 31886. This early 19th-century former rectory is set in 20 ha (50 acres) of parkland, woods and farmland, and is peaceful and attractive. *Rooms: 7*	MC V AE	●	■	··	
RIVERSTOWN: *Coopershill House* ££ — Co Sligo. Road map C2. 071 65108. FAX 071 65466. Very civilized, elegant 17th-century house surrounded by a vast estate. Fine rooms with lovely antiques, huge bedrooms and excellent food. *Rooms: 8*	MC V AE DC	●	■	●	
ROSSNOWLAGH: *Smuggler's Creek* £ — Co Donegal. Road map C2. 072 52366. This is a very cosy place in a wonderful position on top of the cliff looking down over the Rossnowlagh beach. There's a choice of bar food or the restaurant, and all the bedrooms have sea views. *Rooms: 5*	MC V	●	■	●	■
ROSSNOWLAGH: *Sand House* ££ — Co Donegal. Road map C2. 072 51777. FAX 072 52100. An imposing, white castellated building right on a sandy beach overlooking Donegal Bay, this long-established hotel is very comfortable and well decorated and has a relaxed atmosphere. *Rooms: 45*	MC V AE DC	●	■	●	■
STRANORLAR: *Kee's Hotel and Leisure Club* ££ — Ballybofey, Co Donegal. Road map C2. 074 31018. FAX 074 31917. A coaching inn and mail staging post in the 19th century, the hotel maintains a tradition of generous hospitality. Freshly refurbished with a new leisure centre and well located for exploring Donegal. TV *Rooms: 36*	MC V AE DC	●	■	●	■

THE MIDLANDS

ARDEE: *Red House* ££ — MC V
Co Louth. **Road map** D3. 041 53523. **FAX** 041 53523.
This very attractive Georgian manor house is a member of Hidden Ireland.
The rooms are comfortable and there is a floodlit tennis court. **Rooms:** 3

BIRR: *Tullanisk* ££ — MC V AE
Co Offaly. **Road map** C4. 0509 20572. **FAX** 0509 21783.
This well-restored, 18th-century dower house for Birr Castle is a member
of the Hidden Ireland group. It is a comfortable, relaxing place to stay,
with large, stylishly decorated bedrooms. **Rooms:** 7

CARLINGFORD: *Viewpoint* £ — V
Omeath Rd, Carlingford, Co Louth. **Road map** D3. 042 73149. **FAX** 042 73149.
Motel-style, modern accommodation. Well-equipped bedrooms with
wonderful views across Carlingford Lough. **TV Rooms:** 10

CARLINGFORD: *McKevitt's Village Hotel* ££ — MC V AE DC
Market Sq, Carlingford, Co Louth. **Road map** D3. 042 73116. **FAX** 042 73144.
Popular village inn at the heart of the local scene. Rooms have real fires
and a great atmosphere, bedrooms are pristine and pretty. **TV Rooms:** 13

CLONES: *Hilton Park* ££ — MC V
Co Monaghan. **Road map** C2. 047 56007. **FAX** 047 56033.
Superb mansion in magnificent parkland. A member of Hidden Ireland
and extremely civilized. The rooms have a relaxed grandeur. **Rooms:** 5

CROSSDONEY: *Lisnamandra Farmhouse* £ — MC V AE DC
Lisnamandra, Crossdoney, Co Cavan. **Road map** C3. 049 37196. **FAX** 049 37111.
Simple but comfortable accommodation in hospitable 17th-century
farmhouse. Plenty of activities on the farm and nearby. **Rooms:** 6

DROGHEDA: *Boyne Valley* ££ — MC V AE DC
Co Louth. **Road map** D3. 041 37737. **FAX** 041 39188.
A much extended and refurbished 18th-century manor house. Although
most of the decor and furnishings are modern, the hotel preserves much
of the house's traditional feel. **TV Rooms:** 38

DULEEK: *Annesbrook* ££ — MC V
Co Meath. **Road map** D3. 041 23293. **FAX** 041 23024.
This 17th-century house is a member of Hidden Ireland. It has a lovely
welcoming atmosphere and spacious, comfortable bedrooms. **Rooms:** 5

KILMESSAN: *Station House Hotel and Restaurant* £ — MC V AE DC
Co Meath. **Road map** D3. 046 25239. **FAX** 046 25588.
The railway used to run through Kilmessan, but now this Victorian station
building is a comfortable hotel with a good restaurant. **TV Rooms:** 10

LONGFORD: *Carrigglas Manor* ££ — MC V AE
Co Longford. **Road map** C3. 043 45165. **FAX** 043 41026.
The magnificent ancestral home of the Lefroys *(see pp232–3)* is a member
of Hidden Ireland. Being treated as private guests and staying in lovely
surroundings make for a special stay. Open May to October. **Rooms:** 6

MOUNTRATH: *Roundwood House* ££ — MC V AE DC
Co Laois. **Road map** C4. 0502 32120. **FAX** 0502 32711.
A beautiful, 18th-century Palladian villa set in lovely grounds close to the
Slieve Bloom Mountains. Civilized but informal atmosphere. **Rooms:** 10

MULLINGAR: *Bloomfield House Hotel* ££ — MC V AE DC
Co Westmeath. **Road map** C3. 044 40894. **FAX** 044 43767.
A manor house on Lough Ennell with great views. Traditional in atmosphere
but recently refurbished, it's comfortable and friendly. **TV Rooms:** 33

MULLINGAR: *Greville Arms* ££ — MC V AE DC
Co Westmeath. **Road map** C3. 044 48563. **FAX** 044 48052.
Centrally located, this traditional hotel caters for both locals and tourists.
Good facilities with a large bar and restaurant. **TV Rooms:** 40

SLANE: *Conyngham Arms* ££ — MC V DC
Co Meath. **Road map** D3. 041 24155. **FAX** 041 24205.
In the heart of the estate village, this traditional family hotel is welcoming
and comfortable. Good base for touring the Boyne Valley. **TV Rooms:** 16

Price categories are for a standard double room (not per person) for one night, including tax, service charges and breakfast.
£ under £50
££ £50–100
£££ £100–150
££££ £150–200
£££££ over £200

CHILDREN'S FACILITIES
Cots and high chairs are available and some hotels will also provide a baby-sitting service.

PARKING FACILITIES
Parking provided by the hotel in either a private car park or a private garage close by.

RESTAURANT
The hotel has a restaurant for residents which also welcomes non-residents – usually only for evening meals.

PUBLIC BAR
The hotel has a bar that is open to non-residents and residents alike.

NORTHERN IRELAND

	Price	Credit Cards	Children's Facilities	Parking Facilities	Restaurant	Public Bar
ANNALONG: *Glassdrumman Lodge* Mill Rd, Annalong, Co Down. **Road map** D2. **(** 013967 68451. **FAX** 013967 67041. Set deep in the "Kingdom of Mourne", the hotel looks out on the region's famous dry-stone walls. Excellent reputation for food. **Rooms:** 10	££	MC V AE DC		■	●	
ARMAGH: *Charlemont Arms* Co Armagh. **Road map** D2. **(** 01861 522028. **FAX** 01861 526979. A country-style hotel perfectly located for the major attractions. What it lacks in luxury it makes up for in the warmth of its welcome. **Rooms:** 14	£	MC V	●	■		
BALLYGALLY: *Ballygally Castle* 274 Coast Rd, Ballygally, Co Antrim. **Road map** D1. **(** 01574 583212. **FAX** 01574 583681. Reputedly haunted, the castle showpiece is the Ghost Room, a tiny old tower bedroom with a macabre legend. Musicians provide a more friendly atmosphere in the Dungeon Bar of the old fortress. **Rooms:** 30	££	MC V AE DC	●	■	●	●
BALLYMENA: *Galgorm Manor* Co Antrim. **Road map** D1. **(** 01266 881001. **FAX** 01266 880080. The River Maine sweeps past the hotel, enhancing the view from many of the rooms. Fishing and riding are available on the magnificent estate. There is a first-rate restaurant and a traditional, Irish-style bar. **Room:** 23	£££	MC V AE DC	●	■	●	●
BANGOR: *Clandeboye Lodge* 10 Estate Rd, Bangor, Co Down. **Road map** E2. **(** 01247 853777. **FAX** 01247 852772. Resembling a Victorian church school, the hotel has reasonably priced rooms and a stylish dining room with a great menu. **Rooms:** 43	££	MC V AE DC	●	■	●	■
BELFAST: *Duke's Hotel* 65 University St, Belfast BT7. **Road map** D2. **(** 01232 236666. **FAX** 01232 237177. A modern hotel offering comfort, style and international cuisine in the heart of the city. It has a good public bar. **Rooms:** 21	£££	MC V AE DC	●		●	●
BELFAST: *Malone Lodge Hotel* 60 Eglantine Ave, Belfast BT9. **Road map** D2. **(** 01232 382409. **FAX** 01232 382706. Centrally located, it's ideal for business people and tourists. Modern and functional with good bedroom facilities. **Rooms:** 33	££	MC V AE DC	●	■	●	●
BELFAST: *Europa Hotel* Great Victoria St, Belfast BT2. **Road map** D2. **(** 01232 327000. **FAX** 01232 327800. An imposing building in the heart of the Golden Mile, ideal for business people and tourists, with a very good restaurant. **Rooms:** 184	£££	MC V AE DC	●	■	●	●
BELFAST: *Stormont Hotel* 587 Upper Newtownards Rd, Belfast BT4. **Road map** D2. **(** 01232 658621. **FAX** 01232 480240. Close to Stormont and the airport, it's excellent for business people. Modern and functional with an award-winning restaurant. **Rooms:** 109	£££	MC V AE DC	●	■	●	■
CARNLOUGH: *Londonderry Arms Hotel* 20 Harbour Rd, Carnlough, Co Antrim. **Road map** D1. **(** 01574 885255. **FAX** 01574 885263. Winston Churchill once owned this ivy-covered inn next to the harbour of Carnlough in a breathtaking setting at the foot of Glencloy. Family owned, it has a genuine warmth of welcome. **Rooms:** 35	££	MC V AE DC	●	■	●	●
CRAWFORDSBURN: *The Old Inn at Crawfordsburn* Co Down. **Road map** E2. **(** 01247 853255. **FAX** 01247 852775. One of Ireland's oldest hostelries, this thatched 16th-century inn offers quality and comfort with roaring log fires and four-poster beds in some rooms. A good Irish menu and an excellent wine list. **Rooms:** 33	£££	MC V AE DC	●	■	●	■

DUNGANNON: *Grange Lodge* £££
Grange Rd, Dungannon, Co Tyrone. **Road map** D2.
📞 018687 84212. ᴀx 018687 723891.
The hotel is set in pleasant surroundings and offers good Ulster
home-style cooking and a hospitable family welcome. 🛏 TV *Rooms:* 5

MC V

ENNISKILLEN: *Killyhevlin Hotel* ££
Dublin Rd, Enniskillen, Co Fermanagh. **Road map** C2.
📞 01365 323481. ᴀx 01365 324726.
The grounds sweep down to Lower Lough Erne and many bedrooms look
out on the lough, but you must pay extra for the view. 🛏 TV ♿ *Rooms:* 43

MC V AE

ENNISKILLEN: *Manor House* ££
Killadeas, Enniskillen, Co Fermanagh. **Road map** C2.
📞 013656 21561. ᴀx 013656 21545.
Situated on the shores of Lough Erne, this country hotel has a rich interior,
with antiques and paintings, a warm atmosphere and friendly staff. The emphasis is on healthy eating using local seasonal produce. 🛏 TV *Rooms:* 46

MC V AE

FIVEMILETOWN: *Blessingbourne* ££
Co Tyrone. **Road map** C2. 📞 013655 21221.
An Elizabethan-style Victorian mansion with breathtaking views from its
mullioned windows. One bedroom has a four-poster bed and they all have
an appealing elegance. A member of the Hidden Ireland group. *Rooms:* 4

HOLYWOOD: *The Culloden Hotel* ££££
142 Bangor Rd, Holywood, Co Down. **Road map** E2.
📞 01232 425223. ᴀx 01232 426777.
A very fine hotel, set in gardens and woodlands by Belfast Lough.
Originally the palace of the Bishops of Down, it retains its opulence
with many fine antiques and valuable paintings. 🛏 TV ♿ *Rooms:* 80

MC V DC

KILKEEL: *The Kilmorey Arms Hotel* £
41 Greencastle St, Kilkeel, Co Down. **Road map** D3.
📞 016937 62220. ᴀx 016937 65399.
An excellent base for the Mourne area. The rooms are well furnished and
the Smugglers' Bar's ambience fits well with the area. 🛏 TV ♿ *Rooms:* 28

MC V AE

LIMAVADY: *Streeve Hill* ££
Co Londonderry. **Road map** D1. 📞 015047 66563. ᴀx 015047 66563.
This 18th-century dower house on the Drenagh estate is a good base for
the area. The gardens at Drenagh House are exquisite. Plenty of sports
opportunities nearby. Member of Hidden Ireland. 🛏 *Rooms:* 5

MC V

LONDONDERRY: *Beechill Country House* ££
32 Ardmore Rd, Londonderry, Co Londonderry. **Road map** C1.
📞 01504 349279. ᴀx 01504 345366.
Good service and food and a real "home from home" atmosphere. The
bedrooms, some with beautiful pieces of Victorian furniture, give the
feel of a grand old country home. 🛏 TV ♿ *Rooms:* 17

MC V AE

NEWCASTLE: *Burrendale Hotel and Country Club* ££
51 Castlewellan Rd, Co Down. **Road map** E2.
📞 013967 22599. ᴀx 013967 22328.
An excellent base for climbing, horse riding and golf. Good facilities for
the disabled with a comfortable bar and restaurant. 🛏 TV ♿ *Rooms:* 68

MC V AE DC

NEWCASTLE: *Slieve Donard Hotel* £££
Downs Rd, Newcastle, Co Down. **Road map** E2.
📞 0139 67 23681. ᴀx 0139 67 24830.
A stunning red-brick building overlooking the beach and the famous Royal
County Down Golf Course. Good efficient service. 🛏 TV ♿ *Rooms:* 130

MC V AE DC

NEWTOWNARDS: *Edenvale House* £
130 Portaferry Road, Newtownards, Co Down. **Road map** E2. 📞 01247 814881.
Set in extensive grounds next to a wildfowl reserve, this charming Georgian
house is a haven for nature lovers. Leisure activities include croquet on
the lawns, with watersports, golf and riding nearby. 🛏 *Rooms:* 3

MC V AE DC

PORTAFERRY: *Portaferry Hotel* ££
The Strand, Portaferry, Co Down. **Road map** E2.
📞 0124 77 28231. ᴀx 012477 28999.
This waterside inn on the Ards Peninsula overlooks Strangford Lough.
A pleasant atmosphere and an award-winning restaurant. 🛏 TV *Rooms:* 14

MC V AE DC

RESTAURANTS, CAFÉS AND PUBS

ALTHOUGH the highest concentration of top gourmet restaurants is in Ireland's main cities, equally fine cuisine can be found in some very unlikely, remote locations around the country. Good, plain cooking is on offer at moderately priced, family-style restaurants all over Ireland. The restaurants listed on pages 306–17 are recommended for their high standards of service, quality of food and value

Restaurant sign in Kinsale

for money. To supplement these listings, look out for the *Dining in Ireland* booklet published by Bord Fáilte, the Irish Tourist Board. Pub lunches are one of Ireland's top travel bargains, offering generous portions of fresh vegetables and prime meats, and can often serve as the main meal of the day for a very reasonable price. Light meals, bar food and a variety of takeaways are also widely available.

IRISH EATING PATTERNS

TRADITIONALLY, the Irish have started the day with a huge breakfast: bacon, sausages, black pudding, eggs, tomatoes and brown bread. In Northern Ireland this, plus potato cakes and soda farls (*see p304*), is known as an "Ulster Fry". The main meal, dinner, was served at midday, with a lighter "tea" in the early evening.

Although continental breakfasts are now available, you will be hard-pressed to escape the traditional breakfast, which is included in almost all hotel and bed-and-breakfast rates. Increasingly, however, even the Irish settle for a light salad or soup and sandwiches at midday and save their main meal for the evening. Vestiges of the old eating patterns remain in the huge midday platefuls still served in pubs.

Enjoying breakfast at Adare Manor Hotel (*see p294*)

Arriving at a café in Kinvarra (*see p204*)

TIPS ON EATING OUT

ELEGANT DINING becomes considerably more affordable when you make lunch your main meal of the day. In many of the top restaurants, the fixed-price lunch and dinner menus offer much the same, but lunch will usually come to about half the price. House wines are quite drinkable in most restaurants and can reduce the total cost of your meal. If you are travelling with children, shop around for one of the many restaurants that provide a less expensive children's menu.

Lunch is usually served between noon and 2:30pm, with dinner between 6:30 and 10pm, although many ethnic and city-centre restaurants stay open later. Bed-and-breakfast hosts will often provide an ample home-cooked evening meal if given advance notice, and many will serve tea and scones in the late evening at no extra charge.

In top restaurants, men are expected to wear a jacket, though not necessarily a tie, and women to wear a dress or trouser suit. Elsewhere, the dress code is pretty informal, stopping short of bare chests and too-brief shorts.

Visa (V) and Mastercard/ Access (MC) are the most commonly accepted credit cards, with Diners Club (DC) and American Express (AE) also in use. The abbreviations in brackets are used in the restaurant listings to indicate which cards are accepted.

GOURMET AND ETHNIC DINING

THIS ONCE gourmet-poor land now sports restaurants that rank among Europe's very best, with chefs trained in outstanding domestic and continental institutions. There is a choice of Irish, French, Italian, Chinese and even Russian cuisines, with styles ranging from traditional to

regional to *nouvelle cuisine*.
Locations vary as widely as
the cuisine, from hotel dining
rooms, town house basements
and city mansions to castle
hotels and tiny village cafés
tucked away by the sea. The
small County Cork town of
Kinsale has established itself
as the "Gourmet Capital of
Ireland". Outstanding chefs
also reign over the gracious
houses listed in *Ireland's Blue
Book of Country Houses and
Restaurants*, available from
tourist offices.

BUDGET DINING

IT IS QUITE POSSIBLE to eat well
on a small budget wherever
you are in Ireland. In both
city and rural locations, there
are small cafés, tea rooms and
family-style restaurants with
value-for-money meals. Even
if a café or tea room is at a
main tourist attraction, such
as Bantry House, you can still
expect good, home-made
food and freshly baked bread
and cakes. Sandwiches are
usually made with thick, tasty
slices of fresh, rather than
processed, cheese or meat;
salad plates feature smoked
salmon, chicken, ham, pork
and beef; and hot meals
usually come with large help-
ings of vegetables, with the
beloved potato often showing
up roast, boiled and mashed,
all on one plate.

PUB FOOD

IRELAND'S PUBS have moved
into the food field with a
vengeance. In addition to bar
snacks (soup, sandwiches and

Selection of cakes served at Bantry House café *(see pp160–61)*

so on), available from noon
until late, salads and hot meals
are served from midday to
2:30pm. At rock-bottom prices,
hot plates all come
heaped with mounds
of fresh vegetables,
potatoes in one or
more versions, and
good portions of local
fish or meat. Particu-
larly good value are
the pub carveries that
offer a choice of joints,
sliced to your prefer-
ence. In recent years,
the international staples
of spaghetti, lasagne
and quiche have also
appeared on pub menus. For
a list of recommended pubs,
see pages 318–21.

Café sign at
Baltimore

FISH AND CHIPS AND OTHER FAST FOODS

THE IRISH, from peasant to
parliamentarian, love their
"chippers", immortalized in
Roddy Doyle's novel *The Van*,
and any good pub night will
end with a visit to the nearest

fish-and-chip shop. At
virtually any time of day,
however, if you pass by Leo
Burdock's in Dublin, there
will be a long queue
for this international
institution *(see p307)*.
With Ireland's long
coastline, wherever
you choose, the fish
will usually be the
freshest catch of the
day – plaice, cod,
haddock, whiting or
ray (a delicacy). The
many other fast-food
outlets include a host
of familiar interna-
tional names, such as
McDonald's and Kentucky
Fried Chicken, as well as a
wide variety of burger and
kebab shops. Relatively new
arrivals on the scene are
several quite good pasta and
pizza chains, such as Pizza
Express and Milano.

PICNICS

IRELAND IS GLORIOUS picnic
country. Farmhouse cheeses
and flavoursome tomatoes are
picnic treats, or stop by one
of the many small shops that
offer sandwiches made with
fresh local ingredients. As for
where to picnic, the long,
indented coast is ringed with
wide, sandy beaches; with
over 400 forest areas, many
with picnic tables; great views
add to the pleasure of moun-
tainside picnics; and there are
often lay-bys in scenic spots.
Turn off a main road onto
almost any country lane and
you will soon find a picnic
spot by a lakeside, riverbank
or the shady edge of a field.

The 1601 pub in Kinsale *(see p319)*

What to Eat in Ireland

IRELAND'S rich pastureland, unpolluted rivers and extensive coastline provide tender lamb, beef and pork, an array of fish and seafood and fresh fruit and vegetables. From hearty rural fare that makes the most of the ingredients available, Irish cooking has evolved into the gourmet cuisine created by internationally trained chefs. Often you will find the best of both worlds, with Irish stew or ham and cabbage on the same menu as more exotic dishes. The ideal end to a meal is an Irish coffee – coffee, cream and whiskey.

Irish coffee

Wheaten bread / Soda bread / Soda farl / Potato cake

Bread, *invariably baked daily, comes in different guises. Soda bread may be brown or white. In Northern Ireland, brown soda bread is called wheaten bread.*

Sausage / Bacon / Soda farl / Grilled tomato / Potato cake / Fried egg / Black pudding

An Ulster fry *consists of home-baked soda farls (soft bread cakes leavened with soda and buttermilk) and potato cakes (bread made from mashed potato, butter and flour), as well as the basic ingredients of a fry-up. The ultimate Irish breakfast, the "fry" is a perfect way to set yourself up for the day. Without the soda farls and potato cakes, meals like this are consumed with relish all over Ireland at any time of day.*

Mushroom soup *makes a wholesome starter or snack. It is normally made with freshly picked local mushrooms and a generous amount of cream.*

Smoked salmon, *available all over Ireland and very popular, is generally served as simply as possible – enabling you to enjoy the full flavour of the fish.*

Mussel soup *is a substantial dish made with fresh local mussels in a creamy fish stock flavoured with vegetables and herbs. Try it with wheaten bread.*

Fresh oysters, *here served on a bed of seaweed and cracked ice, make a light but delicious lunch – especially when accompanied by a glass of Guinness.*

Dublin coddle, *a traditional Saturday night supper dish, consists of chopped sausages and ham or bacon cooked in stock with potatoes and onions.*

Irish stew, *originally a peasant dish, is a thick casserole made with lamb or mutton, onions, and parsley, topped with potatoes.*

Fresh salmon *is often poached in fish stock or wine and herbs. Galway salmon is particularly sought after for its fine taste.*

Lamb cutlets *are usually served with mint sauce or jelly. Lamb from Kerry and Wicklow is renowned for its tenderness.*

Mashed potato

Roast potatoes

Vegetables *are served in generous portions, usually as an accompaniment to the main course. It is not uncommon to be given potatoes in a number of different forms – roast, boiled, mashed, baked or chipped – together with whichever vegetables happen to be fresh and in season.*

Broccoli

Boiled potatoes

Carrots

Baked ham, *coated with cloves and brown sugar, is commonly served with boiled cabbage in butter and eaten at Christmas or on other festive occasions.*

Strawberries and cream *are the archetypal summer dessert. They are sometimes sweetened with honey rather than sugar.*

Porter cake, *a classic Irish cake made with dried fruit, is most famous for the inclusion of stout, usually in the form of Guinness.*

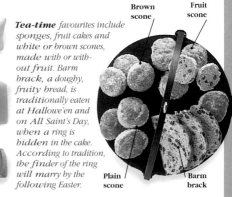

Apple tart, *or "cake" as the Irish often call it, is eaten all year round but is traditionally associated with Hallowe'en.*

CHEESES

For centuries, cheese has been made in farms and monasteries throughout Ireland. Cheese-making has expanded in the last 25 years and Ireland now produces cheeses with a worldwide reputation, from semi-soft ones such as Cashel Blue and St Killian, which is similar to Camembert, to Gouda-like Carrigaline and smoked Durrus.

St Killian

Carrigaline

Cashel Blue

Durrus

Tea-time *favourites include sponges, fruit cakes and white or brown scones, made with or without fruit. Barm brack, a doughy, fruity bread, is traditionally eaten at Hallowe'en and on All Saint's Day, when a ring is hidden in the cake. According to tradition, the finder of the ring will marry by the following Easter.*

Brown scone

Fruit scone

Plain scone

Barm brack

Choosing a Restaurant

THIS CHART LISTS restaurants, selected for their good value, food and location, by region, starting with Dublin. Use the colour-coded thumb tabs, which indicate the regions covered on each page, to guide you to the relevant section of the chart. For Dublin map references, see the map on pages 110–11; for road map references, see the inside back cover.

		Credit Cards	Open Lunch Time	Open Late	Fixed-Price Menu	Good Wine List
DUBLIN						
SOUTHEAST DUBLIN: *Bewley's Oriental Café* 78–79 Grafton St, Dublin 2. **Map** D4. (01 6776761. This Dublin institution is open from breakfast time onwards. Its breads, pastries and home-made soups are superb.	£	MC V AE DC	●	■	●	
SOUTHEAST DUBLIN: *Kilkenny Shop Restaurant* The Kilkenny Shop, 6–10 Nassau St, Dublin 2. **Map** E4. (01 6777066. A busy restaurant, overlooking Trinity College playing fields, offering traditional Irish cooking and an extensive cheeseboard.	££	MC V AE DC	●			■
SOUTHEAST DUBLIN: *Gotham Café* 8 Anne St South, Dublin 2. **Map** D4. (01 6795266. The American-style menu at this bright, friendly café includes "Bowery", "Upper East Side" and "Central Park" gourmet pizzas.	£££	MC V	●	■		■
SOUTHEAST DUBLIN: *The Marrakesh* 28 Anne St South, Dublin 2. **Map** D4. (01 6605539. Authentic cooking in a delightfully created Moroccan setting. Excellent soups, tagines and couscous.	£££	MC V DC		■	●	■
SOUTHEAST DUBLIN: *Pier 32* 22–23 Pembroke St Upper, Dublin 2. (01 6761494. The regularly changing menu includes seafood and regional dishes. Try hare and champ (mashed potatoes, spring onions and butter).	£££	MC V	●	■		■
SOUTHEAST DUBLIN: *Rajdoot Tandoori* 26–28 Clarendon St, Dublin 2. **Map** D4. (01 6794274. This North Indian restaurant serves mildly spiced curries and, from the clay oven, tandoori barbecued beef, chicken and lamb.	£££	MC V AE DC	●	■	●	■
SOUTHEAST DUBLIN: *Sandbank Seafood Bar* Westbury Hotel, Grafton St, Dublin 2. **Map** D4. (01 6791122. There is a delightful buzz about this pub and restaurant full of maritime memorabilia. Try the fresh oysters washed down with Guinness.	£££	MC V AE DC	●	■		■
SOUTHEAST DUBLIN: *Ante Room* 20 Baggot St Lower, Dublin 2. **Map** F5. (01 6618832. Lobster, oysters and clams are served fresh from their seawater tanks in this cosy basement restaurant in the Georgian House Hotel.	££££	MC V AE DC	●			■
SOUTHEAST DUBLIN: *The Commons* Newman House, St Stephen's Green South, Dublin 2. **Map** D5. (01 4780530. Specially commissioned paintings by Irish artists share the honours in this tasteful restaurant with gourmet specialities. On sunny days, aperitifs can be taken in the pretty courtyard.	££££	MC V AE DC	●	■	●	■
SOUTHEAST DUBLIN: *Dobbin's Wine Bistro* 15 Stephen's Lane, Mount St Upper, Dublin 2. **Map** F5. (01 6764679. An intimate, friendly bistro with an innovative monthly menu and one of Dublin's best wine lists.	££££	MC V AE DC	●	■	●	■
SOUTHEAST DUBLIN: *L'Ecrivain* 109 Baggot St Lower, Dublin 2. **Map** F5. (01 6611919. In the heart of Georgian Dublin, French classics here have an Irish touch, such as breast of guinea fowl with a black pudding mousse.	££££	MC V AE DC	●	■	●	■
SOUTHEAST DUBLIN: *The Grey Door* Grey Door Hotel, 23 Pembroke St Upper, Dublin 2. (01 6763286. Award-winning Russian-Scandinavian cuisine in elegant surroundings. Specialities include blini with caviar, borscht and gravlax.	££££	MC V AE DC	●	■		■

Average prices for a three-course meal for one, half a bottle of house wine and unavoidable charges such as service and cover:
- ⓔ under IR£10
- ⓔⓔ IR£10–15
- ⓔⓔⓔ IR£15–25
- ⓔⓔⓔⓔ IR£25–50

OPEN LUNCH TIME
Many restaurants open only in the evening, but those in large towns and attached to pubs often open at lunch time.

OPEN LATE
Restaurant remains open with the full menu available after 10pm.

FIXED-PRICE MENU
A good-value fixed-price menu on offer at lunch, dinner or both, usually with three courses.

GOOD WINE LIST
Denotes a wide range of good wines, or a more specialized selection of wines.

Restaurant	Price	Credit Cards	Open Lunch Time	Open Late	Fixed-Price Menu	Good Wine List
SOUTHEAST DUBLIN: *La Stampa* — 35 Dawson St, Dublin 2. **Map** D4. 01 6778611. This up-market Italian restaurant in the heart of Dublin is noted for its sumptuous, highly ornate Georgian decor. Service is efficient and there is a lively atmosphere. Book at weekends.	ⓔⓔⓔⓔ	MC V AE DC	●	■	●	■
SOUTHWEST DUBLIN: *Leo Burdock's* — 2 Werburgh St, Dublin 8. **Map** C4. 01 4540306. Dublin's oldest fish-and-chip takeaway attracts a mix of patrons. The fish are fresh, and the chips made from top-grade Irish potatoes.	ⓔ		●	■		
SOUTHWEST DUBLIN: *Elephant and Castle* — 18 Temple Bar, Dublin 2. **Map** D3. 01 6793121. This boisterous American-style restaurant serves up-market fast food from tortillas to hamburgers. It is popular for brunch on Sunday.	ⓔⓔⓔ	MC V AE DC	●	■		
SOUTHWEST DUBLIN: *Les Frères Jacques* — 74 Dame St, Dublin 2. **Map** C3. 01 6794555. This French restaurant next to the Olympia Theatre adds Irish flair to many of its classical French dishes. Live piano music at weekends.	ⓔⓔⓔⓔ	MC V AE DC	●	■	●	■
SOUTHWEST DUBLIN: *Lord Edward* — 23 Christchurch Place, Dublin 8. **Map** B4. 01 4542420. Dublin's oldest seafood restaurant serves lunch in the ground-floor pub and evening meals in the upstairs restaurant. Service is courteous.	ⓔⓔⓔ	MC V AE DC	●	■	●	■
NORTH OF THE LIFFEY: *Conway's Pub and Restaurant* — 70 Parnell St, Dublin 1. **Map** D1. 01 8732474. Decor in this pub reflects its 1745 origin, and its patrons include Dubliners and actors from the Gate Theatre as well as visitors. The menu features unexpected items, such as tiger prawns in filo pastry.	ⓔ		●	■	●	
NORTH OF THE LIFFEY: *101 Talbot* — 100–102 Talbot St, Dublin 1. **Map** E2. 01 8745011. Vegetarians have a wide choice in this bright restaurant near the Abbey Theatre. Try the broccoli, fennel, courgette and blue cheese strudel.	ⓔⓔ	MC V AE DC	●	■		■
NORTH OF THE LIFFEY: *Flanagan's Restaurant* — 61 O'Connell St Upper, Dublin 1. **Map** D2. 01 8731388. Popular Flanagan's is great value for money with an extensive menu ranging from burgers and salads to vegetarian and pasta choices.	ⓔⓔ	MC V	●	■		■
NORTH OF THE LIFFEY: *Chapter One Restaurant* — Below Dublin Writers Museum, Parnell Square, Dublin 1. **Map** C1. 01 8732266. The decor features Irish writers. Deep-fried Parmesan and sage gnocchi and king scallops with leeks and mussels are on the menu.	ⓔⓔⓔⓔ	MC V AE DC	●	■	●	■
BALLSBRIDGE: *Conservatory Restaurant* — Berkeley Court Hotel, Lansdowne Rd, Dublin 4. 01 6601711. In this bright, conservatory-style room in one of the city's most luxurious hotels, meals from the extensive menu are excellent value for money. Very popular with Dubliners.	ⓔⓔⓔ	MC V AE DC	●	■	●	■
BALLSBRIDGE: *Le Coq Hardi* — 35 Pembroke Rd, Dublin 4. 01 6689070. French classical cuisine uses the best Irish ingredients in this lovely restaurant, winner of countless awards. Book ahead for dinner.	ⓔⓔⓔⓔ	MC V AE DC	●	■	●	■
BALLSBRIDGE: *Roly's Bistro* — 7 Ballsbridge Terrace, Dublin 4. 01 6682611. Lively bistro with Irish cuisine, including seasonal delights such as venison pie with juniper berries and wood mushrooms. Book ahead.	ⓔⓔⓔⓔ	MC V AE DC	●		●	■

For key to symbols see back flap

Average prices for a three-course meal for one, half a bottle of house wine and unavoidable charges such as service and cover:
£ under IR£10
££ IR£10–15
£££ IR£15–25
££££ IR£25–50

OPEN LUNCH TIME
Many restaurants open only in the evening, but those in large towns and attached to pubs often open at lunch time.

OPEN LATE
Restaurant remains open with the full menu available after 10pm.

FIXED-PRICE MENU
A good-value fixed-price menu on offer at lunch, dinner or both, usually with three courses.

GOOD WINE LIST
Denotes a wide range of good wines, or a more specialized selection of wines.

	Price	CREDIT CARDS	OPEN LUNCH TIME	OPEN LATE	FIXED-PRICE MENU	GOOD WINE LIST
DUN LAOGHAIRE: *Restaurant Na Mara* 1 Harbour Rd. 01 2806767. This restaurant, overlooking the harbour, serves the best just-caught seafood in the area. Non-fish dishes are also available.	£££	MC V AE DC	●	■	●	■
HOWTH: *Abbey Tavern* Abbey St. 01 8390307. A 16th-century tavern overlooking Howth Harbour and specializing in seafood. Its Irish music session is an institution. Book ahead.	£££	MC V AE DC	●		●	■
HOWTH: *King Sitric Fish Restaurant* East Pier. 01 8325235. Howth crab and lobster star on the menu in this elegant restaurant. In summer, a seafood bar serves lunch. Reserve for dinner.	££££	MC V AE DC	●	■	■	■
MALAHIDE: *Eastern Tandoori* 1 New St. 01 8454154. Decor and cuisine are authentically Indian in this restaurant located by the marina. Flavours to suit all tastes are served.	£££	MC V AE DC		■	●	■

SOUTHEAST IRELAND

	Price	CREDIT CARDS	OPEN LUNCH TIME	OPEN LATE	FIXED-PRICE MENU	GOOD WINE LIST
BALLYHACK: *Neptune Bistro Restaurant* Ballyhack Harbour. Road map D5. 051 389284. Next to Ballyhack Castle, this attractive bistro specializes in fresh seafood such as poached hake in lobster sauce.	£££	MC V AE DC			●	■
CAPPOQUIN: *Richmond House* Cappoquin. Road map C5. 058 54278. On the banks of the Blackwater River, this 18th-century country home serves French dishes and local salmon and trout.	££££	MC V AE DC			●	■
CARLOW: *The Beams Restaurant* 59 Dublin St. Road map D4. 0503 31824. A family-run restaurant with beamed ceilings and an old wall oven. Dishes include wild Atlantic salmon with white wine sauce, plus a huge choice of Irish cheeses.	£££	MC V		■	●	■
DUNGARVAN: *Merry's* Main St. Road map C5. 058 41974. Set in an atmospheric 19th-century wine merchant's shop, Merry's menu features shellfish and other seafoods, plus game in season.	£££	MC V AE DC	●		●	■
FERRYCARRIG BRIDGE: *Tides Restaurant* Ferrycarrig Hotel. Road map D5. 053 20999. One of the best restaurants in County Wexford, this relaxed room filled with greenery overlooks the Slaney estuary. Book ahead.	££££	MC V AE DC	●		●	■
GOREY: *Marlfield House* Courtown Rd. Road map D4. 055 21124. This Regency mansion houses one of the Southeast's premier dining rooms. Only organically grown vegetables are used.	££££	MC V	●		●	■
KILDARE: *Silken Thomas* The Square. Road map D4. 0455 22232. Located near the Norman castle keep in the town centre, this restaurant includes beef stroganoff and Gaelic steak on its menu.	£££	MC V AE	●			■
KILKENNY: *Kilkenny Design Centre Restaurant* Castle Yard. Road map C4. 056 22118. A bright, self-service restaurant with home-cooked casseroles and other hot dishes, plus salads, quiches, soups and patés.	££	MC V AE DC	●			

KILKENNY: *Edward Langton Restaurant and Bar*   ₤₤₤ | MC
69 John St. **Road map** C4. [056 65133. | V
At Langton's, each of several small rooms has its own distinctive | AE
decor. Stuffed mussels are among local favourites. 🔣 🔣 🔣 🔣 | DC

LEIGHLINBRIDGE: *Lord Bagenal Inn*   ₤₤₤ | MC
Main St. **Road map** D4. [0503 21668. | V
This riverside restaurant has an old-world air and award-winning wine | DC
list. Wild Irish salmon and game dishes appear in season. 🔣 🔣 🔣

LISMORE: *Eamonn's Place*   ₤
Main St. **Road map** C5. [058 54025.
In summer, meals in the stone-walled beer garden here are delightful,
while a cheerful turf fire adds a glow to winter meals inside. 🔣 🔣

NAAS: *Manor Inn*   ₤₤ | MC
Main St. **Road map** D4. [045 897471. | V
A haunt of punters en route to and from the nearby Curragh | AE
racecourse. Fish, steaks, pasta and grills feature on the menu. 🔣 🔣 🔣 | DC

RATHNEW: *Hunter's Hotel*   ₤₤₤ | MC
Rathnew. **Road map** D4. [0404 40106. | V
Cheerful hotel dining room attracting patrons from Dublin and nearby, | AE
with its friendly ambience and superb meat and fish dishes. 🔣 🔣 | DC

ROSSLARE: *The Lobster Pot*   ₤₤₤ | MC
Carne. **Road map** D5. [053 31110. | V
Lobster and oysters come straight from sea tanks in this tradi- | AE
tional pub and restaurant near Rosslare ferry harbour. 🔣 🔣 🔣

THOMASTOWN: *The Loft*   ₤₤₤ | MC
Mount Juliet Estate. **Road map** D5. [056 24455. | V
Traditional Irish cuisine, such as Irish stew and bacon and cabbage, | AE
is on offer at this informal restaurant. Open in summer only. 🔣 🔣 | DC

THOMASTOWN: *Lady Helen McCalmont Room*   ₤₤₤₤ | MC
Mount Juliet Estate. **Road map** D5. [056 24455. | V
The menu, as elegant as the decor, includes chicken breast with fennel | AE
stuffing in a tomato and red pepper sauce. Book ahead. 🔣 🔣 🔣 🔣 | DC

WATERFORD: *The Munster Bar*   ₤ | MC
Bailey's New St. **Road map** D5. [051 74656. | V
One Munster speciality popular among locals is a "blaa" (meat, onion,
tomato and lettuce on a small roll), found only in Waterford City.
Other traditional dishes feature on the extensive menu. 🔣 🔣 🔣

WATERFORD: *The Olde Stand Pub and Restaurant*   ₤₤ | MC
45 Michael St. **Road map** D5. [051 79488. | V
A glowing fireplace adds to the ambience upstairs in this Victorian-style
restaurant. More casual meals are served downstairs. Skip dessert and
indulge in one of their connoisseur coffees. 🔣 🔣 🔣

WATERFORD: *O'Grady's*   ₤₤₤ | MC
Cork Rd. **Road map** D5. [051 78851. | V
Innovative use of fresh local ingredients characterizes the delectable fare | AE
at this bright restaurant near the Waterford Crystal factory. 🔣 🔣 🔣 | DC

WATERFORD: *Waterford Castle Hotel*   ₤₤₤₤ | MC
The Island, Ballinakill. **Road map** D5. [051 878203. | V
A small car ferry crosses to Waterford Castle on its River | AE
Suir estuary island. Fish and seafood are the specialities in | DC
the magnificent wood-panelled dining room. 🔣 🔣 🔣 🔣

WEXFORD: *The Ocean Bed Restaurant*   ₤₤₤ | MC
Westgate. **Road map** D5. [053 23935. | V
Once a grain store, this is now an inviting restaurant specializing in
fresh seafood such as Wexford mussels and Kilmore scallops. 🔣 🔣

WICKLOW: *The Old Rectory Country House and Restaurant*   ₤₤₤₤ | MC
Wicklow. **Road map** D4. [0404 67048. | V
The pretty dining room is the setting for gourmet meals centred | AE
around pure wholefoods, organically grown vegetables and edible
flowers, local meats and seafood. Book in advance. 🔣 🔣 🔣

For key to symbols see back flap

Average prices for a three-course meal for one, half a bottle of house wine and unavoidable charges such as service and cover:
£ under IR£10
££ IR£10–15
£££ IR£15–25
££££ IR£25–50

OPEN LUNCH TIME
Many restaurants open only in the evening, but those in large towns and attached to pubs often open at lunch time.

OPEN LATE
Restaurant remains open with the full menu available after 10pm.

FIXED-PRICE MENU
A good-value fixed-price menu on offer at lunch, dinner or both, usually with three courses.

GOOD WINE LIST
Denotes a wide range of good wines, or a more specialized selection of wines.

CORK AND KERRY

Restaurant	Price	Credit Cards	Open Lunch Time	Open Late	Fixed-Price Menu	Good Wine List
BALLYFERRITER: *Tig an Tobair* Ballyferriter. **Road map** A5. 066 56404. A glassed-over wishing-well is the centrepiece of the small "House of the Well" restaurant. The chef always uses local fish.	£££	MC V	●			■
BALLYLICKEY: *Sea View House Hotel* Bantry Bay. **Road map** B6. 027 50073. The award-winning cuisine at this charming spot centres on fresh fish from Bantry Bay as well as local produce. Open April to October.	£££	MC V AE DC			●	■
BANTRY: *O'Connor's Seafood Restaurant* The Square. **Road map** B6. 027 50221. Bantry Bay's famed mussels take pride of place in this established restaurant. Mountain lamb and steaks are also excellent.	£££	MC V	●			■
BLARNEY: *Phelan's Woodview House* Tweedmount. **Road map** B5. 021 385197. This intimate restaurant often draws diners from nearby Cork. Make sure you sample chef Billy Phelan's hot seafood parcel.	£££	MC V		■	●	■
CASTLETOWNSHEND: *Mary Ann's* Skibbereen. **Road map** B6. 028 36146. Local seafood stars on the menu of this 150-year-old bar. Try the filleted sole stuffed with fish forcemeat and Mornay sauce glaze.	££££	MC V			●	■
CORK: *Beecher's Inn* Faulkner's Lane. **Road map** C5. 021 273144. A little hard to find, Beecher's is in a lane between St Patrick's Street and Emmet Place. Superb home-made lunches and seafood specialities.	£	MC V AE DC	●			
CORK: *Arbutus Lodge Hotel* Montenotte. **Road map** C5. 021 501237. This informal bar provides some of the best-value lunch-time food in Cork. The more formal restaurant in the same hotel offers gourmet dinners mixing Irish, French and other international cuisine.	£££	MC V AE DC	●	■		■
CORK: *Isaac's Restaurant* 48a MacCurtain St. **Road map** C5. 021 503805. The menu in this converted warehouse is extensive. Try the tagliatelle with red pepper sauce, cream cheese and smoked bacon.	£££	MC V AE DC	●	■		
CORK: *The Ivory Tower* The Exchange Buildings, 35 Princes St. **Road map** C5. 021 274665. Unusual and delicious combinations grace the menu of this attractive and rather trendy restaurant.	£££	MC V	●	■	●	■
DINGLE: *Beginish* Green St. **Road map** A5. 066 51588. This award-winning restaurant offers specialities such as breast of duck with honey and mustard sauce. Efficient and friendly service.	£££	MC V AE DC	●			■
DINGLE: *Half Door Restaurant* 3 John St. **Road map** A5. 066 51600. A combination of stone and light woods creates a relaxed ambience at the Half Door. The day's catch determines the menu.	£££	MC V AE DC	●			■
DURRUS: *Blair's Cove House Restaurant* Blair's Cove. **Road map** B6. 027 61127. In this romantic waterside restaurant on the shores of Dunmanus Bay, both wine list and cheeseboard are exceptional.	££££	MC V AE DC			●	■

KANTURK: *Assolas Country House* — £ £ £ £ — MC V AE DC
Kanturk. **Road map** B5. 029 50015.
Hazel Bourke's culinary expertise and emphasis on freshness has gained this lovely 17th-century home an international reputation. Choose from her seasonal menu or from the dishes of the day. V

KENMARE: *The Purple Heather* — £
Henry St. **Road map** B5. 064 41016.
This town-centre pub and restaurant serves up tasty, hearty food. Dishes include chicken liver terrine and Cumberland sauce. V

KENMARE: *Lime Tree Restaurant* — £ £ £ — MC V
Shelbourne St. **Road map** B5. 064 41225.
Housed in a charming 1830s school, the Lime Tree offers an imaginative choice of dishes. Try the goats' cheese potato cakes.

KENMARE: *Packie's* — £ £ £ — MC V
Henry St. **Road map** B5. 064 41508.
On the eclectic menu here, you're likely to find touches of Californian or Mediterranean cuisine along with traditional Irish dishes, such as casserole of beef with Guinness and mushrooms. V

KILLARNEY: *Dingle's Restaurant* — £ £ £ — MC V AE DC
40 New St. **Road map** B5. 064 31079.
Glowing open fires, oak and leather panelling and exposed stone create an inviting decor at Dingle's. Irish stew is a speciality, and there's a terrific vegetarian casserole. V

KILLARNEY: *Gaby's* — £ £ £ £ — MC V AE DC
High St. **Road map** B5. 064 32519.
Gaby's is the best seafood restaurant in town. Its interior incorporates seafaring memorabilia. Specialities include lobster, shellfish, oysters and Atlantic salmon. There is a fixed-price menu at lunch time.

KILLARNEY: *The Strawberry Tree* — £ £ £ £ — MC V AE DC
24 Plunkett St. **Road map** B5. 064 32688.
No chemically treated meats or vegetables are used here. The wild Atlantic salmon with a sorrel sauce is simple and delicious. V

KILLORGLIN: *Nick's Restaurant* — £ £ £ £ — MC V AE DC
Lower Bridge St. **Road map** A5. 066 61219.
Chef Nick Foley's background as a butcher ensures that only the best cuts of meat reach the table. The same care goes into seafood offerings. There are open fires and a pianist plays regularly. V

KINSALE: *Max's Wine Bar* — £ £ £ — MC V
Main St. **Road map** B6. 021 772443.
For more than 20 years, Max's has been in the forefront of Kinsale's gourmet restaurants. Among its culinary specialities is rack of lamb with red wine and rosemary sauce. Open March to October. V

KINSALE: *The Blue Haven* — £ £ £ £ — MC V AE DC
3–4 Pearse St. **Road map** B6. 021 772209.
A pleasant family restaurant, the Blue Haven offers a wide variety of food, from bar lunches to substantial meals. There's always a good selection of farmhouse cheeses. V

KINSALE: *Man Friday* — £ £ £ £ — MC V AE DC
Scilly. **Road map** B6. 021 772260.
Overlooking Kinsale Harbour, this restaurant has won culinary awards galore. No wonder, with specialities such as black sole with seafood stuffing and roast lamb with mint and rosemary sauce. V

LEAP: *Friskey's Restaurant* — £ £ £ — MC V
The Leap Inn. **Road map** B6. 028 33307.
Traditional Irish dishes (Irish stew, bacon and cabbage, roast stuffed chicken) feature on lunch-time menus in this delightful country inn. Locally caught seafoods are also a speciality. V

MALLOW: *Presidents' Restaurant* — £ £ £ £ — MC V AE DC
Longueville House. **Road map** B5. 022 47156.
Portraits of Irish presidents line the walls in this Georgian mansion. An excellent white wine from their own vineyard is available. V

Average prices for a three-course meal for one, half a bottle of house wine and unavoidable charges such as service and cover: ⓔ under IR£10 ⓔⓔ IR£10–15 ⓔⓔⓔ IR£15–25 ⓔⓔⓔⓔ IR£25–50	**OPEN LUNCH TIME** Many restaurants open only in the evening, but those in large towns and attached to pubs often open at lunch time. **OPEN LATE** Restaurant remains open with the full menu available after 10pm. **FIXED-PRICE MENU** A good-value fixed-price menu on offer at lunch, dinner or both, usually with three courses. **GOOD WINE LIST** Denotes a wide range of good wines, or a more specialized selection of wines.	CREDIT CARDS	OPEN LUNCH TIME	OPEN LATE	FIXED-PRICE MENU	GOOD WINE LIST
PARKNASILLA: *Pygmalion Restaurant* ⓔⓔⓔⓔ Great Southern Hotel. **Road map** A6. 📞 064 45122. Overlooking Kenmare Bay on the Ring of Kerry, the Pygmalion's elegant decor and polished service set off a gourmet cuisine. ♿ 🚹 🚭 ▾	MC V AE DC			●	■
SHANAGARRY: *Ballymaloe House* ⓔⓔⓔⓔ Shanagarry, Midleton. **Road map** C6. 📞 021 652531. At Ballymaloe House, acclaimed for its Irish and French classics, vegetables and meats come from their own farm, and seafood is local. ♿ 🚹 🚭 ▾	MC V AE DC	●		●	■
YOUGHAL: *Aherne's Seafood Restaurant* ⓔⓔⓔⓔ 163 North Main St. **Road map** C5. 📞 024 92424. Chef David Fitzgibbon's seafood chowder is positively addictive. His sumptuous platter of six fish and four shellfish recently won Aherne's the prestigious Seafood Dish of the Year Award. ♿ 🚹 🚭 ▾	MC V AE DC	●		●	■
<div align="center">**THE LOWER SHANNON**</div>					
ADARE: *The Inn-Between* ⓔⓔⓔ Dunraven Arms Hotel, Main St. **Road map** B5. 📞 061 396633. A charming restaurant in a thatched cottage, with informal service and a cosy atmosphere. Lunch features soups and soda bread. ♿ 🚹 ▾	MC V AE DC	●		●	■
ADARE: *The Mustard Seed at Echo Lodge* ⓔⓔⓔⓔ Ballingarry. **Road map** B5. 📞 069 68508. The Mustard Seed's move from Adare to a country house nearby means a change of scene but no change to the excellent food, with seasonal dishes prepared with the freshest of ingredients. ♿ 🚭 ▾	MC V AE			●	■
BUNRATTY: *MacCloskey's* ⓔⓔⓔⓔ Bunratty House Mews. **Road map** B4. 📞 061 364082. Downstairs in this 1846 mansion, the original kitchen, staff quarters and wine cellars form one of the best restaurants in the country. 🚭	MC V AE DC			●	■
CAHIR: *Malone's* ⓔⓔ The Galtee Inn, The Square. **Road map** C5. 📞 052 41247. The all-day menu in this family-run restaurant offers prime beef with rich sauces, roasts and seafood dishes as well as light meals. ♿ 🚹 🚭 ▾	MC V	●	■		
CASHEL: *Chez Hans* ⓔⓔⓔⓔ Rockside. **Road map** C5. 📞 062 61177. At the foot of the Rock of Cashel, Chez Hans occupies a former Wesleyan chapel. For several years, Hans-Peter Matthiä has created wonderfully innovative versions of traditional dishes. ♿ 🚹 🚭	MC V				■
CLONMEL: *The Old Bank Restaurant* ⓔⓔ Clonmel Arms Hotel, Sarsfield St. **Road map** C5. 📞 052 21233. The Old Bank is a bright, airy hotel dining room, decorated with strong colours, lots of brass and some interesting art. The European-influenced menu changes with the seasons. ♿ 🚹 🚭 ▾	MC V AE DC	●	■	●	■
DOOLIN: *Bruach na hAille* ⓔⓔⓔ Roadford. **Road map** B4. 📞 065 74120. This charming, cottage-style restaurant (its name means "banks of the river") uses local produce in unexpected ways, such as fillets of sole in cider served with shellfish in a cream sauce. ♿ 🚹 🚭 ▾	MC V AE			●	■
ENNIS: *Cruise's Pub and Restaurant* ⓔⓔ Abbey St. **Road map** B4. 📞 065 41800. The 17th-century building's low, beamed ceilings and the open fires in winter create a cosy ambience in this restaurant. Several nights a week, meals are served to the accompaniment of traditional music. ♿ 🚹 🚭 ▾	MC V AE DC	●		●	■

LIMERICK: *Bridges Restaurant*   £££   MC V AE DC
Jury's Hotel, Ennis Rd. **Road map** B4. 061 327777.
All-day service makes this bright hotel restaurant one of the most convenient in Limerick. Light snacks share the menu with full meals. The more
formal Copper Room serves gourmet and traditional Irish dishes.

LIMERICK: *O' Flaherty's*   £££   MC V AE DC
74 O'Connell St. **Road map** B4. 061 316311.
Well-placed in the city centre, this informal restaurant serves good and
plentiful bistro fare in pleasant surroundings.

NEWMARKET-ON-FERGUS: *Earl of Thomond Room*   ££££ MC V AE DC
Dromoland Castle. **Road map** B4. 061 368144.
A traditional Irish harper accompanies evening meals in this elegant
dining room. The "Taste of Ireland" set menu has no less than six courses.
Try the hot brown-bread soufflé and the creamy lamb ravioli.

THURLES: *Inch House*   £££   MC V
Thurles. **Road map** B4. 0504 51261.
A mixture of traditional and more adventurous dishes in a fine
country house setting.

THE WEST OF IRELAND

ACHILL ISLAND: *The Boley House Restaurant*   £££   MC V
Keel. **Road map** A3. 098 43147.
Owner Tom McNamara uses only the freshest ingredients, with seafood
from local waters. Roasted free-range duckling is a favourite.

ARAN ISLANDS: *Dún Aonghasa Restaurant*   £££   MC V
Kilronan, Inishmore. **Road map** B4. 099 61104.
Overlooking the harbour, in a setting of stone, wood and open fires,
chef Grace Flaherty bases her menu on fish fresh from Galway Bay.
Choices include creamy seafood chowder and grilled shark.

BARNA: *Donnelly's Seafood Restaurant and Bar*   £££   MC V AE DC
Freeport. **Road map** B4. 091 592487.
Fresh seafood is a speciality in this rustic-style restaurant. Among
non-seafood dishes is chicken supreme, Gaelic-style.

CLARINBRIDGE: *Moran's Oyster Cottage*   ££   MC V AE
The Weir. **Road map** B4. 091 796113.
Known as "Moran's of the Weir", this 200-year-old restaurant
in a thatched cottage is loved by both locals and celebrities,
especially during the annual Clarinbridge Oyster Festival.

CLIFDEN: *O'Grady's Seafood Restaurant*   ££££ MC V AE
Market St. **Road map** A3. 095 21450.
Award-winning O'Grady's offers delicious seafood, such as baked fillet of
cod with a Calvados glaze, plus superb vegetarian choices like avocado
and blue cheese mousse in puff pastry. Open May to mid-October.

CLIFDEN: *Rock Glen Restaurant*   ££££ MC V AE DC
Rock Glen Manor House. **Road map** A3. 095 21035.
A converted Connemara shooting lodge is the setting for gracious dining
here, with friendly service enhancing an excellent cuisine.

CONG: *Connaught Room*   ££££ MC V AE DC
Ashford Castle. **Road map** B3. 092 46003.
Only the best local ingredients come to table in this wood-panelled
dining room. Its menu includes rack of Connemara hill lamb and
fillet of turbot with scallops. Open May to October.

GALWAY: *Hooker Jimmy's Steak and Seafood Bar*   £££   MC V AE DC
The Fishmarket, Spanish Arch. **Road map** B4. 091 568351.
This bar in an old stone building beside the river serves meals out
on the terrace in fine weather. Galway salmon and shellfish from their
own boat are on the menu.

GALWAY: *Rabbitt's Bar and Restaurant*   £££   MC V AE DC
23–25 Forster St, Eyre Sq. **Road map** B4. 091 566490.
Dating back to 1872, this atmospheric bar-restaurant has a menu as traditional as its decor. Irish stew with local lamb is excellent.

Average prices for a three-course meal for one, half a bottle of house wine and unavoidable charges such as service and cover: **£** under IR£10 **££** IR£10–15 **£££** IR£15–25 **££££** IR£25–50	**OPEN LUNCH TIME** Many restaurants open only in the evening, but those in large towns and attached to pubs often open at lunch time. **OPEN LATE** Restaurant remains open with the full menu available after 10pm. **FIXED-PRICE MENU** A good-value fixed-price menu on offer at lunch, dinner or both, usually with three courses. **GOOD WINE LIST** Denotes a wide range of good wines, or a more specialized selection of wines.	**CREDIT CARDS**	**OPEN LUNCH TIME**	**OPEN LATE**	**FIXED-PRICE MENU**	**GOOD WINE LIST**

Restaurant	Price	Credit Cards	Open Lunch Time	Open Late	Fixed-Price Menu	Good Wine List
GALWAY: *The Park Room* Forster St, Eyre Sq. **Road map** B4. (091 564924. This tasteful restaurant inside Park House Hotel offers good value and a wide-ranging menu featuring grilled sea trout, honey-glazed rack of lamb and other Irish specialities prepared from local ingredients.	**££££**	MC V AE DC	●		●	■
MOYCULLEN: *Drimcong House* Moycullen. **Road map** B4. (091 555115. This top restaurant is in a 17th-century lakeside house. The menu changes weekly, and there is a five-course set vegetarian menu.	**£££**	MC V AE DC		■	●	
ROSCOMMON: *Abbey Hotel* Galway Rd. **Road map** C3. (0903 26250. Set dinners in this 18th-century turreted mansion feature steak prepared in different ways, grilled sea trout and other fish dishes.	**£££**	MC V AE DC	●		●	■
WESTPORT: *The Asgard Tavern and Restaurant* The Quay. **Road map** B3. (098 25319. The lively bar here dishes up award-winning lunches. Evening meals include a superb seafood chowder and garlic steak.	**£££**	MC V AE DC	●		●	■

NORTHWEST IRELAND

Restaurant	Price	Credit Cards	Open Lunch Time	Open Late	Fixed-Price Menu	Good Wine List
BALLYSHANNON: *Sweeney's White Horse Bar* Assaroe Rd. **Road map** C2. (072 51452. Sweeney's set bar menu offers good food in an inviting atmosphere. There is traditional music in the Cellar Bar on Friday nights.	**£**		●	■		■
CASTLEBALDWIN: *Cromleach Lodge Country House* Ballindoon, Boyle. **Road map** C3. (071 65155. Fabulous views of Lough Arrow and the Bricklieve Mountains form a backdrop for gourmet dining in this hilltop country house.	**££££**	MC V AE DC			●	■
COLLOONEY: *Glebe House Restaurant* Collooney. **Road map** C2. (071 67787. At this Georgian house, there's an emphasis on organically grown produce and imaginative use of local fish and meats. Friendly service.	**£££**	MC V AE DC			●	■
DUNKINEELY: *Castlemurray House* Dunkineely. **Road map** C2. (073 37022. There are wonderful views across the bay from the relaxed restaurant – perfect surroundings for you to enjoy classic dishes expertly prepared.	**£££**	MC V				
INISHOWEN PENINSULA: *Bree Inn* Malin Head. **Road map** C1. (077 70161. At the northernmost point in Ireland, this lively country inn serves home-cooked meals all day. The place is a favourite with locals.	**£**		●	■		
INISHOWEN PENINSULA: *Restaurant St John's* Fahan. **Road map** C1. (077 60289. An atmospheric restaurant on the shores of Lough Swilly offering five- and six-course set menus, with excellent fish dishes and desserts.	**£££**	MC V AE DC			●	■
KILLYBEGS: *Sail Inn* Main St. **Road map** C2. (073 31130. Food is served all day at this traditional inn. Bar food is good value, and fish from the town's fleet is served in the upstairs restaurant.	**££**	MC V AE DC	●			■
RATHMULLAN: *Pavilion Restaurant* Rathmullan Country House. **Road map** C1. (074 58188. The Pavilion offers gourmet food in a glass-walled setting. Sample the seaweed-based dessert of carrageen moss with stewed fruits.	**££££**	MC V AE DC	●		●	■

ROSSES POINT: *The Elsinore*   £££   MC V AE
Rosses Point Road. **Road map** B2. 071 77111.
Set high above Sligo Bay, with great views of the sea, The Elsinore offers fresh seafood dishes such as crab au gratin or baked trout amandine. Hearty pub lunches are served in the summer.

SLIGO: *Gulliver's Restaurant*   £   MC V AE DC
24 Grattan St. **Road map** C2. 071 42030.
A nautical theme dominates the decor here. The menu is mainly bar food but ranges from burgers, salads and sandwiches to fresh fish.

TOBERCURRY: *Killoran's Traditional Restaurant*   £££   MC V AE DC
Teeling St. **Road map** B3. 071 85111.
Irish stew, boxty (potato pancakes) and crubeens (pickled pigs' feet) are on the traditional menu. Snacks and full meals served all day.

THE MIDLANDS

ARDEE: *The Gables*   £££   MC V
Dundalk Rd. **Road map** D3. 041 53789.
The accent here is definitely French, using the freshest local ingredients available. Choose from classics like snails with garlic butter.

ATHLONE: *L'Escale Restaurant*   £££   MC V AE DC
The Hodson Bay Hotel. **Road map** C3. 0902 92444.
Cuisine is a blend of French and Irish. A typical dish is Dublin Bay prawns with shallots, mushrooms and tomato, flamed in whiskey.

BUTLER'S BRIDGE: *Derragarra Inn*   £££   MC V
Butler's Bridge. **Road map** C3. 049 31003.
A thatched cottage inn decorated with relics of rural Ireland by the River Annalea. The restaurant menu is available in the bar all day.

CARLINGFORD: *Jordan's Town House Restaurant*   £££   MC V AE
Newry St. **Road map** D3. 042 73223.
A renovated 19th-century warehouse overlooking the harbour is the setting for culinary gems with organically grown local ingredients.

CARRICKMACROSS: *Nuremore Hotel*   ££££   MC V AE DC
Carrickmacross. **Road map** D3. 042 61438.
This beautiful restaurant has an imaginative menu, including French and Irish cuisine, served in a tranquil setting.

DUNDALK: *Quaglino's Restaurant*   £££   MC V AE DC
88 Clanbrassil St. **Road map** D3. 042 38567.
This bright, town-centre restaurant features superb Continental dishes, which the menu lists in no less than four languages.

KELLS: *Monaghan's*   £   MC V
Kells. **Road map** D3. 046 40100.
Monaghan's is a moderately priced family restaurant. Only local, hormone-free meats are used. Children welcome until 9pm.

MONAGHAN: *Andy's Restaurant*   £££   MC V
Market St. **Road map** D2. 047 82277.
This restaurant in Monaghan town centre is above an award-winning pub. The extensive menu includes sirloin steak in whiskey and beer sauce and half a dozen vegetarian dishes.

MOUNTRATH: *Roundwood House*   £££   MC V AE DC
Mountrath. **Road map** C4. 0502 32120.
Pre-booking is a must in this gracious Palladian mansion. Its compulsory four-course set menu changes daily. Superb Sunday lunches.

MULLINGAR: *Crookedwood House*   £££   MC V AE DC
Crookedwood. **Road map** C3. 044 72165.
This 200-year-old restaurant changes its menu with the seasons. A summer speciality is River Moy salmon with hollandaise sauce.

TULLAMORE: *Moorhill Country House*   £££   MC V AE DC
Clara Rd. **Road map** C4. 0506 21395.
Stone walls, oak beams and open fires welcome you to this traditional but imaginative restaurant in renovated stables.

Average prices for a three-course meal for one, half a bottle of house wine and unavoidable charges such as service and cover:
£ under £10
££ £10–15
£££ £15–25
££££ £25–50

OPEN LUNCH TIME
Many restaurants open only in the evening, but those in large towns and attached to pubs often open at lunch time.

OPEN LATE
Restaurant remains open with the full menu available after 10pm.

FIXED-PRICE MENU
A good-value fixed-price menu on offer at lunch, dinner or both, usually with three courses.

GOOD WINE LIST
Denotes a wide range of good wines, or a more specialized selection of wines.

NORTHERN IRELAND

Restaurant	Price	Credit Cards	Open Lunch Time	Open Late	Fixed-Price Menu	Good Wine List
ARMAGH: *Pilgrim's Table*	£		●			
BALLYCASTLE: *Wysner's Restaurant*	£££	MC V	●		●	■
BELFAST: *Crown Liquor Saloon*	£	MC V DC	●			■
BELFAST: *Duke of York*	£		●			
BELFAST: *Mangetous*	££	MC V AE DC	●	■	●	■
BELFAST: *Malone House*	£££	MC V AE DC	●		●	■
BELFAST: *Nick's Warehouse*	£££	MC V AE DC	●		●	■
BELFAST: *Antica Roma*	££££	MC V AE	●	■		■
BELFAST: *Roscoff*	££££	MC V AE DC	●	■	●	■
BELLEEK: *Rooney's Bar and Restaurant*	££	MC V AE DC	●		●	■

ARMAGH: *Pilgrim's Table*
38–40 English St. **Road map** D2. (*01861 521814.*
Fine home cooking makes use of the best fresh local produce. Non-fussy dishes, especially the soups (such as potato and leek or chicken and bacon), are tasty, filling and superb value.

BALLYCASTLE: *Wysner's Restaurant*
16 Anne St. **Road map** D1. (*01265 762372.*
Wysner's serves excellent meat and fish dishes. Downstairs is in the style of a French café, while upstairs is a more expensive restaurant where the Bushmills Malt cheesecake is a must.

BELFAST: *Crown Liquor Saloon*
46 Great Victoria St. **Road map** D2. (*01232 249476.*
Centrally located with Victorian decor, this bar's snug-like booths provide the table space for a bowl of Irish stew or champ – a local speciality of potatoes, spring onions and butter.

BELFAST: *Duke of York*
11 Commercial Court. **Road map** D2. (*01232 241062.*
Pub grub, including chilli, steak and lasagne is the typical fare at this very reasonably priced restaurant. Near St Anne's Cathedral, it is Irish in style and carefully cluttered with Belfast memorabilia.

BELFAST: *Mangetous*
30 University Rd. **Road map** D2. (*01232 315151.*
A bicycle hangs over the door of this simple French restaurant where the menu changes daily. Portions are adequate rather than generous. The French onion soup is well worth sampling.

BELFAST: *Malone House*
Barnett Demesne. **Road map** D2. (*01232 681246.*
Only the highest quality Ulster produce is used in the traditional and modern Irish food served at this local favourite. Vegetarian dishes are often the house speciality.

BELFAST: *Nick's Warehouse*
35–39 Hill St. **Road map** D2. (*01232 439690.*
Nick Price's converted warehouse, tucked away in the cobbled backstreets of city-centre Belfast, gets top marks for atmosphere. The menu regularly includes Nick's latest culinary innovations.

BELFAST: *Antica Roma*
67 Botanic Ave. **Road map** D2. (*01232 311121.*
The Roman atmosphere and first-rate service complement the Italian menu featuring creative pasta dishes such as tagliatelle with a rich lamb sauce. There is a resident pianist.

BELFAST: *Roscoff*
7 Lesley House, Shaftesbury Sq. **Road map** D2. (*01232 331532.*
Classical French cuisine with Californian influence combine to make Roscoff a wonderful eating experience. Its Michelin star guarantees use of the freshest local produce and great service. Try the fillet of Glenarm salmon with horseradish sauce and chive cream.

BELLEEK: *Rooney's Bar and Restaurant*
Main St. **Road map** C2. (*013656 58279.*
This cosy pub and restaurant offers huge portions of simply cooked fresh food. Steaks, roast ham or rack of Irish lamb are all on the menu, served with vegetables and potatoes.

DUNDRUM: *The Buck's Head*   £££
77 Main St. **Road map** E2. ☎ 013967 51868.
Open fires and hospitable, friendly service make this an excellent stop for
lunch or dinner. There is a conservatory and beer garden. ♿ 🚹 🚭 V
MC V AE DC

DUNGANNON: *Viscount's Great Food Hall*   £££
10 Northland Row. **Road map** D2. ☎ 01868 753800.
A Victorian church has been converted into a medieval-style banqueting
hall with the emphasis on fun as much as food. The large menu caters
to all appetites and is popular with families in the daytime. ♿ 🚹 🚭 V
MC V

ENNISKILLEN: *Tullyhona Farm Restaurant*   £
59 Marble Arch Rd, Florencecourt. **Road map** C2. ☎ 01365 348452.
Beside Marble Arch caves, this farm restaurant offers great food and
service. Produce fresh from the farm is used, and desserts such as
lemon soufflé and fresh fruit pavlova are a speciality. ♿ 🚹 🚭 V

ENNISKILLEN: *Franco's Restaurant*   ££
Queen Elizabeth Rd. **Road map** C2. ☎ 01365 324424.
A warren of nooks and crannies, this hospitable pizzeria often has live
traditional music. The vast menu offers Italian food with an Irish influ-
ence. Seafood dishes include fresh lobster and mussels. ♿ 🚹 🚭 V
MC V AE DC

ENNISKILLEN: *The Sheelin*   ££
Bellanaleck. **Road map** C2. ☎ 01365 348232.
This thatched cottage restaurant on the shores of Lower Lough
Erne is a gourmet experience. Favourites include ham in a honey
and fruit marinade followed by Baileys Cream cheesecake. ♿ 🚹 V
MC V AE

HOLYWOOD: *Iona Bistro*   ££
27 Church Rd. **Road map** E2. ☎ 01232 425655.
Roughcast walls and tightly packed tables make this restaurant,
owned by Dutchman Bart Brave, homely and welcoming. He
offers four-course surprise menus. Bring your own wine. 🚹 V
MC V

LONDONDERRY: *The Metro*   £
3–4 Bank Pl. **Road map** C1. ☎ 01504 267401.
Shadowed by Derry's city walls, this is a favourite with locals. The food,
from soup and sandwiches to beef stew in Guinness, is first rate. ♿ 🚹 V

LONDONDERRY: *Schooners*   ££
59 Victoria Rd. **Road map** C1. ☎ 01504 311500.
Overlooking Lough Foyle, Schooners is a maritime restaurant.
Try the "Captain's Catch" – baked fillet of trout served with
hazelnut butter. Plenty of non-fish options too. ♿ 🚹 🚭 V
MC V

NEWCASTLE: *Pavilion Restaurant*   £££
36 Downs Rd. **Road map** E2. ☎ 013967 26239.
Overlooking miles of sandy beach, this is one of Newcastle's best
restaurants. Lunch-time snacks are served in the downstairs bar
while in the evening a more elaborate menu is offered. ♿ 🚹 🚭 V
MC V DC

NEWCASTLE: *Percy French*   £££
Downs Rd. **Road map** E2. ☎ 013967 24748.
The Tudor-style bar and restaurant offer generous portions of dishes
from ploughman's cheese and pickle to à la carte choices. ♿ 🚹 🚭 V
MC V AE DC

PORTBALLINTRAE: *Sweeny's Wine Bar*   ££
6b Seaport Ave. **Road map** D1. ☎ 012657 32404.
Prices here are cheap and cheerful and the food creatively prepared.
Situated on the Causeway Coast, Sweeny's occupies a converted stable
block overlooking Portballintrae Harbour. ♿ 🚹 V

PORTRUSH: *The Ramore Restaurant*   £££
The Harbour. **Road map** D1. ☎ 012658 24313.
The Ramore looks over Portrush Harbour and is one
of the finest restaurants in Northern Ireland, with excellent
presentation. Gourmet food includes fried squid with salad. ♿ V
MC V

STRANGFORD: *The Lobster Pot*   £££
The Square. **Road map** E2. ☎ 01396 881288.
Only the finest local catches are served in this predominantly
fish restaurant overlooking Strangford Lough. ♿ 🚹 🚭 V
MC V AE DC

For key to symbols see back flap

Pubs in Ireland

THE ARCHETYPAL IRISH PUB is celebrated for its convivial atmosphere, friendly locals, genial bar staff and the "crack" – the Irish expression for fun. Wit is washed down with whiskey or Guinness, the national drinks. Irish pubs date back to medieval taverns, coaching inns and shebeens, illegal drinking dens which flourished under colonial rule. In Victorian times, brewing and distilling were major industries. The sumptuous Edwardian or Victorian interiors of some city pubs are a testament to these times, furnished with mahogany and marble bar counters. Snugs, partitioned-off booths, are another typical feature of Irish pubs. Traditional pubs can be boldly painted, thatched or "black-and-white" – beamed with a white façade and black trim. Some rural pubs double as grocers' shops.

Good pubs are not evenly distributed throughout the country: in the Southeast, Kilkenny is paradise for pub-lovers, while Cork and Kerry possess some of the most picturesque pubs. The Lower Shannon region is noted for its boisterous pubs, especially in County Clare where spontaneous music sessions are common. The West has an abundance of typical Irish pubs, and the many tourists and students guarantee a profusion of good pubs in Galway. The listings below cover a selection of pubs throughout Ireland; for Dublin pubs, see pages 104–7.

SOUTHEAST IRELAND

Dunmore East: *The Ship Inn*
Road map D5. **℃** 051 383141.
This old, ivy-clad pub lies above the harbour, away from the crowds on the beach. It is noted both for its seafood and its seafaring links. Inside, nautical memorabilia and half-barrel seats abound in the front bar. The small garden is an appealing spot for drinking in the summer. Lemon sole, turbot and brill are on the menu. 🍴 🍺

Enniscorthy: *The Antique Tavern*
14 Slaney St. Road map D5.
℃ 054 33428.
This traditional, timbered, black-and-white pub is charming. The dark, intimate bar contains relics such as pikestaffs from Vinegar Hill, the decisive battle in the 1798 uprising that was fought outside town. Pub lunches and local chat are on offer. In good weather, you can sit on the balcony. 🍺

Enniscorthy: *The Cotton Tree*
Slaney Place. Road map D5.
℃ 054 33179.
Although this is essentially a work-aday pub with few pretensions, its site makes it worth a visit – it is built into the base of an old quarry and a vertical cliff forms part of the back wall of the bar. A recent renovation means that a full menu of bar food is now served all day.

Kilkenny: *Kyteler's Inn*
27 St Kieran's St. Road map C4.
℃ 056 21064.
In good weather you can sit in the courtyard of this historic coaching inn and cellar bar. Food is served all day, and meals are served in the restaurant downstairs until 9:45pm (last orders). An effigy of a witch sits in the window frame, a reminder of the story of a former resident, Dame Alice Kyteler. In 1324, Alice and her maid were pronounced guilty of witchcraft after four of Alice's husbands had died in mysterious circumstances; although pardoned, Alice was again accused but escaped, leaving her maid to burn at the stake. 🍴 🍺

Kilkenny: *Langton's*
69 John St. Road map C4.
℃ 056 65133.
Langton's is noted for its black-and-white exterior, Edwardian ambience (most of the time), and the stylish glass interior at the back. The front bar is cosy with a low ceiling. Pub food is on offer, and there's music and dancing three or four nights a week; Tuesday is disco night. 🍴 🍺

Kilkenny: *Maggie Holland's*
St Kieran's St. Road map C4.
℃ 056 62273.
Set in a central spot near the river, this is a dimly lit but welcoming pub. Traditional music on Tuesday evenings draws plenty of locals. 🎵

Kilkenny: *Marble City Bar*
66 High St. Road map C4.
℃ 056 62091.
Marble City Bar, the most famous pub in town, is named after the local limestone, which becomes black when polished. This four-storey building has an Edwardian façade, adorned with a sign lit by an atmospheric gas lamp. 🎵

Kilkenny: *Tynan's Bridge House Bar*
2 John's Bridge. Road map C4.
℃ 056 21291.
This is the most genuine old-world pub in town, with an intimate interior lit by charming lamps. Quaint relics of the former grocery store and pharmacy are on display, from a set of old scales to the drawers labelled with names of nuts and spices. No food, no music, no TV; as publican Michael puts it, "a chat bar".

Kilmore Quay: *The Wooden House Lodge*
Road map D5. **℃** 053 29804.
This traditional – if over-restored – thatched pub is full of nautical memorabilia and quirky sayings while the small terrace is decorated with anchors. Hearty pub fare is served. 🍴 🍺 🎵

Waterford: *T and H Doolin*
George's St. Road map D5.
℃ 051 841504.
Set in the city's most charming pedestrianized street, this traditional, 18th-century black-and-white pub offers an intimate atmosphere and good "crack". Traditional folk music sessions are held every night. 🎵

Waterford: *The Reginald Bar*
The Mall. Road map D5.
℃ 051 855087.
Set beside Reginald's Tower, the pub incorporates part of the Viking city walls and the medieval sallyports (attack exits), which are still visible. The service is rather brusque but the pub offers both reasonable bar snacks (noon–7:30pm) and a restaurant menu (5:30–10:30pm). There is also an adjoining nightclub. 🍴

Wexford: *Centenary Stores*
Charlotte St. Road map D5.
℃ 053 24424.
Tucked away in a converted ware-house, this cosy, dimly lit pub is the most charming in Wexford. The friendly bar staff and a mixed local and bohemian crowd chat in the wood-panelled bar. Drinkers are often entertained with impromptu sessions of traditional music. 🍺 🎵

Wexford: *Westgate Tavern*
Westgate. **Road map** D5.
[C] 053 22086.
Licensed since 1761, this distinctive, timbered tavern faces the path
leading to the famous Selskar Abbey
and Westgate Heritage Centre.
Simple snacks are available in the
welcoming bar and there is
traditional music on Saturday and
Sunday evenings. [♫]

CORK AND KERRY

Clonakilty: *De Barra's*
Road map B6. [C] 023 33381.
This is one of the best-known pubs
in West Cork, with a traditional
folk club open most nights; many
musicians come from the Gaeltacht
(see p221). The bar is lovingly
restored, with hand-painted signs
and traditional whiskey jars. Simple
snacks are served from 11:30am–
2:30pm. [▦] [♫]

Cork: *Chateau Bar*
St Patrick's St. **Road map** C5.
[C] 021 270370.
This bar in the heart of the city
occupies a striking building that
was once on the quayside. Founded
in 1793, this elegant pub has a
stylish Victorian interior and offers
good quality bar fare.

Cork: *Chimes*
27 Church St. **Road map** C5.
[C] 021 304136.
Set in the hilly, old-world Shandon
district, this convivial working-
class pub attracts a mixed, friendly
crowd, from local pensioners to
sports fans and students. Simple
bar food is sometimes on offer,
and on Thursday, Saturday and Sunday nights there's music, usually in
the form of accordion or keyboard
soloists. [♫]

Cork: *Henchy's*
40 St Luke's Cross. **Road map** C5.
[C] 021 507833.
This traditional pub, situated close
to Chimes *(see above)*, dates from
1884 and has retained much of its
Victorian ambience, enhanced by
the mahogany bar, stained glass
and a snug (a private room, in this
case, with a separate entrance). It
has long been associated with
poets and is where young hopefuls
often recite their work. A varied
bar menu is on offer at lunch time.

Cork: *The World's End*
Market Lane, off St Patrick's St.
Road map C5. [C] 021 272716.
Founded in the 18th century, this
tavern was slightly refurbished by
the new management in 1994. The
restaurant has now closed but the
open-plan bar serves food from
12:30–2pm.

Dingle: *Dick Mack's*
Green St. **Road map** A5.
[C] 066 51960.
This individualistic spot is part
shoe shop, part pub, and retains
the original shop and drinking
counters. The pub is a haunt of
local artists, eccentrics and extro-
verts. In the evening, regulars often
congregate around the piano. [♫]

Dingle: *Doyle's Townhouse*
John St. **Road map** A5.
[C] 066 51174.
This charming bar and restaurant is
celebrated for its delicious seafood
(visible in a tank). The pub's rustic,
yet cosy, stone interior is an appealing place for lunch. Doyle's is open
mid-March to mid-November. [▮▮]

Dunquin: *Krugers*
Road map A5. [C] 066 56127.
Situated close to the quays for the
Blasket Islands, this well-known
family pub is also a guesthouse.
The pub is decorated with family
memorabilia and stills from the
films made in the neighbourhood,
such as *Ryan's Daughter.* [♫]

Killarney: *Buckley's Bar*
College St. **Road map** B5.
[C] 064 31037.
This oak-panelled bar is noted for
its regular traditional music sessions
and its filling meals. The pub was
opened in 1926 when Tom
Buckley, a homesick emigrant,
returned from New York. Bar food
is served until 9pm. [▮▮] [♫]

Killarney: *The Laurels*
Main St. **Road map** B5.
[C] 064 31149.
This claims to be Killarney's
liveliest pub and is popular with
the young locals as well as Irish-
Americans who enjoy listening to
the ballads and singing along. The
pub provides excellent bar snacks
or good meals (steak, mussels,
oysters, fish) in a separate restaurant area. Ballads are performed
nightly from 9:15pm between April
and October, and more sporadi-
cally over the winter. [▮▮] [♫]

Killorglin: *The Old Forge*
Road map A5. [C] 066 61231.
Set on the popular Ring of Kerry,
this thatched pub is delightfully
old-fashioned and authentic.
Expect it to be packed during the
Puck Fair in August *(see p47).* [♫]

Kinsale: *Kieran's Folk
House Inn*
Guardwell. **Road map** B6.
[C] 021 772382.
This convivial corner of old
Kinsale draws locals and visitors
alike, including fishermen and
divers. The interior is snug and

welcoming, with live music on
Friday, Saturday and Sunday
evenings. The inn also houses a
pleasant guesthouse and a noted
restaurant, the Bacchus Brasserie,
open for lunch and dinner between
April and October. [▮▮] [♫]

Kinsale: *The Lord Kingsale*
Main St. **Road map** B6.
[C] 021 772371.
This beamed, old-fashioned pub
attracts a quiet, genteel crowd.
Although the pub is several
hundred years old, the interior is,
in part, a clever fake. In summer,
live music is usually performed
at weekends. [♫]

Kinsale: *The 1601*
Pearse St. **Road map** B6.
[C] 021 772529.
The front bar is bedecked as a
tribute to the Battle of Kinsale
(see p164) while the back bar
incorporates an ever-changing art
gallery. The bar food (served at
lunch time and evenings) is tasty
and eclectic but the pub tends to
get rather crowded. On Monday or
Tuesday evenings you might find
live modern or traditional music
performed in the pub. [▮▮] [▦] [♫]

Kinsale: *The Spaniard Inn*
Scilly. **Road map** B6.
[C] 021 772436.
Set on a hairpin bend above the
village of Scilly, this popular
fishermen's pub has the air of a
smugglers' inn. There is often live
traditional music in one of the
bars every night during the
summer. Expect crowds around
the log fire on weekends. Bar food
is simple, but excellent. [▮▮] [▦] [♫]

THE LOWER SHANNON

Ballyvaughan: *Monk's Pub*
The Pier. **Road map** B4.
[C] 065 77059.
This quaint, cosy pub is situated
on the quay. Inside, country furniture and peat fires are matched
by home-cooked seafood and pies
served until 6pm in the winter,
9pm in the summer. There's live
music most evenings; ring for
details. [▮▮] [▦] [♫]

Bunratty: *Durty Nelly's*
Road map B4. [C] 061 364072.
Set beside Bunratty Castle, this
touristy, extremely commercialized
pub appeals to locals as well as
tourists. The 17th-century atmosphere is sustained by the warren
of rooms, inglenook fireplaces and
historical portraits. Traditional
music is performed most evenings, and
wholesome food is available both
from the bar and from the two
restaurants. [▮▮] [▦] [♫]

Doolin: *O'Connor's*
Road map B4. 【 065 74168.
This famous pub is known to lovers
of traditional music the world
over. The pub has been in the
O'Connor family for over 150 years
and combines an authentic grocery
store with a lively pub. This is the
place for spontaneous music,
simple bar food, young company
and great "crack". 🍴 🎵

Ennis: *The Cloister*
Abbey St. **Road map** B4.
【 065 29521.
This historic pub is situated by the
famous Ennis Friary. The pub's
cosy, atmospheric interior is complemented by a patio for summer
dining. Bar food is available as well
as more refined dishes in the restaurant, from Ballyvaughan mussels
to fresh fish from Donegal. 🍴

Ennistimon: *The Archway Bar*
Main St. **Road map** B4.
【 065 71080.
This imposing old pub, situated on
the main street, has several homely
bars and a terrace overlooking
the trout-rich river, waterfall and
stone-arched bridge. On summer
evenings, sessions of spontaneous
traditional music often take place.
The adjoining restaurant serves
such filling dishes as stew, pasta
and chicken. 🍴 🍴 🎵

Killaloe: *Goosers*
Ballina. **Road map** C4.
【 061 376791.
This delightfully picturesque waterfront pub on the Ballina side of
the river has a thatched roof, traditional interior and a welcoming
atmosphere. Noted for its cuisine,
Goosers serves fairly pricey seafood
in the restaurant and satisfying
"pub grub" in the rustic bar. 🍴 🍴

Limerick: *The Locke*
3 George's Quay. **Road map** B4.
【 061 413733.
Set on a quay on the Shannon,
this is a typical black-and-white
pub. In summer, it is a favourite
port of call for riverside strollers.
In winter, blazing fires and snugs
make it a cosy spot. There's live
traditional music on Tuesday and
Sunday nights, and bar snacks are
served all day. 🍴 🎵

Limerick: *Nancy Blake's*
Upper Denmark St. **Road map** B4.
【 061 416443.
As Limerick's best-known bar,
Nancy Blake's has much to offer
in the way of good "crack" and
traditional music. If you prefer
rhythm and blues, try the adjoining
Outback Bar. The cosy main bar
serves soup and sandwiches at
lunch time. Music is played from
Sunday to Wednesday. 🍴 🎵

THE WEST OF IRELAND

Aran Islands: *Joe Watty's Pub*
Kilronan, Inishmore. **Road map** B4.
【 099 61155.
Set along the road between
Kilronan and Kilmurvy Bay, this
island pub is noted for its informality and huge, hearty portions
of food. Cyclists and hikers
appreciate the lamb stews, soups,
sandwiches and stout. 🍴 🎵

Clarinbridge: *Moran's Oyster
Cottage*
The Weir, Kilcolgan. **Road map** B4.
【 091 796113.
Set in a thatched cottage, this bar
was a regular port of call for crews
from passing "hookers" (traditional
ships). Nowadays, you can sample
all kinds of seafood here, though
Moran's is best known as an oyster
bar – the owner holds the local
speed record for shelling oysters.
You can watch fishermen at work
from the terrace tables. 🍴 🍴

Clarinbridge: *Paddy Burke's
Oyster Inn*
Road map B4. 【 091 796226.
Founded in 1835, this authentic
thatched pub has leaded window-
panes and a charming beamed
interior. Apart from the renowned
Clarinbridge oysters and buffet
lunches, gourmet menus are also
on offer some evenings. 🍴

Clifden: *EJ Kings*
The Square. **Road map** A3.
【 095 21330.
This spacious, bustling pub is
situated on several floors, with the
ground floor the most appealing.
Seafood platters or varied pub fare
can be enjoyed by the peat fire.
In summer, live music is often on
offer, especially folk and ballads.
The staff, mainly students, are
exceptionally friendly. 🍴 🍴 🎵

Galway: *Cooke's Thatch Bar*
Cooke's Corner, 2 Newcastle Rd.
Road map B4. 【 091 521749.
Situated on the outskirts of Galway,
this traditional thatched inn has
been in the same family for six
generations and is renowned for
its friendliness. Bar food is available, with over 20 wines on sale
as well as beer and spirits. There
is a beer garden and barbecue,
and customers can use the piano
if the spirit moves them. 🍴

Galway: *The King's Head*
15 High St. **Road map** B4.
【 091 566630.
Founded in 1649, this historic pub
is adorned with a bow-fronted
façade. The homely interior

---

contains authentic 17th-century
fireplaces. Simple lunch snacks
are served in the main bar. In the
back bar, live theatre at lunch
time, jazz on Sunday lunch times,
and various live bands playing in
the evenings attract a youthful
crowd. 🍴 🎵

Galway: *O'Flaherty's*
Great Southern Hotel, 15 Eyre Sq.
Road map B4. 【 091 564041.
This solid cellar bar began as wine
cellars but now offers cosy snugs
and railway memorabilia. The
popular pub provides a contrast to
the more sophisticated hotel
cocktail bar on the floor above.
A carvery lunch is on offer daily
in the bar, while at weekends live
music sessions (from traditional
music to jazz) draw large audiences
of locals and visitors. 🍴 🎵

Galway: *The Quays*
11 Quay St. **Road map** B4.
【 091 568347.
This cavernous pub is the
highlight of a Galway pub crawl.
Set in an old stone mansion in
Galway's "Latin Quarter", the
sprawling pub is noted for its old-
world charm, choice of bars and
variety of live music. The quaint
front bar retains its authenticity
while the rest of the pub has been
sensitively converted, using old
materials. The tasty and filling
cooked pub meals are popular
with locals. 🍴 🎵

Galway: *The Slate House*
Cross St Upper. **Road map** B4.
【 091 563377.
This barn-like city pub occupies
several storeys, including the shell
of a 16th-century convent on the
top floor. Busker Brown's, the pub
next door, is under the same management, and both are popular
with local students. There are jazz
sessions on Sunday mornings. 🍴

Galway: *Tí Neachtain*
Quay St. **Road map** B4.
【 091 568820.
Set in the "Latin Quarter", this
17th-century town house boasts a
distinctive oriel window. Inside, a
musty wood interior is home to
old-world snugs and friendly
service. Traditional music can
often be heard. Upstairs is one of
Galway's best restaurants, run by
a Swiss chef. 🍴 🎵

Maam Cross: *Keogh's Tavern*
Road map B3. 【 091 552306.
Next to a replica of the traditional
cottage used in the 1950s John
Wayne film *The Quiet Man*, this
modern pub is highly popular
with locals. Standard pub food is
available, as well as steaks bar-
becued over the turf fire. 🍴 🍴 🎵

Westport: *The Asgard Tavern*
The Quay. **Road map** B3.
(098 25319.
This old inn facing the pier and
Clew Bay is decorated with a
nautical theme. Both the main
downstairs back bar and the upstairs restaurant provide excellent
seafood and salads. The small
downstairs front bar is the most
atmospheric. ⬛ 🔳 🎵

Westport: *Matt Molloy's*
Bridge St. **Road map** B3.
(098 26655.
Founded by the flautist from the
traditional Irish folk band The
Chieftains, this deceptively
spacious pub is designed along
equally traditional lines. There is
live music in the back room every
evening, when the pub is packed.
No children after 9pm. 🎵

NORTHWEST IRELAND

Crolly: *Leo's Tavern*
Menaleck. **Road map** C1.
(075 48143.
Owned by the father of modern
folk musicians Clannad and of the
singer Enya, this friendly pub
attracts locals and tourists for its
sing-songs round the accordion,
and traditional music nights. 🎵

Dromahair: *Stanford's Inn*
Main St. **Road map** C2.
(071 64140.
Set in a picturesque village, this
traditional pub has been in the
same family for generations. The
tiny, quaint Biddy's Bar remains
unchanged, adorned with family
portraits and old grocery jars. The
main bar contains mellow brick-
work and flagstones from a ruined
castle, the rustic effect reinforced
by tweed lampshades. Delicious
food is on offer all day, and in
summer there are often impromptu
evening music sessions. 🔳 🎵

Rossnowlagh: *Smugglers'
Creek Inn*
Road map C2. **(** 072 52366.
On a clifftop overlooking Donegal
Bay, this pub is popular with surfers
and other water sports enthusiasts.
There is traditional music at
weekends and the beer garden
offers panoramic views. ⬛ 🔳 🎵

Sligo: *Beezie's*
Tobbergal Lane. **Road map** C2.
(071 45030.
The pub is dedicated to Beezie
Gallagher, a hospitable and much-
loved Sligo character who regularly
rowed from her home on Cottage
Island to Sligo until her death in
1951. A Victorian mood is recreated
by the old-fashioned stained glass,
skylights and fireplaces.

Sligo: *Hargadon's*
4–5 O'Connell St. **Road map** C2.
(071 70933.
A scruffy, rather ramshackle
exterior reveals the most traditional pub in town. The timeless
atmosphere is enhanced by the
old-fashioned stove, uneven floors
and wooden grocery drawers.
The pub is lined with cosy snugs,
all individually designed. During
the summer, dinner is served in
the beer garden. ⬛ 🔳

THE MIDLANDS

Abbeyleix: *Morrissey's*
Main St. **Road map** C4.
(0502 31233.
If driving through County Laois, it
is worth stopping at this genuinely
traditional pub. The 18th-century
inn was remodelled in the Victorian
era and has stayed the same ever
since. The grocery section survives
while the plain but unpretentious
bar serves simple bar snacks.

Carlingford: *PJ O'Hare's
Anchor Bar*
Tholsel St. **Road map** D3.
(042 73106.
Known locally as PJ's, this atmospheric pub and grocery store is
popular with sailors and locals alike.
A friendly and often eccentric welcome is matched by bar food such
as oysters and sandwiches. 🔳 🎵

Kilbeggan: *Locke's Distillery
Museum*
Mullingar. **Road map** C3.
(0506 32307.
As well as being the oldest licensed
pot still distillery in the world
(established in 1757), this historic
complex has a tiny whiskey bar –
the ideal place to sample a few
brands of whiskey before buying
(see p241). The adjoining restaurant
is closed in the evening. ⬛

Portlaoise: *Tracey's Pub and
Restaurant*
The Heath, Dublin Rd. **Road map** C4.
(0502 46539.
This charming thatched cottage
pub and restaurant is 5 km (3 miles)
outside of the town, but is well
worth the drive. It is the oldest
family-run pub in these parts, and
there is a good range of pub grub
(roasts, fish, salads) as well as
prime steak at amazingly
reasonable prices. ⬛ 🔳

NORTHERN IRELAND

Bangor: *Jenny Watt's*
41 High St. **Road map** E2.
(01247 460682.
Likeable and very popular, this bar
with Victoriana trimmings is found
in the centre of town. The walls

are adorned with local photos and
memorabilia. There's live jazz at
Sunday lunch times, and folk
music on Tuesday nights. Bar
food is served until 9:30pm, and
there's a beer garden. 🔳 🎵

Belfast: *Crown Liquor Saloon*
46 Great Victoria St. **Road map** D2.
(01232 249476.
This Victorian gin palace ranks as
one of the most gorgeous bars in
Ireland *(see p269)*. Lunch includes
several local specialities including
Strangford Lough oysters which
are almost too good to believe.
The recently renovated Robinson's
pub next door is particularly lively
in the evening. ⬛

Belfast: *Lavery's Gin Palace*
12–14 Bradbury Place. **Road map** D2.
(01232 328205.
Yet another of Belfast's fine old
gin palaces. This one regularly
has discos in the evenings and is
particularly popular with students
from Queen's University.

Belfast: *White's Tavern*
Winecellar Entry. **Road map** D2.
(01232 243080.
Just one of several daylight-free
pubs tucked away in the Entries
(see p269) sector of Belfast city
centre, that are best at lunch time
when decent, reasonably priced
pub food is served. White's lays
claim to be the oldest bar in the
city. Other pubs in this series of
alleys that are worth a look include
the Morning Star and the Globe. 🎵

Bushmills: *Bushmills Inn*
25 Main St. **Road map** D1.
(01265 732339.
Set in an old coaching inn, this
cosy bar is lit by gaslights. There
is also an excellent restaurant on
the premises, with patio tables for
summer dining. ⬛ 🔳

Enniskillen: *Blake's of the
Hollow*
6 Church St. **Road map** C2.
(01365 322143.
One of a number of popular town-
centre pubs, Blake's dates back to
Victorian days and has many of its
original fittings to prove it.

Hillsborough: *Plough Inn*
The Square. **Road map** D2.
(01846 682985.
Dating back to the 1750s, this
quintessential village pub has
wooden ceiling beams and a
selection of crockery, china and
other ornaments on the walls.
There's a bistro upstairs open
during the day, serving oysters,
and a good beer garden. The
Hillside, just down the main street,
is also worth a visit. ⬛ 🔳

SHOPPING IN IRELAND

IRELAND OFFERS a wide range of handmade goods, usually regionally based and highly individual. Its most renowned products include chunky Aran sweaters, Waterford crystal, demure Irish linen, hand-loomed Donegal tweed and tasty farmhouse cheeses. The thriving crafts industry is based on traditional products with an innovative twist. Typical of contemporary Irish crafts are good design, quality craftsmanship and a range spanning Celtic brooches and bone china, knitwear and designer fashion, carved bogwood and books of Irish poetry. Kitsch souvenirs also abound, from leprechauns and shamrock emblems to Guinness tankards and garish religious memorabilia. In the directory on page 325, a map reference is given for each address. Dublin references are to the map on pages 110–11; road map references are to the towns and cities shown on the inside back cover.

Linen shirt and tweed waistcoat

Fruit and vegetable market in Moore Street, Dublin

WHERE TO SHOP

THE CHOICE of places to shop in Ireland ranges from tiny workshops to large factory outlets, from elegant boutiques to high-street chain stores. Bargains can often be had at bric-a-brac shops and local markets, although the banter is sometimes the best thing on offer. This guide lists market days for every town featured. For last-minute purchases of traditional Irish goods and foods, try the airport duty-free shops.

SHOPPING IN DUBLIN

IN DUBLIN there are two major shopping quarters: the more plebeian north side of the Liffey, centred on O'Connell and Henry Streets, and the more prestigious south side, around Grafton and Nassau Streets. The Temple Bar area contains a number of trendy craft shops. The two main markets are Mother Redcap's indoor flea market in Christchurch at weekends, and the fruit and vegetable market in Moore Street from Monday to Saturday. Dublin's largest shopping centre is **St Stephen's Green Shopping Centre,** full of clothes and craft shops. Near chic Grafton Street is the Powerscourt Townhouse Shopping Centre *(see p76),* encased by a Georgian shell. Traditional department stores in the city include **Brown Thomas** and **Clery's**.

WHEN TO SHOP

MOST SHOPS are open from Monday to Saturday, 9am to 5:30 or 6pm. In shopping centres and large towns, shops tend to have at least one late-night opening, usually Thursday or Friday (Thursday in Dublin). In tourist areas, craft shops are generally open on Sundays too. Shops are closed at Easter and Christmas and on St Patrick's Day but are open on most other public holidays. In Killarney, Ireland's tourist capital, most shops are open until 10pm in summer.

HOW TO PAY

MAJOR CREDIT CARDS are generally accepted in department stores and larger retail outlets, but smaller shops prefer cash. Most traveller's cheques are accepted in major stores with a passport as identification. Eurocheques are slightly less acceptable in shops but can be cashed at certain banks *(see p347).*

SALES TAX AND REFUNDS

MOST PURCHASES are subject to VAT (sales tax) at 21 per cent, a sum included in the sales price. However, visitors from outside the European Union (EU) can reclaim VAT prior to departure. If you are shipping goods overseas, refunds can be claimed at the point of purchase. If taking your goods with you, look for the CashBack logo in shops, fill in the special voucher, then visit CashBack offices at Dublin or Shannon Airport.

A traditional fiddle maker in his workshop in Dingle

Colourful bric-a-brac shop in Kilkenny

BOOKS

READING is a national passion so bookshops are generally good. In larger shops expect solid sections on Irish archaeology and architecture, folklore, history, politics and cuisine. **Eason and Son** is one of the biggest bookshops in Dublin with a wide range of Irish literature and national and international newspapers; seek out the smaller, "Irish interest" shops too. In Galway, **Kennys Bookshop and Art Gallery** is full of both new and second-hand Irish books.

MUSIC

TRADITIONAL MUSICAL instruments (see pp22–3) are made in many regions, especially County Clare, known as "the singing county". Handmade harps are a speciality in Mayo and Dublin. In Dublin, several shops sell musical instruments, such as handcrafted bodhráns (traditional goatskin hand-held drums) and uillean pipes (bagpipes). **Waltons** sells traditional instruments and sheet music, while **Claddagh Records** sells Irish folk and traditional music.

CRAFTS

CRAFTS are a flourishing way of life in rural Ireland. The **Crafts Council of Ireland**, with branches in Dublin and Kilkenny, recommends good small-scale outlets, and tourist offices provide lists of local workshops, where you can often watch the production process. Many craft shops, such as the **Kilkenny Design Centre** and **Bricín**, and especially those at large tourist sights, sell good examples of several different crafts. Some regions are traditionally associated with specific crafts. In Cork and Kerry there is an abundance of workshops; the *Guide to Craft Outlets* is available from local tourist offices. Distinctive products from this area are traditional tiles based on designs found in Kilkenny Cathedral and nearby medieval abbeys. Further west, Connemara marble, green mottled stone, is made into "worry stones", small charms like worry beads. Also made in Connemara, particularly Clifden, are wall hangings, hand-knits and woollen rugs.

Kylemore Abbey teapot

Other crafts in Ireland include metalwork, leatherwork and carpentry. Local woods are used for ash or beech furniture, blackthorn walking sticks and sculptures made of 1,000-year-old bogwood.

CERAMICS AND CHINA

ESTABLISHED in 19th-century Ulster, the Belleek Pottery (see p261) produces creamy china with a lustrous sheen and subtle decorative motifs, including shamrocks and flowers. **Royal Tara China**, in Galway, is Ireland's leading fine bone china manufacturer, with designs incorporating Celtic themes. Also in County Galway, Kylemore Abbey produces handpainted pottery (see p200). **Louis Mulcahy's Pottery** in Ballyferriter is noted for its fine decorative glazes, while **Nicholas Mosse Pottery** in Bennettsbridge, County Kilkenny, is well known for its colourful handpainted designs. Enniscorthy in County Wexford is another centre for ceramics.

CRYSTAL AND GLASSWARE

IN THE WAKE of Waterford Crystal (see p139), the brand leader, come countless followers. The price depends on reputation, the quantity of lead used in the glass and the labour-intensiveness of the design. In the North, **Tyrone Crystal** is rated almost as highly as Waterford but is less expensive. Like Waterford, the factory runs an illuminating tour. **Tipperary Crystal** offers a number of lines, including trophies, lamps and gifts. **Galway Irish Crystal** is another elegant brand.

In County Kilkenny, the famous Jerpoint Abbey inspires local designs by **Jerpoint Glass**. Decorated with simple yet stylish motifs, the small vases, candlesticks, jugs and bowls make pleasing gifts. Most stores will pack and send glassware overseas for you.

Pottery display in Kilkenny Design Centre

Sign for the linen department at Dublin's Brown Thomas store

JEWELLERY

IN ITS GOLDEN AGE, Celtic metalwork was the pride of Ireland (see pp30–33). Many contemporary craftspeople are still inspired by traditional designs on Celtic chalices and ornaments. Hand-crafted or factory-made silver, gold, enamel and ceramic jewellery is produced all over Ireland in a huge variety of designs. The Claddagh ring from Galway is the most famous – the lovers' symbol of two hands cradling a crowned heart. In Dublin's Powerscourt Townhouse Shopping Centre (see p76), shops display handmade and antique jewellery. Ceramic Design, a studio that produces Celtic-influenced brooches, is based here. Gold- and silversmiths can also be seen at work in the shopping centre.

KNITWEAR AND TWEED

ARAN SWEATERS are sold all over Ireland, but particularly in County Galway and on the Aran Islands themselves. One of Ireland's best

buys, these oiled, off-white sweaters used to be handed down through generations of Aran fishermen. Legend has it that each family used its own motifs so that if a fisherman was lost at sea and his body unidentifiable, his family could recognize him by his sweater.

Given the Irish experience of wet weather, warm and rain-resistant clothes are generally of good quality, from waxed jackets and duffel coats to sheepskin jackets. Knitwear is on sale all over Ireland, with **Avoca Handweavers** and **Blarney Woollen Mills** the best-known outlets. Good buys include embroidered sweaters and waistcoats and hand-woven shawls and scarves.

Donegal tweed is a byword for quality, noted for its texture, tension and subtle colours (originally produced by dyes made from lichens, local plants and minerals). Tweed caps, hats, scarves, ties, jackets and suits are sold in outlets such as **Magee and Co** in Donegal.

Second-hand furniture shop in Kenmare

LINEN

DAMASK LINEN was brought to Armagh by Huguenot refugees fleeing French persecution. As a result, Belfast became the world linen capital. Ulster is still the place for linen, with sheets and double-damask table linen on sale in Belfast – at **Smyth's Irish**

Linen, for example – and in other towns. There are also outlets in the Republic. Hand-embroidered linen is made in County Donegal. Linen-making can be seen at Wellbrook Beetling Mill (see p260).

FASHION

INSPIRED by a predominantly young population, Ireland is fast acquiring a name for fashion. Conservatively cut tweed and linen suits continue to be models of classic good taste, while younger designers are increasingly experimental, using bold lines and mixing traditional fabrics.

A-Wear is a quality boutique that has branches in major cities. Here, and in the Design Centre in Powerscourt Townhouse Shopping Centre in Dublin, are clothes by the best Irish designers including John Rocha, Paul Costelloe, Louise Kennedy, Quin and Donnelly and Mariad Whisker. Clothing and shoe sizes are identical to British fittings.

FOOD AND DRINK

SMOKED SALMON, home-cured bacon, farmhouse cheeses, soda bread, preserves and handmade chocolates make perfect last-minute gifts. Several shops will package and send Irish salmon overseas.

Bewley's teas and coffees are sold in **Bewley's Oriental Café** and Bewley shops all over Ireland. Guinness travels less well and is best drunk in Ireland. Irish whiskey is hard to beat as a gift or souvenir. Apart from the cheaper Power and Paddy brands, the big names are Bushmills (see p258) and Jameson (see p171). Rich Irish liqueurs include Irish Mist and Baileys Irish Cream.

Selection of hand-knitted sweaters at a craft shop in Dingle

DIRECTORY

DEPARTMENT STORES AND SHOPPING CENTRES

Brown Thomas
88–95 Grafton St, Dublin 2.
Dublin map D4.
[01 6795666.

Clery's
18–27 O'Connell St
Lower, Dublin 1.
Dublin map D2.
[01 8786000.

St Stephen's Green Shopping Centre
St Stephen's Green West,
Dublin 2. **Dublin map** D4.

BOOKS

Eason and Son
80 Abbey St Middle,
Dublin 1. **Dublin map** D2.
[01 8733811.

Fred Hanna
27–29 Nassau St, Dublin 2.
Dublin map E4.
[01 6771255.

Kennys Bookshop and Art Gallery
High St, Galway.
Road map B4.
[091 562739.

Waterstone's
7 Dawson St, Dublin 2.
Dublin map D4.
[01 6791415.

MUSIC

Claddagh Records
2 Cecilia St, Temple Bar,
Dublin 2. **Dublin map** C3.
[01 6770262.

J McNeill
140 Capel St, Dublin 1.
Dublin map C2.
[01 8722159.

Waltons
2–5 Frederick St North,
Dublin 1.
[01 8747805.

CRAFTS

Bricín
26 High Street, Killarney,
Co Kerry. **Road map** B5.
[064 34902.

Connemara Marble Factory
Moycullen, Co Galway.
Road map B4.
[091 555102.

Crafts Council of Ireland
Powerscourt Townhouse
Shopping Centre, William
St South, Dublin 2.
Dublin map D4.
[01 6797368.
Crescent Workshop,
Castle Yard, Kilkenny.
Road map C4.
[056 61804.

Craftsworks Gallery
13 Linenhall St, Belfast.
Road map D2.
[01232 326087.

Doolin Crafts Gallery
Ballyvoe, Doolin, Co Clare.
Road map B4.
[065 74309.

Kilkenny Design Centre
Castle Yard, Kilkenny.
Road map C4.
[056 22118.

The Kilkenny Shop
6 Nassau St, Dublin 2.
Dublin map E4.
[01 6777066.

Standuin
Spiddal, Co Galway.
Road map B4.
[091 553357.

Tower Enterprise Centre
Pearse St, Dublin 2.
[01 6775655.

CERAMICS AND CHINA

Cré Irish Porcelain
Wellpark, Galway.
Road map B4.
[091 752786.

Hogg's
10 Donegal Sq West,
Belfast. **Road map** D2.
[01232 243898.

Louis Mulcahy's Pottery
Clogher, Ballyferriter, Tralee,
Co Kerry.
Road map A5.
[066 56229.

Nicholas Mosse Pottery
Bennettsbridge, Co
Kilkenny. **Road map** D5.
[056 27105.

Royal Tara China
Tara Hall, Mervue, Galway.
Road map B4.
[091 751301.

Treasure Chest
31-33 William St, Galway.
Road map B4.
[091 567237.

CRYSTAL AND GLASSWARE

Galway Irish Crystal
Merlin Park, Galway.
Road map B4.
[091 757311.

Jerpoint Glass
Stoneyford, Co Kilkenny.
Road map D5.
[056 24350.

Sligo Crystal
Grange, Co Sligo.
Road map C2.
[071 63251.

Tipperary Crystal
Ballynoran, Carrick-on-
Suir, Co Tipperary.
Road map C5.
[051 641188.

Tyrone Crystal
Killybrackey, Coal Island Rd,
Dungannon, Co Tyrone.
Road map D2.
[01868 725335.

Waterford Crystal
Kilbarry, Waterford.
Road map D5.
[051 73311.

JEWELLERY

Brian de Staic
18 High St, Killarney,
Co Kerry. **Road map** B5.
[064 33822.

Hilser Brothers
Grand Parade, Cork.
Road map C5.
[021 270382.

Saller's Jewellers
Williamsgate St, Galway.
Road map B4.
[091 561226.

KNITWEAR AND TWEED

Avoca Handweavers
Kilmacanogue, Bray, Co
Wicklow. **Road map** D4.
[01 2867466.

Blarney Woollen Mills
Blarney, Co Cork.
Road map B5.
[021 385280.

Exclusively Irish
14–15 O'Connell St Upper,
Dublin 1. **Dublin map** D2.
[01 8746064.

Magee and Co
The Diamond, Donegal.
Road map C2.
[073 21100.

Quills Woollen Market
1 High St, Killarney, Co
Kerry. **Road map** B5.
[064 32277.

Studio Donegal
Kilcar, Co Donegal.
Road map B2.
[073 38194.

LINEN

Forgotten Cotton
Savoy Centre, St Patrick's
St, Cork.
Road map C5.
[021 276098.

Smyth's Irish Linen
65 Royal Ave, Belfast.
Road map D2.
[01232 242232.

FASHION

A-Wear
26 Grafton St, Dublin 2.
Dublin map D4.
[01 6717200.

FOOD AND DRINK

Bewley's Oriental Café
78 Grafton St, Dublin 2.
Dublin map D4.
[01 6776761.

Butler's Irish Hand-made Chocolates
51 Grafton St, Dublin 2.
Dublin map D4.
[01 6710599.

What to Buy in Ireland

St Brigid's cross

Hundreds of gift and craft shops scattered throughout Ireland make it easy to find Irish specialities to suit all budgets. The best buys include linen, tweeds and crystal from factory shops which invariably offer an extensive choice of good quality products. Local crafts make unique souvenirs, from hand-made jewellery and ceramics to traditional musical instruments. Religious artifacts are also widely available. Irish food and drink are evocative reminders of your trip.

Traditional hand-held drum (*bodhrán*) and beater

Connemara marble "worry stone"

Traditional Claddagh ring

Enamel brooch

Modern jewellery and metalwork *draw on a long and varied tradition. Craftspeople continue to base their designs on sources such as the* Book of Kells *(see p62) and Celtic myths. Local plants and wildlife are also an inspiration. County Galway produces Claddagh rings – traditional betrothal rings – in gold and silver as well as "worry stones".*

Fuchsia earring from Dingle

Celtic-design enamel brooch

Bronzed resin Celtic figurine

Donegal tweed jacket and waistcoat

Tweed skirt and jacket

Clothing *made in Ireland is usually of excellent quality. Tweed-making still flourishes in Donegal where tweed can be bought ready-made as clothing or hats or as lengths of cloth. Knitwear is widely available all over the country in large factory outlets and local craft shops. The many hand-knitted items on sale, including Aran jumpers, are not cheap but should give years of wear.*

Tweed cap

Aran jumper

Tweed fisherman's hat

Irish linen is world-famous and the range unparalleled. There is a huge choice of table and bed linen, including extravagant bedspreads and crisp, formal tablecloths. On a smaller scale, tiny, intricately embroidered handkerchiefs make lovely gifts as do linen table napkins. Tea towels printed with colourful designs are widely available. You can also buy linen goods trimmed with fine lace, which is still hand-made in Ireland, mainly in Limerick and Kenmare.

Set of linen placemats and napkins

Fine linen handkerchiefs

Nicholas Mosse plate

Belleek teapot

Nicholas Mosse cup

Irish ceramics come in traditional and modern designs. You can buy anything from a full dinner service by established factories, such as Royal Tara China or the Belleek Pottery, to a one-off contemporary piece from a local potter's studio.

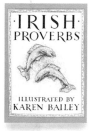

·IRISH· PROVERBS

ILLUSTRATED BY KAREN BAILEY

Book of Irish Proverbs

Irish crystal, hand-blown and hand-cut, can be ordered or bought in many shops in Ireland. Visit the outlets of the principal manufacturers, such as Waterford Crystal, Tyrone Crystal and Jerpoint Glass, to see the full range – from glasses and decanters to elaborate chandeliers.

Books and stationery are often beautifully illustrated. Museums and bookshops stock a wide range.

Celtic-design cards

Waterford crystal tumbler and decanter

Food and drink will keep the distinctive tastes of Ireland fresh long after you arrive home. Whiskey connoisseurs should visit the Old Bushmills Distillery (see p258) or the Jameson Heritage Centre (see p171) to sample their choice of whiskeys. Good regional food can be found at local shops all over Ireland. Try the dried seaweed, which is eaten raw or added to cooked dishes.

Jameson whiskey

Bushmills whiskey

Fruit cake made with Guinness

Jar of Irish marmalade

Packet of dried seaweed

ENTERTAINMENT IN IRELAND

IF THERE IS ONE SPHERE in which Ireland shines, it is entertainment. For details about entertainment in Dublin, see pages 102–7. Elsewhere in Ireland, nightclubs and concerts by international entertainers tend to be concentrated in large cities, but many other events including theatre, arts festivals, traditional music and dance, cultural holidays and even medi-

Morris Minor van advertising the Clonakilty Folk Club

eval banquets take place all over the country. Most towns and cities also have one or two cinemas showing the latest films on release. Not to be overlooked is the free entertainment (planned or spontaneous) provided by a night in a pub. For more active forms of entertainment, covered on pages 332–5, the list is even longer, from golf to pony trekking and cycling to scuba diving. Those who prefer their sports sitting down can go along as spectators to Ireland's famous horse race meetings, as well as Gaelic football, hurling, soccer and rugby matches. Best of all, a happy mix of these activities can easily be put together with almost any itinerary.

Ulster Symphony Orchestra at the Ulster Hall in Belfast

INFORMATION SOURCES

THE TOURIST BOARD for the Republic, **Bord Fáilte**, and the **Northern Ireland Tourist Board** both publish a yearly *Calendar of Events* that lists major fixtures around the country, and all the regional tourist offices have information about events in each locality. To supplement these listings, check regional newspapers and enquire locally to find on-the-spot entertainment.

BOOKING TICKETS

TICKETS can usually be bought at the door on the day or evening of most events. Advance booking is a must, however, for popular concerts and plays. Many cultural and arts festivals require tickets only for the key performances, but for internationally famous festivals, such as the Wexford Opera Festival, you will need to book well in advance through the festival office for all performances.

Credit-card bookings for major plays, concerts and other events around the country can be made by telephone through **Keith Prowse Travel (IRL) Ltd** and **HMV** in Dublin.

MAJOR VENUES

IN MANY IRISH CITIES, the main theatres host a huge variety of events. In Cork, the **Opera House** presents predominantly Irish plays during the summer months, with musical comedy, opera and ballet at other times of year. The city's **Everyman Palace Theatre** stages plays by local and visiting companies interspersed with concerts of both classical and popular music. Sligo's **Hawks Well Theatre** and Limerick's **Belltable Arts Centre** are venues for drama and concerts. In the centre of Belfast, the **Grand Opera House**, **Arts Theatre** and **Lyric Theatre** present a varied programme which includes Irish and international plays, experimental drama, pantomime and opera.

THEATRE

FROM INTERNATIONAL TOURS to amateur productions, there is excellent theatre to be seen in virtually every location in Ireland. In Galway, the **Druid Theatre** specializes in avant-garde plays, new Irish plays and Anglo-Irish classics, with frequent lunch-time and late-night performances, while Gaelic drama, Irish music, singing and dancing have all thrived at the **Taibhdhearc Theatre** since 1928. Waterford boasts its resident Red Kettle Theatre Company which performs at the **Garter Lane Theatre**, while the **Theatre Royal** brings amateur drama and musicals to the city.

Keep an eye out for small theatre groups performing in local halls around the country. Many of them are superb and they have spawned several of Ireland's leading actors.

Home of the Druid Theatre Company in Galway *(see p202)*

The Moscow Ballet at Belfast's Grand Opera House *(see p268)*

CLASSICAL MUSIC, OPERA AND DANCE

MAJOR VENUES for classical music include the **Crawford Art Gallery**, Opera House and Everyman Palace in Cork; the Theatre Royal in Waterford; the Hawks Well Theatre in Sligo; and the Belltable Arts Centre in Limerick. Belfast's **Ulster Hall** hosts concerts from rock bands to the Ulster Symphony Orchestra.

Opera lovers from around the world arrive in their thousands for the **Wexford Opera Festival** in October and November and the **Waterford Festival of Light Opera** in late September and early October. At Wexford, neglected operas are revived, while Waterford selects more mainstream operas and musicals. Elsewhere, opera is performed in Cork's Opera House and in Belfast's Grand Opera House.

Ireland has no resident ballet or avant-garde dance companies, but leading international companies perform occasionally at the major venues around the country.

ROCK, JAZZ AND COUNTRY

WHEN INTERNATIONAL rock and pop stars such as Prince tour in Ireland, concerts outside Dublin are held at large outdoor sites. **Semple Stadium** in County Tipperary and Slane Castle *(see p237)* in County Meath are popular venues. Tickets and information are available from HMV.

Musical pubs *(see pp318–21)* are your best bet for good rock and jazz performed by Irish groups. Check local tourist offices and newspapers for rock and jazz nights, which usually take place midweek, with country and traditional music at weekends. For some of Ireland's "big band" jazz music, keep an eye out for Waterford's Brass and Co who play at dances around the country. Jazz lovers have a field day at the **Cork Jazz Festival** in late October, when music pours from every pub and international jazz greats play in the city's theatres.

Pub scene at Feakle Traditional Music Weekend, County Clare

TRADITIONAL MUSIC AND DANCE

THE COUNTRY PUB has helped keep Irish music alive and provided the setting for the musical revival that began in the 1960s. Today, sessions of informal or impromptu music are still commonplace. In pubs, traditional music embraces ballads and rebel songs, as well as the older *sean-nos* – unaccompanied, understated stories, often sung in Irish.

Nights of Irish music and song are scheduled in many pubs, such as The Laurels and the Danny Mann in Killarney, the Yeats Tavern in Drumcliff, near Sligo, and An Phoenix and The Lobby in Cork. In Derry, the Gweedore Bar, Castle Bar and Dungloe Bar are among the cluster of musical pubs along Waterloo Street. Wherever you are, a query to the locals will send you off to the nearest musical pub. For more pub listings, see pages 318–21.

In Tralee, **Siamsa Tire**, the National Folk Theatre, stages marvellous folk drama incorporating traditional music, singing and dance. The Barn, in Bunratty Folk Park, is the setting for the **Shannon Ceili** – traditional music nights during the summer months.

Comhaltas Ceoltóirí Éireann, in Monkstown near Dublin, has branches around the country and organizes traditional music and dance nights all year. Traditional Irish dancing can be stylish step dancing or joyous set dancing. Visitors are usually encouraged to join in the fun.

The **Fleadh Cheoil** (national traditional music festival) is a weekend of music, dance, song and stage shows that spill over into colourful street entertainment. It takes place at the end of August in a different town each year. Earlier in August, the **Feakle Traditional Music Weekend** in County Clare is a more intimate celebration of traditional music, song and dance.

A large audience for open-air music at the Cork Jazz Festival

Knappogue banquet at Knappogue Castle, County Clare

Most famous are the medieval banquets – the one at Bunratty Castle *(see pp184–5)* was the first and is the liveliest, with year-round performances. From May to October, there is a glittering pageant at Knappogue Castle *(see p181),* and at Dunguaire Castle *(see p204)* there is a quieter, more intimate programme of music and poetry. From March until November, the highly enjoyable Killarney Manor Banquet, held at the stately manor on the Loreto road just south of Killarney, creates an early 19th-century atmosphere.

FESTIVALS

THE IRISH are experts at organizing festivals, staging a week of street entertainment, theatre, music and dance to celebrate almost everything under the sun *(see pp46–9).*

In mid-July the lively town of Galway is host to the **Galway Arts Festival**, one of the largest festivals in Ireland. Here you will find Irish and international theatre and music, street entertainment and events for children. Taking place over two weeks in late July and early August is the **Boyle Arts Festival**. The events here include art exhibitions, poetry and drama performances as well as classical, traditional, folk and jazz concerts. Creative workshops are run for both adults and children.

Kilkenny Arts Week in August, another major festival, features poetry, classical music concerts, films and a range of crafts. The **Cork Film Festival** takes place in the first week of October when international feature, documentary and short films are screened at venues all over the city. The **Belfast Festival at Queen's** is held for three weeks in mid- to late November. The lively and cosmopolitan programme includes a mixture of drama, ballet, comedy, cabaret, music and cinema. These take place over the Queen's University campus plus theatres and other venues throughout Belfast.

In May and June, the **County Wicklow Gardens Festival** entices gardening enthusiasts to wander around the county's most beautiful gardens. In mid-June, the **Music Festival in Great Irish Houses** opens the doors to many of Ireland's historic homes to which the public seldom has access, with classical music performed by top-rate musicians. Venues include Strokestown Park House *(see pp210–11),* Mount Stewart House *(see pp274–5)* and University College, Cork.

Kilkenny Arts Week street theatre

TRADITIONAL BANQUETS WITH ENTERTAINMENT

IRELAND'S BANQUETS have gained international fame and are great fun. Each of the banquets features costumed waiters and performers, as well as traditional food and drink of the chosen period.

CULTURAL HOLIDAYS

A HOLIDAY IN IRELAND focused on any one of the cultural aspects of Irish life is enriching as well as fun. Choose from a variety of cultural topics and study courses: Irish music and literature, great houses and gardens, Irish language and folklore, crafts and cookery.

One of the most fascinating possibilities is the exploration of Ireland's 5,000-year history as revealed in the many relics strewn across the landscape. The **Achill Archaeological Summer School** in County Mayo, for example, runs a course that includes the active excavation of ancient sites.

To learn the secret of Irish cooking, there is no better place than the **Ballymaloe School of Cookery** in County Cork; it is run by Darina Allen, Ireland's most famous cook.

For literature enthusiasts, the **Yeats International Summer School** studies the works of Yeats and his contemporaries, while **Listowel Writers' Week** brings together leading writers for lectures and workshops.

Folk dancers in traditional Irish costume

DIRECTORY

INFORMATION SOURCES

Bord Fáilte
Baggot St Bridge,
Dublin 2.
[01 6024000.

Northern Ireland Tourist Board
St Anne's Court, 59 North St, Belfast.
[01232 246609.

BOOKING TICKETS

Keith Prowse Travel (IRL) Ltd
10 St Stephen's Green,
Dublin 2.
[01 6795444.

Ticket Shop
Grafton House,
70 Grafton St, Dublin 2.
[01 4569569.

MAJOR VENUES

Arts Theatre
41 Botanic Ave, Belfast.
[01232 316900.

Belltable Arts Centre
69 O'Connell St, Limerick.
[061 319866.

Everyman Palace Theatre
MacCurtain St, Cork.
[021 501673.

Grand Opera House
Great Victoria St, Belfast.
[01232 240411.

Hawks Well Theatre
Temple St, Sligo.
[071 61526.

Lyric Theatre
55 Ridgeway St, Belfast.
[01232 381081.

Opera House
Emmet Place, Cork.
[021 270022.

THEATRE

Druid Theatre
Chapel Lane, Galway.
[091 568617.

Garter Lane Theatre
22A O'Connell St,
Waterford.
[051 77153.

Taibhdhearc Theatre
Middle St, Galway.
[091 562024.

Theatre Royal
The Mall, Waterford.
[051 74402.

CLASSICAL MUSIC, OPERA AND DANCE

Crawford Art Gallery
Emmet Place, Cork.
[021 273377.

Ulster Hall
Bedford St, Belfast.
[01232 323900.

Waterford Festival of Light Opera
60 Morrissons Ave,
Waterford.
[051 375437.

Wexford Opera Festival
Theatre Royal, High St,
Wexford.
[053 22144.

ROCK, JAZZ AND COUNTRY

Cork Jazz Festival
20 South Mall, Cork.
[021 270463.

Semple Stadium
Thurles, Co Tipperary.

TRADITIONAL MUSIC AND DANCE

Comhaltas Ceoltóirí Éireann
32 Belgrave Sq,
Monkstown, Co Dublin.
[01 2800295.

Feakle Traditional Music Weekend
Maghera, Caher, Co Clare.
[061 925125.

Fleadh Cheoil
32 Belgrave Sq,
Monkstown, Co Dublin.
[01 2800295.

Shannon Ceili
Bunratty Castle and Folk Park, Bunratty, Co Clare.
[061 360788.

Siamsa Tíre
National Folk Theatre, The Town Park, Tralee,
Co Kerry.
[066 23055.

FESTIVALS

Belfast Festival at Queen's
Festival House, 25 College Gardens, Belfast.
[01232 667687.

Boyle Arts Festival
Festival Office,
Great Meadow, Boyle,
Co Roscommon.
[079 63085.

Cork Film Festival
Hatfield House, Tobin St, Cork.
[021 271711.

County Wicklow Gardens Festival
St Manntan's House,
Kilmantin Hill, Wicklow.
[0404 66058.

Galway Arts Festival
7 Upper Dominic St,
Galway.
[091 583800.

Kilkenny Arts Week
Rose House, Parliament St, Kilkenny.
[056 63663.

Music Festival in Great Irish Houses
1st floor Blackrock
Post Office, Blackrock,
Co Dublin.
[01 2781528.

CULTURAL HOLIDAYS

Archaeology
Achill Archaeological Summer School
St O'Hara's Hill, Tullamore,
Co Offaly.
[0506 21627.

Belcoo Archaeology Summer School
Enterprise Centre,
Railway Rd, Belcoo,
Co Fermanagh.
[01365 386536.

Oideas Gael
Glencolumbkille,
Co Donegal.
[073 30248.

Cookery
Ballymaloe School of Cookery
Shanagarry, Midleton,
Co Cork.
[021 646785.

Crafts
Ardess Craft Centre
Ardess House, Kesh,
Co Fermanagh.
[01365 631267.

Great Houses and Gardens
Irish Heritage Properties
Hillsbrook, Dargle Village,
Bray, Co Wicklow.
[01 2862777.

National Trust
Rowallane House,
Saintfield, Ballynahinch,
Co Down.
[01238 510721.

Irish Language
Irish Conversation Courses
Oidhreacht Chorca
Dhuibhne, Ballyferriter,
Co Kerry.
[066 56100.

Literary
Goldsmith Summer School
Rathmore, Ballymahon,
Co Longford.
[0902 32374.

James Joyce Summer School
University College Dublin,
Belfield, Dublin 4.
[01 7068480.

Listowel Writers' Week
PO Box 147, Listowel,
Co Kerry.
[068 21074.

William Carleton Summer School
Leisure Services Dept,
Dungannon District
Council, Circular Rd,
Dungannon, Co Tyrone.
[018687 25311.

Yeats International Summer School
Yeats Society, Yeats
Memorial Building, Douglas
Hyde Bridge, Sligo.
[071 42693.

Music
South Sligo Summer School of Traditional Music, Song and Dance
Tubbercurry, Co Sligo.
[071 85010.

Willie Clancy Summer School
Miltown Malbay, Co Clare.
[065 84148.

Sports and Outdoor Activities

EVEN IN THE LARGEST CITIES, the countryside is never far away, and it beckons to all lovers of the outdoors. Topping the list of spectator sports is Ireland's famous horse racing, while hurling, Gaelic football and soccer also make for exciting viewing. Those who want to do more than just watch can choose between fishing, golf, horse riding, cruising, cycling, walking and water sports. Entire holidays can be based around any of these activities. In addition to the contacts on page 335, Bord Fáilte in the Republic, the Northern Ireland Tourist Board and all local tourist offices have information on spectator and participant sports. For details of the main events in Ireland's sporting calendar, see pages 26–7.

Horse riding in Killarney

SPECTATOR SPORTS

THE IRISH PASSION for horse racing is legendary. Major courses include the Curragh *(see p121)*, where the Irish Derby is held, Fairyhouse, the venue for Ireland's Grand National, and Leopardstown. Apart from these Dublin-based courses, there are smaller ones al over the Republic (and two in Northern Ireland), where the atmosphere is exciting and informal. Galway Race Week in late July is a great social event. A racing calendar that covers the whole of Ireland, available from the **Irish Horse Racing Authority**, enables you to choose from both National Hunt and flat race meets, which are scheduled for over 230 days of the year.

Sign outside a fishing tackle shop in Donegal

In Dublin, **Croke Park** hosts Gaelic football and hurling matches *(see pp26–7)*, while international rugby and soccer matches are held at Lansdowne Road Stadium. Ticket details for soccer internationals are available from the **Football Association of Ireland**.

For keen golfers, the annual highlight is the Irish Open Golf Championship in July. The venue varies from year to year. For tickets and the latest information, contact the **Irish Open Office**.

FISHING

THE CLAIM that Ireland is a paradise for anglers is no exaggeration. Coarse, game and sea fishing all enjoy widespread popularity. The lakes and rivers are home to bream, pike, perch

Fishing in the canal at Robertstown, County Kildare *(see p120)*

and roach. The **Kingfisher Angling Centre**, near the River Bann, is one of many centres to provide accommodation for anglers on holiday. Coastal rivers yield the famous Irish salmon, and, among other game fish, sea trout and brown trout also offer anglers a real challenge.

Flounder, whiting, mullet, bass and coalfish tempt the sea angler; deep-sea excursions chase abundant supplies of dogfish, shark, skate and ling. You can organize sea-angling trips from many different places – the Cork and Kerry coastline being a particularly popular starting point.

Maps and information on fishing locations are provided by the **Central Fisheries Board** and Bord Fáilte in the Republic, and the **Department of Agriculture (Fisheries)** and Northern Ireland Tourist Board. Check permit requirements before you go.

GOLF

OF THE 300 or more golf courses in the whole of Ireland, over 50 are championship class, and many are by spectacular stretches of coast. Mount Juliet's world-class, Jack Nicklaus-designed course in County Kilkenny has won international acclaim, and many others are also kept in top condition. Northern Ireland's best-known courses are Royal Portrush and Royal

Golfers at Portstewart in Northern Ireland *(see p252)*

Walking in the Gap of Dunloe, Killarney *(see p155)*

County Down. The **Golfing Union of Ireland** and the tourist boards have information on courses, conditions and green fees throughout the Republic and Northern Ireland. Some have clubs for hire, but it is better to bring your own.

Golfing Ireland organizes tailor-made golfing holidays for individuals and groups in the Republic, while **Golfers Abroad** does the same for Northern Ireland.

CYCLING

Cycling is one of Ireland's most popular sports. There is an exhilarating range of countryside to be explored and the comparatively traffic-free roads make cycling a pleasure. Limerick, Waterford and Galway make good bases for cycling holidays. Several organizations, such as **Celtic Cycling**, will plan an itinerary and book accommodation.

If you bring your own bike, you can transport it around the country fairly cheaply by train or bus.

Alternatively, try the many **Raleigh Rent-a-Bike** dealers with depots in the Republic and Northern Ireland, or the **Bike Store**, based in Dublin and with branches in several cities in the Republic.

HORSE RIDING AND PONY TREKKING

The Irish are rightly proud of their fine horses. Many riding centres, both residential and non-residential, offer trail riding and trekking along woodland trails, deserted beaches, country lanes and mountain routes. Dingle, Donegal, Connemara, and Killarney are all renowned areas for trail riding. There are two types of trail riding – post-to-post and based. Post-to-post trails follow a series of routes with accommodation in a different place each night. Based trail rides follow different routes in one area and you stay at the same

place for the whole holiday. Also on offer at many riding centres are lessons for everyone from beginners to more advanced riders to those who want to learn show jumping.

Bord Fáilte and the Northern Ireland Tourist Board publish details of riding centres and courses. **Equestrian Holidays Ireland** organizes holidays for riders of various abilities.

WALKING AND MOUNTAINEERING

A walking holiday puts you in the very middle of the glorious Irish landscape. The network of waymarked trails all over the country takes you to some of the loveliest areas. Information on long-distance walks is available from Bord Fáilte and the Northern Ireland Tourist Board. Routes include the Wicklow Way *(see p131)*, Dingle Way, Munster Way, Kerry Way and Barrow Towpath. All may be split into shorter sections for less experienced walkers or those short of time. The 800-km (500-mile) Ulster Way encircles Northern Ireland passing through a wide range of locations from the spectacular scenery around the Giant's Causeway *(see pp254–5)* to the peaks of the Mountains of Mourne *(see pp276–7)*. **Irish Ways** offers walking holidays in the Republic. For activities in Northern Ireland, call the **Ulster Federation of Rambling Clubs**.

Sign for the Ulster Way, the trail around Northern Ireland

Hill walking, rock climbing and mountaineering holidays are also available. For information, contact the **Association for Adventure Sports**. Always be sure to go well-equipped for the notoriously changeable Irish weather.

Cycling through the Muckross House estate near Killarney *(see p151)*

Surfing at Bundoran *(see p222)*

WATER SPORTS

WITH A COASTLINE of over 4,800 km (3,000 miles), small wonder that water sports are among Ireland's favourite recreational activities. Surfing, windsurfing, water-skiing, scuba diving and canoeing are the most popular, and there are facilities for all of these right around the coastline.

Conditions in Donegal are the best in Ireland for surfing, but many other coastal locations offer good conditions. The **Irish Surfing Association** will put you in touch with surf clubs all over the Republic and Northern Ireland. Windsurfing centres are mainly found near Dublin, Cork and Westport in County Galway.

There is a wide range of diving conditions off the coast of Ireland – visibility is particularly good on the west coast. The **Irish Underwater Council** will put you in touch with courses and facilities. **DV Diving** organizes scuba diving courses and offers accommodation near Belfast Lough and the Irish Sea where there are a number of historic wrecks to be explored.

Inland, Lower Lough Erne *(see pp262–3)* and Killaloe by Lough Derg *(see p182)* are popular holiday centres. The **Lakeland Canoe Centre**, between Upper and Lower Lough Erne, gives canoeing courses and organizes canoeing holidays (with overnight camping), including one down

the Shannon-Erne Waterway *(see p227)*. **Irish Canoeing Holidays** hires out canoeing equipment, with or without a guide, for trips on the Shannon and Barrow rivers.

CRUISING AND SAILING

A TRANQUIL CRUISING holiday is an ideal alternative to the stress and strain of driving, and Ireland's 14,500 km (9,000 miles) of rivers and some 800 lakes offer a huge variety of conditions for those who want a waterborne holiday. Stopping over at waterside towns and villages puts you in touch with the Irish on their home ground. Whether you opt for Lough Derg or elsewhere on the Shannon *(see p177)*, or the Grand Canal *(see p99)* from Dublin to the Shannon, a unique view of the Irish countryside opens up all along the way.

Running between Carrick-on-Shannon in County Leitrim and Upper Lough Erne in Fermanagh is the **Shannon-Erne Waterway** *(see p227)*, a disused canal reopened in 1993. From here it is simple to continue through Upper and Lower Lough Erne to Belleek *(see p262)*. **Emerald Star** has a fleet of cruisers for use on the waterway.

A popular sailing area is between Cork and the Dingle Peninsula. The **International Sailing Centre**, near Cork, offers tuition. In Carrickfergus the **Ulster Cruising School** provides lessons at all levels; more experienced sailors can charter a yacht and sail up to the western coast of Scotland.

HUNTING AND SHOOTING

IRELAND'S HUNTING season runs from October to March, and although fox-hunting predominates, stag and hare hunts also take place. Clay-pigeon (year-round) and pheasant (from November to January) shooting are increasing in popularity. **Mount Juliet Estate**, in County Kilkenny, offers both with guns and cartridges to hire. For details, contact the **Irish Master of Foxhounds Association** in the Republic and, in Northern Ireland, the **British Field Sports Society**.

Yachting off Rosslare *(see p143)*

SPORTS FOR THE DISABLED

SPORTS ENTHUSIASTS with a disability can obtain details of facilities for the disabled from the **Irish Wheelchair Association**. Central and local tourist boards and many of the organizations listed in the directory under each sport will also advise on available facilities. The **Share Centre** provides a range of activity holidays for both disabled and able-bodied people.

Boats moored at Carnlough Harbour on the Antrim coast *(see p259)*

DIRECTORY

SPECTATOR SPORTS

Croke Park
Dublin 3. 01 8363222.

Football Association of Ireland
80 Merrion Sq, Dublin 2.
01 6766864.

Irish Horse Racing Authority
Leopardstown Racecourse,
Foxrock, Dublin 18.
01 2892888.

Irish Open Office
35 Upper Mount St,
Dublin 2. 01 6622433.

FISHING

Central Fisheries Board
Balnagowan House,
Mobhi Boreen, Glasnevin,
Dublin 9.
01 8379206.

Department of Agriculture (Fisheries)
Annex 5, Castlegrounds,
Stormont, Belfast.
01232 523434.

Irish Federation of Sea Anglers
Mr Hugh O'Rorke,
67 Windsor Drive,
Monkstown, Co Dublin.
01 2806901.

Kingfisher Angling Centre
24A Hiltonstown Rd,
Portglenone, Ballymena,
Co Antrim.
01266 821301.

GOLF

Golfers Abroad
6 Park St, Wombwell,
Barnsley, S Yorks, England.
01226 751704.

Golfing Ireland
18 Parnell Sq, Dublin 1.
01 8726711.

Golfing Union of Ireland
Glencar House, 81
Eglinton Rd, Dublin 4.
01 2694111.

CYCLING

Ardclinis Activity Centre
High St, Cushendall,
Co Antrim.
01266 771340.

Bike Store
58 Lower Gardiner St,
Dublin 1.
01 8725399.

Celtic Cycling
Lorum Old Rectory,
Bagenalstown, Co Carlow.
0503 75282.

Raleigh Rent-a-Bike
PO Box 3520, Raleigh
House, Kylemore Rd,
Dublin 10.
01 6261333.

HORSE RIDING AND PONY TREKKING

Association of Irish Riding Establishments
11 Moore Park,
Newbridge, Co Kildare.
045 431584.

British Horse Society
House of Sport, Upper
Malone Rd, Belfast.
01232 381222.

Equestrian Holidays Ireland
1 Sandyford Office Park,
Foxrock, Dublin 18.
01 2958928.

WALKING AND MOUNTAINEERING

Association for Adventure Sports
House of Sport, Longmile
Rd, Dublin 12.
01 4509845.

Irish Ways
Old Rectory,
Ballycanew, Gorey,
Co Wexford.
055 27479.

Ulster Federation of Rambling Clubs
12B Breda House,
Drumart Drive, Belfast.
01232 648041.

WATER SPORTS

Ballyronan Marina
Watersports Centre,
Ballyronan, Co
Londonderry.
01648 418399.

DV Diving
138 Mountstewart Rd,
Newtownards,
Co Down.
01247 464671.

Irish Canoeing Holidays
Multifarnham,
Co Westmeath.
044 71324.

Irish Surfing Association
Easkey House,
Easkey,
Co Sligo.
096 49020.

Irish Underwater Council
78a Patrick St, Dun
Laoghaire, Co Dublin.
01 2844601.

Irish Water Ski Federation
Desmond Burke-Kennedy,
Advance House, JFK Drive,
Dublin 12.
01 4502122.

Irish Windsurfing Association
Haydock,
Westminster Road,
Blackrock, Dublin.
01 2895636.

Lakeland Canoe Centre
Castle Island, Enniskillen,
Co Fermanagh.
01365 324250.

Out and Out Activities
Garrison, Co Fermanagh.
01365 658105,
658072.

CRUISING AND SAILING

Athlone Cruisers
Jolly Mariner, Athlone,
Co Westmeath.
0902 72892.

Derg Line Cruisers
Killaloe, Co Clare.
061 376364.

Emerald Star
47 Dawson St, Dublin 2.
01 6798166.

Erne Marine
Bellanaleck, Enniskillen,
Co Fermanagh.
01365 348267.

International Sailing Centre
East Beach, Cobh, Cork.
021 811237.

Lough Melvin Holiday Centre
Garrison, Co Fermanagh.
01365 658142.

Shannon-Erne Waterway
Ballinamore, Co Leitrim.
078 44855.

Silver Line Cruisers
The Marina, Banagher,
Co Offaly.
0509 51112.

Ulster Cruising School
The Marina, Carrickfergus,
Co Antrim.
01960 368818.

HUNTING AND SHOOTING

British Field Sports Society
Shane's Castle, Antrim,
Co Antrim.
01849 428216.

Irish Master of Foxhounds Association
Thornton, Dunlavin,
Co Kildare.
045 401294.

Mount Juliet Estate
Thomastown, Co Kilkenny.
056 24455.

SPORTS FOR THE DISABLED

Irish Wheelchair Association
Aras Chuchulain,
Blackheath Drive,
Clontarf, Dublin 3.
01 8338241.

Share Centre
Smith's Strand, Lisnaskea,
Co Fermanagh.
01365 722122.

SURVIVAL
GUIDE

PRACTICAL INFORMATION

ALTHOUGH IRELAND is quite a small island, visitors should not expect to see everything in a short time, since many of the country's most magnificent attractions are in rural areas. In remote parts of the island the roads are narrow, the pace of life is very slow, banks often open for only one or two days of the week and public transport tends to be infrequent. However, although the Republic of Ireland remains one of

Bord Fáilte logo

Europe's most unspoilt nations, its economy is developing fast. Any decent-sized town in the Republic is likely to have a tourist information centre and offer a full range of facilities for the traveller. Northern Ireland has its own tourist board with offices in most towns. The standard of facilities available to those travelling in the North equals that across the border and, as with the Republic, the level of hospitality is first-rate.

TOURIST INFORMATION

IN BOTH THE REPUBLIC and Northern Ireland there is an impressive network of tourist information offices. As well as providing lots of free local information, the tourist offices in large towns sell maps and guide books and can reserve accommodation for a nominal charge. There are also tourist information points in some of the smaller towns and villages. The opening hours can be somewhat erratic and many are open only during the summer season. The local museums and libraries often stock a selection of useful tourist literature.

Before leaving for Ireland you can get information from **Bord Fáilte** (Irish Tourist Board) or **Northern Ireland Tourist Board** (NITB) offices, which will supply you with maps and leaflets. Bord Fáilte offices can be found in major cities all over the world – a reflection of the universal appeal of Ireland. It's also worth contacting the regional tourist offices in Dublin, Cork, Limerick and Galway for more information on destinations, including accommodation and car rental. If you call at a tourist office in the Republic and pick up a list of places to stay, you shouldn't expect every local hotel and guesthouse to be included – these lists recommend only those establishments that have been ap-proved by Bord Fáilte.

The Dúchas-run Parke's Castle in County Sligo (see p225)

ADMISSION CHARGES

MOST OF IRELAND'S major sights, including ancient monuments, museums and national parks, have an admission fee. For each place of interest in this guide, we specify whether or not there is a charge. The entrance fees in the Republic of Ireland are normally between IR£1 and IR£5, with discounts for students and the elderly.

Heritage card giving access to historic sites

Dúchas (The Heritage Service) manages and maintains national parks, museums, monuments and inland waterways. At most Dúchas sites you can buy a Heritage Card, which allows

unlimited, free admission to all sites managed by Dúchas for a year. At IR£15 for adults, IR£10 for senior citizens and IR£6 for children and students, the card is a good investment. Popular Dúchas sites that deserve a visit include Céide Fields (see p196), Cahir Castle (see p190) and the Blaskett Centre (see p150). Entrance fees in Northern Ireland are about the same as in the Republic, with discounts for students and senior citizens. North of the border the **National Trust** has a scheme similar to the Heritage Card, but membership costs more (around £25 per annum per person or £45 for families) and there are fewer sites. It doesn't represent very good value for money unless you are also intending to visit National Trust sites elsewhere in the UK.

Northern Ireland Tourist Board logo

Interpretative centre at Connemara National Park *(see p200)*

OPENING TIMES

THE OPENING DAYS of sights are listed in this guide. Few places are open on a Sunday morning, and some museums are shut on Monday. Opening hours are generally between 10am and 5pm; some sights stay open a little later and others close for lunch.

From June to September all the sights are open but the crowds are at their biggest. In winter many tourist attractions are closed several days per week and keep shorter hours; some close down completely. There are also variations on public holidays – many places open for Easter and then close again until summer.

INTERPRETATIVE CENTRES

MANY OF IRELAND'S major sights are ruins or Stone Age archaeological sites and can be difficult to appreciate. In recent years, however, money has become available for building interpretative or visitors' centres which explain the historical significance of sites. Entry to the site may be free, but you have to pay to visit the interpretative centre.

In areas of natural beauty, such as Connemara National Park, an interpretative centre acts as a useful focal point. The centre typically provides information leaflets and has reconstructions of sights. Connemara has 3D models and displays, as well as an audiovisual presentation on the development of the local landscape over the last 10,000 years. There is also a shop for postcards, books and posters.

RELIGIOUS SERVICES

IRELAND is a deeply religious country and for much of the population, churchgoing is a way of life. Because the Republic of Ireland is 95 per cent Roman Catholic, finding a non-Catholic church may sometimes be difficult. In the Republic and Northern Ireland, the tourist offices, hotels and B&Bs all keep a list of local church service times.

DIRECTORY

IRISH TOURIST BOARD (BORD FÁILTE) OFFICES

Republic of Ireland
Baggot St Bridge,
Dublin 2.
☎ 01 6024000.

United Kingdom
150 New Bond St,
London W1Y 0AQ.
☎ 0171 493 3201.

United States
345 Park Avenue,
New York, NY 10154.
☎ (212) 418-0800.

NORTHERN IRELAND TOURIST BOARD OFFICES

Northern Ireland Tourist Board
St Anne's Court, 59 North St,
Belfast BT1 1NB.
☎ 01232 246609.

United Kingdom
11 Berkeley St,
London
W1X 5AD.
☎ 0171 355 5040.

United States
551 Fifth Ave, Suite 701,
New York, NY 10176.
☎ (212) 922-0101.

OTHER USEFUL ADDRESSES

National Trust
Rowallane House, Saintfield,
Ballynahinch, County Down
BT24 7LH. ☎ 01238 510721.

Dúchas (The Heritage Service)
51 St Stephen's Green, Dublin 2.
☎ 01 6613111.

LANGUAGE

The Republic of Ireland is officially bilingual – almost all road signs have place names in both English and Irish. English is the spoken language everywhere apart from a few parts of the far west, called Gaeltachts *(see p221)*, but now and then you may find signs written only in Irish. Here are some of the words you are most likely to come across.

USEFUL WORDS

an banc – **bank**
an lár – **town centre**
an trá – **beach**
ar aghaidh – **go**
bád – **boat**
bealach amach – **exit**
bealach isteach – **entrance**
bus – **bus**
dúnta – **closed**
fáilte – **welcome**
fir – **men**
gardaí – **police**
leithreas – **toilet**

Sign using old form of Gaelic

mná – **women**
oifig an poist – **post office**
oscailte – **open**
óstán – **hotel**
siopa – **shop**
stop/stad – **stop**
ticéad – **ticket**
traein – **train**

Additional Information

European Youth Card

IRELAND IS DIVIDED between the state of the Republic of Ireland, and Northern Ireland – a province of the United Kingdom. Each has a separate currency, postal service and telecommunications system *(see pp344–9)*. However, there are many similarities between them: they are part of the European Union, English is their first language and, both north and south of the border, the tourist industry is well advanced. These two pages describe the regulations that affect the Republic and Northern Ireland, and the special facilities that are available to travellers, including students and the disabled. There is also a general guide to the media in both the North and South as well as a directory of useful names and addresses.

Students at Trinity College, Dublin

VISAS

VISITORS FROM the EU, US, Canada, Australia and New Zealand require a valid passport but not a visa for entry into the Republic or Northern Ireland. All others, including those wanting to study or take up work, should check with their local Irish or British Embassy first. UK nationals born in Britain or Northern Ireland do not strictly need a passport to enter the Republic of Ireland but should take one with them for car rental, cashing of traveller's cheques and medical services.

DUTY-FREE GOODS AND CUSTOMS ALLOWANCES

ADULTS TRAVELLING between Ireland and countries outside the British Isles can buy duty-free goods at the airport, on the plane or on the ferry. This also applies to those going between the Republic and Great Britain but not between North and South. Duty-free is not available when travelling between Northern Ireland and other parts of the UK. Current allowances include a litre of spirits, 50 grams of perfume and 200 cigarettes. 1993 EU regulations also allow travellers within the European Union a quantity of duty-paid goods. Present quotas include 55 litres of beer, 45 litres of wine and 800 cigarettes.

STUDENT INFORMATION

STUDENTS WITH a valid ISIC card (International Student Identity Card) benefit from numerous travel discounts as well as reduced admission to museums and concerts. Buy a Travelsave stamp from any branch of **USIT** and affix it to your ISIC card to get a 50 per cent discount on Irish Rail, NIR train services and Irish Ferries. A Travelsave stamp will also get you discounts on Bus Éireann routes in the South and special rates on commuter tickets (Sep–Jun only) in Dublin, Limerick, Cork, Galway and Waterford. In the North, an ISIC card gives a 15 per cent discount on Ulsterbus services and 20 per cent on Belfast Citybus "Gold Card" commuter services. ISIC cards can be obtained from branches of USIT travel in Dublin, Belfast and other college towns.

USIT will also supply non-students under 26 with an EYC (European Youth Card) for discounts in restaurants, shops and theatres. The name of the card, which is recognized in over 20 European states, varies from country to country but can be identified by its distinctive logo.

FACILITIES FOR THE DISABLED

MOST SIGHTS in Ireland have access for wheelchairs. This book gives basic information about disabled access for each sight, but it's worth phoning to check details. The Access Department of the **National Rehabilitation Board** provides information for the Republic and publishes county-by-county guides to accommodation, restaurants and amenities. In the North, **Disability Action** can advise on accessibility, while the Open Arts organization has a list of entertainment venues and museums providing wheelchair access.

Duty-free shop at Shannon Airport

Relaxing with newspapers in Eyre Square, Galway

RADIO AND TELEVISION

IRELAND has three television channels, RTE 1, Network 2 and the Irish-language Teilifís na Gaelige. All are run by the state-controlled RTE. There are three national radio stations, including an Irish-language service, and many local ones.

The four British TV channels can be picked up in most parts of Ireland. Cable TV is quite common in the Republic, where most hotels offer it.

A selection of daily newspapers from North and South

NEWSPAPERS AND MAGAZINES

THE REPUBLIC of Ireland has five national daily papers and five Sunday papers. Quality dailies include the *Irish Independent*, the *Examiner* and the *Irish Times*, the latter being well known for its journalistic excellence. The broadsheets are useful for up-to-date information on theatre and concerts. Ireland's daily

tabloid is the *Star*. The North's top local paper is the *Belfast Telegraph*, on sale in the afternoon. The province's morning papers, the *News Letter* and *Irish News*, are less rewarding.

In larger towns throughout Ireland, British tabloids are on sale. Broadsheets such as *The Times* are also available and cost less than the quality Irish press. Most towns have a local or regional paper, which will tell you what's on and where.

USA Today, *Newsweek* and *Time* magazine are sold in major cities but are very hard to find in the countryside.

IRISH TIME

THE WHOLE of Ireland is in the same time zone as Great Britain, i.e. five hours ahead of New York and Toronto, one hour behind Germany and France, and ten hours behind Sydney. In both the North and the South, clocks go forward one hour for summer time.

CONVERSION CHART

Imperial to Metric
1 inch = 2.5 centimetres
1 foot = 30 centimetres
1 mile = 1.6 kilometres
1 ounce = 28 grams
1 pound = 454 grams
1 pint = 0.6 litres
1 gallon = 4.6 litres

Metric to Imperial
1 millimetre = 0.04 inches
1 centimetre = 0.4 inches
1 metre = 3 feet 3 inches
1 kilometre = 0.6 miles
1 gram = 0.04 ounces
1 kilogram = 2.2 pounds
1 litre = 1.8 pints

METRICATION

THE CHANGE towards metrication is slow in Ireland, particularly the North, where distances are still measured in miles. In the Republic, all new road signs show distances in kilometres, but there are still many old ones left that use miles *(see p.356)*. However, throughout Ireland all speed limits are shown in miles. In both Northern Ireland and the Republic, petrol is sold in litres but draught beer is always sold in pints. And just to add to the confusion, food may be weighed out either in imperial or in metric measures.

One of the new metric road signs used in the Republic of Ireland

Personal Security and Health

IRELAND IS PROBABLY one of the safest places to travel in Europe. Petty theft, such as pickpocketing, is seldom a problem outside certain parts of Dublin and a few other large towns. Tourist offices and hoteliers gladly point out the areas to be avoided. In the recent past, the main security risk in Northern Ireland has been the threat of bombings, though this has hardly ever affected tourists. In fact, crimes against the individual tend to be fewer than in other parts of the UK and Europe.

Pharmacy in Dublin showing old-fashioned snake and goblet symbol

Pearse Street Garda Station, Dublin

PERSONAL SECURITY

THE POLICE, should you ever need them, are called the Gardaí in the Republic of Ireland and the Royal Ulster Constabulary (RUC) in Northern Ireland. Violent street crime in Ireland – North or South – is relatively rare but it's still advisable to take suitable precautions, such as avoiding poorly lit streets in the cities and larger towns. Poverty and a degree of

Male garda   RUC policeman

heroin addiction in inner-city Dublin has been known to cause a few problems, and Limerick isn't the most inviting of places after dark, but if you avoid the backstreets at night there should be little cause for concern. In some of the larger southern towns you may be approached in the street by people asking for money. This rarely develops into a troublesome situation, but it is still best to avoid eye contact and leave the scene as quickly as possible.

PERSONAL PROPERTY

BEFORE YOU LEAVE, make sure that your possessions are insured, as it might be difficult and more expensive to do this in Ireland. Travel insurance for the UK will not cover you for the Republic, so make sure you have an adequate policy. As pickpocketing and bag-snatching can be a problem in some of the larger towns in the Republic, it's best not to carry around your passport or large amounts of cash, or leave them in your room. Most hotels have a safe and it makes sense to take advantage of this facility. Those carrying large amounts of money around should use traveller's cheques (see pp346–7). When out and about, use a bag that can be held securely, and be alert in crowded places and restaurants. A money belt may be a good investment.

If travelling by car, ensure all valuables are locked in the boot and always lock the car, even when leaving it for just a few minutes. If visiting

Garda Station

RUC Station

Northern Ireland, do not leave any of your bags or packages unattended, as they are likely to result in a security scare.

LOST PROPERTY

REPORT ALL LOST or stolen items at once to the police. To make an insurance claim, you'll need to get a copy of the police report. Most rail and bus stations in the Republic operate a lost-property service.

MEDICAL TREATMENT

RESIDENTS OF COUNTRIES in the European Union can claim free medical treatment in the Republic of Ireland by getting form E111 before setting out. In the event of illness, to avoid having to pay for any treatment and prescribed medicines, you'll need to show your E111 and a form of identification, such as a driving licence or passport. Also, be sure to let the doctor know that you want treatment under the EU's social security regulations.

In Northern Ireland, British citizens need no documentation; visitors from other EU countries should follow the same procedure as for the Republic. Non-EU travellers should either have their own accident and health insurance or be willing to pay for any treatment received.

EMERGENCY NUMBERS

Police, Fire, Ambulance and Coastguard Services
Dial 999 in both the Republic and Northern Ireland.

PHARMACIES

A WIDE RANGE of medical supplies is available over the counter at pharmacies. However, many medicines are available only with a prescription authorized by a local doctor. If you are likely to require specialized drugs during your stay, take your own supplies or ask your doctor to write a letter with the generic name of the medicine you require. Always obtain a receipt for insurance claims.

Until recently, condoms were not freely available in the Republic but are now relatively easy to obtain, in the big cities at least. In some of the small towns you may discover that the pharmacist is opposed to contraception and does not sell condoms.

Small rural health centre in County Donegal

Dublin ambulance

Dublin fire engine

Garda patrol car

RUC patrol car

PERSONAL SAFETY IN NORTHERN IRELAND

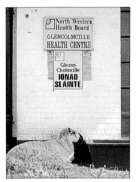

Checkpoint signs

Even at the height of the Troubles in Northern Ireland, there was never a significant threat to the tourist, and travelling around the province was deemed to be as safe as in the Republic. As long as peace exists north of the border, no extra precautions need to be taken there, but in the event of the Troubles resurfacing, first-time visitors should be prepared for certain unfamiliar situations. When driving, if you see a sign that indicates you are approaching a checkpoint, slow down and use dipped headlights. To keep fuss down to a minimum in these situations, it is a good idea to keep a passport or some other form of identification close at hand. When parking in the province's towns and cities, be sure to avoid leaving your vehicle unattended in an area that is marked by a Control Zone sign. If you are walking around the city centres of Belfast and Londonderry, you may notice a strong police or military presence. This is unlikely to inconvenience you. Occasionally, however, you may be asked by shop security to reveal the contents of your bags – don't be

RUC armour-plated Land Rover

Local Currency

THE REPUBLIC and Northern Ireland have different currencies. Although punts, or Irish pounds, and pounds sterling are issued in the same note and coin denominations, they are not interchangeable. Many retailers in the Republic accept sterling if the exchange rate is in their favour, but don't rely on this. When travelling between Northern Ireland and the Republic, there's no shortage of money-changers – official and unofficial – in towns on either side of the border. However, for the best exchange rates, avoid shops and petrol stations and use the *bureaux de change* or banks.

Ulster Bank sub-office in Delvin, County Westmeath

CURRENCY IN THE REPUBLIC OF IRELAND

THE UNIT OF CURRENCY in the Republic is the punt (IR£), often called the Irish pound. It is divided into 100 pence (p). Though there are no restrictions on bringing currency into the Republic, you cannot take more than IR£150 in banknotes out. However, you can take out the same amount of foreign currency as you bring in, up to IR£1,200.

Banknotes
The Republic's banknotes are issued in denominations of IR£100, IR£50, IR£20, IR£10 and IR£5. They increase in size according to value and depict famous figures from the country's past.

IR£50 note

IR£20 note

IR£10 note

IR£5 note

Coins
The Republic of Ireland issues the following coins: IR£1, 50p, 20p, 10p, 5p, 2p and 1p. Although the denominations are the same as those used north of the border, the appearance of the coins is very different.

IR£1   50p

20p   10p   5p   2p   1p

CURRENCY IN NORTHERN IRELAND

NORTHERN IRELAND uses British currency – the pound sterling (£), which is divided into 100 pence (p). As there are no exchange controls in the UK, there is no limit to the amount of cash you can take into and out of Northern Ireland. In addition to the British currency, four provincial banks issue their own banknotes, worth the same as their counterparts. To tell them apart, look for the words "Bank of England" on British notes.

Banknotes

British banknotes are issued in the denominations £50, £20, £10 and £5. Their different colours help make them easily distinguishable.

£50 note

£20 note

£10 note

£5 note

Coins

Coins come in the following denominations: £1, 50p, 20p, 10p, 5p, 2p and 1p. All have the Queen's head on one side and are the same as those elsewhere in the UK, except that the pound coin has a different detail - a flax plant - on the reverse side.

PROVINCIAL BANKNOTES

Banknotes issued by the four provincial banks are not normally accepted by retailers in other parts of the UK, so if you intend to travel on to Great Britain, exchange them for Bank of England notes. Provincial banknotes are not legal tender in the Republic of Ireland.

Bank of Ireland £5 note   Ulster Bank £5 note

Northern Bank £5 note   First Trust Bank £10 note

£1   50p

20p   10p   5p   2p   1p

Banks in Ireland

THE OPENING TIMES of banks in Ireland vary depending on whether the banks are situated in the town or country, in the Republic or Northern Ireland. Both north and south of the border, banks in small towns are often sub-offices where banking services may be provided on only one or two days of the week, so it's advisable to make the most of facilities in the bigger towns whenever you can. Banks throughout Ireland generally provide a very good service and, along with many of the larger post offices, will exchange traveller's cheques, often without charging commission.

Bank of Ireland sub-office in Sneem, County Kerry

USING BANKS

THE FIVE RETAIL BANKS in the Republic of Ireland are the Bank of Ireland, the Allied Irish Bank (AIB), the Ulster Bank, the National Irish Bank and the TSB Bank. In Northern Ireland there are four retail banks: the Ulster Bank, the Bank of Ireland, the Northern Bank and the First Trust Bank.

Cash dispenser

In the Republic of Ireland the usual banking hours are Monday to Friday from 10am to 12:30pm and from 1:30 to 3pm. Some of the larger branches do stay open during lunch time – a custom which more and more of the banks are adopting. There is extended opening (till 5pm) on one day of the week. In Dublin, Cork and

First Trust Bank logo

most other cities and towns, late opening is on Thursdays but in rural areas banks often stay open late on market day instead. Branches of the TSB Bank remain open at lunch time and till 7pm on Thursdays and up to 5pm on other weekdays. Most of the banks in Northern Ireland open from 10am till 3:30pm, though some of them close for lunch between 12:30 and 1:30pm. In both the Republic and in Northern Ireland, all the banks are closed on public holidays, some of which differ from North to South *(see p49)*. Banks in the cities and most of the towns are provided with automated teller machines, or cash dispensers, so if you happen to discover the local bank is closed, it isn't necessarily a major catastrophe.

CREDIT CARDS

THROUGHOUT IRELAND you can pay by credit card in most hotels, petrol stations, large shops and supermarkets. VISA or Mastercard (known also as Access) are the most commonly accepted credit cards. Fewer businesses take American Express and Diners Club cards. Cash can be withdrawn from banks displaying the appropriate sign.

TRAVELLER'S CHEQUES

TRAVELLER'S CHEQUES are the safest way to carry around large amounts of money. These are best changed at one of the main banks but, failing this, many shops and restaurants accept them – usually for a small charge.

Traveller's cheques can be bought before setting out at American Express, Thomas

Ornate post office and *bureau de change* in Ventry, County Kerry

Cook or your own bank. In Ireland, traveller's cheques can be purchased at banks or from *bureaux de change*, which can be found in the larger cities and at airports.

EUROCHEQUES

INSTEAD OF traveller's cheques you can get a Eurocheque book and guarantee card from your local bank. When buying from a store in Ireland that takes Eurocheques, you make out the cheque for the exact amount in punts or pounds. The Eurocheque card can also be used to withdraw cash up to your card limit.

Drawing money from an Allied Irish Bank cash dispenser

BUREAUX DE CHANGE

IN ADDITION to the foreign exchange counters at the main banks, there are some private *bureaux de change* in Dublin. As with most other exchange facilities, *bureaux de change* open later than banks. However, it's worth checking their rates before undertaking any transactions.

BUREAUX DE CHANGE

American Express
Dublin Tourism Centre,
Suffolk Street, Dublin 2.
☎ 01 6057709.
Also in Galway, Killarney & Belfast.

Thomas Cook
118 Grafton Street, Dublin 2.
☎ 01 6770476.
11 Donegall Place, Belfast.
☎ 01232 550030.
Branch also at Belfast International Airport and offices in Ballymena, Bangor, Coleraine, Lisburn, Londonderry & Portadown.

Sending a Letter

Northern Ireland Post Office sign

MAIN POST OFFICES in the Republic and Northern Ireland are usually open from 9am to 5:30pm during the week and from 9am to around 1pm on Saturdays, although times do vary. Some smaller offices close for lunch on weekdays and do not open on Saturdays. Standard letter and postcard stamps can also be bought from certain newsagents. The Republic of Ireland does not have a first- and second-class system, but sending a postcard is a few pence less expensive than a letter. Though it is improving all the time, the postal service in the Republic is still quite slow – allow three to four days when sending a letter to Great Britain and at least six days

Republic of Ireland Post Office logo

for the United States. In Northern Ireland, letters to other parts of the UK can be sent by either first- or second-class mail. First-class postage is slightly more expensive but most letters sent this way reach their UK destination the next day. A letter to any EU country (including the Republic) costs the same as first-class mail.

POSTBOXES

POSTBOXES in Ireland come in two colours – green in the Republic and red in the North. Many of Ireland's postboxes are quite historic. Some of those in the Republic even carry Queen Victoria's monogram on the front, a relic from the days of British rule. Even the smallest towns in Ireland have a postbox, from which the mail is collected regularly – anything from once to four times daily.

Letter and parcel stamps for the Republic of Ireland

Second-class, parcel and first-class stamps used in the North

First-class and overseas slot

Second-class slot

List of the daily collection times

Insignia of the British monarch

Monogram of Queen Victoria

Postbox in the Republic

Northern Ireland double postbox

Using Ireland's Telephones

THE TELEPHONE SYSTEM in the Republic of Ireland is run exclusively by Telecom Eireann and provides a modern and efficient service. Today, TE has a network of up-to-date coin and card telephones. For those intending to spend more than IR£4 on calls during their stay, it can be cheaper to use phonecards as they offer reasonable discounts. Also, there are now more card phones in the Republic than coin phones. Northern Ireland, like the rest of the United Kingdom, has British Telecom coin and card public phones. BT and TE phonecards are available from newsagents, post offices, supermarkets and other retail outlets.

TELECOM EIREANN

The Telecom Eireann logo

USING A TE COIN PHONE

1 Lift the receiver and wait for the dialling tone.

2 Insert any of the coins below. The illuminated display shows the minimum amount required.

3 Dial the number and wait to be connected.

4 The display indicates how much money you have put in and the credit left. A rapid bleeping noise means your money has run out. Insert more coins.

5 If you want to make a further call and you have money left in credit, do not replace the receiver, press the follow-on-call button.

6 When you have finished speaking, replace the receiver and collect your change. Only wholly unused coins are refunded.

USING A TE CARD PHONE

1 Lift the receiver and wait for the dialling tone.

3 The display shows how many units are left. The minimum charge is one unit (20p).

4 Dial the number and wait until you are connected.

5 When your phonecard runs out you will hear a rapid bleeping noise. To continue, press the "change card" button and the old card will come out. Remove it and insert a new card.

6 If you want to make a further call and you have money left in credit, do not replace the receiver, press the follow-on-call button.

2 Insert a TE Callcard in the direction of the arrow on the card.

7 To adjust the volume in your earpiece, press the button with the upward-pointing arrow to increase it, and the button with the downward-pointing arrow to decrease it.

IR£1   50p   20p   10p

TE phonecards come in 10, 20, 50 and 100 units. A unit is worth 20p.

PHONING FROM THE REPUBLIC OF IRELAND

Cheap rate calls within the Republic and to the UK are from 6pm to 8am weekdays and all day at weekends. Off-peak times for international calls vary from country to country, but are generally as above.
• To call Northern Ireland: dial 08, then the area code, followed by the number.
• To call the UK: dial 0044, the area code (minus the leading 0), then the number.
• To call other countries: dial 00, followed by the country code (for example, 1 for the USA, 61 for Australia), the area code (minus the leading 0), then the number.

• For directory enquiries: call 1190 for numbers in the Republic and Northern Ireland, 1197 for numbers in Great Britain and 1198 for numbers in other countries.
• For assistance in making a call: dial 10 for numbers within Ireland and Britain, 114 for international calls.
• Credit cards issued in certain countries including the USA, Australia and Canada are accepted as payment for calls to the country from where the card was issued.
• To send a telemessage: dial 196.
• For emergencies: dial 999.

Telephone boxes
Most of the phone boxes in the Republic are modern. There are two styles in Northern Ireland – new ones and the traditional red boxes – but both are issued with the same type of telephone. In both North and South, the wording around the top of each box indicates whether it is a coin, phonecard or credit card phone.

Telecom Eireann phone boxes

Old BT phone box   **New BT phone box**

USING A BT COIN PHONE

1 Lift the receiver and wait for the dialling tone.

2 Insert any of the coins shown below. The display shows the minimum amount of money you must put in.

3 Dial the number and wait to be connected.

4 The display indicates how much money you have put in and the credit left. A rapid bleeping noise means your money has run out. Insert more coins.

5 If you want to make another call and you have money left in credit, do not replace the receiver, press the follow-on-call button.

6 When you have finished speaking, replace the receiver and collect your change. Only wholly unused coins are refunded.

£1   50p   20p   10p

USING A BT CARD PHONE

1 Lift the receiver and wait for the dialling tone.

3 The display shows how many units you have left. The minimum charge is one unit (10p).

4 Some of the BT. phones take credit cards as well as phonecards. With the black strip on the right-hand side and away from you, insert and slide through.

5 Dial the number and wait until you are connected.

6 When your phonecard runs out you will hear a rapid bleeping noise. Press the eject button and remove the old card, replacing it with a new one.

2 Insert a BT phonecard, green side up, in the direction of the arrows on the card.

7 If you have credit on your card and want to make another call, just press and quickly release the receiver rest.

BT phonecards come in 20, 40, 100 and 200 units. The value of each unit is 10p.

PHONING FROM NORTHERN IRELAND

Cheap rate calls within the province, to other parts of the UK and to the Republic are from 6pm to 8am on weekdays and all day at weekends. Times for off-peak international calls vary from country to country but are generally as above.

• For calls within the UK: dial the area code and the number you want.

• For international calls: dial 00, then the country code (for example, 1 for Canada, 64 for New Zealand), then the area code minus the first 0 and finally, the number you require.

• For calls to the Republic of Ireland: dial 00 353 then the area code minus the first 0, then the number.

• For assistance with making a call: contact the operator on 100 for calls within the UK and 155 for all other countries, including the Republic of Ireland.

• For directory enquiries: call 192 for UK and Republic of Ireland numbers and 153 for all other countries.

• For telemessages: dial 0800 190191.

• For the 24-hour speaking clock: call 8081.

• For emergency services: call 999.

TRAVEL INFORMATION

IRELAND'S THREE main airports, Dublin, Shannon and Belfast, are well served by flights from Britain, the United States and an increasing number of countries around the world. If you are travelling by sea from the UK, there is a very good choice of ferry routes from ports in Britain to both the Republic and Northern Ireland. Instead of buying separate tickets, you can purchase combined coach/ferry and rail/ferry tickets from almost all of the towns in mainland Britain. The less-than-comprehensive public transport systems in both the North and South reflect the rural nature of the island. With this in mind, travelling around Ireland is probably best enjoyed if you embrace the Irish way of thinking and just take your time.

Aer Lingus Airbus in flight

The modern exterior of Dublin International Airport

FLYING TO THE REPUBLIC OF IRELAND

FLIGHTS from most of the major cities in Europe arrive at **Dublin Airport**, which is the country's busiest airport. Regular services to the Republic depart from all five of the London airports (Heathrow, City, Gatwick, Luton and Stansted) and 15 other cities in Britain, plus the Channel Islands and the Isle of Man.

The major airline operating scheduled flights between Britain and the Republic is **Aer Lingus**, although since deregulation the rival **Ryanair** firm has grown fast due to its policy of cheap fares from Stansted, Luton, Gatwick and other British airports. Aer Lingus and **Delta Airlines** fly direct from the US to Dublin Airport and **Shannon Airport**, ten miles outside Limerick – gone is the old ruling that all

planes flying eastward to Dublin must first touch down at Shannon. As well as flying from Moscow, **Aeroflot** has non-stop flights from Miami, New York and Washington, DC to Shannon Airport.

Cork Airport is served by flights from London (Heathrow and Stansted), Birmingham, Manchester, Bristol, Plymouth, Exeter and Newquay. Although there are no direct flights to any of Ireland's airports from Australia and New Zealand, popular connecting points are London and Moscow.

The other airports in the Republic are smaller with fewer regular flights. There are many charter flights for pilgrims to **Knock International Airport**, which also has flights from Dublin, London (Stansted) and Manchester; there are flights into Kerry Airport from Dublin, Luton, Düsseldorf and Munich; Waterford Airport is served by flights from London (Stansted), Luton and Manchester, and at Galway Airport there are twice-daily flights from Dublin.

One of the Airlink coaches which take passengers from Dublin Airport into the city centre

GETTING TO AND FROM THE AIRPORT

THE REPUBLIC'S three main airports are all served by regular bus services, whereas the smaller airports depend mainly on local taxi services. An express bus service runs between Dublin Airport and the city's main rail and bus stations about every 20 minutes, from early morning to midnight. The journey takes half an hour. At Cork, Bus Éireann provides an express bus service, taking 15 minutes, to get from the airport to the city. Buses run every 45 minutes on weekdays and hourly at the weekends. At Shannon Airport, Bus Éireann has a regular service to Limerick, taking 35 minutes to the city centre. Also, several buses a day go to the town of Ennis, about 30 km (18 miles) away. All airports in the Republic have both long- and short-stay parking facilities.

Information signs in the main concourse of Shannon Airport

Passengers checking in at Belfast International Airport

FLYING TO NORTHERN IRELAND

THERE ARE HOURLY FLIGHTS, operated by either **British Airways** or **British Midland**, from London Heathrow to **Belfast International Airport** (BIA), 30 km (18 miles) northwest of Belfast city centre. BIA is also served by flights from Luton and some regional airports like Manchester and Glasgow. There is a daily **KLM** flight from Amsterdam and a weekly **American Trans Air** flight from New York.

Belfast City Airport is used by smaller aircraft, but is favoured by many because of its location – it is just 6 km (4 miles) from the city centre. The airport also has more flights from the UK – around 15 cities plus Gatwick, Stansted and Luton – than BIA. The City of Derry Airport is Northern Ireland's smallest, with one flight daily from Manchester and Glasgow.

AIRPORT CONNECTIONS IN NORTHERN IRELAND

THE ARRANGEMENTS for getting to and from the airports in Northern Ireland are generally good. BIA's Airbus service will take you from the airport to the Europa Bus-centre via Oxford Street Bus Station and Central Railway Station. This runs every half hour and takes about 30 minutes from end to end. At Belfast City Airport the number 21 bus passes every half hour, taking around 10 minutes to get to the Belfast City Hall bus depot. There are trains from the airport to Central Station about every 30 minutes. Derry's airport is on a local bus route: the number 143 goes into the city centre once an hour (less frequently at weekends). All airports in Northern Ireland have taxi ranks and both long- and short-term parking facilities.

Airport sign in English and Gaelic

AIR FARES

AIRLINES OFFER a host of options on air fares to Ireland from Britain. Usually, the amount you pay is determined by how flexible you are prepared to be and how far in advance you book. The best bargains tend to be on flights for which the dates are not changeable. It's not difficult to get a return flight from mainland UK to Dublin for well under £100. However, these tickets often stipulate that your stay must include a Saturday night. The cheapest place to fly from is usually London – in recent years, the air fares from Stansted and Luton to both Dublin Airport and Belfast International have been particularly low.

Ticket prices are generally fairly constant throughout the year except at Christmas, during summer and on bank holidays, when there are comparatively few discounted fares available. During these periods, due to the increased demand by visiting friends and relatives – referred to by airline companies as "VFR" – seats are taken well in advance. Many airlines offer discounts to those under 25, while USIT (*see p340*), Campus Travel and other specialist travel agents often have cheaper rates for students and under-26s.

Arriving by Sea

TRAVELLING BY FERRY is a popular way of getting to Ireland, especially for groups or families intending to tour the country by car. Eight ports in Great Britain and four in France provide ferry crossings to Ireland's six ports. Nowadays, all ferries are of the modern drive-on/drive-off variety with lounges, restaurants and, if you're sailing to the Republic, duty-free shops. Crossing the Irish Sea is now faster than ever before, thanks to a new generation of high-speed ferries.

Logo of Irish Ferries

Stena Sea Lynx leaving Dun Laoghaire harbour

FERRIES TO DUBLIN AND DUN LAOGHAIRE

THERE IS A GOOD CHOICE of ferry services from Wales to Ireland. **Irish Ferries**, the country's largest shipping company, is the sole operator on the Holyhead–Dublin route and has two crossings a day. Unlike the service to Dun Laoghaire, there is no high-speed service – only the conventional ferry, which takes about 3½ hours. Like most ferry companies, Irish Ferries does not operate on Christmas Day or Boxing Day.

The service from Holyhead to the Dublin suburb of Dun Laoghaire – traditionally the busiest port in Ireland – is operated by **Stena Sealink**. This route is served by conventional ferries and the Stena HSS (High-speed Sea Service) newly introduced into service in September 1995. As the world's largest fast ferry, the HSS has the same passenger and vehicle capacity as the conventional ferries but its jet-engine propulsion gives it twice the speed.

Vehicle loading and unloading times on the Stena HSS are also considerably shorter than with other ferries – the loading time for cars is about 20 minutes as opposed to a minimum of 30 minutes with most other ferries. Passengers requiring special assistance at ports or on board the ship should contact the company they are booked with at least 24 hours before the departure time. Like most other ferry companies, Irish Ferries and Stena Sealink take bicycles free of charge, but this should be mentioned when making your reservation.

FERRIES TO ROSSLARE

ROSSLARE, in County Wexford, is the main port for crossings from South Wales to Ireland. Stena Sealink runs a service from Fishguard using both the conventional ferry and the speedier Sea Lynx catamaran-style ferries. Those intending to take a car on Sea Lynx should make sure the measurements of their vehicle, when fully loaded, are within those specified by Stena Sealink. The maximum dimensions allowable per vehicle on Sea Lynx are: height 3 m (10 ft), length 6 m (20 ft) and weight 3 tonnes.

Irish Ferries operates two crossings to Rosslare from Pembroke all year round, which take about 4½ hours. There are also Irish Ferries services to Rosslare from Le Havre (20 hours), Cherbourg (16½ hours) and Roscoff (15 hours). On all crossings to Rosslare, cabins and berths are available but these should be booked in advance.

FERRIES TO CORK

THE PROSPECT of a 10-hour sea journey could be enough to deter some from taking the ferry to Cork, but for those heading for south-west Ireland, sailing to the small town of Ringaskiddy, near Cork, can help cut out a cross-Ireland car journey of

FERRY ROUTE	OPERATORS
Holyhead–Dun Laoghaire	Stena Sealink
Fishguard–Rosslare	Stena Sealink
Pembroke–Rosslare	Irish Ferries
Stranraer–Belfast	SeaCat Scotland Stena Sealink
Liverpool–Belfast	Norse Irish Ferries
Cairnryan–Larne	P&O European Ferries
Swansea–Cork	Swansea Cork Ferries

Gallery overlooking the quayside at Rosslare Harbour

up to 250 miles. During the high season, **Swansea Cork Ferries** has up to six crossings per week between the two cities but the service doesn't operate between early January and mid-March. The crossing takes about 10 hours. There are also several routes direct to Cork from France. Between May and September, Irish Ferries operates weekly sailings from Le Havre to Cork, taking about 22 hours, and Roscoff to Cork, which takes

Directions for ferry passengers

around 15 hours. Brittany Ferries has a 14-hour Roscoff–Cork service from March to October and an 18-hour St Malo–Cork crossing during the same period. Cabins and berths are available on routes to Cork but should be booked in advance. There is a small charge for taking bicycles on Swansea Cork Ferries.

PORT CONNECTIONS

ALL IRELAND'S PORTS have adequate bus and train connections. At Dublin Port, buses are laid on (fare payable) to take all ferry passengers into the city centre. From Dun Laoghaire, DART trains run into Dublin every 10 to 15 minutes calling at Pearse Street, Tara Street and Connolly Stations. These go from the railway station near the main passenger concourse. Buses run from Dun Laoghaire to Eden Quay and Fleet Street in the city centre every 10 to 15 minutes. At all ports, taxis are there to meet arrivals.

Irish Ferries ship loading up at Rosslare Harbour

DIRECTORY

FERRY COMPANIES

Brittany Ferries
☎ 021 277801 (Cork).
☎ 01752 227941 (UK).
☎ 98 29 28 00 (France).

Irish Ferries
☎ 01 8552222 (Dublin).
☎ 0990 171717 (UK).
☎ 2 35 22 50 28 (France).

Isle of Man Steam Packet Co Ltd
☎ 01624 661661 (Isle of Man).

Norse Irish Ferries
☎ 01232 779090 (Belfast).
☎ 0151 9441010 (UK).

P&O European Ferries
☎ 1800 409049 (in Ireland).
☎ 0990 980980 (UK).

Stena Sealink Line
☎ 01 2047777 (Dublin).
☎ 01233 647022 (UK).

Swansea Cork Ferries
☎ 021 271166 (Cork).
☎ 01792 456116 (UK).

SeaCat
☎ 0990 523523 (UK).

THROUGH-TICKET BUS COMPANIES

Citylink/Ulsterbus
☎ 01232 337002 (Belfast).
☎ 0990 505050 (UK).

Eurolines
☎ 01 8366111(Dublin).
☎ 01582 404511 (UK).

National Express
☎ 0990 808080 (UK).

LENGTH OF JOURNEY	CROSSINGS TO IRELAND	BUS AND TRAIN CONNECTIONS
HSS: 1 hr 40 mins Ferry: 3 hrs 30 mins	6–8 per day	DART train or local bus to Dublin: 14 km (9 miles)
Sea Lynx: 1 hr 40 mins Ferry: 3 hrs 20 mins	Mid-Jul–mid-Oct: 5–7 per day Mid-Oct–mid-Jul: 2–5 per day	Train or bus to Wexford: 19 km (12 miles); or Dublin: 162 km (101 miles)
4 hrs	2 per day	Train or bus to Wexford: 19 km (12 miles); or Dublin: 162 km (101 miles)
SeaCat: 1 hr 30 mins HSS: 1 hr 45 mins	9–10 per day	Local bus to city centre: 1 km (0.6 miles)
8 hrs 30 mins	1–2 per day	Taxi to city centre: 4 km (2.5 miles)
Jetliner: 1hr Ferry: 2 hrs 20 mins	7–9 per day	Bus or train to Belfast: 37 km (23 miles)
10 hours	Mid-Mar–early Jan: 3–5 per week Early Jan–mid-Mar: no service	Bus to Cork: 18 km (11 miles)

FERRIES TO BELFAST AND LARNE

THE FASTEST CROSSING to Belfast is the 90-minute **SeaCat** service from Stranraer in Scotland. This catamaran-style ferry sails four or five times per day, all year round. On the same route, Stena Sealink have introduced the second of their new HSS ferries. On these the sailing time is only 15 minutes longer than that of the SeaCat.

A Liverpool to Belfast service is run by **Norse Irish Ferries**, leaving Liverpool every evening and three mornings a week, all year, and taking over 8 hours to reach Belfast. Crossing the Irish Sea with the **Isle of Man Steam Packet Co** lets you visit the Isle of Man en route. Leaving from both Liverpool and Heysham, this summer-only service provides the added advantage of allowing you to disembark at Dublin and return from Belfast or vice versa.

There is only one sea route to Larne (north of Belfast) – from Cairnryan in Scotland. The service is operated by **P&O European Ferries**, who run both conventional ferries, which take about 140 minutes to make the crossing, and the new high-speed Jetliner, which takes only an hour. During the week in high season there are 9 sailings each day from Cairnryan to Larne.

Port of Belfast logo

Cars and lorries disembarking at Larne Port

PORT CONNECTIONS

ALTHOUGH it takes only ten minutes on foot into the city centre from Belfast Port, Flexibus shuttles are on hand to take ferry passengers into the city centre via the Europa Buscentre and Central Railway Station. A regular bus service connects Larne Harbour to the town's bus station, and from here, buses run every hour into Belfast city centre. From Larne Port, there are trains to take ferry passengers to Belfast's Yorkgate and Central railway stations. At both Belfast and Larne ports, there are usually taxis waiting to meet each arriving ship.

FARES AND CONCESSIONS

FARES ON FERRY CROSSINGS to Ireland vary dramatically according to the season – prices on certain days during the peak period of mid-June to mid-September can be double those at other times of the year. Prices increase greatly during the Christmas and New Year period, too. It is also advisable to book your journey both ways before setting out. Those travelling to ports without a reservation should always check availability before setting out.

Often, the cheapest way for families or groups of adults to travel is to buy a ticket that allows you to take a car plus a maximum number of passengers. At certain times of the year on particular routes, the return ticket for a car and five adults (two children count as one adult) can cost less than £50. The cheapest crossings are usually those where the passenger must depart and return within a specified period. Fares are normally reduced for midweek travel and early-morning or late-night crossings. Ferry companies offer discounts for students bearing an ISIC card *(see p340)* and some have cut-price deals for those with InterRail tickets *(see p359)*.

RAIL AND COACH THROUGH-TICKETS

IT IS POSSIBLE TO TRAVEL from any railway station in Great Britain to any specified destination in Ireland on a combined sea/rail ticket. This can be bought from most British Rail stations.

Eurolines runs a through-bus service from about 35 towns in Britain to over 100 destinations in the Republic. **Citylink/Ulsterbus** offers the same service to destinations in Northern Ireland. Tickets for both these coach companies can be booked through **National Express**, which has over 2,000 agents in Great Britain. Travellers from North America, Australia, New Zealand and certain countries in Asia can buy a BritIreland pass. As well as including the return ferry crossing to Ireland, it allows unlimited rail travel throughout Great Britain and Ireland on any five or ten days in a month.

Hitchhiker waiting for a lift at Larne Harbour

On the Road

ONE OF THE BEST WAYS to see Ireland's magnificent scenery and ancient sites is by car. Driving on the narrow, twisting country roads can be a pleasure; often you don't see another vehicle for miles. It can also be frustrating, especially if you find yourself stuck behind a slow-moving tractor or a herd of cows. If you don't want to take your own vehicle, car rental in Ireland is no problem. All the international car hire firms operate in the Republic and are also well represented in the North. Touring by bicycle is another enjoyable way of seeing the best parts of the island at your own leisurely pace.

Gaelic road sign instructing motorists to yield or give way

TAKING YOUR OWN CAR

IF YOU INTEND to take your own car across on the ferry *(see pp352–4)* check your car insurance to find out how well you are covered. To prevent a fully comprehensive policy being downgraded to third-party cover, ask your insurance company for a Green Card. Carry your insurance certificate, Green Card, proof of ownership of the car and, importantly, your driver's licence. If your licence was issued in Great Britain, you should also bring your passport with you for ID.

Membership of a reputable breakdown service like the **AA**, **RAC** or **Green Flag National Breakdown** is advisable unless you are undaunted by the prospect of breaking down in remote parts. Non-members can join up for just the duration of their holiday. Depending on the type of cover, breakdown organizations may offer only limited services in Ireland.

RENTING A CAR

CAR RENTAL FIRMS do good business in Ireland, so in summer it's wise to book ahead. Car hire – particularly in the Republic – is quite expensive and the best rates are often obtained by hiring in advance. Broker companies, such as **Holiday Autos**, use the major rental companies and will shop around to get you the best deal. Savings can also be made by choosing a fly-drive or even a rail-sail-drive holiday, but always check for hidden extras. Car rental usually includes unlimited mileage plus passenger

One for the road

indemnity insurance and cover for third party, fire and theft, but not damage to the vehicle. If you plan to cross the border in either direction, however briefly, you must tell the rental company, as there may be a small insurance premium to be paid.

To rent a car, you must show a full driving licence, which you should have held for two years without endorsement. Cars are usually rented only to those aged between 23 and 70, but some companies may make exceptions.

BUYING PETROL

UNLEADED PETROL and diesel fuel are available just about everywhere in Ireland. Although prices vary from station to station, petrol in the Republic is quite expensive. In Northern Ireland it is slightly cheaper. Almost all the petrol stations accept VISA and Mastercard, although it is worth checking before filling up, particularly in rural areas.

ROAD MAPS

THE ROAD MAP on the inside back cover shows all the towns and villages mentioned in this guide. In addition, each chapter starts with a map of the region showing all the major sights and providing tips on getting around. However, if you plan to do much driving or cycling, you should equip yourself with a more detailed map. Ordnance Survey Holiday Maps are among the best road maps. You can usually get town plans free from tourist offices *(see p338)*. The tourist boards of the Republic and Northern Ireland both issue free lists of suggested routes for cyclists.

A busy Hertz car rental desk at Dublin Airport

The familiar sight of a farmer and cattle on an Irish country road

RULES OF THE ROAD

E VEN FOR THOSE unused to driving on the left, motoring in Ireland is unlikely to pose any great problems. For many, the most difficult aspect of driving on Ireland's roads is getting used to overtaking on the right and giving way to traffic on the right at roundabouts. On both sides of the border, the wearing of safety belts is compulsory for drivers and all front-seat passengers; where fitted, rear safety belts must be worn. All children must have a suitable restraint system. Motorcyclists and passengers must wear crash helmets. Northern Ireland uses the same Highway Code as Great Britain. The Republic of Ireland's Highway Code is very similar – copies of both

Speed limit signs in mph on a country road in County Cork

are available from bookstores. In Northern Ireland, you will notice some cars carrying a red "R" plate. These identify "restricted" drivers who have passed their driving test within the previous 12 months and have to keep to lower speeds.

SPEED LIMITS

I N THE REPUBLIC and Northern Ireland the maximum speed limits, which are shown in miles, are more or less the same as those in Britain:
• 30 mph (50 km/h) in built-up areas.
• 60 mph (95 km/h) outside built-up areas.
• 70 mph (110 km/h) on motorways.
On certain roads, which are clearly marked, the speed limits are either 40 mph (65 km/h) or 50 mph (80 km/h). Where there is no indication, the speed limit is 60 mph (95 km/h). In the Republic, vehicles towing caravans must not exceed 55 mph (90 km/h) on any road. Speed limits are more strictly enforced in the North than in the Republic.

ROAD SIGNS

M OST ROAD SIGNS in the Republic are in both Gaelic and English. Ireland is striving toward metrication so all the new-style green and white signs are in kilometres. However, nothing's quite that simple in Ireland, so expect to come across some black-on-white signs showing distances in miles. As in Britain, road signs in the North are always

in miles. One road sign that is unique to the Republic is the "Yield" sign – in the UK this is worded "Give Way". Throughout both the Republic and Northern Ireland, brown signs with white lettering indicate places of historic, cultural or leisure interest.

SIGNS IN THE REPUBLIC

Unprotected quay or river ahead   **Junction ahead**

Children or school ahead   **Dangerous bends ahead**

SIGNS IN NORTHERN IRELAND

Motorway direction sign

Primary route sign

ROAD CONDITIONS

N ORTHERN IRELAND'S roads are well surfaced and generally in better condition than those in the Republic, though there are just as many winding stretches requiring extra caution. The volume of traffic, particularly in the South, is much lower than in Britain. On some of the more rural roads you may not come across another motorist for miles. Even the major roads can be surprisingly quiet. There are only a few sections of motorway in the whole of Ireland, though recent years have seen extensive construction of dual carriageways in the Republic, including rural areas such as County Donegal.

PARKING

PREDICTABLY, in a country with so little congestion, finding a parking place is rarely a problem in Ireland. Most towns have at least one free car park. Dublin, Belfast and a few other cities have either parking meters or (fairly expensive) car parks. Parking on the street is allowed, though a single yellow line along the edge of the road means there are some restrictions (there should be a sign nearby showing the permitted parking times). Double yellow lines indicates no parking at any time.

Parking disc sign

Disc parking – a version of "pay & display" – operates in most large towns and cities in the Republic of Ireland. Discs can be purchased from local newsagents, petrol stations, tourist offices and many small shops. In Northern Ireland, almost all towns and villages have Control Zones, which are indicated by large yellow or pink signs. For security reasons, unattended parking in a Control Zone is not permitted at any time of the day.

Warning sign in Northern Ireland

CYCLING

THE QUIET ROADS of Ireland help to make touring by bicycle a real joy. The **Raleigh Rent-a-Bike** network of cycle dealers operates a reasonably priced rental scheme throughout Ireland. Also local shops, such as **Rent-a-Bike** in Dublin, rent cycles to tourists and are open at least six days a week.

You can often hire a bike in one town and drop it off at another for a small charge. Many dealers can also provide safety helmets, but bring your own lightweight waterproof clothing to help cope with the unpredictable weather. Buses and trains will usually carry bikes for a surcharge.

SECURITY ROADBLOCKS IN NORTHERN IRELAND

IN THE LATE 1960s, when the Northern Ireland conflicts began, roadblocks were introduced on to the roads of the province. These days if you are travelling by road, whether in the centre of Londonderry or the remote Sperrin Mountains, you may come across several roadblocks or none at all, depending on the political climate at the time. Checkpoints can be staffed by either the army or the police, who will simply ask for proof of identity. In the unlikely event of being stopped, show your driving licence and insurance certificate or rental agreement when asked and don't make any sudden movements. As long as you are polite, it should be a smooth encounter.

Cyclists checking their directions in Ballyvaughan, County Clare

Travelling by Train

THE REPUBLIC OF IRELAND'S RAILWAY NETWORK is run by
Irish Rail (Iarnród Éireann) and is state-controlled.
The rail network is far from comprehensive and quite
expensive, but the trains are generally reliable and
comfortable and can be a good way of covering long
distances. The service provided by **Northern Ireland
Railways** (NIR) is more limited but fares are slightly
cheaper. In 1996 the line connecting North to South is
being modernized, with high-speed trains taking
passengers from Belfast to Dublin in under 95 minutes.

Logo of the Iarnród Éireann
InterCity service

TRAIN SERVICES IN NORTHERN IRELAND

OTHER THAN an express
service out to Larne
Harbour and a commuter line
to Bangor, there are only two
main routes out of Belfast: a
line westward to Londonderry
via Coleraine (for the Giant's
Causeway) and Ireland's only
cross-border service, operating
between Belfast and Dublin
six times daily. All trains leave
from Central Station except
for the Larne Harbour link,
which departs from Yorkgate.
A new station, Great Victoria
Street, opens in September
1995 and intends to bring rail
travellers right to the heart of
the city's business and shopping district. Bear in mind that
there are no left-luggage facilities at any of Northern Ireland's
train or bus stations.

Platform of Heuston station in Dublin

TRAIN SERVICES IN THE REPUBLIC OF IRELAND

ALTHOUGH the more rural
areas in the Republic of
Ireland are not served by
railways, Irish Rail operates a
satisfactory service to most of
the large cities and towns.
Going by rail is probably the
fastest and most convenient
way of travelling from Dublin
to places like Waterford,
Cork, Limerick and Galway.
However, there are glaring
gaps in the rail network; for
example, Donegal is totally
devoid of train services, so if
you are planning to explore
the west coast of Ireland using
public transport, you will have
to continue westward from
towns such as Galway, Sligo,
Limerick and Westport using
the local bus services.

The two main rail stations
in Dublin are Connolly, for
trains to the north, northwest
and Rosslare, and Heuston,
which serves the west, midlands and southwest. These
two stations are connected
by the No. 90 bus service
which runs every 10
to 15 minutes and
takes a quarter of an
hour – traffic permitting.
All trains in the Republic of

Ireland have standard and
super-standard (first-class)
compartments. A supplement
is charged for all first-class
travel. Bicycles can be taken
on trains but for this there is
a supplement of up to IR£6,
depending on the length of
journey. For information on
times and routes, InterCity
rail timetables are available
from most Irish Rail stations
and cost around 50p.

DART SERVICE

THE HANDY electric rail
service known as DART
(Dublin Area Rapid Transit)
serves 25 stations between
Howth, County Dublin and
Bray, County Wicklow, with
several stops in Dublin city
centre. A Dublin Explorer
ticket allows four consecutive
days' travel on DART trains as
well as Dublin Bus services.
Tickets can be purchased at
any of the DART Stations.
Bikes can be taken on the
trains if there is room, but
you'll have to pay extra.

DART Stáisiún

DART station sign

DART STATIONS

HOWTH
Sutton
Bayside
HOWTH JUNCTION
Killbarrack
Raheny
Harmonstown
Killester
CONNOLLY
Tara Street
PEARSE
Lansdowne Road
Sandymount
Sydney Parade
Booterstown
Blackrock
Seapoint
Salthill & Monkstown
DUN LAOGHAIRE
Sandycove & Glasthule
Glenageary
Dalkey
Killiney
Shankill
BRAY

TICKETS AND FARES

THROUGHOUT IRELAND, train tickets are generally quite expensive, but there are lots of good value incentive or concessionary passes. Most of these include bus travel, so you can get virtually anywhere in Ireland on one ticket.

The most comprehensive ticket available is the Emerald Card, which can be used on all Irish Rail, Northern Ireland Railways, Dublin Bus and Ulsterbus services. For around IR£100 the Emerald Card gives eight days' unlimited travel in a 30-day period. An eight-day Irish Explorer ticket is slightly cheaper and is valid on all Irish Rail and Bus Éireann transport. For rail travellers, the Irish Rover ticket can be good value for money. It is valid on all Irish Rail and Northern Ireland Railways journeys for five days within a 15-day period.

The modern ticket office at Belfast's Central Station

CONCESSIONS

STUDENTS CAN BUY a Travel-save Stamp *(see p340)* to affix to their ISIC cards for discounts on train fares. For those under 26, Faircards give 50 per cent off all Irish Rail single journeys, and can be bought from USIT *(see p340).*

Under-26 InterRail passes allow unlimited rail travel for 15 days or one month in the Republic and 25 other European countries. Older travellers can get InterRail Plus 26 cards costing slightly more. However, InterRail cards allow only a one-third discount on Northern Ireland Railways.

IRELAND'S RAIL NETWORK

Irish Rail (Iarnród Éireann)
35 Abbey St Lower, Dublin 1.
[📞] 01 8366222.

Northern Ireland Railways
Central Station, East Bridge St,
Belfast BT1 3PB.
[📞] 01232 899411.

KEY

— Irish Rail

— NIR

0 kilometres 100

0 miles 50

Travelling by Bus and Taxi

T HE BUS SERVICES THROUGHOUT IRELAND are quite good, for such a rural island. However, longer journeys often involve changing buses en route so extra travelling time should be allowed for. Touring by coach is also a good way to see Ireland – local tourist offices have details of tours as well as prices and often take bookings. Taxi services are available in all major cities and towns in Ireland. In the Republic, taxis are usually saloon cars and are identified by a yellow light on the roof. In the North, cities like Belfast and Londonderry have both mini-cabs and London-style black cabs.

Boarding a bus at the Europa Buscentre in Belfast

Logo on Bus Éireann local and express buses

GETTING AROUND BY BUS

T HE REPUBLIC OF IRELAND'S national bus company, Bus Éireann, operates a country-wide network of buses serving all the cities and most of the towns. In Dublin, the main bus station is the Busáras on Store Street, a short walk from O'Connell Street. There are also numerous private bus companies which either compete with the national network or provide services on routes not covered by Bus Éireann. In rural Donegal, for example, there are several private bus services. Some are not fully licensed, so it might be best to check whether you would be covered in the unlikely event of an accident. Local tourist offices should be able to point out the most reputable firms.

Ulsterbus runs an excellent service throughout Northern Ireland including express links between all the major towns. Belfast has two main

bus stations – the Europa Bus-centre off Great Victoria Street and Oxford Street Station. Check before setting out that you are going to the right one. Note that there are no left-luggage facilities at any of the stations in Northern Ireland.

FARES AND TICKETS

I N THE REPUBLIC, long-distance buses are about half the price of the equivalent rail journey. If you are making the return trip on the same day, ask for a day-return ticket, which is much cheaper than the normal return fare. Also, between Tuesday and Thursday you can buy a "period" return ticket for the price of a single journey. Under 16s pay half the adult fare. Students with a Travelsave stamp *(see p340)* get a 30 per cent reduction. For those intending to do a lot of travelling it is cheaper to buy a "Rambler" ticket. This allows unlimited bus travel through-out the Republic for a certain

number of days in a set period, for example, 15 days' travel out of 30 consecutive days.

A "Freedom of Northern Ireland" ticket gives you un-limited travel on all Ulsterbus routes for either a day or a week. Ulsterbus also offers cheap day-return tickets. Stu-dents can get a 15 per cent discount by showing their ISIC card. There are also a number of period passes available that combine bus and rail travel *(see p359).*

COACH TOURS

W HILE THE BUS SERVICES in Ireland are generally adequate for getting from town to town, using public transport isn't a very practical way of exploring specific areas or regions in great detail – unless you have a lot of time on your hands. If you find yourself in a remote area like Connemara *(see pp198–201)* but have only a very limited amount of time in which to see its main attractions, a local guided tour of the area is a good idea. For about IR£10 per adult you can do the picturesque "figure of eight" circuit by coach, starting from Galway and taking in Spiddal, Kylemore, Letter-frack, Oughterard and then returning to Galway. The coach sets out at 10am and returns at about 5:30pm, making regular stops at places of interest. The price does not include admission fees or lunch. Bookings are made at Galway Tourist Information Centre and can be arranged

Express service coach in Northern Ireland

in advance or on the day. Four-hour or one-day tours such as this are available in many of Ireland's main tourist areas. Other popular tours of rural Ireland include Glendalough *(see pp132–3)*, Donegal *(see pp216–23)*, and the Ring of Kerry *(see pp156–7)*. In Dublin and other cities in the Republic, Bus Éireann and some local companies run half- and one-day excursions. Dublin Bus (Bus Átha Cliath) runs a Dublin City tour, which leaving from O'Connell Street Upper. This guided tour takes in the city's most famous sights.

In Northern Ireland, Ulster-bus operates a number of tours from the Europa Buscentre in Belfast to all the major places of interest. These tours include the Causeway Coast, the Glens of Antrim, the Ulster-American Folk Park, near Omagh. Ulsterbus prefers bookings to be made in person at their Belfast office rather than over the phone. During the summer, Belfast Citybus operates up to three guided bus tours a week around the city.

Passengers alighting from a Waterford city bus

Dublin Bus logo

Waterford are operated by Bus Éireann. Buses in Dublin city centre run from about 6am until 11:30pm. If you're using the bus more than two or three times in a day, it's worth getting a one-day pass, costing around IR£3. In the rest of the Republic the bus services are operated mainly by Bus Éireann. In some places, though, the bus routes connecting towns and villages are served by private companies as well as Bus Éireann. Bus times (and stops) in villages and the more remote places are often best found by asking the locals. All Bus Éireann routes and times can be found in its timetable, which costs 50p and is available at main bus stations.

Except for Belfast, Northern Ireland's bus network is run by Ulsterbus. In the province's capital the comprehensive local service is operated by Citybus. A wide variety of travel passes are available for Citybus and Ulsterbus lines. Regional timetables are available at bus stations.

CITY AND LOCAL BUSES

LOCAL BUS SERVICES in cities and large towns throughout the Republic are generally well-run and reasonably priced. Dublin Bus runs all the services in the Greater Dublin area (which includes parts of Wicklow, Kildare and Meath), while city buses in Cork, Galway, Limerick and

Taxis lined up outside the arrivals building at Dublin Airport

TAXIS IN THE REPUBLIC

EXCEPT in the most rural of places, there is usually a local taxi service – your hotel or B&B will provide details. In Dublin, taxis are large saloon cars. Cruising taxis are a rarity: the best places to find cabs are at rail or bus stations, hotels and taxi ranks. Prices are based on metered mileage. If your taxi does not have a meter, always ask the fare to your destination.

TAXIS IN NORTHERN IRELAND

TAXIS IN NORTHERN IRELAND are reasonably priced. Journeys within the centre of Belfast usually cost no more than £3 by mini-cab or black cab. In most decent-sized towns in the North you will find at least one taxi office or rank where you can queue for a cab. Otherwise, ask for the number of a taxi firm at a local hotel or B&B.

DIRECTORY

NATIONAL BUS COMPANIES

Bus Éireann
01 8366111 *(including day tour enquiries)*.

Ulsterbus
01232 333000.
01232 337004 *(day tours)*.

CITY BUS COMPANIES

Dublin Bus
01 8734222 *(including day tour enquiries)*.

Belfast Citybus
01232 246485.
01232 458484 *(day tours)*.

COACH TOUR COMPANIES

Gray Line Tours
The Malt House,
Grand Canal St, Dublin 2.
01 6619666.

McGeehan Coaches
Fintown PO, Co Donegal.
075 46101.

General Index

Acknowledgments

DORLING KINDERSLEY would like to thank the following people whose contributions and assistance have made the preparation of this book possible.

MAIN CONTRIBUTORS

LISA GERARD-SHARP is a writer and broadcaster who has contributed to numerous travel books, including the *Eyewitness Travel Guide to France*. She is of Irish extraction, with roots in County Sligo and County Galway, and a regular visitor to Ireland.

TIM PERRY, from Dungannon, County Tyrone, writes on travel and popular music for various publishers in North America and the British Isles.

ADDITIONAL CONTRIBUTOR

Douglas Palmer.

ADDITIONAL PHOTOGRAPHY

Peter Anderson, Joe Cornish, Andy Crawford, Michael Diggin, Steve Gorton, Anthony Haughey, Mike Linley, Stephen Oliver, Magnus Rew, Clive Streeter, Matthew Ward.

ADDITIONAL ILLUSTRATIONS

Richard Bonson, Brian Craker, John Fox, Paul Guest, Stephan Gyapay, Ian Henderson, Claire Littlejohn, Gillie Newman, Chris Orr, Kevin Robinson, John Woodcock, Martin Woodward.

ADDITIONAL PICTURE RESEARCH

Miriam Sharland.

EDITORIAL ASSISTANCE

Marion Broderick, Margaret Chang, Guy Dimond, Fay Franklin, Caroline Radula-Scott.

DESIGN ASSISTANCE

Martin Cropper, Yael Freudmann, Sally Ann Hibbard, Annette Jacobs, Erika Lang, Michael Osborn.

INDEX

Hilary Bird.

SPECIAL ASSISTANCE

Dorling Kindersley would like to thank all the regional and local tourist offices in the Republic and in Northern Ireland for their valuable help. Particular thanks also to: Ralph Doak and Egerton Shelswell-White at Bantry House, Bantry, Co Cork; Vera Greif at the Chester Beatty Library and Gallery of Oriental Art, Dublin; Alan Figgis at Christ Church Cathedral, Dublin; Labhras Ó Murchu at Comhaltas Ceoltóirí Éireann; Catherine O'Connor at Derry City Council; Patsy O'Connell at Dublin Tourism; Tanya Cathcart at Fermanagh Tourism, Enniskillen; Peter Walsh at the Guinness Hop Store, Dublin; Gerard Collet at the Irish Shop, Covent Garden, London; Dónall P Ó Baoill at ITE, Dublin; Pat Cooke at Kilmainham Gaol, Dublin; Angela Shanahan at the Kinsale Tourist Office; Bill Maxwell, Adrian Le Harivel and Marie McFeely at the National Gallery of Ireland, Dublin; Philip McCann at the National Library of Ireland, Dublin; Willy Cumming at the National Monuments Divison, Office of Public Works, Dublin; Eileen Dunne and Sharon Fogarty at the National Museum of Ireland, Dublin; Joris Minne at the Northern Ireland Tourist Office, Belfast; Dr Tom MacNeil at Queen's University, Belfast; Sheila Crowley at St Mary's Pro-Cathedral, Dublin; Paul Brock at the Shannon Development Centre; Tom Sheedy at Shannon Heritage and Banquets, Bunratty Castle, Co Clare; Angela Sutherland at the Shannon-Erne Waterway, Co Leitrim; Máire Ní Bháin at Trinity College, Dublin; Anne-Marie Diffley at Trinity College Library, Dublin; Pat Maclean at the Ulster Museum, Belfast; Harry Hughes at the Willie Clancy School of Traditional Music, Miltown Malbay, Co Clare.

ADDITIONAL ASSISTANCE

Kathleen Crowley, Rory Doyle, Peter Hynes, David O'Grady, Mary O'Grady, Madge Perry, Poppy.

PHOTOGRAPHY PERMISSIONS

THE PUBLISHER would like to thank all those who gave permission to photograph at various cathedrals, churches, museums, restaurants, hotels, shops, galleries and other sights too numerous to list individually.

PICTURE CREDITS

tl = top left; tc = top centre; tr = top right; cla = centre left above; ca = centre above; cra = centre right above; cl = centre left; c = centre; cr = centre right; clb = centre left below; cb = centre below; crb = centre right below; bl = bottom left; bc = bottom centre; br = bottom right.

Every effort has been made to trace the copyright holders and we apologize in advance for any unintentional omissions. We would be pleased to insert the appropriate acknowledgments in any subsequent edition of this publication.

Works of art have been reproduced with the permission of the following copyright holders: © DACS, London 1995 68tr, 88tr.

The publisher would like to thank the following individuals, companies and picture libraries for permission to reproduce their photographs:

AER LINGUS/AIRBUS INDUSTRIE: 350tc; AKG, LONDON: National Museum, Copenhagen/Erich Lessing 24cl; ALLSPORT: David Rogers 26cb; Steve Powell 45tc; APPLETREE PRESS LTD, BELFAST (*Irish Proverbs* © illustrations Karen Bailey) 327cl.

BORD FÁILTE/IRISH TOURIST BOARD: Brian Lynch 22–23, 23tl, 238tl, 238tr, Pat Odea 330c; © BRISTOL CITY MUSEUMS AND ART GALLERY: 30bl; © BRITISH LIBRARY: *Richard II's Campaigns in Ireland* Ms.Harl.1319, f.18 35tl; © BRITISH MUSEUM: 31bl; © BUSHMILLS LTD: 258bl.

© CENTRAL BANK OF IRELAND: *Lady Lavery as Cathleen ni Houlihan*, John Lavery 13ca, 344 (all banknotes and coins except for tr), 345; © CHESTER BEATTY LIBRARY, DUBLIN: 75t; © CLASSIC DESIGNS/LJ YOUNG LTD, BLARNEY: 327c; Mark Boulton 17tr; Patrick Clement 16clb, 16bl; Adrian Davies 16br; Rodney Dawson 17cl; Frances Furlong 16tl; David Green 200bl; Pekka Helo 17cr; Jan Van de Kam 178bl; Gordon Langsbury 16cl, 178cr; John Markham 244br; George McCarthy 17tl, 17bl,17br, 130tl, 201bl; MR Phicon 16crb; Eckhart Pott 17cb; Hans Reinhard 17tcb, 154tl, 262tl; Kim Taylor 17tc, 244t; R Wanscheidt 17cbr; Uwe Walz 16cr, 177cb; G Ziesler 201bl; © CORK EXAMINER: 27tl; © CORK PUBLIC MUSEUM: 33cla; JOE CORNISH: 17cla, 204b, 262tr, 336–7; CRAWFORD MUNICIPAL ART GALLERY: *The Meeting of St Brendan and the Unhappy Judas*, Harry Clarke 166bl.

DERRY CITY COUNCIL: 250tr; MICHAEL DIGGIN: 18tl, 145b, 155cr, 156cla, 157tr, 177tl, 198bl, 217t, 218tr, 218cl, 219cra, 332tl, 333tl, 333b, 339br, 341b, 343cl, 346b; BILL DOYLE: 206bl; GA DUNCAN: 44cb, 44bl; © DUNDEE ART GALLERIES AND MUSEUMS: *The Children of Lir*, John Duncan 25tc.

ET ARCHIVE: 25bl; MARY EVANS PICTURE LIBRARY: 9 (inset), 22tl, 24tr, 24bl, 24br, 25cla, 32bl, 35bc, 36bl; 42bl, 51 (inset), 75cl, 87bl, 113 (inset), 273br, 279 (inset), 337 (inset).

© STEPHEN FALLER LTD, GALWAY: 326cla; © FAMINE MUSEUM CO ROSSCOMMON: 211tr; JIM FITZPATRICK: 77bl.

GILL AND MACMILLAN PUBLISHERS, DUBLIN: 43bl; RONALD GRANT ARCHIVE: *The Commitments*, Twentieth Century Fox 21br; © GUINNESS IRELAND LTD: 96bl, 96br, 97tl, 97tr, 97bl, 97br.

HULTON DEUTSCH COLLECTION: 20clb, 21tr, 37t, 40br, 40cbl, 44crb, Reuter 45crb, 60bl.

IMAGES COLOUR LIBRARY: 46bl, 53tl; 221bc; INPHO, DUBLIN: 26cla, Billy Stickland 26br, Lorraine O'Sullivan 27br; IRISH PICTURE LIBRARY, DUBLIN: 36cla, 39tl, 42tl; © IRISH TIMES: 126br; © IRISH TRADITIONAL MUSIC ARCHIVE, DUBLIN: 23bl.

JARROLD COLOUR PUBLICATIONS: JA Brooks 60br;

MICHAEL JENNER: 235cr.
TIMOTHY KOVAR: 76bl; 103tl, 106bl.

© LAMBETH PALACE LIBRARY, LONDON: Plan of the London Vintners' Company Township of Bellaghy, Ulster, 1622 (ms. Carew 634 f.34) (detail) 37cra; FRANK LANE PICTURE AGENCY: Roger Wilmshurst 178bc; © LEEDS CITY ART GALLERY: *The Irish House of Commons*, Francis Wheatley 38cla.

HUGH McKNIGHT PHOTOGRAPHY: 99t; MANDER AND MITCHESON THEATRE COLLECTION: 22cl; MANSELL COLLECTION: 38bl, 43cra, 79bl, 260bc; ARCHIE MILES: 200br; JOHN MURRAY: 49bl, 94cl, 120c; © MUSEUM OF THE CITY OF NEW YORK: Gift of Mrs Robert M Littlejohn, *The Bay and Harbor of New York 1855*, Samuel B Waugh 40–41.

NATIONAL CONCERT HALL, DUBLIN: Frank Fennell 107bl; © NATIONAL GALLERY OF IRELAND, DUBLIN: *WB Yeats and the Irish Theatre*, Edmund Dulac 20tr, *George Bernard Shaw*, John Collier 20cr, *Carolan the Harper*, Francis Bindon 22tr, *Leixlip Castle*, Irish School 39cla, *The Custom House, Dublin*, James Malton 39bc, *Queen Victoria and Prince Albert Opening the 1853 Dublin Great Exhibition*, James Mahoney 41bl, *The Houseless Wanderer*, JH Foley 68tl, *Pierrot*, Juan Gris 68tr, *For the Road*, JB Yeats 68cla, *The Taking of Christ*, Caravaggio 69cra, *The Castle of Bentheim*, Jacob van Ruisdael 69cl, *Judith with the Head of Holofernes*, Andrea Mantegna 69crb, *The Sick Call*, Matthew James Lawless 69bl, *Jonathan Swift, Satirist*, Charles Jerval 80bc, *James Joyce*, Jacques Emile Blanche 88t, *Interior with Members of a Family*, P Hussey 124br, *William Butler Yeats, Poet*, JB Yeats 225tl, *The Last Circuit of Pilgrims at Clonmacnoise*, George Petrie 242tr; © NATIONAL GALLERY, LONDON: *Beach Scene*, Edgar Degas 89br; © NATIONAL LIBRARY OF IRELAND, DUBLIN: 21cla, 21crb, 29b, 32tl, 32clb, 34bl, 36tl, 36clb, 38clb, 40tl, 40cla, 40bl, 41crb, 41tl, 42clb, 43tl, 43crb, *St Stephen's Green*, James Malton 50–51, 133tr, 170cra, 236b; © NATIONAL MUSEUM OF IRELAND, DUBLIN: 3, 30tl, 30clb, 30cb 30crb, 30–31, 31c 31clb, 31br, 32cla, 33cb, 33br, 53bl, 57cr, all 64–5, 99b; THE NATIONAL TRUST, NORTHERN IRELAND: *Lord Castlereagh* after Lawrence 274tl, *Hambletonian*, George Stubbs 275tl, 275cra; THE NATIONAL TRUST PHOTOGRAPHIC LIBRARY: Mathew Antrobus 265b, John Bethell 276tl, Patrick Pendergast 264bl, Will Webster 269br, 278–9; NATURE PHOTOGRAPHERS: B Burbridge 179bc, Paul Sterry 178clb; NORTHERN IRELAND TOURIST BOARD: 26tr, 250cl, 265tr, 328cl, 329tl; NORTON ASSOCIATES: 72 clb.

KYRAN O'BRIEN 107tr; © THE OFFICE OF PUBLIC WORKS, IRELAND: 164bl, 238cl, 239tl, 239cr, 240br,

242tl; OXFORD SCIENTIFIC FILMS: Frithjof Skibbe 178tl.
WALTER PFEIFFER STUDIOS, DUBLIN: 23tr, 23cra, 23c,
23cr, 23crb, 23br; PHOTO FLORA: Andrew N Gagg
178br; PHOTOSTAGE: Donald Cooper 106tr, 107tl;
POPPERFOTO: 44cla, 44br, 45tl, Reuter/Crispin
Rodwell 45tr; POWERSCOURT ESTATE, ENNISKERRY: 127c.

RANGE PICTURES: 41cra; THE REFORM CLUB, LONDON:
40cla; REPORT/DEREK SPIERS, DUBLIN: 44tl, 44tr,
270bl, 270br; RETNA PICTURES: Chris Taylor 22bl,
Jay Blakesberg 22br; RETROGRAPH ARCHIVE, LONDON:
© Martin Ranicar-Breese 63br; REX FEATURES: 45ca;
Sipa Press 45clb, 45br, 45bl.

SHANNON DEVELOPMENT PHOTO LIBRARY: 330tl;
SHANNON-ERNE WATERWAY: 227bc; THE SLIDE FILE,
DUBLIN: 14bc, 15t, 15c, 16cla, 16cra, 20cla,
27cra, 27clb, 27bl, 30cla, 46cla, 46bl, 47cb,
48cla, 48cra, 48cb, 48bl, 49cra, 75tr, 75br,
106br, 114cla, 121br, 130cl 130br, 143br, 177br,
203tl, 205tr, 206cb, 206br, 207bc, 216br,
219tr, 222tl, 222b, 224tr, 229b, 232tl, 234tl,
240tl, 242–3, 244cra, 262clb, 329br, 330br;
SPORTSFILE, DUBLIN: 27tc; DON SUTTON
INTERNATIONAL PHOTO LIBRARY: 282br.

© TATE GALLERY PUBLICATIONS: *Captain Thomas Lee*,
Marcus Gheeraedts 36br; TOPHAM PICTURE SOURCE:
39br, Tim Graham 94t; © TRINITY COLLEGE, DUBLIN:
Ms.1440 (Book of Burgos) f.20v 35clb; Ms.58
(Book of Kells) f.129v 4tr, *The Marriage of
Princess Aoite and the Earl of Pembroke*, Daniel
Maclise 34cla, Ms.57 (Book of Durrow) f.84v 53cr,
Ms.57 (Book of Durrow) f.85v 61cr, Ms.58 (Book
of Kells) f.129v 62cra, Ms.58 (Book of Kells) f.34r
62cl, Ms.58 (Book of Kells) f.28v 62crb, Ms.58
(Book of Kells) f.200r 62b; TRIP: R Drury 15br, 132c.

© ULSTER MUSEUM, BELFAST: *The Festival of St Kevin
at the Seven Churches, Glendalough*, Joseph
Peacock 28, *The Relief of Derry*, William Sadler II
36–7, 37crb, 42cla, 249crb, 270clb.

VIKING SHIP MUSEUM, STRANDENGEN, DENMARK:
watercolour by Flemming Bau 33tl.

© WATERFORD CORPORATION: 33bl, 34tl, 34clb, 35bl;
© WRITERS MUSEUM, DUBLIN: 20tl.

PETER ZÖLLER: 12, 14tl, 46tc, 46cr, 47cra, 47bl,
138br, 192, 208–9, 211bl, 212, 228, 241tr, 334tl.

Front endpaper: all commissioned photography
with the exception of PETER ZÖLLER: tl, tc, cb.

Jacket: all commissioned photography with the
exception of © TRINITY COLLEGE, DUBLIN: front tl;
Michael Jenner: spine t.